Roles in Interpretation

Fifth Edition

Judy E. Yordon

Ball State University

Boston   Burr Ridge, IL   Dubuque, IA   Madison, WI   New York   San Francisco   St. Louis
Bangkok   Bogotá   Caracas   Kuala Lumpur   Lisbon   London   Madrid   Mexico City
Milan   Montreal   New Delhi   Santiago   Seoul   Singapore   Sydney   Taipei   Toronto

McGraw-Hill Higher Education

*A Division of The **McGraw-Hill** Companies*

ROLES IN INTERPRETATION
Published by McGraw-Hill, an imprint of The McGraw-Hill Companies, Inc. 1221
Avenue of the Americas, New York, NY, 10020. Copyright © 2002, 1999, 1993, 1989,
1982, by The McGraw-Hill Companies, Inc. All rights reserved. No part of this
publication may be reproduced or distributed in any form or by any means, or stored in a
data base or retrieval system, without the prior written consent of The McGraw-Hill
Companies, Inc., including, but not limited to, in any network or other electronic storage
or transmission, or broadcast for distance learning.
Some ancillaries, including electronic and print components, may not be available to
customers outside the United States.

This book is printed on acid-free paper.

2 3 4 5 6 7 8 9 0 DOC/DOC 0 9 8 7 6 5 4 3 2

ISBN   0-07-243181-4

Publisher: *Phillip A. Butcher*
Sponsoring editor: *Nanette Kauffman*
Developmental editor: *Jennie Katsaros*
Marketing manager: *Kelly May*
Project manager: *Ruth Smith*
Production supervisor: *Debra Sylvester*
Coordinator freelance design: *Damian Moshak*
Cover design: *Joanne Schopler*
Compositor: *ElectraGraphics, Inc.*
Typeface: *11/13 Palatino*
Printer: *R. R. Donnelley & Sons Company*

Library of Congress Cataloging-in-Publication Data

Yordon, Judy E.
   Roles in interpretation / Judy E. Yordon.—5th ed.
      p. cm.
   Includes bibliographical references and index.
   ISBN 0-07-243181-4 (alk. paper)
   1. Oral interpretation. 2. Social role. I. Title.
PN4145.Y67 2002
808.5'4—dc21   2001018715

www.mhhe.com

Preface

I think it was Ann Landers—or perhaps her sister—who penned that if something is not broken, it shouldn't be fixed. Keeping this in mind, we tried to maintain much of what wasn't "broken" in the fourth edition. Reviewers and adoptees of the book suggested some improvements that could enhance the usability and accessibility of the text, and we have taken their advice.

Experimentation in performance styles and formats is in vogue right now, so in this edition, we encourage you to do the same. If you examine recent productions, you will find that many of them defy classification because they shatter traditional conventions. How would you characterize Blue Man Group, for example, which is a contemporary art satire employing polyrhythmic percussion, food tricks, and crepe paper orgies? How do you categorize the work of Barry Humphries whose Dame Edna one-woman show opened on Broadway? Or an improvised performance like *Musical! The Musical* by Nancy Howland Walker?

There was controversy surrounding the four nominees in the "Best Musical" category during the 2000 Tony Award broadcast. The controversy involved the four nominated shows in the musical category that many believed did not fit the category as it had customarily been defined. Is a show that contains primarily or all dance, for example, a musical? The Tony-Award winning "musical" *Contact* that looks a lot like a ballet is a dance-driven one act with music by such artists as Squirrel Nut Zippers and Dion. James Joyce's *The Dead* is based on a story by the Irish author. *Swing!* is primarily a revue of dance and music that re-creates the excitement of the swing revival. *The Wild Party* is based on a book-length poem of the same title by Joseph Moncure March, a mid-twentieth-century writer and editor. Ultimately, though, we see this as a positive evolution of contemporary theatre. As Edgar Dobie, managing producer of the Tony Awards Productions, put it in his defense of the "imperfect process" of the Tony Awards, "One wonders how the Broadway musical landscape will look in five years and if the decision to take a chance in 2000 by allowing 'Contact' into the musical category was prescient . . . Things change in life . . . [and] being flexible is good for Broadway, because theater people continue to create new works that defy categorization."

NEW TO THIS EDITION

We realize that some of the "rules" we have used to define genres and performance analogues for those genres might seem a bit prescriptive and limiting. We have consequently added a section in Chapter 1 on metaphoric versus metonymic performances. The fourth edition of this text discussed metaphoric versus metonymic productions, but we have found that this information relates equally well to solo performance. We have thus given more attention to the idea of being more creative and personal when constructing an interpretation.

Included in Chapter 4 is improved and expanded material on vocal and physical responsiveness, some of which was formerly in Chapter 7. In addition, there is much more information on composing introductions, including more sample introductions. Chapter 4 also includes new information and practical guidelines on coping with performance anxiety or stage fright, including some suggestions from students themselves.

Many reviewers commented on the difficulty of understanding and applying the information on structural and transactional analysis in Chapter 7, so we eliminated this entire section and expanded the "why" section of this chapter to include information on characters' goals, obstacles, and strategies to achieve those goals.

Included in Chapter 9 is information on using the Internet and on how to incorporate presentation software, particularly the use of PowerPoint™ slides, in the development of media performances.

In addition, the inside cover of the book displays a timeline that traces the historical evolution of this performance medium. It is our hope that this timeline will help to put this art form into historical perspective for the student.

There are also added anthology materials—including even more multicultural selections, particularly in Chapters 2 and 4—and an updated appendix, glossary, and bibliography.

There is now a website for this text, www.mhhe.com/yordon, with links to performance sites, the online Instructor's Manual and Test Bank, and to the author. Should instructors or students have questions or issues about the text, please feel free to access this site.

ACKNOWLEDGEMENTS

Many people are responsible for the completion of this edition. Primary thanks go to my editor, Jennie Katsaros, whose compassion and understanding were greatly appreciated. I would like to thank colleague Michael O'Hara for help with the revisions in Chapter 9, Lysa Franklin for her able work on the historical timeline, and Gina Nicewonger, my secretary, for her valued assistance with the permissions. In addition, I owe a large debt of gratitude to the following individuals for their thoughtful and constructive comments on the fourth edition: Lisa Abramson, Western Oregon University; Shirley Basfield Dunlap, Iowa State University; Diana Enloe, Alton High School; Derek Goldman, University of North Carolina at Chapel

Hill; and Kelly S. Taylor, University of North Texas. I would also like to thank again all my previous reviewers, the students who posed for the photos used throughout this text, photographer Sam Clemmons who took most of the photos, and especially to my students who have taught me so much.

As always, it is my hope that this new edition will help to illuminate the world of literature through performance for all who delve with it.

Judy E. Yordon
Distinguished Professor of Performance Studies

Contents

PART 1: INITIAL ROLES

2 | Your Role with Literature: Appreciation   44

3 | Your Role with Literature: Analysis   80

4 | Your Role in Rehearsal and Performance   114

5 | Your Role as Audience and Evaluator   162

PART 2: LITERARY ROLES

8 | Your Role with Poetry   262

Initial Roles

EMILY DICKINSON

Because I Could Not Stop for Death

Because I could not stop for Death—
He kindly stopped for me—
The Carriage held but just Ourselves—
And Immortality.

We slowly drove—He knew no haste
And I had put away
My labor and my leisure too,
For His Civility—

We passed the School, where Children strove
At Recess—in the Ring—
We passed the Fields of Gazing Grain—
We passed the Setting Sun—

Or rather—He passed Us—
The Dews drew quivering and chill—
For only Gossamer,[8] my Gown—
My Tippet[9]—only Tulle[²]—

We paused before a House that seemed
A Swelling of the Ground—
The Roof was scarcely visible—
The Cornice—in the Ground—

Since then—'tis Centuries—and yet
Feels shorter than the Day
I first surmised the Horses' Heads
Were toward Eternity—

ca. 1863

INTRODUCING SOLO INTERPRETATION PERFORMANCE

The Roles We Play

Interpretation is an artistic process of studying literature through performance and sharing that study with an audience. When we study interpretation, we are primarily interested in the relationship between you and a text, in this case, literary texts, through the medium of performance. But are texts only "literary," and what do we mean by "performance"? The meanings of both these terms have greatly expanded since the discipline of interpretation was incorporated into an academic field entitled performance studies. Performance studies is an interdisciplinary field of knowledge that focuses on elements of texts, performers, and audiences, individually or in groups, to advance understanding of the aesthetic, historical, psychological, political, and sociocultural dimensions of performance and performative events.[1]

When we consider "text," we include literary texts (prose, drama, poetry), as well as aesthetic objects (a quilt, for example, is a "text" of a particular family, time period, culture), oral texts (personal narratives, everyday conversations), and ethnographic studies of a particular culture or minority group, for example. Rituals are social or cultural texts; demonstrations, rallies, and sit-ins are political texts; drawings and dance are texts of self-expression. Text, then, is a metaphor for all kinds of experience, and we "read" texts, we understand them, through other texts that we have read, seen, experienced.

By "performing" we mean the traditional notion of performance as in theatrical productions, but we also include performances in a more general sense—including the roles you play on a daily basis. Performance is a human activity involving fixed texts such as literary texts and those used in stage, film, and television and more spontaneous texts, including everyday conversation, cultural rituals, and storytelling. Human beings always act or play roles—throughout childhood, for example, we often rehearse being adults. Your everyday behavior (actions), appearance (costume), and language (dialogue) alter depending on the situation you are in and the role you assume. For example, try starting a conversation about what you did last night with a close friend. Then discuss the same subject with a teacher, a boss, a grandparent. How did the conversation change? How did you adjust or modify your behavior, your language—your "performance"? How does your behavior differ at job interviews or formal dinners or holiday gatherings or religious services or political rallies or dances? How do you "act" with your friends as opposed to your mother, or your lover, or the president of a large corporation? Our daily lives are filled with performance events. Richard Schechner includes a wide spectrum of events in his discussion of performance, including "theatre, dance, music, sacred ritual, secular ritual, sports, social drama, . . . a bar mitzvah, . . . Hindu temple services, title boxing matches, TV soap operas, etc."[2] Schechner would also include such events as the 1991 Gulf War, the Clarence Thomas Supreme Court hearings, and the William Kennedy Smith and Mike Tyson rape trials. Everyday life and performance have intermingled.

The chef of a four-star restaurant in Mississippi, for example, acknowledged the metaphoric relationship between his restaurant and a theatrical production. He said that a restaurant is like theatre—it's show time every night. Your dining room is filled with an audience you are trying to please. The chef is the director, and the kitchen and the staff are role players. They all have a role and it all comes together. We create a show for our customers and hopefully at the end of the night, they will applaud and say it was a great show.

During the O. J. Simpson civil trial NBC news legal analyst Jay Monahan consistently used theatrical metaphors to describe the proceedings: "It sounded dramatic. . . . It was high theatre and he [attorney Daniel Petrocelli] performed it well." In *The Trial of O. J.*, Charles B. Rosenberg places the "trial of the century" in a theatrical context by entitling his chapters: "The Trial as a Story," "The Storytellers—the Lawyers," "The Story's Editor—the Judge," "The Story's Audience—the Jury," and so on.

After Bill Clinton and Bob Dole squared off during their second "town hall" debate during the 1996 campaign, CBS brought in none other than *The New York Times* theatre critic Frank Rich as political commentator. Dan Rather explained that the debate was really not about politics but about theatre, and he asked Rich to comment on the "subtext" of the exercise. In fact, Edmund Morris, Ronald Reagan's biographer, admitted outright that most good leaders are theatrical by nature.

Although we may assume that talk shows rely on spontaneous interaction, they are really tightly scripted theatrical events.

From these examples, it is easy to conclude that much of our daily life is involved in participating in and viewing performances—in playing roles. Thus, the title of this book.

While it is not possible in a beginning textbook to cover all of these text and performance possibilities, our focus on the analysis and performance of literary texts—on the diverse literary roles available for you to play—will provide you with experiences that will help enrich and inform the roles you play in daily life. While performance studies as a discipline has become more and more interested in the study and performance of nonliterary texts, we are of the opinion that the study of literature should not be jettisoned in this time of discipline reassessment, but recognized as a window on broader societal concerns. The study of literature is essential; it helps us understand more about ourselves and the world in which we live.

As you study and perform literature, see what connections you can make to the everyday events of your own life. As you perform dialogues created by another, what do you learn about your own communicative strategies? As you assume another's perspective, what do you learn about your own? In general, ask yourself, What do I learn about myself and others by studying and performing literary texts?

Literature and Solo Interpretation Performance

In the following poem, the connection between life and literature is made manifest.

> He ate and drank the precious Words—
> His spirit grew robust—
> He knew no more that he was poor,
> Nor that his frame was Dust—
> He danced along the dingy Days
> And this Bequest of wings
> Was but a Book—What Liberty
> A loosened spirit brings—
>
> Emily Dickinson
>
> Reprinted by permission of the publishers and the Trustees of Amherst College from THE POEMS OF EMILY DICKINSON, Thomas H. Johnson, ed., Cambridge, Mass.: The Belknap Press of Harvard University Press, Copyright 1951, © 1955, 1979, 1983 by the President and Fellows of Harvard College.

The study of literature has been and shall continue to be one of the most exciting endeavors we can undertake. The man in the poem above, for example, was able to exist on the love of "the precious Words" alone. Although you need not go to his extreme, the study of literature is often as stimulating, liberating, and rewarding for you as for the man in this poem. Literature expands your experiences, stimulates your imagination, and exposes you to different kinds of people and cultures. Literature allows you to experience the power of language. Literature persuades, moves, affects you—this is why you read it. Literature can offer you a fantasy world in which to escape, a realistic world to contemplate, or a surrealistic vision of the future. Writers of literature create characters with whom you cry, laugh, scream—characters who may be like you or unlike you, but who by their universality have something to say to us all. Through literature, you expand your knowledge of the world and consequently your knowledge of yourself and others.

Our focus in this text is on the study of literature—more specifically, the process of studying literature (prose fiction, drama, and poetry) through performance. (Chapter 9 discusses nonfiction, children's literature, and postmodern literature as well as some experimental performance possibilities.) We are especially interested in bringing a literary text and a student closer together than is possible with silent reading alone. Performance encourages—even demands—this closeness.

Although interpretation may be new to you, perhaps two related fields are not. If you have ever been involved in acting or public speaking classes, you have been exposed to styles of presentation similar to those used in the interpretation classroom.

Acting and Solo Interpretation Performance

Acting, like interpretation, asks that you take on the role of another, attempting to create the character in the play. As an actor, your goal is to project your understanding of the character—physically, vocally, psychologically. The more specifically you can suggest this character's identifying traits, the more successful your portrayal. In interpretation, you engage in this same role-playing process. Clearly, however, there are some practical differences between the art of the actor and the art of the interpreter, which is why the two art forms exist. Let us briefly outline the basic components that individualize each of these art forms.

Acting	Solo Interpretation Performance
Performers usually deal only with drama (plays)	Performers deal with all literary texts.
Performers usually face each other during the performance (onstage focus).	Performers project scenes out front during the performance (offstage focus).
Performers memorize their lines. No scripts are present on stage.	Performers are very familiar with their lines but may have a script.
Performers rely on costumes, makeup, scenery, and the like to help them create the illusion of reality.	Performers rely on their performance and the audience's imaginations to create the scenes.
Performers act on a stage, usually separated from the audience, and use a great expenditure of gesture and movement.	Performers are often in a room, close to the audience, and employ economy of gesture and movement.
Performers usually play only one role.	Performers often play many roles, including roles they might not be cast to play in conventional theatre.
Performers are guided in their interpretations by a director's production concept.	Performers are their own directors and devise their own concepts or interpretations.

In the past, interpretation was hampered by arbitrary rules that stated (1) interpreters who moved were acting, (2) interpreters who sat down were acting, and (3) interpreters who did not use a script were acting, among others. Rules like these are proscriptive, limit creativity, and do not make allowances for individual texts or individual interpretations. Rules limit choices, and when they are rigidly followed, rules can be detrimental to the literature as well as to the performance.

The differences between the actor and the interpreter, then, are differences in degree and not in kind. Sharing a performance with an audience is central to both artists. Aside from the interpreter's need to practice economy of movement and action, to suggest rather than actually demonstrate the character's movement and interaction, the actor and the interpreter have much in common, as earlier suggested. Both artists role play, engage in acting. Speaking is an action—and no one would deny that interpreters speak. Actors, in turn, must interpret their roles. Howard R. Martin puts it well as he describes the similarities between these two complementary arts:

> After all, acting is an "interpretive" art in the sense of deriving from a clear understanding of previous givens (e.g., texts, scenarios, characters), and conversely, interpretation is a dramatic art involving empathy, transformation, characterization, and the like.[3]

Public Speaking and Solo Interpretation Performance

Just as acting and interpretation are two similar but distinct art forms, so are public speaking and interpretation. Let's examine the similarities and differences between the two.

In public speaking, you stand before an audience to share ideas and feelings, just as you do in interpretation. The public speaker addresses an audience directly—facing the members and receiving their immediate responses—like politicians delivering campaign speeches. The interpreter, too, faces the audience, and both have the advantage of receiving the responses of the audience at the moment of performance.

One difference is that public speakers may deliver their speeches extemporaneously; they know the outlines of their speeches, but the exact wording may change. Interpreters, on the other hand, are bound by the exact words of the texts.

Another difference between these two situations is that the public speaker's text is an original speech (although some orators hire speech writers to compose their speeches) which conveys the speaker's personal feelings and attitudes (backed by research, in some cases). The interpreter's text, on the other hand, is a literary selection which conveys the speaker in the text's feelings and attitudes as interpreted by the performer. The interpreter may or may not share these feelings and attitudes.

Finally, public speakers normally remain themselves, whereas interpreters often attempt to suggest someone other than themselves. Thus, while interpreters share similarities with actors and public speakers, interpretation is different from either of these other types of performance.

This chapter introduces the essentials of the art of interpretation, including its primary characteristics and values for you as a student. In addition, the chapter includes a sample analysis, including performance suggestions, of a literary selection.

WHAT ARE THE VALUES OF SOLO INTERPRETATION PERFORMANCE?

A question often asked by beginning interpretation students is, What value is an interpretation course to me? Many of you are taking this course because it fulfills a requirement, not necessarily because you want to. Some of you may have never heard of interpretation and are curious. If either of these descriptions fits you, consider the possible values you can receive from this course—regardless of your chosen major or future vocational goals. Values gained from participating in the fine arts include the ability to work under pressure, to be goal-oriented, to be self-disciplined, to be self-motivated, to think on your feet, to budget time, and to take the initiative—all valuable skills, traits, or qualities. We concentrate here on three primary values derived from participating in solo performance.

First, solo interpretation performances enable you to study the world's best literature. Your exposure to literature begins as you search for a selection that you would like to study and share with an audience. You will probably have to read many selections before you find the right one for you. In addition, performance brings you closer to these texts than mere silent reading. As you practice your selection aloud, you discover many intricacies that silent reading alone may never have revealed. Widening your personal literary text repertory is one of the primary values of solo interpretation performance.

Second, you expand your knowledge of yourself and your world through solo interpretation performance. As you work to create the speaker(s) in the selection, you begin to ask yourself, How does this speaker look? How does this speaker sound? How does this speaker feel? How does this speaker think? What does this speaker want? What does this speaker need? How are these speakers different from one another? From me? As you begin to understand and create the experiences of the speaker(s), you learn what others think and feel. You hear other social voices and take on other social roles. You discover more about your culture and traditions as well as about other cultures and other times. Because you select the characters you will portray, you avoid the typecasting dilemma common in the theatrical world of an actor's having to play the same type of role over and over again because of the way he or she looks. In solo performance, all roles are available to you, regardless of your gender, age, or ethnicity. Playing a variety of roles fosters change and growth as you take risks and dare yourself to become involved in unique experiences. By creating characters in literature, you learn to view the world through another's eyes. You are exposed to different values, attitudes, and beliefs and are thereby able to gain a wider perspective on your own life, perhaps modifying your world view. You are able to increase your communication competence outside of the classroom as you come to understand the intentions and motives of others. You learn to judge yourself and others less harshly as you express other people's points of view. Each new study expands your experiences, and the accumulation of your experiences affects your study of every text.

The third value of solo interpretation performance is the direct result of the performance experience itself. This value has two parts: one comes from performing and the other comes from viewing the performances of others.

Although you probably will experience some stage fright (figure skater Nancy Kerrigan admitted that she is always nervous before she performs, but that she has learned to use that to her advantage) at the thought of performing before a group of people, knowing that everyone in the class is in the same situation should alleviate much of the fear. If you read any of the many "confessions" written by professional actors concerning their early performances, they invariably say that their first response was fear—fear of failure, fear of inadequacy, fear of not meeting expectations. So, if you are fearful, you are in good company! The best remedy for stage fright, however, is preparation. The more time you spend learning about and living with your material, the less stage fright is likely to overcome you. (Keep in mind, however, that some stage fright is inevitable and even useful if it can be channeled into performance energy.) If you are prepared and feel confident on the day you are to perform, you will find that the benefits of performing far outweigh the temporary anxiety. (See Chapter 4 for specific guidelines on coping with performance anxiety or stage fright.) Performing before an audience develops poise, self-confidence, and an awareness of yourself that may be gained in no other way. In addition to the development of poise and self-confidence, performance helps you to develop better vocal control, quality, and flexibility, as well as improved diction. The performance experience also helps to improve your oral delivery in other communication situations.

Viewing the performances of others, and discussing these performances, helps sharpen your critical skills. You develop the ability to support your opinions. You discover the importance of explaining why something worked for you or how it might be improved. Postperformance discussions help you learn how to constructively evaluate your own performances as well as the performances of others.

Expanding your knowledge of good literature, increasing your awareness of other people and cultures, developing self-confidence, and improving your critical skills are just some of the important values derived from the solo performance experience.

WHAT IS THE DIFFERENCE BETWEEN SOLO INTERPRETATION PERFORMANCE AND ORAL READING?

Interpretation involves performance, but how does this type of performance differ from the oral reading you have been doing since you first learned to read? Often the terms *interpretation* and *oral reading* are used interchangeably. For clarity, we will draw a distinction between these terms. There are three basic differences between interpretation and oral reading.

First, oral reading is a skill you developed early in your education. Oral reading is the sounding of words so that they may be heard. Although you read the words orally, you do not necessarily understand the words or what they mean to you. Can you recall reading aloud from a text you did not understand? Can you remember hearing another person read who had no comprehension of the ideas being expressed?

Interpretation, on the other hand, is more sophisticated than oral reading. Interpretation is an artistic process that begins with silent and oral reading, but then asks that you make choices. When interpreting a written text, you do not merely sound words; you must come to some personal understanding of them— this is your interpretation. You make a determination as to who is speaking and to whom. In this way, you experience another's feelings, emotions, attitudes, and share those with your audience in performance.

Second, in an oral reading, you sound the words in your own voice. You make no attempt to change the way you normally speak. In interpretation, as we previously suggested, you may have to alter your voice to suggest the voice of the speaker. You change the pitch, volume, rate, or quality of your voice to correspond with your concept of this speaker.

Third, oral reading usually involves only vocal reinforcement of the text. In interpretation, nonverbal reinforcement is essential: you try to suggest your understanding not only of the speaker's voice, but also of the speaker's physical stance, walk, gestures, and facial expressions. You not only sound words, but also suggest the voice and body of the speaker and suggest the mind behind the words.

In interpretation, then, you create an impression of the speaker and share your creation with the audience. This created impression is based on your past experiences, preoccupations, memories, aspirations, interests. We call this weaving of text and personal experience *intertextuality.*

WHAT IS INTERTEXTUALITY?

Earlier we mentioned that one of your primary responsibilities in solo interpretation performance is to discover the nature of the speaker in a text. It is important that you know that a text is merely a construct the reader has the potential to create. Thanks to some current literary theories (see Chapter 3), the reader (you) is empowered with a greater responsibility than ever before in determining what a text means. As Beverly Whitaker Long so aptly put it at a performance festival, "When we read texts, we write or produce them. We relate them to texts we already know. We connect them to other texts and to other performances of those texts. . . . We make sense of a text in terms of another—and in terms of what we already know is similar."[4] As Mark Twain once wrote, "You can find in a text whatever you bring." Perhaps Bartholomae and Petrosky sum it up best when they describe reading as an act of aggression. They call for students to "make their mark" on the text, to be interactive with it: "Reading involves a fair measure of push and shove. You make your mark on a book and it makes its mark on you. Reading is not simply a matter of hanging back and waiting for a piece, or its author, to tell you what the writing has to say."[5]

During the Romantic period and throughout the nineteenth century, critics were primarily interested in studying the *writer's* contribution to a text. These critics studied biographical details of the writer, assuming they would find a direct correspondence between the writer's life and the literature he or she produced. During the first half of the twentieth century, the emphasis shifted to the *text* itself, quite separate from the writer or from the world in which the text was created. These New Critics believed that the only way to understand a text was to study it, that nothing outside the text could help unlock the secrets to understanding the tone, images, sounds, rhythms that made up the text. Today, the *reader* is responsible for determining what a text is about. The reader is considered as vital (perhaps, to some critics, more vital) than the author in determining what a text has to say. On a broad level, a text is an interweaving of language and experience, and you bring your own "text" (your own experiences with and ownership of language) with you whenever you interact with a work of literature. Wolfgang Iser, for example, believes that a "copartnership" exists between reader and text. Iser says that there is no single correct interpretation of a text which will exhaust its semantic potential.[6] This does not mean that you cannot get help in making your interpretation. It is always useful to read other works by the same author as well as critical commentaries, but, in the end, what a text means is determined by your unique relationship with it.

Our lives, then, may be viewed as "texts" through which we interpret other texts—thus the term, *intertextuality*. Our lives are influenced and shaped by books we have read, movies we have seen, experiences we have had, as well as by our relationship with language. As Louise Rosenblatt writes, "The reader's attention to the text activates certain elements in his past experience—external reference, internal response—that have become linked with the verbal symbols. Meaning will emerge from a network of relationships among the things symbolized *as he senses them*."[7] Thus, when you study a literary selection, you do not simply or objectively perceive it. Your interpretation of the text is always influenced and affected by what you have already experienced, by your interests, hobbies, preoccupations, as well as by your ownership of language. Suppose you were to listen to performance artist Laurie Anderson's version of *Hansel and Gretel*, or read Anne Sexton's version of the same tale in her book *Transformations*. How would your reception of these versions be affected by your knowledge of the original Brothers Grimm tale? Newlyweds, for example, will view a film about a couple who are divorcing much differently from how a couple on the verge of their own breakup might view the film. Your background and experiences influence and contribute to your interpretation of texts.

Your responsibility, then, is to read and study the text carefully, decide what *you* think it means, ask yourself who is speaking, to whom, about what, where, when, how, and why. (These are the questions posed in a dramatistic analysis of a literary text, which we shall discuss in more detail in Chapter 3.) You will create *your* conception of the speaker and his or her situation in performance. You "project" the speaker in the text as you understand that speaker from your interaction with the language in the text.

It is each reader's subjective response to a literary text that accounts for the many different interpretations any one text may produce. This encourages healthy discussion as we try to understand the way language communicates different images to different people.

Class Exercises

1. Look at this poem by Henry Reed. As you read the poem, ask yourself, Through what personal texts do I interpret this text? After you have decided what the poem means to you, answer the questions that follow it and discuss your responses with others.

NAMING OF PARTS   Henry Reed

To-day we have naming of parts. Yesterday,
We had daily cleaning. And to-morrow morning,
We shall have what to do after firing. But to-day,
To-day we have naming of parts. Japonica
Glistens like coral in all of the neighbouring gardens.
    And to-day we have naming of parts.

This is the lower sling swivel. And this
Is the upper sling swivel, whose use you will see,
When you are given your slings. And this is the piling swivel,
Which in your case you have not got. The branches
Hold in the gardens their silent, eloquent gestures.
    Which in our case we have not got.

This is the safety-catch, which is always released
With an easy flick of the thumb. And please do not let me
See anyone using his finger. You can do it quite easy
If you have any strength in your thumb. The blossoms
Are fragile and motionless, never letting anyone see
    Any of them using their finger.

And this you can see is the bolt. The purpose of this
Is to open the breech, as you see. We can slide it
Rapidly backwards and forwards: we call this
Easing the spring. And rapidly backwards and forwards
The early bees are assaulting and fumbling the flowers
    They call it easing the Spring.

They call it easing the Spring: it is perfectly easy
If you have any strength in your thumb: like the bolt,
And the breech, and the cocking-piece, and the point of balance,
Which in our case we have not got; and the almond-blossom
Silent in all of the gardens and the bees going backwards and forwards,
    For to-day we have naming of parts.

From Henry Reed, *A Map of Verona.* Reprinted by permission of Jonathan Cape Ltd. on behalf of the Estate of Henry Reed.

What does this text mean to you? What other texts does this text bring to mind? How many different voices do you hear? Who do you think is the audience for this text? Where is (are) the speaker(s)? When do you think this poem takes place? Why do you think the speaker(s) speaks? How would you describe the style of language the speaker(s) uses? How do you account for different interpretations of this poem?

2. Find one short poem that you really like and perform it for the class. Then lead a discussion about what other "texts" (past experiences, other literature read, movies seen, and so on) the audience, as well as you, "read" this poem through. If you perform a poem about the death of someone, for example, and you just lost someone close to you, how is your performance affected by this experience? How would your performance of a poem about war be affected if someone close to you had been at a battlefront? How would your knowledge of the painting "The Fall of Icarus" by Breughel influence your performance of "Musée des Beaux Arts" by W. H. Auden?

IS INTERPRETATION DIFFERENT FROM OTHER LITERATURE COURSES?

The question of whether interpretation is different from other literature courses is a legitimate question, since literature is the ultimate concern of English classes as well as of many interpretation classes. The difference resides in the method used to undertake and demonstrate literary study. In an English class, you analyze literature through preliminary silent reading, class discussion, and, occasionally, oral reading. In the interpretation classroom, you create your idea of the speaker(s) in a text and share the feelings, beliefs, desires, and so on, of that speaker with an audience. In the interpretation classroom, performing a text is a way of knowing that text.

In both classes, a discussion of whether Hamlet is really mad or is feigning madness might take place. In the interpretation class, however, you manifest your decision in performance. How to involve yourself personally in a particular literary text, and how to share the experience you discover in the text with an audience, are the central concerns of this book. The process of studying literature, then, is common to both the English and the interpretation classrooms. The manner in which you study the literature is the primary difference.

WHAT IS INTERPRETATION?

We have already stated that interpretation is the process of studying and performing texts, and we have discussed the diverse ways both "text" and "performance" may be defined. In this book, however, our focus is on the performance of literary texts in particular. For our purposes, then, interpretation is defined as *an artistic process of studying literature through performance and sharing that study with an audience.* The three basic ingredients of the interpretation process are a performer (you), a piece of literature, and an audience. Figure 1.1 shows a model of the interpretation ingredients. The boundaries which separate what we mean by text, performer, and audience are more indeterminate than ever before; thus, the broken circles. The shaded area is the interplay of text, performer, and audience—where all the variables come together during performance.

Let us examine each element of this definition individually.

Interpretation Is an Art

The artist creates a feeling, an idea, or an image through some means of expression. Some of these means of expression are music, dance, sculpture, literature, and painting. Each of these art objects involves an audience to a greater or lesser degree and causes them to experience various emotions. The artist creates an object which can be studied, analyzed, evaluated, and appreciated by others.

Interpreters, too, create art objects. In the interpretation process, you deal with works of art written by authors who are skillful in causing an audience to experience vicariously the feelings of the characters. As you project these characters for an audience, you, too, are creating art. You are helping the audience members to experience feelings, attitudes, and beliefs they may never have experienced.

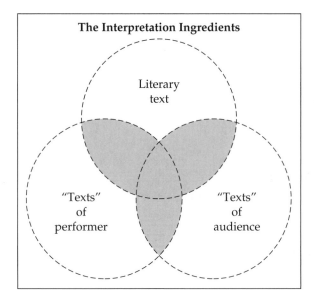

Figure 1.1

Interpretation Is a Process

Interpretation is a process, because from the moment you engage in the search for the right selection to perform, you never really come to a time when your study is culminated. The process continues for as long as you work with a text, and is different for each person who studies that text. You learn about the selection you have chosen for performance every time you study, rehearse, and perform it—just as you gain new insights from films by seeing them more than once, or from books by rereading them several times.

The process begins when you select a text to perform. The selection you choose should be one you like and feel compelled to perform. Once you have made your selection, you will want to spend time seeking to understand it, analyzing what you think it means, and creating your impression of the speaker(s) and audience(s). Analysis as well as rehearsal helps you make choices about the text which are then communicated in performance. Your choices are based on your interpretation, and you share that interpretation with others in performance. *But neither the analysis nor the performance is an end in itself.* Your analysis, as well as your performance, often leads to further analytic discoveries, to further insights into the text.

Look how this process works in relation to Emily Dickinson's poem "Because I Could Not Stop for Death."

16

BECAUSE I COULD NOT STOP FOR DEATH   Emily Dickinson

Because I could not stop for Death—
He kindly stopped for me—
The Carriage held but just Ourselves
And Immortality.

We slowly drove—He knew no haste
And I had put away
My labor and my leisure too,
For His Civility—

We passed the School, where Children strove
At Recess—in the Ring
We passed the Fields of Gazing Grain—
We passed the Setting Sun—

Or rather—He passed Us—
The Dews drew quivering and chill—
For only Gossamer, my Gown—
My Tippet—only Tulle—

We paused before a House that seemed
A swelling of the Ground—
The Roof was scarcely visible—
The Cornice—in the Ground—

Since then—'tis Centuries—and yet
Feels shorter than the Day
I first surmised the Horses' Heads
Were toward Eternity—

Upon first impression, you might decide that because this poem is about death, the speaker must necessarily be depressed and morose. After some time analyzing, rehearsing, and performing the poem, you could alter your original opinion. You might decide that death, to this speaker, is not viewed as a cold, hard, finale to life, but instead is viewed as a carriage ride with Death as the courtly driver carrying the speaker to Eternity. You might decide that this poem has nothing to do with literal death, but more about reliving one's life. Your interpretation may go through many transformations as a result of rereadings, additional study, rehearsal, and performance. New interpretations may be demonstrated in later performances of the same text.

Begin to view rehearsals as trial performances, and your performances as sophisticated rehearsals. Performances, then, are not ends to literary study, but rather parts of your study. Analysis, rehearsal, and performance are all means of studying literature common to interpretation.

The more time you spend with a piece of literature in analysis, rehearsal, and performance, the more you learn about it. One of your performances of a literary work might be completely different both from someone else's and from subsequent ones you present of the same text. From this comes the saying, "It's a matter of interpretation!" No two people describe a phenomenon in the same way, because no two people view things from the same perspective. Likewise, students of literature view the same selection differently because of their varying perspectives. Also, as we have intimated before, language is slippery, and what a word signifies may cause disagreement. The play of language is one of the major reasons we may have so many possible interpretations of a given text. The poet Wallace Stevens, for example, wrote in a highly ambiguous vein that allowed for the possibility of multiple interpretations. Stevens once wrote to R. P. Blackmur, "For the life of me, I don't . . . see why a poem should not mean one thing to one person and something else to another. The merest block of wood is anything that can be made out of it."[8] You are in the creative role of producing meaning, of making something identifiable out of that block of wood! In time, even your own perspective may change, and a literary selection you once thought meant one thing may come to mean something very different. The process of interpretation allows for and even encourages these kinds of alterations.

We have talked throughout this chapter about your empowerment in determining what a text means. We must offer a caveat, however, concerning your ethical responsibility in this process. Although you ultimately decide what a text means to you, as a beginning student you should gather as much information as you can to help you devise your interpretation. You could read information about the author's life, other works by the same author, as well as critical accounts of the author's work. This is especially true of texts from cultures other than your own. Be sure you familiarize yourself with background information about that culture so that your performance does not suffer from a lack of sensitivity to the elements that that culture holds sacred.

Interpretation Is the Study of Literature

You have now seen that you engage in the study of literature both prior to and during performance. This study is often what frightens beginning interpretation students. You may worry that your interpretation of a text is "wrong." You may feel ill-equipped to understand a piece of literature well enough to decide on an interpretation and share it with an audience. Although these feelings are common, they are unwarranted. All that is required at this time is your present knowledge and your desire to learn.

Many works of literature are not meant for our immediate understanding; understanding may come later, eventually, ultimately, or sometimes not at all. As you read a text, write down your initial impressions without censoring yourself. Try to avoid feeling that you are not entitled to an interpretation because you may not have had much experience devising one. This is not true. *Your impressions of a text are valid, and you have the power to decide what a text means to you.* Keep a record of your impressions after several rereadings, continued study, and analysis. These impressions will help you devise your own interpretation.

The more time you spend studying literature, the more you will learn about it, and the easier it will be for you to recognize textual clues that lead to an interpretation.

The first step in interpretation is to choose a piece of literature that you really like and want to spend some time with. Once you have chosen a selection, ask yourself what kind of communication is taking place. The two questions to ask yourself as you begin your study of a text are, Who is speaking? and Whom is the speaker addressing? Since your responsibility is ultimately to create your conception of the speaker in the text, you will want to know as much as possible about this person. You will also want to know who is addressed.

Literary Speakers

Begin analyzing your selection by gathering your impressions of the speaker. There are three general categories of speakers in literary texts: *personae, characters,* and *narrators.* Let us identify each of these three types of speakers.

Persona literally means "mask of the poet." The persona is an undefined speaker who is the writer's disguised self. Oftentimes writers create personae, rather than defined speakers, when they want to emphasize an experience rather than the person having it. In other words, the experience in the text is so universal (covering themes such as love, hate, war, marriage, sex, death) that a person of either gender or of any age could be expressing the words. Although it is often true that if the writer is male the persona is male and if the writer is female the persona is female, this may not always be the case. When you create a persona, you work to suggest the attitude you hear, the personal experience you sense—you do not have to worry about establishing a defined character.

Speakers who are dramatized are called *characters.* When the speaker in a text is defined and is clearly male or female, young or old, then that speaker is called a character and specific clues to characterization are provided in the text. The speaker may have a name, a style of language peculiar to him or her, as well as a specified age, height, or weight. Defined characters usually exist in specific settings and within a definite time period. When you deal with a text having a defined speaker, your job is to create that speaker as fully as possible.

Speakers who tell stories are called *narrators*. When a selection focuses on a series of events in time, the speaker is a narrator. Narrators are as varied as the stories they tell. Works that tell a story usually are framed in the past tense—the narrator is remembering something that has already happened—and the work creates a feeling of time progression.

To discover who is speaking, then, begin by deciding whether a persona, defined character, narrator, or a combination of speakers inhabits the text. Your decision always should be supported by lines from that text. Read your selection aloud several times. Ask yourself: Is there a particular style of language or word choice, use of the present tense, a defined time and place that seem to signal that a character speaks? Is the speaker an undramatized persona sharing a personal experience? Is the speaker narrating a series of past events? Let your rehearsal sessions help you decide the nature of the speaker and of the experience in the selection.

We need to make two additional points concerning the speaker in a selection. When you ask yourself, Who is speaking? two answers can immediately be ruled out. First, the speaker is not the author (although some exceptions to this exist— see Chapter 9 for a discussion of literary texts where the distinction between speaker and author is often blurred). Second, the speaker is not you.

Although writers often write from and about personal experiences, they create speakers to project these experiences for them. Sometimes the speaker is very close to the author (persona), and sometimes the speaker and the author seem very different from each other (character). In any case, though, we should not confuse the writer and the speaker any more than we confuse a self-portrait with the living artist who painted it. Your responsibility is to create the speaker *in* the work and not the writer *of* it.

There is certainly more room for interpretation when you attempt to create the speaker from clues provided in the text as opposed to trying to impersonate the writer. If you perform a short story by Mark Twain, for example, you suggest the speaker and not Twain. Your responsibility is to use your own experience with language and your own feelings about the text to create the speaker you see and hear. There was only one Mark Twain, and many people know what he looked and sounded like. There is not, therefore, much room for creativity or choice were you to try to suggest Twain. (Of course, were you to do a one-person show with the intent of re-creating the writer—such as Hal Holbrook did with Mark Twain, Julie Harris did with Emily Dickinson, or Robert Morse did with Truman Capote— impersonating the writer would be highly desirable.) Many more choices are available to you when you attempt to project the fictive speakers Twain creates. To assume a congruence between author and speaker turns a literary work into an autobiography, and this may not be the case. When Stephen King was asked during an interview on HBO if the film *Stand By Me*—which was an adaptation of his novella "The Body"—were autobiographical, he admitted that "writers always start to lie after awhile—they don't mean to, but they do."

The speaker, then, is not the author; the speaker is also not exactly the same as you. Although the speaker may be your gender and age and may be undergoing experiences or expressing feelings similar to those you have had, there will always be a difference between the experiences and feelings of a fictive speaker and your own. It is fine to begin by determining what you and the speaker have in common. Use these commonalities to help you identify with and create the speaker, but then ask yourself how you and the speaker are different. You may feel there is an advantage to performing speakers who seem to be as much like you as possible, but on the other hand, this may not provide the richest learning experience. To limit yourself to performing only those selections which express experiences similar to your own is to close yourself off from vicarious experiences that may help broaden your awareness. It may prevent you from tackling such larger-than-life characters as King Lear, Hamlet, Macbeth, Antigone, or Medea, among others. Remember, your responsibility is to create the speaker—to experience life through another's eyes. If you remain yourself, one of the primary benefits of interpretation is lost.

Literary Audiences

After you have determined who the speaker in a selection is, ask yourself, Whom is the speaker in this work addressing? The audience in a selection is sometimes very obvious and sometimes very obscure. Although the possible audiences are as numerous and varied as the types of speakers, there are four generalized audience categories. A speaker may address (1) himself or herself, (2) an inanimate object, a deceased or absent person, a muse, God, or some other mute listener, (3) a character or characters created in the work, or (4) the general public. Understanding the audience the speaker is addressing helps you create your interpretation of the speaker as well as the situation.

Interpretation Is Sharing Literature with an Audience

The performer must consider not only the audience within a work, but the audience for whom the work is presented. Sharing the study of a text with an audience is a performer's joy. Poets, lyricists, choreographers, painters, musicians—all artists create works of art to share them with others. Art is meant to be shared.

Interpretation gives you the opportunity to share your creation with an audience. Your audience includes yourself as well as those for whom you perform. As your own audience, you function as critic and self-evaluator. You may begin to see aspects of the text differently as you perform, and you also appraise your performance and the audience's response to it. The audience for whom you perform also may increase your understanding of the text by their responses.

In interpretation, a reciprocal sharing occurs between performer and audience. You offer the literature to an audience with your performance, and they, in turn, share primarily nonverbal responses with you as you perform, and eventually verbal responses during a postreading discussion. During this discussion, you find out how others interpreted your performance; you receive their personal impressions of what you did. Do keep in mind, though, that their opinions of your performance are influenced by their particular perspectives and by the "texts" they bring to your performance. They receive your interpretation and interpret or constitute it from their points of view. You try to minimize discrepancies between what you send and what the audience receives, but some discrepancies are inevitable and quite natural and may become the stimulus for valuable and revealing discussions (see Chapter 5).

In summary, the art of interpretation, like all artistic endeavors, asks that you give something of yourself. You engage in close study of a text—you give time and thought and feeling to this study—and you communicate this study to an audience. In performance, you bring your study of a literary selection to life, you grow from the experience and create the impetus for growth in the audience. In a sense, you "publish" your interpretation through performance, and the audience "reads" or "constitutes" it from their various perspectives.

WHAT LITERARY SELECTION SHOULD I CHOOSE?

There is no simple answer to this question, but we can make some suggestions. The first criterion, as we have already suggested, is to select a text you like, understand, and feel compelled to perform. We cannot stress the importance of this enough. You must care about a text to motivate yourself to spend the time it takes to prepare it for performance. Liking your selection must be of primary concern.

Since you spend a good deal of time with literature in the interpretation process, you will want to spend your time wisely by choosing the best literature to perform. Although deciding what is "best" is often a subjective process, certain characteristics are obvious. Good literature is characterized by *universality, individuality,* and *suggestion.* These qualities of good literature (along with the quality of aesthetic distance—see Chapter 4) were distilled as being important to the evaluation of literature as early as 1941 by Cornelius Corman Cunningham.[9]

Although this is a simplification of a complex process, examining a piece of literature in terms of universality, individuality, and suggestion helps you to determine if the literature is worth your time. Let's look at each quality more closely.

Literature is universal if it has something to say to all people for all time. Aspects of our common humanity are promoted in universal literature. Literature which deals with the common themes of love, hate, war, childhood, and death, among others, is universal. (Though we include universality as one of the three components of good literature as most good writers deal with universal themes, we also realize that all written texts deal with themes that are to some extent common to all human beings because we share a common humanity. The telephone book, by this definition, is universal because it deals with our common need for communicating with others, but that does not mean that the phone book would be an appropriate vehicle for solo performance! Individuality and suggestion are probably more important to defining good literature than is universality.)

Literature is individualistic if it is written by an author who has a unique way of expressing a universal subject. Even though we have encountered the theme before, we are still moved by the freshness of the approach the writer uses. Good literature must also leave something to the reader's imagination—this is the quality we call suggestion. In all good literature, the reader must be able to read between the lines and fill in and flesh out the experience the writer creates. In literature that is highly suggestive, the reader must work even harder to fill in the gaps, to flesh out the indeterminacies. We might say that poetry is the most highly suggestive type of literature because so much content is condensed in so few words. Postmodern literature (see Chapter 9) is also highly suggestive, asking quite a bit from the interpreter.

Let us now consider E. E. Cummings's poem "anyone lived in a pretty how town" and apply the characteristics of universality, individuality, and suggestion to it.

ANYONE LIVED IN A PRETTY HOW TOWN   E. E. Cummings

anyone lived in a pretty how town
(with up so floating many bells down)
spring summer autumn winter
he sang his didn't he danced his did.

Women and men (both little and small)
cared for anyone not at all
they sowed their isn't they reaped their same
sun moon stars rain

children guessed (but only a few
and down they forgot as up they grew
autumn winter spring summer)
that noone loved him more by more

when by now and tree by leaf
she laughed his joy she cried his grief
bird by snow and stir by still
anyone's any was all to her

someones married their everyones
laughed their cryings and did their dance
(sleep wake hope and then) they
said their nevers they slept their dream

stars rain sun moon
(and only the snow can begin to explain
how children are apt to forget to remember
with up so floating many bells down)

one day anyone died i guess
(and noone stooped to kiss his face)
busy folk buried them side by side
little by little and was by was

all by all and deep by deep
and more by more they dream their sleep
noone and anyone earth by april
wish by spirit and if by yes.

Women and men (both dong and ding)
summer autumn winter spring
reaped their sowing and went their came
sun moon stars rain

Universality

The poem "anyone lived in a pretty how town" appears to be about love. It seems to be about two people who meet, fall in love, die, and are buried side by side. This is a universal theme, and the ritual is common to most people everywhere for all time. The universality is captured also by the poet's use of the natural passage of time throughout the poem—spring, summer, autumn, winter—and by the emphasis on the elements of nature—sun, moon, stars, rain.

Individuality

In addition to having a universal theme, this poem has a distinctive, individualistic style. What exactly is it about this poem that makes it individualistic? There are many qualities that make it unique.

The most apparent aspect is Cummings's unique style. The lack of traditional punctuation or capitalization makes this poem distinctive, and the use of language is also unusual. Cummings seems to be using pronouns like "anyone" and "noone" to signify particular people, verbs like "isn't" and "didn't" as nouns, and phrases like "when by now and tree by leaf" to alter our usual expectation of language. All these qualities make this poem original.

The love theme is also uniquely expressed. Cummings seems to be telling the story of true love in contrast to a society of "how town" residents who are indifferent, apathetic, and mechanical in action and feeling—where the "how" of what they do is always the same. This is a town where the people ("Women and men," "someones and everyones," "busy folk") "slept their dreams," as opposed to "anyone" and "noone," who "dream their sleep." Despite the "how town's" apathy, "anyone" and "noone" love one another, even after death: "all by all and deep by deep/and more by more they dream their sleep/noone and anyone earth by april/wish by spirit and if by yes." At the end, they seem to transcend their physical lives to merge with the harmony of Nature in a spiritual existence. The "busy folk" learn nothing from them, but continue their routine: they "reaped their sowing and went their came/sun moon stars rain." The poem is built on the relative contrasts between the "how town" residents and "anyone" and "noone." For all of these reasons (and probably many more), this poem has an individualistic quality.

Suggestion

The last quality that determines whether a piece of literature is "good" is suggestion. The suggestive elements of this poem are those elements that produce a new meaning for the reader every time the poem is read, spoken, or heard. The qualities that make this poem individualistic also contribute to its suggestiveness. The more you read this poem, the more you learn about it.

Although we have talked of "anyone" and "noone" as distinct people living in a "how town," this is only one way to interpret this poem. "anyone" and noone" could be literally "anyone" in the world and "noone" at all. "noone" could be "anyone's" soul, which developed an identity of its own and became immortal through "anyone's" distinct individuality. Another interpretation might see "anyone" as a real person complete in himself and needing "noone" to complement him. The fact that there are so many possible interpretations of just the words "anyone" and "noone" makes this poem suggestive.

In addition to the many connotations of "anyone" and "noone," Cummings's unusual use of language and syntax adds to the poem's suggestive quality. Lines like "he sang his didn't he danced his did," "they sowed their isn't they reaped their same," "bird by snow and stir by still," and "little by little and was by was" each ask you to supply meaning. Much is left up to the imagination of the individual reader within the context of the whole poem.

This poem, then, fulfills our criteria for good literature—universality, individuality, and suggestion. Apply these characteristics to any literary selection you choose to study so that your time is spent on literature worthy of your investigation.

Class Exercise

Apply the characteristics of "good" literature to the following two poems.

THE FRAILTY AND HURTFULNESS OF BEAUTY   Henry Howard, Earl of Surrey

Brittle beauty that nature made so frail,
Whereof the gift is small, and short the season,
Flowering today, tomorrow apt to fail,
Tickle treasure, abhorred of reason,
Dangerous to deal with, vain, of none avail,
Costly in keeping, past not worth two peason,
Slipper in sliding as an eelës tail,
Hard to attain, once gotten not geason,
Jewel of jeopardy that peril doth assail,
False and untrue, enticëd oft to treason,
En'my to youth (that most may I bewail!),
Ah, bitter sweet! infecting as the poison,
Thou farest as fruit that with the frost is taken:
Today ready ripe, tomorrow all to-shaken.

THE FACE   Randall Jarrell

Die alte Frau, die alte Marschallin!
Not good any more, not beautiful—
Not even young.
This isn't mine.
Where is the old one, the old ones?
Those were mine.

It's so: I have pictures,
Not such old ones; people behaved
Differently then . . . When they meet me they say:
You haven't changed.
I want to say: You haven't looked.

This is what happens to everyone.
At first you get bigger, you know more,
Then something goes wrong.
You are, and you say: I am—
And you were . . . I've been too long.

I know, there's no saying no.
But just the same you say it. No.

I'll point to myself and say: I'm not like this.
I'm the same as always inside.
—And even that's not so.

I thought: if nothing happens . . .
and nothing happened.

Here I am.
But it's not *right*.
If just living can do this,
Living is more dangerous than anything:
It is terrible to be alive.

"The Face" from *The Complete Poems* by Randall Jarrell. Copyright © 1950, 1969 by Mrs. Randall Jarrell.

Now, see if you can decide which of these two poems is the better poem by applying the qualities of universality, individuality, and suggestion. Read the poems aloud and answer the following questions. (As you proceed, keep in mind that the answer to each question is a matter of interpretation. Try to support your decision by pointing to specific elements in each poem.)

1. Does each poem deal with a universal theme? What do you think the themes are? What makes the themes universal?
2. Which poem has a more individual style? Why do you think so?
3. In which poem has something been left up to your imagination? In which poem is there more creative involvement called for from the reader? Why do you think so?

HOW DO I PREPARE A SELECTION FOR PERFORMANCE?

Although the following six-step procedure greatly simplifies the complex process of preparing a selection for performance, it does help you know how to begin.

1. *You receive an assignment.* Let us say you are asked to perform a prose fiction selection (a section from a short story or novel) of five-to-seven minutes in length, including an introduction.

2. *You choose a selection.* Be sure the selection you choose is one you enjoy and want to share and is an example of good literature. There are many possible sources for selections. Check your own library of sources or those of a friend. Choose one of the selections in this text or in other interpretation texts. Go to the library and look up fiction writers you have heard of or whose works you have

read in the past. Alternatively, you could search the Internet, now a global resource for students. It is estimated by IDC's Internet Commerce Market Model that in 2003, over 200 million people in the United States alone will be accessing the Internet. A recent *Newsweek* interview with writers, publishers, and editors revealed that soon "books" and "publishing" will take on completely different definitions as there is "online publishing" and "books on demand." You may check the Internet for biographical information about writers, quotes to use in your introductions, copies of literary selections (mostly selections in the public domain), among hundreds of other uses. Effective search engines for this information include Alta Vista, Excite, Google, Lycos, and Yahoo. If you know the name of a writer that you like, just type in the name of the writer; if you know the name of a specific selection but you do not have a copy, type in the name of the selection (you will get better results if you put the writer's or selection's name in quotation marks) and often you will be able to download a copy of the selection. Should you want to perform a sonnet or a scene from a Shakespearean play, for example, there are over 13,127 web pages if you search under "Shakespeare's plays." The address of one good source is *daphnepalomar.edu/Shakespeare/works.htm.* Here you will find introductory information about Shakespeare, study guides, collected editions of the plays, as well as individual editions of the plays and copies of all of Shakespeare's poems and sonnets. You will be able to download a specific scene from any Shakespearean play. Another good source is *ArdenShakespeare.com,* which provides excellent, reliable texts of the complete works. One good source to access if you need specific questions answered about writers or their texts is *Webhelp.com* where in real time a live person will respond to any inquiries you may have.

Keep in mind, though, that anyone can enter material on the Internet. It is probably a good idea to check with the library or with your instructor if you suspect that information you have downloaded is inaccurate, incomplete, or mere speculation.

You will want to find a selection that can be easily cut, or shortened, to fit the five-to-seven minute time limit. Since you have a time limit, chances are slim that you will be able to perform the entire selection. You will have to take a five-to-seven minute cutting from the whole, trying to maintain a sense of completeness. (We will learn more about cutting in Chapter 4.) If you are unfamiliar with prose fiction writers, consult the "sources to check for selections to perform" at the end of Chapter 2, the list of possible selections at the end of Chapter 6, or consult the *Short Story Index* in the library for possible selections. Another excellent source is *Masterpieces of World Literature in Digest Form.* (This book will give you plot summaries, and then you can find and read the complete work.) Book reviews in magazines may give you some ideas, and bestseller lists posted in libraries, book stores, and in the book sections of many magazines can also be of use. You might also ask your instructor for suggestions.

3. *You analyze and rehearse your selection.* You will now want to analyze and rehearse your selection to answer those two important initial questions: Who is

speaking, and to whom? Use all sources available to you, including other works by the same writer, biographical accounts, and critical commentary.

You analyze your selection through study, rehearsals, and eventually through performance. We suggest that you apply the two means of analysis discussed in Chapter 3: the dramatistic and the modal. With the dramatistic analysis, you decide who is speaking, to whom, about what, where, when, how, and why. With the modal approach, you categorize and analyze literature. When you categorize literature modally, you look at the work as a whole and determine its literary classification by investigating the relationship between the writer and the speaker. Does someone very much like the writer—a persona—seem to be speaking (lyric mode)? Does a defined character(s) seem to be speaking (dramatic mode)? Are both a persona and a character speaking (epic mode)? We call this decision the "Speaker Mode."

When you analyze literature modally, you look at the work line by line or moment by moment and examine the relationship between the speaker and his or her audience. Is the speaker, at any given time, addressing himself or herself, God, a muse, or an absent or deceased person (lyric mode)? Is the speaker addressing a character or characters (dramatic mode)? Is the speaker addressing the audience (epic)? We call these decisions "Audience Modes." Rehearse the selection several times aloud after preliminary silent reading. As you rehearse, you will learn more and more about the nature of the speaker—how this person looks, sounds, and feels—and the speaker's audience. Remember, short rehearsal sessions over an extended period of time will be more beneficial to you than a long rehearsal session the night before you perform! Work back and forth between silent analysis and rehearsals. Both will help you answer performance questions and solve performance problems.

4. *You compose an introduction.* As you analyze and rehearse your selection, you should also be thinking about the introduction. Most interpretation performances are preceded by an introduction which prepares the audience for what is to come. You will want the audience to know the title of the selection, the author's name, and any additional information pertinent to your cutting. You need only introduce your cutting; do not attempt a plot summary of the whole novel or story. (We will learn more about introductions in Chapter 4.)

5. *You perform your selection.* Walk confidently up to the front of the room, and pause—look at your audience to be sure they are all prepared to listen. Deliver your introduction directly to them. Pause again to give the audience time to digest what you have said and to give yourself a moment to create the speaker. (This "moment before" is an essential aspect of performance that is often disregarded. This performance medium allows the audience to see you transform into the speaker before their eyes—a transformation that normally takes place off stage. As David Black puts it, "While you are concentrating, the audience experiences a dramatic moment. This is something a normal theatre audience does not get to see— that magical moment in time when you become someone else. While you are

concentrating on what you are about to do, you are also preparing your audience for their journey to the imaginary world to which you are taking them. And you are creating anticipation as if the houselights were going down in the theatre."[10] During this moment before, you should be thinking about what prompts the first line, what has gone on before [if you are not starting at the beginning of the selection], that motivates your first line.) Then begin your selection by establishing the scene out front and varying your voice, body, focus, gestures, and so forth as necessary to present your interpretation. When you come to the end of your performance, slow down the last line to prepare the audience for the ending, pause, and walk back to your seat. This is not an audition, so there is no need to say "thank you." (We should thank you for sharing your gifts with us.) Try not to show any displeasure you might have experienced if things did not go just as planned. Chances are the audience will not know you've made a mistake unless you draw attention to it.

6. *You participate in an evaluation session.* In an evaluation session, both your performance and the performances of your peers are evaluated. Among the qualities a good evaluator should have is objectivity. (We will discuss evaluation in more detail in Chapter 5.)

This simple formula is merely a skeletal list of the order of events you will go through as you prepare a piece of literature for performance. Depending on the nature of the text you have selected, some steps may take longer than others, some may need to be drastically altered, and some may need to be repeated several times.

A SAMPLE ANALYSIS AND PERFORMANCE SUGGESTIONS FOR "THE USE OF FORCE"

The rest of this chapter provides the specific kinds of information you will need to prepare your first selection for class. We will study William Carlos Williams's short story "The Use of Force" because it offers multiple levels for investigation and is an excellent selection for performance. After the story, an analysis and some performance suggestions are provided, along with sample introductions.

THE USE OF FORCE   William Carlos Williams

They were new patients to me, all I had was the name, Olson. Please come down as soon as you can, my daughter is very sick.

When I arrived I was met by the mother, a big startled looking woman, very clean and apologetic who merely said, Is this the doctor? and let me in. In the back, she added. You must excuse us, doctor, we have her in the kitchen where it is warm. It is very damp here sometimes.

The child was fully dressed and sitting on her father's lap near the kitchen table. He tried to get up, but I motioned for him not to bother, took off my overcoat and started to look things over. I could see that they were all very nervous, eyeing me up and down distrustfully. As often, in such cases, they weren't telling me more than they had to, it was up to me to tell them; that's why they were spending three dollars on me.

The child was fairly eating me up with her cold, steady eyes, and no expression to her face whatever. She did not move and seemed, inwardly, quiet; an unusually attractive little thing, and as strong as a heifer in appearance. But her face was flushed, she was breathing rapidly, and I realized that she had a high fever. She had magnificent blonde hair, in profusion. One of those picture children often reproduced in advertising leaflets and the photogravure sections of the Sunday papers.

She's had a fever for three days, began the father, and we don't know what it comes from. My wife has given her things, you know, like people do, but it don't do no good. And there's been a lot of sickness around. So we tho't you'd better look her over and tell us what is the matter.

As doctors often do I took a trial shot at it as a point of departure. Has she had a sore throat?

Both parents answered me together, No . . . No, she says her throat don't hurt her.

Does your throat hurt you? added the mother to the child. But the little girl's expression didn't change nor did she move her eyes from my face.

Have you looked?

I tried to, said the mother, but I couldn't see.

As it happens we had been having a number of cases of diphtheria in the school to which this child went during that month and we were all, quite apparently, thinking of that, though no one had as yet spoken of the thing.

Well, I said, suppose we take a look at the throat first. I smiled in my best professional manner and asking for the child's first name I said, come on, Mathilda, open your mouth and let's take a look at your throat.

Nothing doing.

Aw, come on, I coaxed, just open your mouth wide and let me take a look. Look I said opening both hands wide, I haven't anything in my hands. Just open up and let me see.

Such a nice man, put in the mother. Look how kind he is to you. Come on, do what he tells you to. He won't hurt you.

At that I ground my teeth in disgust. If only they wouldn't use the word "hurt" I might be able to get somewhere. But I did not allow myself to be hurried or disturbed but speaking quietly and slowly I approached the child again.

As I moved my chair a little nearer suddenly with one cat-like movement both her hands clawed instinctively for my eyes and she almost reached them too. In fact she knocked my glasses flying and they fell, though unbroken, several feet away from me on the kitchen floor.

Both the mother and father turned themselves inside out in embarrassment and apology. You bad girl, said the mother, taking her and shaking her by one arm. Look what you've done. The nice man . . .

For heaven's sake, I broke in. Don't call me a nice man to her. I'm here on the chance that she might have diphtheria and possibly die of it. But that's nothing to her. Look here, I said to the child, we're going to look at your throat. You're old enough to understand what I'm saying. Will you open it now by yourself or shall we have to open it for you?

Not a move. Even her expression hadn't changed. Her breaths however were coming faster and faster. Then the battle began. I had to do it. I had to have a throat culture for her own protection. But first I told the parents that it was entirely up to them. I explained the danger but said that I would not insist on a throat examination so long as they would take the responsibility.

If you don't do what the doctor says you'll have to go to the hospital, the mother admonished her severely.

Oh yeah? I had to smile to myself. After all, I had already fallen in love with the savage brat, the parents were contemptible to me. In the ensuing struggle they grew more and more abject, crushed, exhausted while she surely rose to magnificent heights of insane fury of effort bred of her terror of me.

The father tried his best, and he was a big man but the fact that she was his daughter, his shame at her behavior and his dread of hurting her made him release her just at the critical moment several times when I had almost achieved success, till I wanted to kill him. But his dread also that she might have diphtheria made him tell me to go on, go on though he himself was almost fainting, while the mother moved back and forth behind us raising and lowering her hands in an agony of apprehension.

Put her in front of you on your lap, I ordered, and hold both her wrists.

But as soon as he did the child let out a scream. Don't you're hurting me. Let go of my hands. Let them go I tell you. Then she shrieked terrifyingly, hysterically. Stop it! Stop it! You're killing me!

Do you think she can stand it, doctor! said the mother.

You get out, said the husband to his wife. Do you want her to die of diphtheria?

Come on now, hold her, I said.

Then I grasped the child's head with my left hand and tried to get the wooden tongue depressor between her teeth. She fought, with clenched teeth, desperately! But now I also had grown furious—at a child. I tried to hold myself down but I couldn't. I know how to expose a throat for inspection. And I did my best. When finally I got the wooden spatula behind the last teeth and just the point of it into the mouth cavity, she opened up for an instant but before I could see anything she came down again and gripping the wooden blade between her molars she reduced it to splinters before I could get it out again.

Aren't you ashamed, the mother yelled at her. Aren't you ashamed to act like that in front of the doctor?

Get me a smooth-handled spoon of some sort, I told the mother. We're going through with this. The child's mouth was already bleeding. Her tongue was cut and she was screaming in wild hysterical shrieks. Perhaps I should have desisted and come back in an hour or more. No doubt it would have been better. But I have seen at least two children lying dead in bed of neglect in such cases, and feeling that I must get a diagnosis now or never I went at it again. But the worst of it was that I too had got beyond reason. I could have torn the child apart in my own fury and enjoyed it. It was a pleasure to attack her. My face was burning with it.

The damned little brat must be protected against her own idiocy, one says to one's self at such times. Others must be protected against her. It is a social necessity. And all these things are true. But a blind fury, a feeling of adult shame, bred of a longing for muscular release are the operatives. One goes on to the end.

In a final unreasoning assault I overpowered the child's neck and jaws. I forced the heavy silver spoon back of her teeth and down her throat till she gagged. And there it was—both tonsils covered with membrane. She had fought valiantly to keep me from knowing her secret. She had been hiding that sore throat for three days at least and lying to her parents in order to escape just such an outcome as this.

Now truly she *was* furious. She had been on the defensive before but now she attacked. Tried to get off her father's lap and fly at me while tears of defeat blinded her eyes.

William Carlos Williams, *The Farmers' Daughters.* Copyright 1933 by William Carlos Williams. Reprinted by permission of New Directions Publishing Corporation.

A Sample Analysis of "The Use of Force"

The first important question to ask is, Who is speaking? The speaker in this story is both a character (the doctor) and the narrator of the story, and he speaks from a *first-person, major character* point of view. He is inside the story (he is a character in the story who refers to himself in the first person as "I" or "me"), and he is telling us of a firsthand experience in which he was the central figure (major character). But what kind of a person is he? What do we know about him? We know that he is a doctor who makes house calls, who is determined to carry out his examination of a patient despite all obstacles, and that he has to use some force to make a diagnosis. We know, also, that the patient is new to him. The doctor describes both the actions he took and the reasons or rationales behind those actions. Little physical detail of the doctor is given other than that he wears glasses.

The next important question is, Whom is the speaker addressing? We said earlier that a speaker usually has one of four audiences in mind. The narrator in this story would address the general audience. But ask yourself who that "general audience" *might* be. Any time you address the "general audience," you will want to make the identification of your audience one of your interpretation choices. Who will you imagine the actual audience to be as you address them as the doctor? You discover this by analyzing the way the narrator speaks to the audience, the language he uses to tell the story, as well as the subject matter itself.

The nature of the audience in this story is not immediately apparent (this is true of much prose fiction). We can assume that the doctor is not talking to others in the medical profession, for if he were talking to peers, he would probably not say, "As doctors often do I took a trial shot at it as a point of departure." Other doctors would know what "doctors often do." Though the specific nature of the audience is unclear, we can say that the doctor seems to be talking to people he trusts and feels confident will understand his confrontation with the patient and her family.

The language the narrator uses is extremely simple and conversational. Williams says his stories "were written in the form of a conversation which I was partaking in."[11] The conversational style is highlighted by the fact that Williams refrains from using any quotation marks for the dialogue in the story. The effect created by this stylistic device is that the story reads as though only the doctor is speaking, and as though he is paraphrasing in his own words what others—including himself— once said. The lack of quotation marks also gives the effect that this story is being spoken—not written. Oral communication does not need quotation marks. The narrator, then, is conscious of telling a story, and his language style indicates that he is comfortable telling it.

Let us now consider two possible interpretations of this story. One way to view it is as an experience in the life of a doctor as he undergoes his daily routine of patient care. The doctor finds this case worth telling perhaps because of the unusual attractiveness of the child, the pervasive poverty of her surroundings, or the fear that she might have had diphtheria. In this interpretation of the story, the doctor is relating the events surrounding a particularly difficult case where he lost control for a moment. Knowing that Williams was himself a doctor lends credence to this interpretation.

This story can be interpreted in a completely different way as well. (As we said earlier, good stories have room for many different interpretations.) The doctor's examination of the child could be viewed as a metaphor for rape. In this reading of the story, we see a doctor rationalizing his behavior after forcing a child to submit to him against her will. The story now becomes a doctor's confession to vindicate himself and alleviate guilt. Although this interpretation is on a *figurative* (or connotative) level as opposed to a *literal* (or denotative) level, it is supportable. There are lines in the story that suggest the rape motif: "At that I ground my teeth in disgust," "I had already fallen in love with the savage brat," "I could have torn the child apart in my own fury and enjoyed it. It was a pleasure to attack her." In addition, there are phrases like "a longing for muscular release," and "a final unreasoning assault." The placing of objects inside the child's mouth is also suggestive, as is the child's feeling of fury and defeat. R. F. Dietrich supports this figurative reading of the story when he writes, "The connotations of rape are unmistakable."[12]

As we have shown, there is more than one level of meaning in this story, and there is more than one possible interpretation. As an interpreter, you must decide what you think the story means, based on your understanding of it. As long as you can support your interpretation with lines from the text, it is a viable interpretation. Remember, though, that performance decisions do not always *follow* analytic decisions. You may discover more about a text by performing it than by hours of silent pondering. As suggested, work back and forth between silent study of text and rehearsals.

Let us look at ways to perform this story.

Performance Suggestions for "The Use of Force"

When you translate analysis into performance, you decide how each character who appears in your scene will look, sound, act, and feel. You make these decisions by reading your selection aloud several times and responding to the language the author uses. Try to develop a character from the inside out. Let the kind of language and the style of speech a character uses determine how that character will be projected in performance. Try to feel as the character would feel and let your voice, body, and mind respond naturally. Although this inward development of character often takes time and lots of rehearsal, certain specific performance suggestions can help you develop a character. These performance suggestions can be divided into three categories: vocal responsiveness, physical responsiveness, and emotional responsiveness. Let us examine "The Use of Force" with these elements in mind.

Vocal responsiveness

When you decide on the vocal response for each character, you decide how to adjust your own pitch, rate, volume, emphasis, and quality to project the character's unique vocal pattern. In "The Use of Force," the doctor-narrator is the only speaker. He is telling us now about an event that happened to him in the past. Since there are no quotation marks around the lines said by the other characters in this story, the doctor-narrator is the only character who actually speaks. He seems to be paraphrasing rather than directly quoting what the other characters said in the past when this event occurred. When performing this story, you create the doctor-narrator, and he suggests the other characters from his point of view. The characterization, then, of the parents and child in the story will depend on how "dramatic" and "credible" you believe the doctor-narrator to be and on how vividly he wishes to re-create the past scene.

The vocal responsiveness of the doctor-narrator depends on your interpretation of the story. The doctor's rate, volume, pitch, and intensity could vary greatly, depending on whether you decide that this story is a recounting of a typical day in the life of a doctor or a metaphor for rape. Try to deliver the following lines, keeping in mind these two different interpretations (of course, other interpretations are also possible). Pay close attention to vocal responsiveness: how is it affected by your interpretation?

> But the worst of it was that I too had got beyond reason. I could have torn the child apart in my own fury and enjoyed it. It was a pleasure to attack her. My face was burning with it.
>
> The damned little brat must be protected against her own idiocy, one says to one's self at such times. Others must be protected against her. It is a social necessity. And all these things are true. But a blind fury, a feeling of adult shame, bred of a longing for muscular release are the operatives. One goes on to the end.

The doctor-narrator's vocal responsiveness would also be affected by whom you decide he is addressing. We speak differently to friends, for example, than to superiors or to strangers.

The doctor-narrator in the present suggests the vocal quality of the other three characters as well as of himself in the past, and his characterization of these others is again dependent on your interpretation of the story and on how the doctor remembers them. The doctor in the past should sound quite similar to the narrator, as they are the same person, separated only by a seemingly short period of time. The doctor may be presented as becoming more emotionally involved as he begins to relive the scenes from the past. The doctor-narrator might use a high-pitched voice with clenched teeth for the child, a lower pitch and softer vocal quality with a more intense delivery for the mother, and a low pitch and slow, deliberate quality for the father.

Physical responsiveness

As you tell the story as the doctor-narrator, you will probably want to stand. The doctor-narrator might stand straight with a bit of tautness in the shoulder area. The doctor in the remembered scene would look similar to the doctor-narrator, but might be a little less straight and taut. The experience he is reliving might cause his body to become more tense as he becomes angry in the story, then a bit more tired and bent as the story winds down.

The doctor projects the physical as well as the vocal qualities of each character in the past scene. He may decide to project the child's body as rigid and impenetrable. Her body should seem "as strong as a heifer"—as the doctor describes her. The mother's body should be taut and tense. At one point, she is "raising and lowering her hands in an agony of apprehension." The doctor could pace a bit when she speaks, to underscore her fear and anxiety. The father's body might also show tension as he is trying to maintain control and hold on to his daughter. Since the father is seated most of the time with the child on his lap, the doctor would not move or walk around as he repeats the father's lines. To suggest the height differences between the standing doctor and the seated child and father, the doctor in the past would look slightly down when speaking to them, and they would look slightly up when addressing him.

One additional consideration involved in physical responsiveness is the use of *focus* and *character placement*. In this story, the doctor projects himself as well as three other characters. This means that you must indicate to the audience a place where each character can be imagined to exist. Actors, when performing in a play, look at each other using *onstage focus*. Since the interpreter performs alone, looking onstage (turning profile to the audience to deliver a line as though another person were present) would be awkward and would cause some audience members to miss some nonverbal expressions. In interpretation, the scene exists not onstage, as it does for the actor, but in the audience's imagination. Therefore, the interpreter projects out front, using offstage focus. The use of *offstage focus* enables the audience to see the performer's full face throughout the performance and encourages them to participate by imagining the scene the performer creates around them.

Character placement is an aspect of focus used as a rather arbitrary means of keeping characters separate during passages of dialogue. When a character speaks a line of dialogue, the interpreter does not look at the audience (since the audience is not being addressed), but out front above the audience. Each character who speaks receives his or her own placement in space, and this placement does not

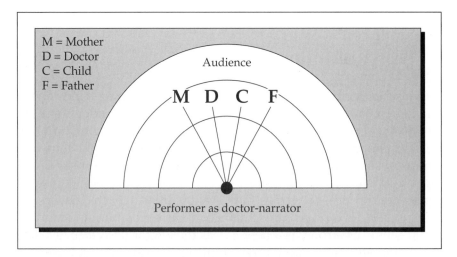

Figure 1.2

vary, no matter whom the character addresses or where the character might move. We call this assignment of specific locations for each character out in the audience *character placement*. The avoidance of eye contact with the audience is called *closed focus.*

In "The Use of Force," the doctor-narrator must use character placement when he suggests the other characters through himself. He might visualize the characters in the imagined scene as diagramed in Figure 1.2.

The doctor-narrator looks directly at the audience, telling the story to them. When he does this, he uses *open focus,* and makes direct contact with members of the audience. The doctor-narrator looks at and addresses the audience as he shares the events of the story. When he presents the characters' dialogue from the past, he uses closed focus and character placement to suggest that they were looking at and speaking to each other.

Narrator: Uses open focus, looks at and talks to the audience.
Characters: Use closed focus, and look at and speak to each other out in the imagined scene in the audience. Each character receives one placement and appears to see the character or characters being addressed from that placement. That placement does not change regardless of what the character does, where the character goes, or to whom the character speaks. Characters speaking lines of dialogue rarely, if ever, look at the audience.

Emotional responsiveness

The emotional responsiveness, as well as the vocal and physical responsiveness, of the doctor-narrator also depends upon your interpretation of the story as a whole. Since the events the doctor-narrator relates have already happened, he would probably be less emotionally involved than he is in the remembered scene. The doctor-narrator remains fairly calm and objective in the present as he describes and explains what happened in the past. At times, though, he does seem to get caught up in the remembered scene and relives the emotions he felt then. Lines such as "I had to smile to myself" and "I tried to hold myself down" indicate that the doctor-narrator is not quite as objective as he may initially seem.

The doctor projects the child and the mother as highly emotional and tense. The father seems to be more calm and controlled. The doctor seems to have a little less contempt for the father than for the mother, and he might thus project the father more favorably.

The attitudinal tone the doctor-narrator uses is also important. Once again, the way the narrator relates the events of the story will be determined by your choice of interpretation. The story's tone could be humorous or devastating. If you view the story as an examination that is simply more difficult than most because of a strong-willed little brat and her ignorant parents, then the story might have a light-hearted tone, and you would make the narrator look and sound kind and sympathetic. If you view the story as a metaphor for rape, the tone will depend on how aware the doctor-narrator is of his "use of force" both now and in the past, and on how aware he thinks his audience is of what he is "confessing."

Composing and Presenting the Introduction

One additional consideration is the introduction (see Chapter 4 for more extensive information on the content and delivery of introductions). As we stated earlier, most interpretation performances are preceded by a well-planned introduction that captures attention and prepares the audience for what is to come. Each time you rehearse your performance, you should rehearse your introduction as well.

An introduction should include the title of the work, the name of the author, and the time and location in which the selection takes place, if significant. The introduction should also carve out your approach to the material so that the audience knows what to expect once your performance begins. If time does not permit you to perform the entire selection, your introduction should also briefly explain what has gone on before your scene begins. (If you are performing from the beginning of a selection, however, you need not tell the audience what happens afterward. In fact, refraining from revealing the ending may motivate them to read the selection for themselves.) In addition, if you directly address the general audience (i.e., use open focus) at any time during the performance—as would the narrator in "The Use of Force," you should explain in the introduction who that audience *might* be. As you perform, then, you speak to those in the room as though they were the intended audience. Lastly, your introduction should be composed with the people in the room in mind. For example, if someone before you has performed something serious and you are performing something humorous, you may want to say something like, "And now for a complete change of mood," to alter the atmosphere in the room. The delivery of your introduction should set an appropriate mood and be flexible enough to allow for changes should the audience send feedback that they do not understand something.

Read the sample introductions below for "The Use of Force." We have composed two different introductions to coincide with the two different views of the story presented above. Notice how in each instance the interpreter identifies the intended audience and carves out an interpretation of the selection in the introduction. This allows the audience to listen to the performance with the performer's concept in mind and aids them during a postperformance evaluation, when two relevant questions could be, What did you say you were going to do? and Did you do it?

Sample introduction 1

Doctors often encounter patients who are particularly memorable because the patients have unusual characteristics or are particularly difficult. This is certainly true in William Carlos Williams's short story "The Use of Force." This story involves the doctor-narrator's confrontation with Mathilda Olson and her parents in their home during the 1930s when doctors made house calls and only charged $3.00! Knowing that Williams was himself a doctor underscores the sense of light-heartedness the narrator feels as he shares this story with family and friends.

Sample introduction 2

At first look, "The Use of Force" by William Carlos Williams seems to be a simple short story that reveals the conflict that occasionally ensues when doctor meets patient. But I believe that much more is suggested beneath the surface. In my interpretation, the doctor-narrator is riddled with guilt because of his unethical treatment of Mathilda Olson, his patient, and he is now trying to alleviate this guilt by confessing and attempting to justify his behavior to therapists. The story took place in the 1930s in the Olson home. "The Use of Force" by William Carlos Williams.

   After delivering the introduction, pause. Use this pause to transform yourself into the doctor-narrator, then begin the story.

   Now that we have given you an idea of a traditional approach to this art form, let us suggest a more experimental approach to performance.

METAPHORIC AND METONYMIC PERFORMANCES

What we have demonstrated up to this point can best be described as *metaphoric* interpretations. By metaphoric we mean interpretations which affirm, respect, or conserve the perceived integrity of a text. Texts are open to many alternative possibilities and there are many viable performances of the same text. Beverly Whitaker Long and Mary Frances Hopkins believe that some interpretations reflect *certainties,* some *probabilities,* some *possibilities,* and some *distortions* of literary texts.[13] Certainties imply that there is direct evidence for the decisions you make. We assume, for example, that in Elizabeth Barrett Browning's sonnet "How Do I Love Thee" (see Chapter 8), the speaker addresses a significant other, proclaiming an undying love. We learn this from the literal (denotative) meaning of the words in the sonnet and from doing research on Elizabeth Barrett Browning, which would reveal her intense love for her husband, Robert Browning, at the time she wrote the sonnet. Probabilities and possibilities are metaphoric interpretations that may be only implied or suggested, but are still viable. A probable or possible interpretation of the sonnet would be to assume that the speaker is addressing herself or God, for example. Distortions are interpretations that cannot be supported either with lines from the text or outside research. To say, for example, that Browning's sonnet is a sarcastic diatribe against love or the musings of an introspective prisoner dealing with thoughts of life and death in a confined space are distortions. Assuming that Wilfred Owen's poem "Dulce et Decorum Est" is a pro-war poem because the title and last lines translate "it is sweet and appropriate to die for one's country," seems to be a distortion as every image in the poem depicts the horrors of war. Owen saw his friends die in war and was ultimately a victim of World War I himself. The title and last line seem to be ironic, as the poem itself suggests the opposite point of view.

But what if your intention **is** to distort; that is, to subvert, challenge, or transgress beyond the perceived integrity of a text? If this is your goal, you are engaged in a *metonymic* interpretation of a text. Most metonymic performances intentionally set out to undermine rather than reify the values implicit in a text. Metonymic performances often expose new ramifications of a text and reveal creative possibilities for performance. Although the performer's intertextuality is involved in creating both metaphoric and metonymic interpretations, metonymic interpretations are often more deeply personal and idiosyncratic. Often in metonymic performances, performers reveal very personal texts—personal information about self—which can be risky and takes courage. Look at this poem by Robert Frost entitled "The Road Not Taken:"

THE ROAD NOT TAKEN   Robert Frost

Two roads diverged in a yellow wood,
And sorry I could not travel both
And be one traveler, long I stood
And looked down one as far as I could
To where it bent in the undergrowth.

Then took the other, as just as fair,
And having perhaps the better claim,
Because it was grassy and wanted wear;
Though as for that the passing there
Had worn them really about the same.

And both that morning equally lay
In leaves no step had trodden black.
Oh, I kept the first for another day!
Yet knowing how way leads on to way,
I doubted if I should ever come back.

> I shall be telling this with a sigh
> Somewhere ages and ages hence:
> Two roads diverged in a wood, and I—
> I took the one less traveled by,
> And that has made all the difference.

This poem has been variously interpreted. Some see in it the theme of individualism; some, the theme of anxiety and angst. Many performance majors are drawn to it because they see themselves as the persona attempting to choose between a stable, secure, clear career path (e.g., doctor, lawyer) and the tangled, thorny path of the performer, even if this interpretation is not what Frost literally implies or intends (since the persona tells us that the paths were worn about the same).

Performers may also use literature to serve political or social agendas. What issues are raised, for example, when someone other than a black woman speaks the poem "I am a Black Woman" (see Chapter 2)? Could we perhaps divorce the poem from its content and deal instead with what we learn from the language play? What happens when a male performs a poem about a female, and vice versa? What happens when Catholics perform texts about Jews, and vice versa? Interpretation allows for and, indeed, promotes this divergency—*but we must always be aware of what we are doing and why.* We must also avoid stereotyping the other instead of trying to understand and respect.

One of the most cogent arguments for the metonymic comes from Terence Hawkes who compares the experimental approach described above to the jazz musician:

> The abstract model I reach for is of course that of jazz music: that black American challenge to the Eurocentric idea of the author's, or the composer's, authority. For the jazz musician, the "text" of a melody is a means, not an end. Interpretation in that context is not parasitic but symbiotic in its relationship with its object. Its role is not limited to the service, or the revelation, or the celebration, of the author's/composer's art. Quite the reverse: interpretation constitutes the art of the jazz musician.[14]

Metonymic interpretations are probably NOT the best place to begin your study of interpretation. We suggest that you rely on certainties, probabilities, and possibilities and know and obey the "rules" we have delineated in this chapter before you attempt to ignore them. We admit, however, that many of the most memorable and impactful performances come from appreciating and knowing the rules and then artfully breaking them, stretching the forms, not out of recklessness or lack of close textual study, but out of a deeply personal and subjective relationship with a text. Metonymic performances can be very exciting because they empower the performer to speak *of* the text, not just *in* the text. Should you prepare a metonymic performance, be aware of the choices you are making and know why you are making them. You should, however, check with your instructor before deciding on a metonymic interpretation or performance.

You should now feel a bit more confident in approaching your first interpretation assignment. The remaining chapters in Part 1 provide more detailed information on literature, hints on selecting the right literary selection, rehearsal and performance techniques, and suggestions on how to be a good audience member and evaluator.

SUMMARY

The study of literature through interpretation helps you to know and understand yourself and your world. The experience of performing literature demands a closer type of reading and a more personal involvement than mere oral or silent reading. The performer, in creating the speaker in a text, learns to view the world from another's perspective. The performer also brings his or her own text—experiences, memories, interests, hopes—to the performance. This weaving of the literary text with the performer's personal text is called *intertextuality*.

The many values of interpretation include an opportunity to study the world's best literature; to expand self-knowledge; to develop poise, self-confidence, and improved diction; and to sharpen your critical faculties. You gain these benefits because interpretation is an artistic process of studying literature through performance and sharing that study with an audience. The three components of the interpretation process are a performer (you), a literary selection, and an audience.

The first step in interpretation is choosing a literary selection to perform. When looking for a selection, make sure that it truly appeals to you and that it has the three qualities of good literature: universality, individuality, and suggestion. After choosing your selection, the process of interpretation involves several more steps—analyzing the selection, rehearsing, composing an introduction, giving a performance, and participating in an evaluation.

Metaphoric performances attempt to reinforce or affirm the perceived integrity of a text, while metonymic performances challenge or transgress beyond this perceived integrity.

Notes

1. Mary S. Strine, Beverly Whitaker Long, and Mary Frances HopKins, "Research in Interpretation and Performance Studies: Trends, Issues, Priorities," in *Speech Communication* (1990): 181.
2. Richard Schechner and Willa Appel, eds., *By Means of Performance: Intercultural Studies of Theatre and Ritual* (Cambridge: Cambridge University Press, 1990), p. 1.

3. Howard R. Martin, "The Issue: The Future—A Response by Howard R. Martin," in *Issues in Interpretation,* vol. 3, no. 2, eds. Michael Kelly and Tony Lentz (Ann Arbor, MI: University of Michigan, Department of Speech Communication and Theatre, 1978).

4. Beverly Whitaker Long, in an address to the participants attending the Ozarks/Flint Hills Performance Festival, Emporia State University, Emporia, Kansas, April 1991.

5. David Bartholomae and Antony R. Petrosky, eds. *Ways of Reading: An Anthology for Writers* (New York: St. Martin's Press, 1993), p. 5.

6. Terry Eagleton, *Literary Theory: An Introduction* (Minneapolis: University of Minnesota Press, 1983), p. 81.

7. Louise Rosenblatt, *The Reader, The Text, The Poem: The Transactional Theory of the Literary Work* (Carbondale and Edwardsville, IL: Southern Illinois University Press, 1978), p. 11.

8. From a letter to R. P. Blackmur dated November 16, 1931, in Holly Stevens, "Flux," *Southern Review* 15 (1979): 774.

9. Cornelius Corman Cunningham, *Literature as a Fine Art: Analysis and Interpretation* (New York: Ronald Press, 1941), p. 36. See also Charlotte I. Lee and Timothy J. Gura, *Oral Interpretation,* 7th ed. (New York: Houghton Mifflin, 1987), pp. 8–15.

10. David Black, *The Actor's Audition* (New York: Vintage Books, 1990), pp. 10–11.

11. Linda Wagner, ed., *Interviews with William Carlos Williams: Speaking Straight Ahead* (New York: New Directions, 1976), p. 81.

12. R. F. Dietrich, "Connotations of Rape in 'The Use of Force,' " *Studies in Short Fiction* 3 (1966): 450.

13. Beverly Whitaker Long and Mary Frances HopKins, *Performing Literature: An Introduction to Oral Interpretation* (Englewood Cliffs, NJ: Prentice Hall, 1982), pp. 132–34.

14. Terence Hawkes, "Telmah," in *Shakespeare and the Question of Theory,* eds. Patricia Parker and Geoffrey Hartman (New York: Methuen, 1985), p. 330.

YUKIO MISHIMA

Swaddling Clothes

H E WAS ALWAYS BUSY, Toshiko's husband. Even tonight he had to dash off to an appointment, leaving her to go home alone by taxi. But what else could a woman expect when she married an actor—an attractive one? No doubt she had been foolish to hope that he would spend the evening with her. And yet he must have known how she dreaded going back to their house, unhomely with its Western-style furniture and with the bloodstains still showing on the floor.

Toshiko had been oversensitive since girlhood: that was her nature. As the result of constant worrying she never put on weight, and now, an adult woman, she looked more like a transparent picture than a creature of flesh and blood. Her delicacy of spirit was evident to her most casual acquaintance.

Earlier that evening, when she had joined her husband at a night club, she had been shocked to find him entertaining friends with an account of "the incident." Sitting there in his American-style suit, puffing at a cigarette, he had seemed to her almost a stranger.

"It's a fantastic story," he was saying, gesturing flamboyantly as if in an attempt to outweigh the

The three main ingredients of the interpretation process are a piece of literature, an interpreter, and an audience to listen and respond. Each of these three ingredients is essential to make the interpretation experience complete. In Chapter 1, we concentrated on introducing you to interpretation and explaining the benefits and values you would derive from participating in the interpretation process. In this chapter, we concentrate on your appreciation of literature. We begin by defining what we mean by "literature," and then we explain the basic characteristics of the three main *genres,* or types, of literary texts—prose, drama, and poetry. We offer some advice on what to consider in choosing the right selection to perform. The last section of this chapter includes an anthology of material for performance, focusing on those aspects of each text that foster appreciation. An annotated bibliography listing sources to check for performance selections appears at the end of this chapter.

Throughout time, literature has enjoyed a variety of functions and uses. Some persons read literature merely for enjoyment—for the pleasure of a good story. Some read it to appreciate the language play or to study the interaction of characters. Some read to escape into a fictive world, some to experience vicariously the life of another. And some read literature to understand how various writers view the world. Recently, some have even used literature for therapeutic purposes. Disturbed children and prisoners, for example, have been helped through role playing dramatic scenes. Often people read because the act represents a refuge against the pressures of public life—a retreat enabling one to regroup and refresh. Because of these numerous functions, people define literature in numerous ways.

WHAT IS LITERATURE?

All of the functions of literature just listed have one element in common. In each case, readers of literature are involved in some type of experience. Every piece of literature expresses a certain type of experience which the writer shares with others. In much of her work, southern fiction writer Eudora Welty depicts life along the Natchez Trace; poet Anne Sexton writes about what it is like to be institutionalized; and playwright Molière often points out the hypocrisy he finds in society by depicting exaggerated, stereotyped characters. Each writer asks us to become involved in the experience he or she creates in the literature. The experiential emphasis is central to a definition of literature.

René Wellek and Austin Warren define literature as "a potential cause of experiences."[1] Their definition is critical to the interpreter because it implies that the reader of a text is the primary element in releasing the experience that the words on the page suggest. As Louise Rosenblatt writes, "A person becomes a reader by virtue of his activity in relationship to a text, which he organizes as a set of verbal symbols. A physical text, a set of marks on a page, becomes the text of a poem or of a scientific formula by virtue of its relationship with a reader who can thus interpret it and reach through it to the world of the work."[2] Literature is alive—a "living essence"—with the potential to affect us and, indeed, to be affected by us. As literature acts on you—you act on it. There is a symbiotic relationship. Literature, however, cannot affect or be affected unless it is read, heard, or shared. It takes a reader or a performer to bring out these potential experiences in literature through interpretation. The reader activates the potential experiences in literature by participating with it. As Rosenblatt writes, ". . . a text, once it leaves its author's hands, is simply paper and ink until a reader evokes from it a literary work—sometimes, even, a literary work of art."[3] In a sense then, literature is an event—a performance—a verb, not a noun. Finally for some, literature is the interweaving of "texts," the texts the writer writes, the texts the reader reads, and the texts in which the social context of this interaction occurs.

When you are preparing a selection for performance, the two initial questions for you to ask, as we stated in Chapter 1, are, Who do you think is speaking, and Who do you think is being addressed? We suggested that there are three kinds of speakers: personae, characters, and narrators. Examine the "potential experiences" in each of the following three poems, and see if you can identify the type of speaker.

JUDGE SELAH LIVELY   Edgar Lee Masters

Suppose you stood just five feet two,
And had worked your way as a grocery clerk,
Studying law by candle light
Until you became an attorney at law?
And then suppose through your diligence,
And regular church attendance,
You became attorney for Thomas Rhodes,
Collecting notes and mortgages,
And representing all the widows
In the Probate Court? And through it all
They jeered at your size, and laughed at your clothes
And your polished boots? And then suppose
You became the County Judge?
And Jefferson Howard and Kinsey Keene,
And Harmon Whitney, and all the giants
Who had sneered at you, were forced to stand
Before the bar and say "Your Honor"—
Well, don't you think it was natural
That I made it hard for them?

"Judge Selah Lively" from *Spoon River Anthology* by Edgar Lee Masters. Originally published by the Macmillan Company. Permission by Ellen C. Masters.

DISILLUSIONMENT OF TEN O'CLOCK   Wallace Stevens

The houses are haunted
By white night-gowns.
None are green,
Or purple with green rings,
Or green with yellow rings,
Or yellow with blue rings.
None of them are strange,
With socks of lace
And beaded ceintures.
People are not going
To dream of baboons and periwinkles.
Only, here and there, an old sailor,
Drunk and asleep in his boots,
Catches tigers
In red weather.

TO AN ATHLETE DYING YOUNG   A. E. Housman

The time you won your town the race
We chaired you through the market-place;
Man and boy stood cheering by,
And home we brought you shoulder-high.

To-day, the road all runners come,
Shoulder-high we bring you home,
And set you at your threshold down,
Townsman of a stiller town.

Smart lad, to slip betimes away
From fields where glory does not stay
And early though the laurel grows
It withers quicker than the rose.

Eyes the shady night has shut
Cannot see the record cut,
And silence sounds no worse than cheers
After earth has stopped the ears:

Now you will not swell the rout
Of lads that wore their honours out,

Runners whom renown outran
And the name died before the man.

So set, before its echoes fade,
The fleet foot on the sill of shade,
And hold to the low lintel up
The still-defended challenge-cup.

And round that early-laurelled head
Will flock to gaze the strengthless dead,
And find unwithered on its curls
The garland briefer than a girl's.

In the Edgar Lee Masters poem, the title and first line tell us that the speaker is a defined character: a judge, short of stature; we learn in the last few lines that this person derives great satisfaction from the "giants" who are forced to stand before him at the bar. These are essential elements to communicate in performance, as anything contrary to these facts contradicts the information the poet provides for us.

In the Wallace Stevens poem, the personal experience—the disillusionment or dream—is more important than the nature of the person having the dream. All we really know is what happened one night at ten o'clock. We do not know the particulars about the person to whom this happened; there doesn't seem to be anything in this poem that clarifies or characterizes this speaker. In this poem, then, we call the speaker a *persona.* If you were to perform this poem, you would concentrate on defining the experience as you perceive it, and on how this experience affected the speaker, rather than trying to create a dramatized character.

The Housman poem seems to center on a *narrator* telling the story of an athlete who died young. The focus in the poem is on the narrator's address to the dead athlete, who died before his fame disappeared. The performer would want to decide what the narrator's perspective is as he or she tells this story. Does he or she project a sense of loss? Does he or she communicate irony in this situation?

All decisions you make about a text should be substantiated with lines from that text. Thus, to say that the speaker in "Disillusionment of Ten O'Clock" is a tall man with a beard who bowls on Wednesday nights would be an interesting and creative decision, but difficult to support textually! If you cannot envision a defined character in a specific setting and time period, you need not attempt to create a defined character in performance.

Once you have answered the question, Who is speaking? and decided whether the speaker is a persona, a character, or a narrator, the second important initial question comes into play: Who is being addressed? As stated in Chapter 1, there are four potential audiences for any speaker: (1) himself or herself, (2) a silent listener—an inanimate object, deceased or absent person, muse, or God, (3) a character(s) created in the work, or (4) the general audience (or a combination of any of these four). Look at the openings of the following three poems, and see if you can detect what kind of audience is suggested.

From DEATH BE NOT PROUD   John Donne

Death, be not proud, though some have called thee
Mighty and dreadful, for thou art not so,
For those whom thou think'st thou dost overthrow
Die not, poor Death, nor yet canst thou kill me.

This poem by metaphysical poet John Donne begins with the persona's valiant struggle with death. The speaker calls on all the forces of his or her intellect (although the poet is male, a persona of either gender could be speaking) in an attempt to vanquish this enemy. The persona also attempts to overcome the barriers that separate life, death, and eternal life. The persona seems to be thinking aloud, trying to come to terms with mortality. The persona is also apostrophizing Death (addressing Death as though it were a character), attempting to bring Death down to a human level to deal with it on an equal basis. In performance, you would want to suggest that the persona is speaking both to himself or herself and to Death. To get the kind of effect you need for this poem, try to imagine what you look and sound like when you are alone and thinking aloud. Now try to imagine what you would act like if you addressed someone not present in the room with you. Try to reproduce these experiences as you perform this poem. Find a place directly above the audience for Death to be located, so that when Death is obviously being addressed, you can focus on Death. Do not stare fixedly at that place, however: Death is being addressed figuratively, not literally. Do not make it appear as though you expect a reply!

From THE APPLICANT   Sylvia Plath

First, are you our sort of a person?
Do you wear
A glass eye, false teeth or a crutch,
A brace or a hook,
Rubber breasts or a rubber crotch,

Stitches to show something's missing? No, no? Then
How can we give you a thing?

The audience in the Plath poem seems to be a character—the "applicant" of the title. When performing this poem, you would place the applicant in and directly above the audience, as you did for Death in the Donne poem. In this poem, however, the applicant *does* seem to be physically present and is responding—nonverbally, at least, as his imagined responses motivate the speaker's questions so you would want to maintain more direct contact with him in his imagined location.

> **From IN JUST-   E. E. Cummings**
>
> in Just-
> spring   when the world is mud-
> luscious the little
> lame balloonman
>
> whistles   far   and wee
>
> and eddieandbill come
> running from marbles and
> piracies and it's
> spring
>
> The lines from "in Just-" are reprinted from *Tulips & Chimneys* by E. E. Cummings, edited by George James Firmage, by permission of Liveright Publishing Corporation. Copyright 1923, 1925 and renewed 1951, 1953 by E. E. Cummings. Copyright © 1973, 1976 by the Trustees for the E. E. Cummings Trust. Copyright © 1973, 1976 by George James Firmage.

The audience for the Cummings poem seems very generalized. The speaker seems to be addressing anyone, explaining the events of spring to anyone who will listen. As we stated in Chapter 1, however, it is difficult to know how to address a generalized audience—you must make a definitive choice that reflects your interpretation. Try to imagine that this generalized audience is some particular group who would be appropriate for your interpretation, for example, friends or children. As we have stated several times, the definition of the audience may reveal itself once you have decided on your interpretation and have analyzed the speaker's intentions. As this Cummings poem continues, we learn that the innocent-seeming balloonman is "goat-footed" suggesting an alliance with the devil—known to be a "shape-shifter." The speaker, then, could be warning children to beware of "lame, goat-footed balloonmen"—of people who are not what they seem. Try performing this by looking directly at the actual audience while imagining them to be the particular group you have defined. Try to imagine yourself having a "dialogue" of sorts with this particular audience.

As you prepare a selection for performance, see if you can decide who is speaking and to whom. The answers to these two questions guide you in making initial performance choices.

WHAT TYPES OF LITERATURE ARE AVAILABLE?

All literature is a "potential cause of experiences," and you are free to select whatever type of experience appeals to you within the limitations of the assignment you are given. Usually you will be asked to choose a prose, drama, or poetry selection. Literature has traditionally been divided into these three genres, or types. Following is a description of each of these three literary genres.

Generic Classification

Prose

There are two subgenres within this category: prose fiction and prose nonfiction.

1. *Fiction:* Narrative literature that creates an imaginary reality in the form of a story written in sentences and paragraphs with no strong rhythmic base. Fiction usually creates a sense of vicarious experience, of a narrator recreating in the present events that occurred in the past.
2. *Nonfiction:* Works of fact or theory. Included are letters, diaries, essays, autobiographies, biographies, histories, newspapers, and so forth.

Drama

Plays are written with characters, implied action, and dialogue, and are usually intended for actors to perform on a stage. Plays may be written in prose or verse. Plays create scenes that seem to be taking place now—the audience witnesses a present-tense event.

Poetry

Poetry is highly imagistic, and it is written in condensed, heightened language, stylized syntax, and figures of speech not found in ordinary communication. Poetry usually creates a strong rhythm or metrical feel and a sense of crystallized experience. Acclaimed Shakespearean scholar G. Wilson Knight says "the specific nature of poetry [is] to express the intangible and spiritual in terms of the concrete and physical."[4]

HOW DO I FIND THE RIGHT SELECTION?

The first criterion for selecting the "right" text is to choose a selection you like. If you care about the piece of literature you have selected, you will find it easier to share it fully in performance. Liking the selection doesn't necessarily mean that you have had a similar experience. It simply must be an experience you can imagine, expressed by a speaker you feel you can understand.

The second criterion is to be sure that the literature is "good." Apply the characteristics of universality, individuality, and suggestion discussed in Chapter 1 to decide if your chosen selection is worth your time and effort. A "good" text is usually one that has a universal message expressed individualistically with suggestive elements that appeal to the imagination.

The third criterion is to select a text you feel would offer you the most valuable experience. Since in performance you achieve a more visceral relationship with a text than is possible in any other way and since performance is a way of knowing, select a text that creates a world you would like to know more about. As we stated in Chapter 1, an advantage of solo interpretation performance is that you do not have to fall victim to typecasting—the roles you select to play are limitless. You are free to taste another's reality—the reality of someone of another gender, age, race, religion, or culture.

The fourth criterion is to choose a selection you feel you can understand. Does this text speak to your "text" (background, experiences, and so on)? As stated earlier, your interpretation of a text is based on your understanding of language, your past experiences with other texts, your interests, preoccupations, and other personal characteristics. As you study and rehearse a text, these individual experiences help you form a unique understanding of it. Be sure you have done the basics, such as looking up all unfamiliar words, engaging in outside research, studying the images, deciding on the identities of the speaker and the audience, and defining their relationship to help you create your interpretation. Do not be concerned if others in class do not agree with your interpretation. Their views of your selection will differ because the "texts" they bring to it determine their understanding of it. They are different from you, and consequently their perspectives will make their interpretations different.

Since there is no one definitive, universally agreed-upon meaning in a text, you have the power to devise your own. Many authors admit that they write to discover what they mean, to find out what they want to say: they do not write with preconceived intentions. Southern writer Flannery O'Connor, for example, admits that she discovered "the meaning" in many of her short stories *after* the stories were written. Discussing her story "Good Country People," O'Connor says:

> I doubt myself if many writers know what they are going to do when they start out. When I started writing that story ["Good Country People"] I didn't know there was going to be a Ph.D. with a wooden leg in it. I merely found myself one morning writing a description of two women that I knew something about, and before I realized it, I had equipped one of them with a daughter with a wooden leg. As the story progressed, I brought in the Bible salesman, but I had no idea what I was going to do with him. . . . This is a

story that produces a shock for the reader, and I think one reason for this is that it produced a shock for the writer.[5]

As O'Connor points out, a work of literature may not always contain a pre-conceived meaning which it is your responsibility to find. *You bring meaning to a text.* Ask not only, What does this work mean? but perhaps more importantly, What does this text mean to me? The text means what you think it means, based on your study of it and your experience with its language. You and the text have a unique relationship, and you affect each other uniquely. As Wolfgang Iser writes:

> If interpretation has set itself the task of conveying meaning of a literary text, obviously the text itself cannot have already formulated that meaning. How can the meaning possibly be experienced if—as is always assumed by the classical norm of interpretation—it is already there, merely waiting for a refer-ential exposition? . . . If he [the author] clarifies the *potential* of a text, he will no longer fall into the fatal trap of trying to impose one meaning on his reader, as if that were the right, or at least the best, interpretation.[6]

Following are three lists of some general suggestions for the beginning inter-preter. The right text for you probably will have most of the qualities on the lists. However, *if you have good reasons for not following the suggestions, then by all means, don't. Feel free to follow your own instincts as to what will work best for you.* (We focus here primarily on prose fiction, drama, and poetry. For information on other liter-ary forms, see Chapter 9.)

If you are working with prose fiction:

1. A story with a first-person narrator—a storyteller who tells the story using the pronoun "I" to refer to himself or herself—is usually easier for novice interpreters to perform. In early assignments, you may find defined character-narrators (such as the narrator in "The Use of Force") easier to analyze and understand than noncharacterized third-person narrators.
2. A selection with a minimum number of speakers poses fewer performance difficulties than a text with many speakers. The more characters who speak dialogue in a scene, the more vocal and physical differentiation necessary.
3. A serious story might be easier to perform than a comedic story. The timing required to do comedy well often takes time and experience to develop.
4. You might find it less difficult to choose a short story or a scene from a short story rather than a scene from a novel. Because time limits are necessary in interpretation classes, it is easier to find a good scene to perform when deal-ing with the more tightly written, more condensed short story. (The intro-duction is usually less difficult to compose as well.)

5. If you select a story whose flavor and charm depend upon the characters' speaking in dialect, be sure you can comfortably and consistently speak in the dialect.

6. A story with a narrator and characters not too far from your own age might be easier to perform than a story whose characters have a wide range of different ages (although on the other hand some performers find that they have less difficulty differentiating when they depict widely divergent characters).

Some of these suggestions for prose fiction are certainly applicable to your choice of a drama selection as well. Other suggestions for drama and poetry selections follow. If you are working with drama:

1. A scene from the middle or end of a play might be better for performance than a scene from the beginning. A scene which contains conflict, emotional variety, builds and releases, and highs and lows holds the attention of your audience and is easier to pace.

2. Rapid-paced dialogue is very difficult to perform well. The more rapid the dialogue, the faster the pace must be and the freer you must be of your script (if you use one). (This may also rule out those dramatic scenes having very brief one-word or one-sentence dialogue passages.)

3. Choosing a scene in which all of the characters are of a different gender and age from your own may give you additional problems. Be aware of the challenge this type of selection presents for the novice performer (although as stated above, some performers find that they are better able to differentiate among characters when they are widely divergent).

If you are working with poetry:

1. Again, since your choices are limitless, select a poem that allows you to have the most rewarding experience. Although it is often easier (some actually find it more difficult!) to depict a speaker of your own gender, age, culture, and so on, the opportunity to become someone quite different from you is one of the exciting challenges interpretation offers. Ask yourself, though, what is my responsibility to this speaker? What must I do to suggest this speaker who is so different from myself?

2. A poem that is too short (approximately fourteen lines or less) often causes problems because the performance may be over before you have become totally involved. If you find a short poem that you really like, perhaps you could perform more than one poem and relate them in some way.

3. If you select poems with refrains or highly regular rhythmic patterns, like ballads, be aware of the challenge of presenting such material. These poems often present pacing and variety problems.

Finding the right text is a very personal matter, but the preceding suggestions, the anthology to follow shortly, and the list of source materials at the end of this chapter (as well as the lists of possible performance selections found at the ends of Chapters 6, 7, and 8) will, we hope, be useful in helping you make choices. Many beginning interpreters may want to experiment, to try more difficult material, and they should be encouraged to do so. The foregoing suggestions are meant to be descriptive and not prescriptive. Feel free to choose any literary selection that appeals to you, but consult these suggestions and the list of source materials if you are fearful of choosing a text that may initially present too many problems.

APPRECIATING LITERATURE

Why do we appreciate a text? Certainly there are as many reasons as there are texts to appreciate. We appreciate a literary text because of its intrinsic qualities: subject matter, beauty of the language, rhythmic qualities, sound appeal, freshness of image, the clever way it is written or constructed. We also admire texts because of what they are able to help us understand about ourselves, others, and the world in which we live.

But who determines what kinds of texts we are to appreciate? The most highly anthologized texts, and probably the most often read and performed texts, are canonical texts of the dominant culture. There are, however, literally hundreds of texts that reveal cultural diversity and minority points of view that are available to be explored, studied, and performed. We must try to embrace both our similarities and differences if we are to begin to bridge cultural communication gaps. Black writer Maya Angelou made a passionate plea for the need to recognize our shared humanity in a 1989 television interview: ". . . human beings are more alike than we are unalike, and the minute we begin to understand just the slightest part of that we recognize ourselves as family. The moment I see a fifteen-year-old Jewish boy with braces on his teeth and know that boy is mine, and a very oversized white woman in Kansas, that she is mine and I am hers, and that Arab woman in the Palestinian concentration camp is mine and I am hers, then I am liberated." Similarly, we must become more aware of the value of the contributions of persons of other cultures for our own personal liberation. During this era of multiculturalism, we can empower ethnic and minority voices and raise the consciousness levels of our audiences through performance. We give voice to works that may not otherwise be heard.

The texts that follow are for your appreciation; all are particularly suitable for performance. Feel free to choose any of these literary selections for class performances, but in the case of selections that are cuttings from longer works, be sure to read the complete work. These texts deserve our attention because many of them are revelatory of a particular cultural or minority point of view and because all of them manifest the intrinsic qualities (image, sound, rhythm, and so forth) previously mentioned.

AN ANTHOLOGY OF TEXTS
FOR YOUR APPRECIATION

From GHETTO   Joshua Sobol
Translated by Jack Viertel

(The play takes place in a ghetto in Vilna, Lithuania, during World War II. The Jews in this ghetto have formed an acting company which entertains the Nazis and keeps the Jews alive. Chaja is the singer in the acting company, but, as we learn, also a resistance fighter intent on escaping. Kruk is the socialist who runs the ghetto library. Kittel is the S.S. officer who, at twenty years of age, has total power over the ghetto inhabitants. The first part of this scene takes place in Kruk's library, and the second part in the ghetto courtyard.)

Kruk: May I help you?

Chaja: No thanks. Just looking . . .

Kruk: Excuse me, but you come here every day and search for hours, Surely I could help you . . . you must be looking for something.

Chaja: (*A little defensive, protecting something*): I like to browse.

Kruk: I thought you were wonderful in the revue—"Pesche from Resche."

Chaja: Wonderful?

Kruk: There's no need to be ashamed. It's a fine thing to be an actress.

Chaja: Is it? I don't think so.

Kruk: No?

Chaja: What good is theatre in our situation? It's trivial . . . even insulting.

Kruk: I thought that way once. I was against the theatre company from the beginning.

Chaja: I know. You were right. You are right.

Kruk: (*Shakes his head*): No. Every form of cultural activity is essential here in the ghetto. It's the battle plan in our fight to remain human beings. The fascists can kill us at will—it's not even a challenge for them. But they can't achieve their real aim: They can't obliterate our humanity—not as long as we cling to a spiritual life, not as long as we reach for the good and the beautiful. They forbid flowers in the ghetto, we give one another leaves. And suddenly, leaves are the most beautiful flowers in the world. Theatre is essential. (Silence) You must be looking for a book on theatre. Come.

Chaja: I don't want a book on theatre. I want a book . . . on explosives.

Kruk:	(*Smiling*): Why didn't you say so? I could have saved you precious time. (*He climbs a ladder and takes a thin book from the top of the shelf. He climbs back down and hands her the book. She looks through it quickly.*)
Chaja:	Is this Russian?
Kruk:	It's a Soviet army manual. I stole it from the university. It's the only book I've ever stolen.
Chaja:	But I don't know the language.
Kruk:	You must have friends. Show it to your friends. Unless I'm mistaken, one of your friends will know Russian.
Chaja:	Thank you. I'll bring it back.
Kruk:	Please, I don't even know you took it. A thief who steals from a thief is no thief.
Chaja:	Thank you. (*She heads for the door.*)
Kruk:	(*When she is almost there*): Wait. (*From a tin box he takes a leafy stem and hands it to her. She takes it, leaves the library, and unfortunately runs into Kittel.*)
Kittel:	Where have you been? Rehearsal?
Chaja:	Yes. Working on a new piece. (*He reaches for her book.*)
Kittel:	You sang very well at the party. Is this your new play? (*He looks it over.*) In Russian?
Chaja:	That's right. Do you . . . know Russian?
Kittel:	Sorry.
Chaja:	Pity. It's a good play.
Kittel:	What's it called?
Chaja:	*Beneath the Bridge.*
Kittel:	And you're performing it in Russian?
Chaja:	No, no. We'll adapt and improve it. (*She reaches for the book. Kittel holds on to it.*)
Kittel:	You dance and sing your way through the war, eh?
Chaja:	When I'm happy I laugh. When I'm sad I sing.
Kittel:	(*Laughs*): Very good. (*He hands her the book.*) Perhaps—I hope—you'll wipe out your debt to me with this one.
Chaja:	I'll try. (*She runs off suddenly. Kittel looks after her.*)

I AM A BLACK WOMAN   Mari Evans

I am a black woman
the music of my song
some sweet arpeggio of tears
is written in a minor key

and I
can be heard
                    humming
in the night

I saw my mate leap screaming to the sea
and I/with these hands/cupped the lifebreath
from my issue in the canebrake
I lost Nat's swinging body in a rain of tears
and heard my son scream all the way from Anzio
for Peace he never knew. . . . I
learned Da Nang and Pork Chop Hill
in anguish
Now my nostrils know the gas
and these trigger tire/d fingers
seek the softness in my warrior's beard

I
am a black woman
tall as a cypress
strong
beyond all definition still
defying place
and time
and circumstance
    assailed
        impervious
            indestructible

Look
    on me and be
renewed

"I Am a Black Woman," from *I Am a Black Woman,* published by Wm. Morrow & Co., 1970, by permission of the author.

FROM SWADDLING CLOTHES   Yukio Mishima
Translated by Ivan Morris

He was always busy, Toshiko's husband. Even tonight he had to dash off to an appointment, leaving her to go home alone by taxi. But what else could a woman expect when she married an actor—an attractive one? No doubt she had been foolish to hope that he would spend the evening with her. And yet he must have known how she dreaded going back to their house, unhomely with its Western-style furniture and with the bloodstains still showing on the floor.

Toshiko had been oversensitive since girlhood: that was her nature. As the result of constant worrying she never put on weight, and now, an adult woman, she looked more like a transparent picture than a creature of flesh and blood. Her delicacy of spirit was evident to her most casual acquaintance.

Earlier that evening, when she had joined her husband at a night club, she had been shocked to find him entertaining friends with an account of "the incident." Sitting there in his American-style suit, puffing at a cigarette, he had seemed to her almost a stranger.

"It's a fantastic story," he was saying, gesturing flamboyantly as if in an attempt to outweigh the attractions of the dance band. "Here this new nurse for our baby arrives from the employment agency, and the very first thing I notice about her is her stomach. It's enormous—as if she had a pillow stuck under her kimono! No wonder, I thought, for I soon saw that she could eat more than the rest of us put together. She polished off the contents of our rice bin like that. . . ." He snapped his fingers. "'Gastric dilation'—that's how she explained her girth and her appetite. Well, the day before yesterday we heard groans and moans coming from the nursery. We rushed in and found her squatting on the floor, holding her stomach in her two hands, and moaning like a cow. Next to her our baby lay in his cot, scared out of his wits and crying at the top of his lungs. A pretty scene, I can tell you!"

Yukio Mishima: *Death in Midsummer and Other Stories.* Copyright © 1966 by New Directions Publishing Corporation. Reprinted by permission of New Directions Publishing Corporation.

NEW YORK TAXIS   Yevgeny Yevtushenko
Translated by Albert Todd with the author

New York is all mankind in the same casserole.
Don't ask New York for mercy,
                              you'll get cooked anyway.
Crawling like yellow turtles,
                    flying like golden bullets,
New York taxis,
              taxis,
                    taxis.
Skirts scream,
          both mini,
                and maxi:
"Taxi! Taxi!
Two little dachshunds,
          two ink spots on a leash, not foolish patsies

hopelessly bark at the taxis.
"Driver, are you from Odessa?
                              Do you pay taxes?"
"Sir, you underestimate people who work in taxis."
Moscow doesn't believe in tears,
          What does New York do with tears?
                                    It merely waxes.
            Taxi!
                  Taxi!
                        Where are the bloody taxis?
You're completely dressed by Armani,
                              from cufflinks to condoms,
you are completely free from any syndromes,
you are completely shining and fresh,
but you open the taxi door
                        and you are in Bangladesh,
where the driver's turban
                  looks like bandages on invisible wounds.
Everybody wants to be happy.
It's a little bit crappy.
You couldn't make happy
this patchwork world—
                  this quarreling quilt.
It is our common guilt.
Inside one taxi—Sri Lanka,
Inside the second—Santa Domingo,
Inside the third—starving Zaire,
almost without hope or desire.
New York taxi,
            you always hide something
                        behind your doors.
I'm afraid of you,
              but I couldn't live without
              the fragrant smell of your dirty floors.
This morning I jumped into Poland,
            at mid-day into Haiti.
Charge me double price, Taxi driver,
                  my head has become too weighty.
At night I found myself in a fever in Sarajevo.
I am trying to speak Russian.
                  Drive to the left—
                        nalevo!

Where will I be tomorrow?
> In Jakarta?
>> In Punjab?
Where on this globe will you drop me,
> my cab?
What kind of new wound from somebody's body
>> will end up on mine?
From where comes this wound?
>> From the Amazon?
>>> The Volga?
>>> The Main?
Probably here in New York,
> that I never leave,
I will jump more often into Moscow,
> into Kiev.
And such a pity that I can't say in Chinese
> even on bended knees—
TAXI! TAXI!
> Where are you, damned taxis?

Reprinted by permission of the author.

A LION AND A MOUSE   Aesop

A Mouse one day happened to run across the paws of a sleeping Lion and wakened him. The Lion, angry at being disturbed, grabbed the Mouse, and was about to swallow him, when the Mouse cried out, "Please, kind Sir, I didn't mean it; if you will let me go, I shall always be grateful; and, perhaps, I can help you some day." The idea that such a little thing as a Mouse could help him so amused the Lion that he let the Mouse go. A week later, the Mouse heard a Lion roaring loudly. He went closer to see what the trouble was and found his Lion caught in a hunter's net. Remembering his promise, the Mouse began to gnaw the ropes of the net and kept it up until the Lion could get free.
Moral: Little friends might prove to be great friends.

From TWELFTH NIGHT, Act II, Scene iv   William Shakespeare

Scene: The Duke Orsino's palace in Illyria.
Characters: Orsino, Duke of Illyria, in love with Olivia—countess of Illyria
Viola, a young woman disguised in male garb as Cesario—attendant to the Duke
Curio—an attendant to the Duke

Duke: Give me some music. Now good morrow, friends.
Now, good Cesario, but that piece of song,

	That old and antique song we heard last night;
	Methought it did relieve my passion much,
	More than light airs and recollected terms
	Of these most brisk and giddy-paced times.
	Come, but one verse.
Curio:	He is not here, so please your lordship, that should sing it.
Duke:	Who was it?
Curio:	Feste the jester, my lord, a fool that the Lady Olivia's father took much delight in. He is about the house.
Duke:	Seek him out, and play the tune the while. (*Exit Curio. Music plays.*)
	Come hither, boy. If ever thou shalt love,
	In the sweet pangs of it remember me;
	For such as I am, all true lovers are,
	Unstaid and skittish in all motions else,
	Save in the constant image of the creature
	That is belov'd. How dost thou like this tune?
Viola:	It gives a very echo to the seat
	Where Love is thron'd.
Duke:	Thou dost speak masterly.
	My life upon't, young though thou art, thine eye
	Hath stay'd upon some favor that it loves.
	Hath it not, boy?
Viola:	A little, by your favor.
Duke:	What kind of woman is't?
Viola:	Of your complexion.
Duke:	She is not worth thee then. What years, i' faith?
Viola:	About your years, my lord.
Duke:	Too old, by heaven. Let still the woman take
	An elder than herself, so wears she to him;
	So sways she level in her husband's heart.
	For, boy, however we do praise ourselves,
	Our fancies are more giddy and unfirm,
	More longing, wavering, sooner lost and won,
	Than women's are.
Viola:	I think it well, my lord.
Duke:	Then let thy love be younger than thyself,
	Or thy affection cannot hold the bent;
	For women are as roses, whose fair flow'r
	Being once display'd doth fall that very hour.
Viola:	And so they are; alas, that they are so!
	To die, even when they to perfection grow!

THE WISE MERCHANT

A Jewish tale adapted by Allan B. Chinen

Once upon a time, a merchant and his grown son set out on a sea voyage. They carried a chest full of jewels to sell on the journey, but told no one about their fortune. One day, the merchant overheard the sailors whispering among themselves. They had discovered his treasure and were plotting to kill him and his son to steal the jewels!

The merchant was beside himself with fear, and he paced back and forth in his cabin, trying to figure a way out of the predicament. His son asked what was the matter, and his father told him.

"We must fight them!" the younger man declared.

"No," the old man replied, "they will overpower us!"

Sometime later, the merchant stormed out on the deck. "You fool of a son!" he cried out, "you never heed my advice!"

"Old man!" the son yelled back, "you have nothing to say worth hearing!"

The sailors gathered round curiously as father and son started cursing at each other. Then the old man rushed to his cabin, and dragged out his chest of jewels. "Ungrateful son!" the merchant shrieked. "I would rather die in poverty than have you inherit my wealth!" With that, the merchant opened his treasure chest and the sailors gasped at the sight of all the jewels. Then the merchant rushed to the railing and before anyone could stop him, he threw his treasure overboard.

In the next moment, father and son stared at the empty box, and then they collapsed upon each other, weeping over what they had done. Later, when they were alone in their cabin, the father said, "We had to do it, son. There was no other way to save our lives!"

"Yes," the son replied, "your plan was best."

The ship soon docked, and the merchant and his son hurried to the magistrate of the city. They charged the sailors with piracy and attempted murder, and the magistrate arrested the sailors. The judge asked the sailors if they had seen the old man throw his treasure overboard, and they agreed. So he convicted them all. "What man would throw away his life's savings, except if he feared for his life?" the judge asked. The pirates offered to replace the merchant's jewels, and in return for that the judge spared their lives.

Excerpt from Allan B. Chinen, "The Wise Merchant," *In the Ever After: Fairy Tales and the Second Half of Life,* © 1989 by Chiron Publications, pp. 39–40. Reprinted by permission of the publisher.

TRYING TO CONCEIVE #2   Marion Cohen

Whaddaya mean, Mother Nature? Nature's no
  mother.
If nature were a mother, women would ovulate once

64

a day not once a month And umbilical cords
would be rigid pipes not flexible ropes
that can twist and turn and do God-knows-
what to the baby And placentas wouldn't have
all those veins and be so complicated And
it would be impossible for embryos to implant
anywhere but the uterus and all babies that
were meant to be miscarriages wouldn't implant
in the first place And women wouldn't have
morning sickness when their babies were
doing just fine and feel top o' the morning
when their babies were suffocating
And if Nature were a mother, it wouldn't be
survival of the fittest; it would be survival
of the sweetest.
So whaddaya mean, Mother Nature? Nature's no
mother. If nature were a mother, there would
be no "accidents of Nature" If Nature
were a mother, Nature would be perfect.

"Trying to Conceive #2" by Marion Cohen. Appeared in Marion Cohen's book *She Was Born She Died*. Centering Corp., Nebraska, 1984. Used by permission of the author.

EVEN THE BIRDS ARE LEAVING THE WORLD   Hwang Chiu

Before the film begins
We all stand up for our national anthem.
On Ulsuk Island
In the "Splendid Land of Three Thousand Ri,"*
A flock of white birds
Leaving the field of reeds
Fly in one, two, three files,
Honking, giggling
Carrying their own world,
Separating their world from ours,
To some place beyond this world.
I wish we could fly off too,
Giggling, crackling,
Forming a file,
Carrying our world

*"Splendid Land of Three Thousand Ri": an epithet for Korea.

To some place beyond this world.
But with "Preserve forever the integrity of Korea to Koreans"
We sit down,
Sinking into our seats.

"Even the Birds Are Leaving the World" by Hwang Chiu. *Modern Korean Literature: An Anthology.* Ed. Peter H. Lee. Honolulu: University of Hawaii Press, 1990, p. 308.

DEAR PAUL NEWMAN   Marie Kennedy Robins

After all these years
it's over between you and me.
There's a younger man.
I get to see him five times a week
and he tries to bring me the world.
I worried a lot about your racing
in them fast cars, your beer drinking,
the fact that the color of your eyes
is fading a little with age.
Them eyes always reminded me of Ed Kozelka
who sat next to me in American History.
When you and Ed turned them blues on me,
it sure made my pilot light blaze up.
When reporters asked why you was
faithful to Joanne, you once said,
"Why should I go out for hamburger
when I can have steak at home?"
Now that Joanne is looking so plain,
I wonder if you are going to Wendy's.
Paul baby, it was fun, and
I'll never forget your spaghetti sauce.
I gotta move on.
I'm the same age as you, but in the dark
Peter Jennings will never notice.

"Dear Paul Newman" by Marie Kennedy Robbins. Reprinted by permission of the author.

From M. BUTTERFLY   David Henry Hwang

This play is based on a real incident between a former French diplomat and a Chinese opera singer, an account of which was published in *The New York Times* in May 1986. The play, though, says Hwang, is not docudrama but speculation. A lover of the opera

Madame Butterfly, the diplomat (Rene Gallimard, the symbol of Western Pinkertons), sees in a Chinese opera singer (Song Liling, the Butterfly) qualities he admires, qualities he believes are true of all Oriental women: diffidence, delicacy, submissiveness, and modesty. The diplomat falls in love with the opera singer and proceeds to have a twenty-year affair with her, only to discover that the opera singer is a spy who ultimately causes him to be charged with espionage. The most astounding discovery the diplomat makes, however, is that the woman he loved for so many years is really a man. So, the diplomat, duped by love, turns out to be the Butterfly, and the Chinese spy who exploited the love, is the real Pinkerton. Hwang writes of our need for cultural interchange and understanding in the afterword to his play:

> *M. Butterfly* has sometimes been regarded as an anti-American play, a diatribe against the stereotyping of the East by the West, of women by men. Quite to the contrary, I consider it a plea to all sides to cut through our respective layers of cultural and sexual misperception, to deal with one another truthfully for our mutual good, from the common and equal ground we share as human beings.
>
> For the myths of the East, the myths of the West, the myths of men, and the myths of women—these have so saturated our consciousness that truthful contact between nations and lovers can only be the result of heroic effort. Those who prefer to bypass the work involved will remain in a world of surfaces, misperceptions running rampant. This is, to me, the convenient world in which the French diplomat and the Chinese spy lived. This is why, after twenty years, he had learned nothing at all about his lover, not even the truth of his sex.

The scene below is one of the early meetings between Gallimard and Song Liling—the first time he has been invited to her apartment.

Act One, Scene 10

Song Liling's apartment, Beijing, 1960.

> **Gallimard:** I returned to the opera that next week, and the week after that . . . she keeps our meetings so short—perhaps fifteen, twenty minutes at most. So I am left each week with a thirst which is intensified. In this way, fifteen weeks have gone by. I am starting to doubt the words of my friend Marc. But no, not really. In my heart, I know she has . . . an interest in me. I suspect this is her way. She is outwardly bold and outspoken, yet her heart is shy and afraid. It is the Oriental in her at war with her Western education.
>
> **Song** (*Offstage*): I will be out in an instant. Ask the servant for anything you want.
>
> **Gallimard:** Tonight, I have finally been invited to her apartment. Though the idea is almost beyond belief, I believe she is afraid of me. (*Gallimard looks*

around the room. He picks up a picture in a frame, studies it. Without his noticing, Song enters, dressed elegantly in a black gown from the twenties. She stands in the doorway looking like Anna May Wong.)

Song: That is my father.

Gallimard (*surprised*): Mademoiselle Song . . .

> (*She glides up to him, snatches away the picture.*)

Song: It is very good that he did not live to see the Revolution. They would, no doubt, have made him kneel on broken glass. Not that he didn't deserve such a punishment. But he is my father. I would've hated to see it happen.

Gallimard: I'm very honored that you've allowed me to visit your home.

> (*Song curtsies.*)

Song: Thank you. Oh! Haven't you been poured any tea?

Gallimard: I'm really not—

Song (*To her offstage servant*): Shu-Fang! Kwai-lah! (To Gallimard) I'm sorry. You want everything to be perfect—

Gallimard: Please.

Song: —and before the evening even begins—

Gallimard: I'm really not thirsty.

Song: —it's ruined.

Gallimard (*Sharply*): Mademoiselle Song!

> (*Song sits down.*)

Song: I'm sorry.

Gallimard: What are you apologizing for now?

> (*Pause: Song starts to giggle.*)

Song: I don't know!

> (*Gallimard laughs.*)

Gallimard: Exactly my point.

Song: Oh, I am silly. Lightheaded. I promise not to apologize for anything else tonight, do you hear me?

Gallimard: That's a good girl.

> (*Shu-Fang, a servant girl, comes out with a tea tray and starts to pour.*)

Song (*To Shu-Fang*): No! I'll pour myself for the gentleman!

> (*Shu-Fang, staring at Gallimard, exits.*)

Song: No, I . . . I don't even know why I invited you up.

Gallimard: Well, I'm glad you did.

> (*Song looks around the room.*)

Song: There is an element of danger to your presence.

Gallimard: Oh?

Song: You must know.

Gallimard: It doesn't concern me. We both know why I'm here.

Song: It doesn't concern me either. No . . . well perhaps . . .

Gallimard:	What?
Song:	Perhaps I am slightly afraid of scandal.
Gallimard:	What are we doing?
Song:	I'm entertaining you. In my parlor.
Gallimard:	In France, that would hardly—
Song:	France. France is a country living in the modern era. Perhaps even ahead of it. China is a nation whose soul is firmly rooted two thousand years in the past. What I do, even pouring the tea for you now . . . it has . . . implications. The walls and windows say so. Even my own heart, strapped inside this Western dress . . . even it says things—things I don't care to hear.

(*Song hands Gallimard a cup of tea. Gallimard puts his hand over both the teacup and Song's hand.*)

Gallimard:	This is a beautiful dress.
Song:	Don't.
Gallimard:	What?
Song:	I don't even know if it looks right on me.
Gallimard:	Believe me—
Song:	You are from France. You see so many beautiful women.
Gallimard:	France? Since when are the European women—?
Song:	Oh! What am I trying to do, anyway?

(*Song runs to the door, composes herself, then turns towards Gallimard.*)

Song:	Monsieur Gallimard, perhaps you should go.
Gallimard:	But . . . why?
Song:	There's something wrong about this.
Gallimard:	I don't see what.
Song:	I feel . . . I am not myself.
Gallimard:	No. You're nervous.
Song:	Please. Hard as I try to be modern, to speak like a man, to hold a Western woman's strong face up to my own . . . in the end, I fail. A small, frightened heart beats too quickly and gives me away. Monsieur Gallimard, I'm a Chinese girl. I've never . . . never invited a man up to my flat before. The forwardness of my actions makes my skin burn.
Gallimard:	What are you afraid of? Certainly not me, I hope.
Song:	I'm a modest girl.
Gallimard:	I know. And very beautiful. (*He touches her hair.*)
Song:	Please—go now. The next time you see me, I shall again be myself.
Gallimard:	I like you the way you are right now.
Song:	You are a cad.
Gallimard:	What do you expect? I'm a foreign devil.

(*Gallimard walks downstage. Song exits.*)

Gallimard (*To us*): Did you hear the way she talked about Western women? Much differently than the first night. She does—she feels inferior to them—and to me.

SUMMARY

According to Wellek and Warren, literature is a "potential cause of experiences." An interpreter brings this experience to life in performance.

There are three literary genres, or types of literature: prose, drama (plays), and poetry. Prose fiction is narrative literature that creates an imaginary reality in the form of a story; prose nonfiction includes works of fact or theory.

When you choose a selection for performance, make sure that you really like and understand it, want to learn more about it, and want to share it with an audience.

There are a wide variety of literary selections to appreciate, and a wide range of reasons to appreciate them. We can appreciate the intrinsic values of a text (sound, image, rhythm, and so on) as well as those elements that help us know ourselves, others, and our world better. In addition, we can empower minority voices by performing texts of other cultures, thereby raising our own and our audience's awareness of cultural similarities and differences.

SOURCES TO CHECK FOR SELECTIONS TO PERFORM

The following lists of sources are provided to help you find the right selection for you. The lists include anthologies which contain prose, drama, poetry, and children's literature selections. Many of the anthologies contain the literature of other cultures and of minorities. Some books listed contain the selections themselves, and some are indexes or compilations of titles and authors.

GENERAL ANTHOLOGIES

Abcarian, Richard, and Klotz, Marvin, eds. *Literature: The Human Experience: The Shorter Edition.* New York: St. Martin's Press, 1980. This edition offers 170 selections of fiction, poetry, and drama, ranging from ancient to present-day writings.

Altenbernd, Lynn, ed. *Anthology: An Introduction to Literature.* New York: Macmillan, 1977. This is an excellent compilation of prose fiction, poetry, and drama, including science fiction selections and detective stories.

Elliott, Emory, et al., eds. *American Literature: A Prentice Hall Anthology.* Volumes One and Two. Englewood Cliffs, NJ: Prentice Hall, 1991.

Lauter, Paul, et al., eds. *The Heath Anthology of American Literature.* Volumes One and Two. Lexington, MA: Heath, 1990.

Miller, James Jr. *Heritage of American Literature.* Volumes One and Two. San Diego: Harcourt, 1991.

Richter, David H. *The Critical Tradition: Classic Texts and Contemporary Trends.* New York: St. Martin's Press, 1989.

NORTON ANTHOLOGIES

These anthologies are large compilations of good literature with excellent commentaries. They include American literature and English literature editions, among others. They contain excellent selections for performance.

Baym, Nina, et al., eds. *The Norton Anthology of American Literature.* Volumes One and Two. 3rd ed. New York: W. W. Norton, 1989.

Cassill, R. V. *The Norton Anthology of Contemporary Fiction.* New York: W. W. Norton, 1988.

Mack, Maynard, et al., eds. *The Norton Anthology of World Masterpieces.* 5th ed. New York: W. W. Norton, 1987.

Reed, Ishmael; Trueblood, Kathryn; and Wong, Shawn, eds. *The Before Columbus Foundation Fiction Anthology: Selections from the American Book Awards 1980–1990.* New York: W. W. Norton, 1992.

PROSE FICTION ANTHOLOGIES

Adrian, Jack, ed. *Twelve Mystery Stories.* New York: Oxford University Press, 1999. The mystery stories in this collection relate episodes of madness and revenge, terror and obsession, and the grotesque and the arabesque. Writers include Wilkie Collins and Arthur Conan Doyle.

Altenbernd, Lynn, and Lewis, Leslie L., eds. *Introduction to Literature: Stories.* 3rd ed. New York: Macmillan, 1980. This is an excellent anthology of short fiction, including writers from Kate Chopin to Donald Barthelme. It also contains study questions, notes on authors, and a glossary of literary terms.

Backscheider, Paul R., and Richetti, John J., eds. *Popular Fiction by Women 1660–1730.* New York: Oxford University Press, 1997. A sparkling selection of shorter fiction by the most successful women writers of the period, including Aphra Behn.

Barmé, Geremie, and Minford, John. *Seeds of Fire: Chinese Voices of Conscience.* New York: Hill and Wang, 1988. A variation in perspective, this collection includes stories and poetry of dissent.

Brown, Clarence, ed. *The Portable Twentieth-Century Russian Reader.* New York: Viking, 1985. For a "portable," this is an exceptional anthology.

Brown, Stewart, and Wickham, John, eds. *The Oxford Book of Caribbean Short Stories.* New York: Oxford University Press, 1999. This text includes fifty-two stories representing over a century's worth of pan-Caribbean short fiction.

Cavitch, David, ed. *Life Studies: A Thematic Reader.* 2nd ed. New York: St. Martin's Press, 1986. A collection of fiction and nonfiction organized thematically. Thematic topics include our self-images, our family relationships, our love for other people outside the family, among others.

Correas de Zapeta, Celia. *Short Stories by Latin American Women: The Magic and the Real.* Houston: Arte Publico Press, 1990. An excellent collection with a number of selections short enough for easy adaptation for interpretation.

Cox, Michael, ed. *Twelve Victorian Ghost Stories.* New York: Oxford University Press, 1997. The editor brings together well-wrought tales of haunted houses, vengeful spirits, spectral warnings, invisible antagonists, and motiveless malignity from beyond the grave.

Dalby, Richard, ed. *Twelve Gothic Tales.* New York: Oxford University Press, 1999. This anthology includes a dozen examples of Gothic literature, spanning more than 150 years from Mary Shelley and Charles Maturin through Gerald Durrell.

Echevarria, Roberto Gonzalez, ed. *The Oxford Book of Latin American Short Stories.* New York: Oxford University Press, 1997. This anthology showcases the work of fifty-two writers, ranging from the 16th-century "Colonial Period" to such storytellers as Cuban Antonio Benitez Rojo and Venezuela's Jose Balza.

Flint, Kate, ed. *Victorian Love Stories: An Oxford Anthology.* New York: Oxford University Press, 1996. This text includes Victorian love stories in all their varied moods. Included are works by Elizabeth Gaskell and Somerset Maugham.

Highwater, Jamake, ed. *Words in the Blood: Contemporary Indian Writers of North and South America.* New York: New American Library, 1984. Prose, poetry, song, and essays by Indian writers of North and South America.

Howe, Irving, and Howe, Ilana Wiener, eds. *Short Shorts: An Anthology of the Shortest Stories.* Toronto: Bantam Books, 1982. This anthology contains thirty-eight excellent short-short stories by writers from all over the world.

Menton, Seymour, ed. *The Spanish American Short Story: A Critical Anthology.* Los Angeles and Berkeley: UCLA Latin American Center Publications and University of California Press, 1980. This anthology is particularly helpful because of its introductory material. Not only is biographical information provided, but the major literary movements (Realism, Modernism, Criollisma, and so on) are described as well.

Moffett, James, and McElheny, Kenneth. *Point of View.* New York: Penguin Books, 1995. This is a fine anthology of stories arranged by narrative technique (e.g., interior monologue, letter narration, subjective narration, etc.). Stories range from "A Bundle of Letters" by Henry James to "Uglypuss" by Margaret Atwood.

Pickering, James H., ed. *Fiction 100: An Anthology of Short Stories.* 3rd ed. New York: Macmillan, 1982. This is a large compilation of excellent short stories, including detective fiction, science fiction, and humorous stories, as well as classics like Joseph Conrad's "The Secret Sharer" and Ernest Hemingway"s "Hills Like White Elephants."

Shapard, Robert, and Thomas, James, eds. *Sudden Fiction: American Short-Short Stories.* Salt Lake City: Peregrine Smith, 1986. A collection of American short-short stories suitable for performance.

Shapard, Robert, and Thomas, James, eds. *Sudden Fiction International.* New York: W. W. Norton, 1989. A collection of international short-short stories.

Siu, Helen F., ed. *Furrows: Peasants, Intellectuals, and the State.* Stanford, Calif.: Stanford University Press, 1990. A thematic anthology which divides its stories into four sections: "The Frailty of Power," "The Force of Dogma," "Critique and Ambivalence," and "Furrows." It also includes a lengthy introduction.

Zahafa, Irene, ed. *Word of Mouth: 150 Short-Short Stories by 90 Women Writers.* Freedom, CA: Crossing Press, 1990. The title explains the contents of this excellent anthology.

DRAMA ANTHOLOGIES

Allison, Alexander W.; Carr, Arthur J.; and Eastman, Arthur M., eds. *Masterpieces of the Drama.* 6th ed. New York: Macmillan, 1986. This book contains thirty plays, ranging in scope from Aeschylus's *Agamemnon* to Anton Chekhov's *The Cherry Orchard* and Caryl Churchill's *Top Girls.*

Brockett, Oscar G., and Brockett, Lenyth, eds. *Plays for the Theatre: An Anthology of World Drama.* 4th ed. New York: Holt, Rinehart & Winston, 1984. This anthology offers an excellent variety of plays from *Oedipus Rex* to *Streamers.*

Chervin, Stan, ed. *Short Pieces from the New Dramatists.* New York: Broadway Play

Publishing, 1985. This text includes many very short scenes and monologues suitable for performance.

Cheung, Martha P.Y., and Lai, Jane, eds. *An Oxford Anthology of Contemporary Chinese Drama.* New York: Oxford University Press, 1997. This anthology introduces readers to fifteen plays which comprise some of the finest Chinese drama of the last twenty years.

Dasgupta, Gautum, and Marranca, Bonnie, eds. *Wordplays* 5. New York: PAJ Publications, 1986. The five plays included in this anthology employ new approaches to writing for the theatre.

Delgado, Ramon, ed. *The Best Short Plays 1989.* New York: Applause Theatre Books, 1989. This is an anthology of eleven contemporary one-act plays covering a wide range of topics.

Nelson, Richard, ed. *Strictly Dishonorable and Other Lost American Plays.* New York: Theatre Communications Group, 1986. A collection of four "lost" plays from the twenties and thirties by writers such as Damon Runyon and Sidney Howard.

Vorenberg, Bonnie L., ed. *New Plays for Mature Actors.* Morton Grove, IL: Coach House Press, 1987. An anthology of ten plays with roles for mature actors.

Wellman, Mac, ed. *7 Different Plays.* New York: Broadway Play Publishing, 1988. A collection of nontraditional plays which chart "the ongoing disaster of current American social discourse."

Wellman, Mac, ed. *Theatre of Wonders: Six Contemporary American Plays.* Los Angeles: Sun & Moon Press, 1985. A variety of unique plays by such playwrights as Len Jenkin, Jeffrey Jones, and Des McAnuff, who have "a unique 'take' on the matter of time."

POETRY ANTHOLOGIES

ah-Udhari, Abdullah, ed. and tr. *Modern Poetry of the Arab World.* New York: Penguin Books, 1987. This is a collection of modern Arabic poetry that gives the outsider an excellent view of Arab thought and history.

Allen, Donald, and Butterick, George, F., eds. *The Postmoderns: The New American Poetry Revised.* New York: Grove Press, 1982. A fine collection of modern and contemporary poems.

Armstrong, Isobel; Bristow, Joseph; and Sharrock, Cath, eds. *Nineteenth-Century Women Poets: An Oxford Anthology.* New York: Oxford University Press, 1997. This new anthology brings to light diverse female traditions that have

74

remained in obscurity. Writers include Elizabeth Barrett Browning and Christina Rossetti.

Baird, Joseph L., and Workman, Deborah S., eds. *Toward Solomon's Mountain: The Experience of Disability in Poetry.* Philadelphia: Temple University Press, 1986. This is the work of thirty-five poets, most of whom battle with some type of health problem while still maintaining a sense of humor.

Bargad, Warren, and Chyet, Stanley F., comps. and trs. *Israeli Poetry: A Contemporary Anthology.* Bloomington: Indiana University Press, 1986. This collection of poetry spans the past forty years of literary accomplishments in Israel.

Besner, Neil; Schnitzer, Deborah; and Turner, Alden, eds. *Uncommon Wealth: An Anthology of Poetry in English.* New York: Oxford University Press, 1998. This text features poems written over a period of 400 years by 426 authors from countries and territories on almost every continent.

Bradley, Anthony, ed. *Contemporary Irish Poetry: An Anthology.* New and rev. ed. Berkeley: University of California Press, 1988. This anthology includes approximately fifty of the major modern Irish poets, including Louis MacNeice and Samuel Beckett.

Brant, Beth, ed. *A Gathering of Spirit: Writing and Art by North American Indian Women.* Montpelier: Sinister Wisdom Books, 1984. This collection highlights the daily experiences of the poets and moves from the adjustment to urban life to the feelings of a child and a prisoner.

Bruchac, Joseph, ed. *Breaking Silence: An Anthology of Contemporary Asian-American Poets.* Greenfield Center: Greenfield Review Press, 1983. This collection includes the dreams and ideas of fifty Asian-American poets.

Bruchac, Joseph, ed. *Songs from This Earth on Turtle's Back: Contemporary American Indian Poetry.* Greenfield Center: Greenfield Review Press, 1983. This guide speaks to human beings who care about the well-being and survival of the earth and all its creatures.

Chang-soo, Koh, comp. *Anthology of Contemporary Korean Poetry.* Boston: C. E. Tuttle, 1987. This collection includes the work of six mainstream Korean poets. This is primarily lyric poetry about nature.

Chipasula, Frank Mkalawile, ed. *When My Brothers Come Home: Poems from Central and Southern Africa.* Hanover: Wesleyan University Press, 1985. This collection includes the work of fifty-one African poets who deal with the troubled relationship between Europe and Africa.

Cocalis, Susan, L., ed. *The Defiant Muse: German Feminist Poets from the Middle Ages to the Present.* New York: Feminist Press, 1986. This collection features mostly uncelebrated female poets from the early part of the thirteenth century to the present day.

Eastman, Arthur M.; Allison, Alexander W.; Barrows, Herbert; Blake, Caesar R.; Carr, Arthur J.; and English, Hubert M., Jr., eds. *The Norton Anthology of Poetry.* New York: W.W. Norton, 1970. This book is a very large and complete anthology of poetry from Chaucer to Ishmael Reed.

Jamil, Maya, ed. *Poetry from Pakistan: An Anthology.* New York: Oxford University Press, 1998. Sixteen poets showcase their talents.

Jayyusi, Salma Khadra, ed. *Modern Arabic Poetry: An Anthology.* New York: Columbia University Press, 1987. This anthology includes poetry written in the latter half of this century that shows a search for identity in the modern world.

Kessler, Jascha, ed. *The Face of Creation: Contemporary Hungarian Poetry.* Minneapolis: Coffee House Press, 1988. This collection mainly compiles the work of Istvan Vas, Sander Csoori, and Marton Kalasz.

Kowit, Steve, ed. *The Maverick Poets: An Anthology.* Santee, Calif.: Gorilla Press, 1988. As the title suggests, this is a collection of "maverick" poems which often are radical, off color, and occasionally subversive.

Linthwaite, Illona, ed. *Ain't I a Woman!: A Book of Women's Poetry from Around the World.* New York: P. Bedrick Books, 1988. This collection covers the important events in the lives of women.

Martz, Sandra, ed. *When I Am an Old Woman I Shall Wear Purple.* Watsonville, CA: Papier-Mache Press, 1987. This is a collection of poetry and prose by and about the elderly.

Nims, John Frederick, ed. *Western Wind: An Introduction to Poetry.* New York: Random House, 1974. This is a fine collection of different kinds of poems with excellent commentary by Nims.

Philip, Neil, ed. *A New Treasury of Poetry.* New York: STC, 1990. The 288 poems by such writers as Emily Dickinson, e. e. cummings, Langston Hughes, and Walt Whitman were selected for their inherent freshness and rhythm.

Pichaske, David, R., ed. *Beowulf to Beatles and Beyond: The Varieties of Poetry.* 2nd ed. New York: Macmillan, 1981. This is a fine anthology of poetry, including "traditional" poetry, rock lyrics, contemporary poetry, prose poetry, and concrete poetry.

Ray, David, and Ray, Judy, eds. *Fathers: A Collection of Poems.* New York: St. Martin's Press, 1997. In this collection of memories about fathers, both daughters and sons—some famous poets, others less well known—introduce and pay tribute to their fathers.

Reaney, James. *Performance Poems.* Ontario, Canada: Moonstone Press, 1990. An anthology of poems with solo and group performance possibilities.

Sanchez, Marta Ester, ed. *Contemporary Chicana Poetry: A Critical Approach to an Emerging Literature.* Berkeley: University of California Press, 1985. All of the poets are women not generally known. The subject matter includes topics of gender, ethnicity, and silence.

Stanton, Donna, C., ed. *The Defiant Muse: French Feminist Poems from the Middle Ages to the Present.* New York: Feminist Press, 1986. This anthology covers poets that date from the twelfth century to contemporary writers. The poems make courageous and defiant statements about male-dominant society.

Strand, Mark, ed. *The Best American Poetry 1991.* New York: Macmillan, 1991. Seventy-five contemporary poems worthy of acclaim.

CHILDREN'S LITERATURE

Arbuthnot, May Hill. *Children and Books.* Glenview, Ill.: Scott, Foresman, 1947.

Arbuthnot, May Hill. *The Arbuthnot Anthology.* Rev. ed. Glenview, Ill.: Scott, Foresman, 1961.

Burack, A. S., ed. *100 Plays for Children.* Boston: Plays, Inc., 1983.

Cole, Joanna, comp. *A New Treasury of Children's Poetry: Old Favorites and New Discoveries.* Garden City, NY: Doubleday, 1984.

Hardendorff, Jeanne, B., ed. and rev. *Stories to Tell: A List of Stories with Annotations.* 5th ed. Enoch Pratt Free Library, 1965.

Iarusso, Marilyn, comp. *Stories: A List of Stories to Tell and to Read Aloud.* 7th ed. New York: New York Public Library, 1977.

Jennings, Coleman A., and Harris, Aurand, eds. *Plays Children Love.* Garden City, NY: Doubleday, 1981.

Livingston, Myra Cohn, ed. *I Like You, If You Like Me: Poems of Friendship.* New York: Macmillan, 1987.

Nolan, Paul T. *Folk Tale Plays Round the World.* Boston: Plays, Inc., 1983.

Olfson, Lewy. *Radio Plays from Shakespeare.* Boston: Plays, Inc., 1983.

Silverstein, Shel. *Where the Sidewalk Ends.* New York: Harper, 1974.

Thane, Adele. *Plays from Famous Stories and Fairy Tales.* Boston: Plays, Inc., 1983.

Tolkien, J. R. R. "On Fairy Stories," in *The Tolkien Reader.* New York: Valentine Books, 1956.

Ward, Winifred, ed. *Stories to Dramatize.* Anchorage, KY: Anchorage Press, 1952.

ADDITIONAL AIDS

The following books contain, for the most part, lists of stories or plays or poem titles, occasionally by author and occasionally by theme. You can consult these books for a synopsis of a story or play or for the title of a poem. You will then have to find an anthology to obtain a copy of the selection.

Barker, Clive, and Trussler, Simon, eds. *New Theatre Quarterly.* New York: Cambridge University Press. This journal informs on all aspects of theatre studies.

Bogart, Gary L., ed. *Short Story Index.* New York: H. W. Wilson, 1979. This is an index to stories in anthologies and periodicals.

Fidell, Estelle, A., ed. *Play Index, 1973–1977.* New York: H. W. Wilson, 1978. The book contains an index to 3,878 plays, and includes the name of the play-wright, title of the play, a brief description of the play, the number of acts and scenes, the size of the cast, and the number of sets required.

Greenfieldt, John, and Yaakov, Juliette, eds. *Play Index 1983–1987.* New York: H. W. Wilson, 1988. This is an index to 3,964 plays indexed by author, title, and subject.

Gross, John, ed. *The Oxford Book of Essays.* New York: Oxford University Press, 1999. This text includes 140 essays by 120 writers: classics, curiosities, medita-tions, diversions, old favorites, and recent examples that deserve to be better known. Writers range from Benjamin Franklin to John Updike.

Guide to Play Selection. 3rd ed. Compiled by the Liaison Committee of the National Council of Teachers of English with the Speech Communication Association and the American Theatre Association. Urbana, IL: National Council of Teachers of English; and New York: R. R. Bowker, 1975. A fine collection of more than 850 plays, described and listed according to playwright. A section on television plays is also included.

Salem, James M., ed. *Drury's Guide to Best Plays.* 4th ed. Metuchen, NJ, and London, England: The Scarecrow Press, 1987. This is an index of 1,500 full-length, non-musical plays in English, covering all dramatic periods from Greek to contem-porary. Included are plays selected for inclusion in *The Best Plays of the Year* series, Pulitzer winners, and the most popular and commonly produced plays.

Shank, Theodore J., ed. *A Digest of 500 Plays: Plot Outlines and Production Notes.* New York: Crowell-Collier Press, 1963. This contains a listing of 500 plays, including title, author, type of play, plot summary, and character descriptions.

Smith, William James, ed. *Granger's Index to Poetry.* New York: Columbia University Press, 1978. The book is organized according to the title and first line of a poem. There are also an author index and a subject index.

Many magazines such as *Saturday Review of Literature, Atlantic,* and *Harper's* contain excellent literary selections and literary reviews.

Notes

1. René Wellek and Austin Warren, *Theory of Literature,* 3rd ed. (New York: Harcourt, Brace & World, 1956), p. 150.
2. Louise M. Rosenblatt, *The Reader, the Text, the Poem: The Transactional Theory of the Literary Work* (Carbondale and Edwardsville, IL: Southern Illinois University Press, 1978), pp. 18–19.
3. Ibid., p. ix.
4. G. Wilson Knight, in *Shakespearian Dimensions* (Sussex: Harvester Press, 1984), p. 12.
5. Flannery O'Connor, in Sally Fitzgerald and Robert Fitzgerald, eds., *Mystery and Manners* (New York: Farrar, Straus & Giroux, 1970), p. 100.
6. Wolfgang Iser, *The Art of Reading: A Theory of Aesthetic Response* (Baltimore: Johns Hopkins University Press, 1978), p. 18.

3

BALLAD OF PEARL MAY LEE

THEN, off they took you, off to the jail,
A hundred hooting after.
And you should have heard me at my house.
I cut my lungs with my laughter,
    Laughter,
    Laughter.
I cut my lungs with my laughter.

They dragged you into a dusty cell.
And a rat was in the corner.
And what was I doing? Laughing still.
Though never was a poor gal lorner,
    Lorner,
    Lorner.
Though never was a poor gal lorner.

The sheriff, he peeped in through the bars,
And (the red old thing) he told you,
"You son of a bitch, you're going to hell!"
'Cause you wanted white arms to enfold you,
    Enfold you,
    Enfold you.
'Cause you wanted white arms to enfold you.

But you paid for your white arms, Sammy boy,
And you didn't pay with money.
You paid with your hide and my heart, Sammy boy,
For your taste of pink and white honey.

Although it might seem like a paradox to you now, your appreciation of a piece of literature grows as you study and analyze it. In general, the more you know about something, the more you understand and admire it. Many students balk at the idea of literary analysis. They are afraid of it because they fear they might come up with the wrong answers—as if there were right and wrong answers! It is true, though, that a literary theory is only as good as the person who applies it, and the more you know about a theory, the more skill you bring to its application. Analysis helps you discover what you think a text means by introducing useful questions to ask and focusing on important elements to consider, and by reinforcing the cues that need your attention. Some texts benefit from the application of one type of a literary analysis over another, and each analysis yields different kinds of information.

In recent years, literary theories have proliferated. You could become intimidated just by the sheer number of possible theories as well as by their seeming complexity. As already stated, we believe that performance itself is a form of criticism—a way of coming to know a text. Many types of analysis may, however, help inform that performance and make it richer and more meaningful.

Because this is not a text in literary analysis, our discussion of these theories must by necessity be cursory. What we have done, though, is to summarize many of the existing forms of literary analysis in terms of intent, apply each analysis to reveal one possible interpretation of an Aesop fable, and then posit performance *analogues*—specific performance choices—which you may employ to communicate that interpretation to an audience. Certainly, you would want to study any theory you might choose to apply in more depth, but we hope the following discussion will introduce the possibilities to you. Check the bibliography at the end of this text for sources of more information on the literary theories introduced.

TYPES OF LITERARY ANALYSIS

As you will see, there are many ways to "unpack" literature. We include these analytical approaches to show you the variety of ways a text may be analyzed. Do not let the variety or complexity overwhelm you, but return to these analytical applications after you have mastered the two types of analysis best employed by beginning solo performers: the dramatistic and the modal. The literary analyses we shall consider are Archetypal, Biographical, Deconstructionist, Dramatistic, Feminist, Formalist, Marxist, Modal, New Historical, Psychoanalytic, Reader-Response, Rhetorical, and Structuralist. Each of these types of literary analysis will be applied in relation to the fable "The Crow and the Pitcher" by Aesop.

THE CROW AND THE PITCHER   Aesop

A thirsty Crow found a Pitcher with some water in it, but so little was there that, try as she might, she could not reach it with her beak, and it seemed as though she would die of thirst within sight of the remedy. At last she hit upon a clever plan. She began dropping pebbles into the Pitcher, and with each pebble the water rose a little higher until at last it reached the brim, and the knowing bird was enabled to quench her thirst.

Necessity is the mother of invention.

From *The Fables of Aesop,* edited by Joseph Jacobs, Macmillan, 1950. By permission of the Macmillan Co., New York.

ARCHETYPAL—Archetypal theorists examine literature in relation to mythological motifs and patterns.

Interpretation: The bird (either trickster or transcendent self) is dropping pebbles (symbols of the immortal and unalterable self) into the water (symbol of the unconscious self—or the female principle). Because the water is in a pitcher, the rebirth of the integrative self is assured.

Performance Analogue: The performer looks at each part of the story as a different voice—aspects of self (bird as transcendent self, pebbles as unalterable self, and water as unconscious self). By the end of the story, the integrated voice of the whole self is apparent.

BIOGRAPHICAL—Biographical theorists examine the relationship between the writer's life and influences and the literature the writer creates.

Interpretation: This fable parallels Aesop's life (if indeed there was an Aesop, and he wasn't just legendary) in terms of his desire to escape from the bonds of slavery. The Crow represents Aesop in his quest to be free and accommodate his needs without depending on anything or anyone else.

Performance Analogue: The speaker would initially communicate the oppressed feelings of the Crow in not being able to reach the water. By the fable's end, the Crow has succeeded in his quest for liberation, and Aesop's persona is heard speaking the moral.

DECONSTRUCTIONIST—Deconstructionist theorists analyze a text by examining the necessary gaps which occur whenever language is used. They question textual closure and authority.

Interpretation: Deconstructionists might examine this text using the word "pebble." They might say that the story drops line by line like the pebbles into the pitcher, climaxing in the overflow of language in the moral. The language cannot be contained in the pitcher, so it all has to burst forth into the final epigram.

Performance Analogue: Approach this like a performance art piece (see Chapter 9). Treat each sentence like a pebble, and drop it into your audience. Each sentence acts as a pebble and builds toward the climax: the moral—which is the overflow or explosion out of the text. The story cannot hold the moral any more; it must release it.

DRAMATISTIC—Dramatistic theorists study the work as though it were a minidrama. A dramatistic analysis answers the questions: Who is speaking? To whom? About what? Where? When? How? and Why? The text is analyzed to come to terms with the dramatic situation inherent in it.

Interpretation: A third-person omniscient narrator (the who) is speaking to a group of children (to whom) about a Crow who wants something and cleverly devises a way to get it (about what). The where and when do not seem significant, as the fable is universal and timeless. The speaker's language (how) is simplistic, employing stark images to best communicate with the intended audience. The speaker is telling the children this so that they will understand that "necessity is the mother of invention" (why).

Performance Analogue: The performer should suggest the positive attitude this third-person omniscient narrator has toward the Crow. The performer should speak directly to the audience, maintaining eye contact with them and making sure they understand the situation and the Crow's success, which culminates in the moral lesson the children are to learn.

FEMINIST—Feminist theorists approach a text in terms of the portrayal of women and the power relations they are involved in during the portrayal.

Interpretation: The feminist critic might first question why the Crow is "she." Is the Crow placed in a domestic role, woman as water carrier? Or does her role as the water carrier (life bringer) reflect a positive image of the female because she is able to achieve her goal independently—without patriarchal intervention? Finally, why is necessity the "mother" of invention?

Performance Analogue: Depending on which of the interpretations you choose, you would project sympathy for the Crow as water carrier, antipathy for the stereotyping of Crow as domestic servant, or possibly total identification.

FORMALIST—Formalist theorists study the work in and of itself—the images, the figures, the structure—especially as they manifest the defamiliarizing character of language. Formalists seek the "literariness" of a text, its style, genre, technique, and so on.

Interpretation: A narrator employs economy of phrase, stark images, and simplistic language to convey a moral. The combination of these elements guarantees the classification of this text as a fable.

Performance Analogue: The performer must emphasize the simplicity of the story and convey the images—that is, really see the Crow, the pitcher, the pebbles; hear the pebbles fall into the pitcher; feel the Crow's satisfaction upon relieving its thirst.

MARXIST—Marxist theorists examine a text in terms of its production, including the means and authority by which it is produced—based on principles devised by Karl Marx.

Interpretation: As a slave, Aesop understood the power of revolution through story. The Crow represents the working class dropping its "pebbles" into the wells of history. While the fable portrays a means by which the dominant class produced a docile public (by keeping them working for a paucity of water), history supports Aesop and his revolutionary vision of the workers controlling the means of production.

Performance Analogue: Like the worker, the performer/Crow drops its pebbles into history's pitcher. The determined speaker communicates the inevitability of history by building the suspense until the pitcher breaks.

MODAL—Modal theorists attempt to analyze a text according to its speaker or audience mode. Speaker mode is concerned with identifying the nature of the speaker in a text. Audience mode studies who is being addressed moment-by-moment or line-by-line in the text.

Interpretation: When the author seems to be much like the speaker (but not the same as) in a text, we say the speaker mode is lyric. There seems to be a lyric relationship between the poet and the third-person omniscient narrator in this fable. A similarity in attitude evidently exists between poet and narrator: both desire to teach a moral lesson. The ideal audience for this story would probably be children young enough to need to know that facing a problem can inspire new and creative solutions. Since the speaker wants to "teach," the audience mode is epic—a general audience is directly addressed.

Performance Analogue: Use open focus, and address the actual audience as if they were the ideal audience for this work. The speaker might want to assume a professorial air to suggest the "lesson" quality of the fable. The speaker suggests the Aesop persona when delivering the moral.

NEW HISTORICAL—New Historical critics examine the social and political contexts that situate a text in a particular ideological framework.

Interpretation: The fable is situated in a culture that prizes individual initiative, but only as far as that initiative is used for self-affirmation in the justification of the culture. The fable is seen as a cultural artifact that privileges the bird's survival, but keeps hidden the conditions that keep the bird thirsty.

Performance Analogue: The performer narrates the story as a moral document, justifying a particular culture. Then, the performer could repeat the story, narrating a cultural voice that challenges the point of the story, or raises questions about how the Crow got thirsty in the first place.

PSYCHOANALYTIC—Psychoanalytic theorists analyze literature as well as the state of mind of the writer in terms of Freudian psychology, especially examining literature for its latent/manifest content.

Interpretation: One possible psychoanalytic interpretation of this fable involves a woman's maternal need for children without relying on the conventional means of conception. The pitcher is the womb, and the pebbles the seed which the Crow controls. The rising water symbolizes the nine-month gestation period, until finally birth is achieved. The "quenching of thirst" is the satisfaction of maternal need.

Performance Analogue: This interpretation involves the reader's sense of self, coming to terms with one's own body, and the satisfaction one receives from achieving success alone.

READER-RESPONSE—Reader-response theorists analyze a text according to a reader's expectations and discoveries.

Interpretation: The suspense of the fable is created by the question of how the Crow will quench her thirst. Each sentence creates new expectations as to how she will accomplish her task. Thus, first the reader discovers the Crow cannot reach the water with her beak. Then she hits upon "a clever plan," giving rise to the question, What plan? Gradually, the reader is given the picture of the Crow's solution, pebble by pebble.

A reader-response critic may also examine why fables are particularly suitable for younger readers. Thus the moral tag at the end is unnecessary for the adult reader, but offers closure to the story for the young reader.

Performance Analogue: Find moments of suspense in the piece—and through pause, vocal/physical variation, and so on, create this suspense for the audience. The performance of the moral would vary depending on the nature of the audience. An audience of children would necessitate a more explanatory delivery, with perhaps more direct audience contact and an upward pitch inflection. For an audience of adults, the delivery of the moral would be more conspiratorial or satiric since adults have probably reasoned this out for themselves.

RHETORICAL—Rhetorical theorists are concerned with the persuasive/communicative strategies within the literary work, and with the effect the work has on its audience/readers.

Interpretation: The author, through the speaker, wishes to communicate the idea that "necessity is the mother of invention." The fable is an illustration employed to communicate that idea. The fable is simplistic, with recognizable images which indicate that the intended audience is children.

Performance Analogue: The speaker's tone would be persuasive; the intention, to teach a lesson. The speaker should clearly separate the illustration from the moral.

STRUCTURALISM—Structuralist theorists examine the fundamental structures underlying the patterns of a text.

Interpretation: An agent drops an object into a container of liquid. The liquid rises, and the cycle is repeated until stasis is achieved.

Performance Analogue: The performer creates a comparative performance, substituting other agents and objects into the slots of the Crow, the pitcher, and the pebble. (For example, Crow = Princess, pitcher = Magic pool, pebble = frog.)

As stated earlier, the two types of literary analysis most applicable for beginning performers are the dramatistic and the modal. When applied, these two approaches yield information which can be easily turned into performance analogues—which, as stated above, are translations of analytic decisions into performance choices that convey your interpretation to an audience. Start with these approaches first and then decide which, if any, of the other approaches just described will reveal additional information necessary to understand your particular selection. Although dramatistic or modal analyses answer only some of the basic inquiries necessary for interpretation, they are good starting points for analysis. The specific questions to ask when analyzing prose fiction, drama, and poetry are discussed in some depth in Chapters 6, 7, and 8.

THE DRAMATISTIC ANALYSIS

The interpreter uses the dramatistic analysis to answer the following seven questions:

Who is speaking?
To whom is the speaker speaking?
About what is the speaker speaking?
Where is the speaker speaking?
When is the speaker speaking?
How is the speaker speaking?
Why is the speaker speaking?

The answers to these questions provide information needed to help you prepare for performance. The dramatistic approach essentially answers the same questions about literature that you would ask in general when you want more information about someone or something. Most literary selections can be examined as though they were dramas—as something being said by someone to someone else in a certain place, at a certain time, in a given style, and for a certain reason.

A Sample Dramatistic Analysis of "Ringing the Bells"

Let us perform a sample dramatistic analysis of Anne Sexton's "Ringing the Bells." As you read the poem, preferably out loud, see if you can decide who is speaking, to whom, about what, where, when, how, and why.

RINGING THE BELLS   Anne Sexton

1   And this is the way they ring
2   the bells in Bedlam
3   and this is the bell-lady
4   who comes each Tuesday morning

5 to give us a music lesson
6 and because the attendants make you go
7 and because we mind by instinct,
8 like bees caught in the wrong hive,
9 we are the circle of crazy ladies
10 who sit in the lounge of the mental house
11 and smile at the smiling woman
12 who passes us each a bell,
13 who points at my hand
14 that holds my bell, E flat,
15 and this is the gray dress next to me
16 who grumbles as if it were special
17 to be old, to be old,
18 and this is the small hunched squirrel girl
19 on the other side of me
20 who picks at the hairs over her lip,
21 who picks at the hairs over her lip all day,
22 and this is how the bells really sound,
23 as untroubled and clean
24 as a workable kitchen,
25 and this is always my bell responding
26 to my hand that responds to the lady
27 who points at me, E flat;
28 and although we are no better for it,
29 they tell you to go. And you do.

The first question posed by the dramatistic analyst is, Who is speaking? The speaker (who) is a woman who has been institutionalized. Although she is speaking about herself, she seems to be speaking for all the women in her group, as she uses the pronouns "us" and "we" throughout. From what she chooses to tell us, we can assume that she is a fairly young woman, for she complains about the grumblings of the old and refers to the old woman next to her as "the gray dress." How sane is this woman who refers to herself and to her fellow patients as "the circle of crazy ladies"? Is it possible that sane people might think they are crazy, while truly crazy people think they are sane? This woman seems to have an awareness and an understanding of what is happening around her that links her to reality. She seems troubled but not "crazy." Could she be a bee caught in the wrong hive? She realizes that she is no better off following the rules, but she does as she is told because to do otherwise would require her to exert more energy and summon more initiative than she seems to possess right now. It is easier to go through each day minding "by instinct."

The audience (to whom) this woman addresses would appear to be people unfamiliar with life in an institution—perhaps a group of people on a tour of the facility. The speaker's attention to details and descriptions of the routine are for the uninitiated or the unaware. There is a kind of "show and tell" feel to her recitation, as though she feels it necessary to point out everything in the room: "this is the bell lady," "this is the gray dress," "this is the small hunched squirrel girl," and "this is how the bells really sound." Her audience seems not too critical or judgmental, for the speaker uses very childlike images, words, and rhythm, and she seems unconcerned about whether this might be inappropriate. (A case could be made that the speaker is addressing herself, reaffirming her belief in her sanity or at least trying to maintain that belief.)

The place (where) is the lounge of a mental institution, and the time (when) is now—an eternal present—during a music lesson.

The speaker is talking about the tedious life in an institution (what). She does not seem to enjoy the life there, and her use of repetitive phrases ("and this is," "and because," and "who comes," "who sit," "who passes," "who points," "who grumbles") and the repetition of certain lines ("to be old" and "who picks at the hairs over her lip") seems to highlight the repetitiveness and routine of her institutional existence. She is out of place there—she is an "E flat."

The language and style of speech (how) is casual and fairly colloquial. The speaker uses common, everyday language, simple and unadorned. The rhythm of the language has a nursery-rhyme quality, almost as if the speaker has become a child again. The poem has only two sentences: a very long one and a short one. The long sentence is full of the repetition and the visual images we previously referred to, and the short one ("And you do.") capsulizes the logical outcome of the instinctive, mechanical life she leads.

The speaker could have any number of purposes (why) in recounting this. On a large scale, the speaker could be saying that we all live life in some kind of institution, and that the ladies in the circle form a microcosm of humanity. On a more specific level, the speaker could be showing us the results of one woman's inability to cope with the pressures of the outside world. She is now in a place where life is less pressured because there are fewer choices and fewer decisions to be made. Here is a place where she does not have to worry about "workable kitchens." She may feel out of place, but she can now respond without having to think—her actions are controlled by outside stimuli. She rings her bell when told and tries to stay in harmony with her institutionalized environment. If the audience is composed of people taking a tour, the persona could simply be pointing people and things out to them as the delegated spokesperson. As she does so, she inadvertently reveals the childlike state to which she has been reduced. There is room in this poem for all of these interpretations, and many more.

Anne Sexton has been called a "confessional" poet because she often writes about personal experiences—experiences that she has lived through herself. Her poetry has the quality of the confessional about it, as though she were revealing her own private pain and innermost thoughts. Knowing that Sexton was for a time institutionalized and that she ultimately committed suicide provides valuable insights to help us understand why she might have written this poem.

Performance Suggestions for "Ringing the Bells"

Let us now translate what we learned from this brief dramatistic analysis into performance suggestions. Although performance suggestions should be made at the same time as each analytical decision, for purposes of simplification we have separated analysis and performance ideas so that each process can be examined individually. One problem many beginning interpreters seem to have is knowing how to turn an analytical decision into a performance analogue. Deciding that the speaker in the selection is a ninety-four-year-old man who is depressed about life and wants others to know about it is an analytical decision. Deciding that to perform the speaker in the selection, you will round your shoulders, hunch over slightly, use a lower than normal pitch, look at the audience, keep eyes downcast, and deliver in a soft, slow voice is translating that analysis into performance.

Let us translate the information we gained from the dramatistic analysis of "Ringing the Bells" into performance suggestions. Before we begin, however, we must reiterate one important point. As we stressed in Chapter 2, there is no one definitive interpretation of any poem, no one way to analyze or perform it. Notice that during the analysis of "Ringing the Bells," we often used the words "could" and "seems." No one—perhaps not even Sexton herself—has *the* right interpretation of this poem. Your responsibility is to study the poem and share what the poem means to you. Every reader of the poem will see it differently and will come up with different conclusions based on his or her special transaction with it. As long as your decisions can be supported by lines from the text they are valid.

The speaker in this poem is very much like Anne Sexton. Although the persona is like Sexton, the speaker is not Sexton, but rather someone she created to speak this poem for her.[1] If the persona were Sexton, your responsibility would be to investigate what Sexton looked like, sounded like, and so forth at the time she wrote this poem and to impersonate her. In texts where the speaker seems to be very like the author, the tendency is to assume that author and speaker are one. Bacon deals with this problem in relation to the letters of John Keats: "The interpreter does not read the letters of Keats in the person of Keats any more than he reads it in his own person. The style may be the inner man; it is not the outer man. He does read it in the style of Keats, which is another matter."[2]

As you become the persona in this poem, you work to embody Sexton's style. A female performer should ask herself, "What is there in my own experience that will help me become this particular woman?" A man should ask himself the same question, but he should also do some thinking about how he is going to suggest a woman in performance. The poem makes it clear that the persona is a woman ("we are the circle of crazy ladies"), and this should be projected in performance—although extreme exaggeration is never necessary. (A common mistake of many beginning interpreters is changing pitch so drastically high to project women and so drastically low to project men that they depict cartoonlike caricatures.) The femaleness of this speaker, however, is not as important as her state of mind and mental attitude. The rhythm, word choices, and tone of the poem suggest a rather childlike, nursery-rhyme quality. You would want to project this in your voice by affecting perhaps a hollow, mesmerized, slightly high-pitched, singsong tone. Your body might feel frail, slightly thin, and small. The persona is seated, so you might want to sit during your performance—though you need not be that literal. Since the persona seems to be explaining what life and the people are like in an institution to persons unfamiliar with the routine, you would want to look directly at the audience and speak right to them. To create the scene, try to imagine where the other characters in the circle are seated out in the audience, directly above the audience members' heads. Try to re-create all the sensory images—the bell lady, the attendants, the circle of crazy ladies, the sound of the bell—out in the audience. The more clearly you seem to see, hear, and sense the images in the poem, the more the members of the audience will be able to participate in the creation of the scene in their imaginations.

As stated earlier, you study literature in interpretation both prior to your performance and during your performance. As you perform "Ringing the Bells," part of you will be listening to your performance—evaluating what you are doing. This is natural, and it happens quite spontaneously. If you listen to yourself each time you perform the same poem, you will gain new insights. These new insights can then become the basis for new performance ideas.

Class Exercise

Try performing a dramatistic analysis of these selections. (In the case of cuttings from longer works, a thorough analysis can be achieved only after the whole work is studied.)

FROM THE TELL-TALE HEART   Edgar Allan Poe

True!—nervous—very, very dreadfully nervous I had been and am; but why *will* you say that I am mad? The disease had sharpened my senses—not destroyed—not dulled them. Above all was the sense of hearing acute. I heard all things in the heaven and earth. I heard many things in hell. How, then, am I mad? Hearken! and observe how healthily—how calmly I can tell you the whole story.

It is impossible to say how first the idea entered my brain; but once conceived, it haunted me day and night. Object there was none. Passion there was none. I loved the old man. He had never wronged me. He had never given me insult. For his gold I had no desire. I think it was his eye! yes, it was this! He had the eye of a vulture—a pale blue eye, with a film over it. Whenever it fell upon me, my blood ran cold; and so by degrees—very gradually—I made up my mind to take the life of the old man, and thus rid myself of the eye forever.

Now this is the point. You fancy me mad. Madmen know nothing. But you should have seen *me*. You should have seen how wisely I proceeded—with what caution—with what foresight—with what dissimulation I went to work! I was never kinder to the old man than during the whole week before I killed him. And every night, about midnight, I turned the latch of his door and opened it—oh so gently! And then, when I had made an opening sufficient for my head, I put in a dark lantern, all closed, closed, so that no light shone out, and then I thrust in my head. Oh, you would have laughed to see how cunningly I thrust it in! I moved it slowly—very, very slowly, so that I might not disturb the old man's sleep. It took me an hour to place my whole head within the opening so far that I could see him as he lay upon his bed. Ha!—would a madman have been so wise as this? And then, when my head was well in the room, I undid the lantern cautiously—oh, so cautiously—cautiously (for the hinges creaked)—I undid it just so much that a single thin ray fell upon the vulture eye. And this I did for seven long nights—every night just at midnight—but I found the eye always closed; and so it was impossible to do the work; for it was not the old man who vexed me, but his Evil Eye. And every morning, when the day broke, I went boldly into the chamber, and spoke courageously to him, calling him by name in a hearty tone, and inquiring how he had passed the night. So you see he would have been a very profound old man, indeed, to suspect that every night, just at twelve, I looked in upon him while he slept.

MOTHER TO SON   Langston Hughes

Well, son, I'll tell you,
Life for me ain't been no crystal stair.
It's had tacks in it.
And splinters,
And boards torn up,
And places with no carpet on the floor—
Bare.
But all the time
I'se been a-climbin' on,
And reachin' landin's,

And turnin' corners,
And sometimes goin' in the dark
Where there ain't been no light.
So, boy, don't you turn back.
Don't you set down on the steps
'Cause you finds it kinder hard.
Don't you fall now—
For I'se still goin', honey,
I'se still climbin',
And life for me ain't been no crystal stair.

From THE LESSON   Eugene Ionesco

Scene: The office of the old professor, which also serves as a dining room.
Characters (in this scene): The Professor, aged 50 to 60
                    The Young Pupil, aged 18

Professor: Good morning, young lady. You . . . I expect that you . . . that you are the new pupil?

Pupil: (*Turns quickly with a lively and self-assured manner; she gets up, goes toward the Professor, and gives him her hand*): Yes, Professor. Good morning, Professor. As you see, I'm on time. I didn't want to be late.

Professor: That's fine, miss. Thank you, you didn't really need to hurry. I am very sorry to have kept you waiting . . . I was just finishing up . . . well . . . I'm sorry. . . . You will excuse me, won't you? . . .

Pupil: Oh, certainly, Professor. It doesn't matter at all, Professor.

Professor: Please excuse me . . . Did you have any trouble finding the house?

Pupil: No . . . Not at all. I just asked the way. Everybody knows you around here.

Professor: For thirty years I've lived in this town. You've not been here for long? How do you find it?

Pupil: It's all right. The town is attractive and even agreeable, there's a nice park, a boarding school, a bishop, nice shops and streets . . .

Professor: That's very true, young lady. And yet, I'd just as soon live somewhere else. In Paris, or at least Bordeaux.

Pupil: Do you like Bordeaux?

Professor: I don't know. I've never seen it.

Pupil: But you know Paris?

Professor: No, I don't know it either, young lady, but if you'll permit me, can you tell me, Paris is the capital city of . . . miss?

Pupil:	(*Searching her memory for a moment, then, happily guessing*): Paris is the capital city of . . . France?
Professor:	Yes, young lady, bravo, that's very good, that's perfect. My congratulations. You have your French geography at your fingertips. You know your chief cities.
Pupil:	Oh! I don't know them all yet, Professor, it's not quite that easy, I have trouble learning them.
Professor:	Oh! it will come . . . you mustn't give up . . . young lady . . . I beg your pardon . . . have patience . . . little by little . . . You will see, it will come in time . . . What a nice day it is today . . . or rather, not so nice . . . Oh! but then yes it is nice. In short, it's not too bad a day, that's the main thing . . . ahem . . . ahem . . . it's not raining and it's not snowing either.
Pupil:	That would be most unusual, for it's summer now.
Professor:	Excuse me, miss, I was just going to say so . . . but as you will learn, one must be ready for anything.
Pupil:	I guess so, Professor.
Professor:	We can't be sure of anything, young lady, in this world.
Pupil:	The snow falls in the winter. Winter is one of the four seasons. The other three are . . . uh . . . spr . . .
Professor:	Yes?
Pupil:	. . . ing, and then summer . . . and . . . uh . . .
Professor:	It begins like "automobile," miss.
Pupil:	Ah, yes, autumn . . .
Professor:	That's right, miss, that's a good answer, that's perfect. I am convinced that you will be a good pupil. You will make real progress. You are intelligent, you seem to me to be well informed, and you've a good memory.
Pupil:	I know my seasons, don't I, Professor?
Professor:	Yes, indeed, miss . . . or almost. But it will come in time. In any case, you're coming along. Soon you'll know all the seasons, even with your eyes closed. Just as I do.

Excerpt from "The Lesson" by Eugene Ionesco. Reprinted by permission of Grove Press. Copyright © 1958 by Grove Press, Inc.

THE MAN AND THE LION   Lisa Cofield and Debbie Dingerson

One day Mr. Aesop told a story in his village. It was about a man and a Lion who traveled together through the forest. They soon began to boast of their respective superiority to each other in strength and prowess.

As they were disputing, they passed a statue carved in stone, which represented "a Lion strangled by a Man." The man pointed to it and said "See there! How strong we are, and how we prevail over even the king of beasts." The Lion replied, "This statue was made by a man. If we Lions knew how to erect statues, you would see the Man placed under the paw of the Lion."

The next day, Mrs. Aesop began writing her own stories. "You can't write stories," said Mr. Aesop. "You know that men tell the best stories."

"Yes, dear," replied Mrs. Aesop with a knowing smile. "But that's only because until now, the men have told all the stories."

Moral: Sometimes the best version of history is herstory.

Published in *Mrs. Aesop's Fables* by Lisa Cofield and Debbie Dingerson. Reprinted by permission of Great Quotations Publishing Company, 1967 Quincy Court, Glendale Heights, IL 60139-2045.

THE MODAL APPROACH

As we stated earlier, the modal approach is divided into two types of analysis: speaker mode and audience mode.

Speaker Modal Analysis

The speaker modal analysis is employed when one is interested in categorizing literature as a whole in terms of who is speaking. If a text contains an undefined, uncharacterized speaker—a persona—the speaker mode is called *lyric*. As we said earlier, "persona" literally means mask of the poet, but you should not assume from this that speaker and writer are one in the same. Remember that the writer is the creator of the work and not necessarily the speaker in it. In Sexton's poem "Ringing the Bells," for example, which we just discussed, the lyric persona is very much like Anne Sexton, but there are differences between Sexton the woman and the persona she creates to speak for her in this poem. Discovering those differences would be part of a speaker modal analysis. Writers, for example, may exaggerate some details of their lives, create fictitious events, alter some details, or leave details out. In a 1986 issue of *Parade Magazine,* Lynn Minton cites Gene Saks (director of the film version of *Brighton Beach Memoirs* by Neil Simon) on this issue. She speculates, "Neil Simon has drawn so much from his own life—adolescence, Army service, marriage, divorce—for his plays and movies that it's natural to wonder if he has a better memory than the rest of us. Not so, says the director Gene Saks: 'Neil doesn't necessarily remember it as it was. He remembers it as he makes it up now.'"

Lyric speaker mode

In a lyric mode text, only one voice is heard—the persona's. This lyric persona is not characterized. Personae in lyric texts share personal experiences, reveal thoughts, or celebrate an occasion. Literature in the lyric mode is usually highly emotional and intimate, and seems to exist in a timeless present. Following is an example of a poem that would be classified in the lyric speaker mode.

IN MY CRAFT OR SULLEN ART   Dylan Thomas

In my craft or sullen art
Exercised in the still night
When only the moon rages
And the lovers lie abed
With all their griefs in their arms,
I labour by singing light
Not for ambition or bread
Or the strut and trade of charms
On the ivory stages
But for the common wages
Of their most sacred heart.

Not for the proud man apart
From the raging moon I write
On these spindrift pages
Not for the towering dead
With their nightingales and psalms
But for the lovers, their arms
Round the griefs of the ages,
Who pay no praise or wages
Nor heed my craft or art.

This is a lyric mode poem since the speaker is not a dramatized character and seems to be speaking as the mask of the poet, Dylan Thomas. The speaker is the "I" of the poem, and he or she is thinking aloud, musing about why and for whom he or she writes. The experience depicted in the poem and the effect the experience has on the persona should be emphasized in performance.

Dramatic speaker mode

In a *dramatic* speaker mode text, defined character or characters speak. Literature written in the dramatic mode is on the opposite end of the continuum from lyric mode literature. In the dramatic mode text, the speaker is always defined, and we receive a particular image of a particular person in a particular place and time. Dramatic mode literature has as its central focus dramatized character(s) in conflict situations. The dramatic mode text is usually written in the present tense, and seems to be taking place now. The text often, though not always, features a style of language that helps to characterize that specific speaker. Here is a poem written in the dramatic mode.

THEM EGGS   Max King

"It was them eggs, Jack!

I tole her
        and
tole her,
'Woman,
I got simple tastes.
I ain't hard to please!
All
I want
      is
two
fried eggs
starin' me in the face ev'ry mornin'.
           I said
starin', girl,
not have one of 'em blind and runnin' all
                 over
               the
                  plate.'

I tole her,
I ain't no jive dude Jack!
She knowed
but she broke
them two yolks anyway!
An' I jus' dunno what
        to do.
If I beat her
she'll break 'em again,
          an'
if'n I
don't
beat her,

the bitch'll keep doin' it!
I jus' dunno
what
to do
    about
        them
        eggs."

"Them Eggs" by Max King, reprinted by permission of the author.

This is a dramatic poem. The speaker is a character—the man in the poem—who is speaking to "Jack," possibly in a diner. The man seems to be a Southerner, perhaps an urban black, disgruntled about his female companion. His background is exemplified by his language usage and grammar. He is in a conflict situation as he explains to Jack the problem he has with his disobedient partner. In this poem, the characterization of the man is an essential element to communicate in performance. *(Notice that in this poem, the speaker refers to himself as "I" just as the speaker did in "In My Craft or Sullen Art." The use of the pronoun "I," then, does not especially denote a lyric or dramatic mode text. Defined and undefined speakers may refer to themselves as "I.")*

Epic speaker mode

If a text contains both a lyric voice and a dramatic voice(s), the mode of the work is *epic*. The epic mode, then, is the combination of the lyric (an undefined narrator) and the dramatic mode (defined characters). In the epic mode, an undefined narrator tells a story in the present, and we also hear the characters who participated in that story in the past. "Old Witherington" is an example of a poem written in the epic mode.

OLD WITHERINGTON   Dudley Randall

Old Witherington had drunk too much again.
The children changed their play and packed around him
To jeer his latest brawl. Their parents followed.

Prune-black, with bloodshot eyes and one white tooth,
He tottered in the night with legs spread wide
Waving a hatchet. "Come on, come on," he piped,
"And I'll baptize these bricks with bloody kindling.
I may be old and drunk, but not afraid
To die. I've died before. A million times
I've died and gone to hell. I live in hell.
If I die now I die, and put an end
To all this loneliness. Nobody cares

Enough to even fight me now, except
This crazy bastard here."

And with these words
He cursed the little children, cursed his neighbors,
Cursed his father, mother, and his wife,
Himself, and God, and all the rest of the world,
All but his grinning adversary, who, crouched,
Danced tenderly around him with a jag-toothed bottle,
As if the world compressed to one old man
Who was the sun, and he sole faithful planet.

"Old Witherington" reprinted from *Poem Counterpoem,* by permission of Dudley Randall.
Copyright 1969 by Margaret Danner and Dudley Randall.

This poem is modally epic, as more than one voice is heard. The first speaker is
an undefined narrator who tells us the story of "Old Witherington," who is the
dramatic voice in the poem. To perform this poem, you need a voice, body, and
attitude for the narrator and a voice, body, and attitude for Old Witherington
whom the narrator suggests. Since the narrator is speaking in the present about
something that happened in the past (notice the verb tenses: "had drunk,"
"changed," "packed"), Old Witherington is not now present. The narrator drama-
tizes Old Witherington from his or her particular narrative perspective.

Another way to describe the speaker mode is to think of a series of paintings. A
self-portrait is in the lyric mode—the painter re-creates a self-image. If the painting
is a picture of the painter's mother, it represents the dramatic mode. If the painting
has images of the painter and the mother, it is in the epic mode.

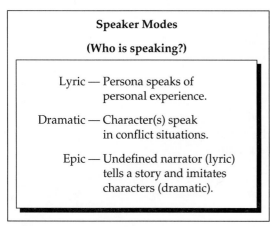

Speaker Modes

(Who is speaking?)

Lyric — Persona speaks of
    personal experience.

Dramatic — Character(s) speak
    in conflict situations.

Epic — Undefined narrator (lyric)
    tells a story and imitates
    characters (dramatic).

Figure 3.1

A speaker modal analysis, then, examines a work in its entirety to determine who is speaking. Figure 3.1 summarizes the characteristics of each speaker mode.

The continuum of lyric, epic, and dramatic texts looks like this:

LYRIC .... EPIC .... DRAMATIC

The lyric is at one end of the continuum, where an undefined speaker—a persona—speaks. The dramatic is at the other end of the continuum where a defined character or characters speak. The epic mode combines the lyric and dramatic with an undefined narrator and characters.

Audience Modal Analysis

Once you have performed a speaker modal analysis and have identified the nature of the speaker in the work, begin an audience modal analysis. An audience modal analysis examines a work line-by-line or moment-by-moment to determine the relationship between the speaker and his or her audience. If the speaker addresses himself or herself, God, a muse, an inanimate object, or a deceased or absent person, the audience mode is *lyric*. If the speaker addresses another character, the audience mode is *dramatic*. If the speaker addresses the general audience, the audience mode is *epic*. Remember, though, that an entire selection may be classified in one speaker mode, and still contain dramatic, epic, and lyric moments within it. The speaker mode of "Ringing the Bells," for example, is lyric—a persona seems to be speaking. If you perform an audience modal analysis, you may discover epic moments (if you decide a general audience is being addressed), dramatic moments (if you decide that a silent character is being addressed), or lyric moments (if you decide the speaker is really thinking aloud or apostrophizing). Returning to Sexton's poem "Ringing the Bells," the line "who picks at the hairs over her lip all day," for example, could be labeled epic if you think the speaker is reemphasizing her frustration regarding the woman's repetitive behavior to the general audience. The line could be labeled dramatic if the speaker were to deliver the line to the "small hunched squirrel girl" as a complaint against her behavior. Finally, the line might be labeled lyric if the speaker is musing about her own possibly disturbing behavior, or if the speaker realizes that there really isn't much else for the "squirrel girl" to do. The decision depends on your interpretation.

Let us try an audience modal analysis of this poem by Alice Walker.

"GOOD NIGHT, WILLIE LEE, I'LL SEE YOU IN THE MORNING"   Alice Walker

1 Looking down into my father's
2 dead face
3 for the last time
4 my mother said without

5   tears, without smiles
6   without regrets
7   but with *civility*
8   "Good night, Willie Lee, I'll see you
9   in the morning."
10   And it was then I knew that the healing
11   of all our wounds
12   is forgiveness
13   that permits a promise
14   of our return
15   at the end.

This poem appears to be in the epic speaker mode because both a lyric and a
dramatic voice speak. The main speaker is a lyric persona who speaks for the
writer. The dramatic voice is the persona's mother. An audience analysis reveals
the many modal shifts in the poem. The first seven lines seem to be epic. The persona describes the behavior of the dramatic character, behavior that took place in
the past and that she (the persona seems to be a woman—the mask of the poet,
Alice Walker) is relating for the benefit and understanding of the audience. The
main speaker describes for the audience an observable event—an event that she
witnessed, and that was significant to her. In lines 8 and 9, the persona allows us to
hear the voice of her mother. These are dramatic lines. The persona suggests how
the mother sounded and looked as she said goodbye to her husband, Willie Lee.
The last six lines (lines 10–15) are complex. The revelation or epiphany that the
persona comes to about grace and forgiveness occurred when she witnessed the
farewell between her mother and deceased father, but she recalls it now. Does she
recall it for the benefit of the general audience? Or does she reaffirm her belief in
that lesson for her own benefit—to reaffirm her own faith? Your answers to these
questions will determine how these final lines are performed. If you decide that the
persona is sharing this lesson with the audience, the lines are epic and would be
addressed directly to the audience. If you decide that the speaker forgets about the
presence of an audience and is reaffirming her own faith for her own benefit, then
the lines are lyric and would be performed as if the speaker were suddenly alone
and speaking aloud. Both interpretations are viable (as are others). Try different
approaches during rehearsal and see which works best for you.

The audience modal analysis, then, examines a text line-by-line or moment-by-
moment to discover who is being addressed. Figure 3.2 summarizes the characteristics of each audience mode.

```
┌─────────────────────────────────────────┐
│              Audience Modes             │
│                                         │
│         (Who is being addressed?)       │
│   ┌─────────────────────────────────┐   │
│   │  Lyric — Speaker addresses self,│   │
│   │        muse, God, inanimate     │   │
│   │        object, absent or        │   │
│   │        deceased person.         │   │
│   │                                 │   │
│   │  Dramatic — Speaker addresses a │   │
│   │        character or characters. │   │
│   │                                 │   │
│   │  Epic — Speaker addresses a     │   │
│   │        general audience.        │   │
│   └─────────────────────────────────┘   │
└─────────────────────────────────────────┘
```

Figure 3.2

Generic and Modal Classifications Combined

Each of the previous literary examples is generically classified as poetry, yet you can see that modal classifications cut across generic lines. In other words, there are lyric, dramatic, and epic poems; lyric, dramatic, and epic plays; and lyric, dramatic, and epic prose selections. The rationale for employing the modal classification system and analysis is not to abandon traditional generic categories, but to expand their dimensions, provide additional information, and aid in the classification of some literary texts which defy conventional generic categorization. Some texts do not fit neatly into any of the three genres, and so the performer is left confused, with no guidelines. The novels of James Joyce, Virginia Woolf, Italo Calvino, and Alain Robbe-Grillet, for example, do not quite fit traditional prose fiction characteristics. The plays of Samuel Beckett, Gertrude Stein, and Bertolt Brecht often defy traditional categorization. The poems of Walt Whitman, Jonathan Williams, and e. e. cummings do not meet conventional standards of classification. Analyzing conventional as well as nonconventional works modally helps the interpreter to gather the information necessary for performance. The marriage of the generic and modal classification systems, then, clarifies a piece of literature from many perspectives and helps interpreters make performance decisions.

The combination of genre and mode delineates nine different literary categories:

Lyric prose	Dramatic prose	Epic prose
Lyric poetry	Dramatic poetry	Epic poetry
Lyric drama	Dramatic drama	Epic drama

Let us look more closely at each of these nine categories and list examples of each.

Generic and Modal Classifications and Examples

Genre	Lyric Mode	Dramatic Mode	Epic Mode
Prose	Prose where someone very much like the author seems to be speaking. *Examples:* most essays, letters, diaries; many stream-of-consciousness works; narrative moments in autobiographies; "On Going Home" by Joan Didion; "The Masks of Minority Terrorism" by Pico Iyer.	Prose that tells a story where the author's voice is effaced and characters seemingly speak for themselves. *Examples:* many Hemingway short stories, "Here We Are" by Dorothy Parker; *As I Lay Dying* by William Faulkner; *Great Expectations* by Charles Dickens.	Prose that tells a story and moves back and forth between a narrator speaking to the reader/audience and characters speaking to each other. *Examples: The Grapes of Wrath* by John Steinbeck; *Tom Sawyer* by Mark Twain; "The Open Window" by Saki.
Drama	Plays where only a character who represents the playwright's voice is heard, or autobiographical plays where the playwright's point of view is dramatically represented. *Examples: The Glass Menagerie* by Tennessee Williams; *Long Day's Journey into Night* by Eugene O'Neill; "Krapp's Last Tape" by Samuel Beckett.	Plays without an intervening narrator; clearly defined characters speak. *Examples:* plays by Shakespeare; *Who's Afraid of Virginia Woolf?* by Albee; *A Raisin in the Sun* by Lorraine Hansberry; "Constantinople Smith" by Mee.	Plays which have an intervening narrator. *Examples: Our Town* and *The Skin of Our Teeth* by Thornton Wilder; plays by Bertolt Brecht; *A View from the Bridge* by Arthur Miller; *Equus* by Peter Shaffer; *Into the Woods* by Stephen Sondheim.

| Poetry | Poems where a persona speaks of a personal experience. *Examples:* "I Wandered Lonely as a Cloud" by William Wordsworth; "When I Have Fears That I May Cease to Be" by Keats; "Because I Could Not Stop for Death" by Emily Dickinson; "Carrion Comfort" by Hopkins. | Poems where the poet's voice is submerged and only a character(s) speaks. *Examples:* "My Last Duchess" and "Porphyria's Lover" by Browning; "The Love Song of J. Alfred Prufrock" by T. S. Eliot; *Spoon River Anthology* by Edgar Lee Masters. | Poems that move back and forth between a narrator speaking and characters speaking for themselves. *Examples: Iliad* and *Odyssey* by Homer; "The Ballad of Sir Patrick Spens"; "Home Burial" and "The Death of the Hired Man" by Robert Frost. |

As you search for a selection to perform, begin to consider the speaker and audience modes to help in formulating your interpretation. Here are some questions to ask yourself:

Speaker Mode:

Is a surrogate for the author speaking?   (lyric category)
Is a dramatized character(s) speaking?   (dramatic category)
Are a narrator and character(s)   (epic category)
  speaking?

Audience Mode:

Is the speaker addressing himself or   (lyric moment)
  herself, a muse, God, or other silent
  listener?
Is the speaker addressing another   (dramatic moment)
  character(s)?
Is the speaker addressing a general   (epic moment)
  audience?

Summary of Lyric, Dramatic, and Epic Mode Characteristics

In addition to helping you discover who is speaking and to whom, modal analysis provides other useful information: the sense of time, the subject matter, the type of focus to employ, as well as vocal and physical analogues. The three summaries that follow provide detailed information on each mode which will help you to make performance decisions.

Lyric mode

Speaker The speaker is very similar to (but not the same as) the writer. You will want to do some research into the life of the writer to discover biographical information which may be essential in understanding the nature of the persona that writer created. Literature in the lyric mode is usually told in the first person ("I"). The speaker is reflecting on a personal, firsthand experience and the performer creates his or her response to this emotional experience.

Audience The speaker addresses himself or herself, a muse, God, or an inanimate object, a deceased or absent person, or some other silent listener. (Some less personal lyric works may be addressed to the general audience.)

Time Lyric texts as well as lyric moments may be written in either the present, past, or future tense, and the speaker is usually engaged either in describing or reflecting. If the text is descriptive (verbs are in the present tense), the speaker is usually more active, physically alert, and responsive; if the text is reflective (verbs are in the past or future tense), the speaker is usually more contemplative and thoughtful. In general, however, there is with the lyric mode a sense of timelessness—of time either not being important or seemingly not "ticking away."

Subject Matter The speaker is usually recounting a personal experience or expressing a moment of private insight, revelation, or self-awareness. The mood is often, though not always, serious, somber, and solemn. The work projects a sense of language as inner life, exposure of interiority.

Focus When performing any literary selection, you must decide at any given moment how the nature of the experience determines where you are to look during the performance. This is called *focus*. There are two kinds of focus to use for lyric lines/moments. Use *inner-closed* focus when you want to create the effect that the speaker is alone and thinking aloud. You may look around the room, but do not catch anyone's eye. (Careful—often in an attempt to avoid the present audience, beginning performers employing inner-closed focus stare at the floor. This directs your energy down, and makes it difficult for the audience to see your facial responses.) If the speaker is addressing a muse, or God, or an inanimate object or, in general, anyone or anything that is not present or responding, use *semi-closed* focus. With semi-closed focus you find a spot in and directly above the audience where you imagine that muse, or God, or object to be, and when the muse, God, etc. is referred to or directly addressed, you look in that spot (as you would when addressing "Death" in the poem "Death, Be Not Proud"). Don't stare fixedly at the spot, however, since you don't want to give the audience the impression that the muse, or God, etc. is actually present or reacting—although the muse or God, etc. may *seem* very present and responsive, imaginatively speaking. During moments when the muse, or God, etc. is not being referred to or addressed, use inner-closed focus.

Additional Performance Analogues There is often in the lyric mode a sense of discovery and flow in delivery—a sense of the speaker free-associating, or getting a thought which leads to other thoughts. We call this *triggering.* The audience should see triggering as you react to whatever sensation or emotion the triggered thought registered. You might use a softer volume, since you are seemingly unaware of the audience (but remember, you still have to be loud enough to be heard). On the other hand, you might speak at a much louder volume, since the knowledge that you are alone frees you to ventilate at will.

Literary Examples Letters, diaries, personal journals, lyric poetry, and essays are examples of literature in the lyric speaker mode. Many soliloquies, thought revelations, self-discoveries, and reflections in prose fiction, drama, or poetry are lyric audience mode moments.

Dramatic mode

Speaker Speakers in the dramatic mode are defined characters, so you will want to discover the unique, individualizing qualities of the character or characters who speak. A close scrutiny of the character's language will help to define his or her personality. The dramatic speaker, as well as the lyric speaker, may refer to himself or herself as "I."

Audience The speaker often speaks to another character or characters in a specific literary setting, though characters may also speak to themselves or to the general audience. When a character speaks to another character, work on keeping the silent character alive by imagining that the silent character's responses are motivating the speaking character. When a character speaks to the general audience, decide ahead of time who that audience might be and speak to them in an appropriate manner. If the character speaks to himself or herself, it is usually during a moment of self-realization or self-reflection. Suggest this lyric triggering in performance.

Time Dramatic moments are usually in the present tense. The performer assumes that the action and dialogue are taking place now. He or she tries to capture the vitality and spontaneity necessary to keep the scene fresh and alive, attempting to coin the language now.

Subject Matter In the dramatic mode, characters are usually in some sort of conflict situation and reveal their own thoughts, emotions, and attitudes. Often what a character says may be at odds with what the author thinks or feels, a fact which helps to distinguish the dramatic from the lyric speaker. Dialogue and character interaction are often evident. The piece creates a sense of dramatized event. Speakers usually are in a specific locale and time period.

Focus If there is an exchange of dialogue and characters speak to each other, the performer uses *closed focus*. With closed focus, the performer projects the scene out front, above the audience, and all characters speak from their own specified *placement* in space. Dramatic mode selections often require character placement. Since you want to keep your imaginary stage balanced, if two characters speak, place one just right and one just left of center. If three characters speak, place the most important character or the character who has the most lines center and the other two on the central character's left and right. If four characters speak, space them equally apart, two left of center and two right of center. Character placement is used to help keep characters physically distinct for the audience and to make it possible for the audience to imagine characters interacting. If only one character speaks and he or she is thinking aloud, use *inner-closed focus*. If the character is aware of the general audience, use *open focus*, directly addressing them (again examine the language and situation to decide who the general audience might be).

Additional Performance Analogues Beginning performers often tend to undercharacterize. Though solo interpretation performance depends on *economy*—suggesting, rather than literalizing, character action and interaction—you must still develop individualized voices and bodies for each character who speaks. Try working on one character at a time, if your text has more than one character, before putting the complete scene together.

There are many ways to suggest different characters vocally. You can change your normal pitch (higher or lower), your rate (faster or slower), your volume (louder or softer), and your quality (vocal timbre). Although pitch, rate, and volume are essential for projecting emotional variety, varying the quality of your voice is one of the best ways to suggest character differences. Check the information on vocal quality in Chapter 7 for assistance.

Physical differentiation between characters is also challenging. In general, men and women carry their weight differently; men usually carry their weight higher, women lower. Stand up and see if you can feel where your center of weight is. Try varying that center to correspond with the character you are portraying.

Literary Examples Interview transcripts, representational dramas, poetic dramas, and dramatic poetry are some examples of literature which could be classified in the dramatic speaker mode. Dialogue in prose fiction, poetry, and plays would be considered examples of dramatic audience mode moments.

Epic mode

Speaker In epic mode literature, an undefined narrator and a character(s) speak. You will want to identify the perspective of the narrator as well as the personality of each character the narrator recreates.

Audience The narrator usually addresses a general audience external to the literature. You should determine who that audience *might* be and speak as though you, as the narrator, were having a kind of "dialogue" with that particular audience. The characters speak to each other.

Time In the epic mode, there is an alternation between present and past. When narrators speak, they are usually remembering the past, but telling the story now. The narrator, then, speaks in the present about past events. Characters seem to be speaking in the present; but, in actuality, the narrator is recounting their dialogue—dialogue that occurred in the past.

Subject Matter The subject matter of most epic mode works is a story. The narrator is telling a story and has a certain attitude or perspective toward the story as well as the characters in it. Epic literature is usually less personal than lyric literature and less immediate than dramatic literature. Epic moments reveal information the audience needs to know that they would not otherwise have, for example, weather conditions, time of day or year, opinions, plans of action, etc.

Focus The narrator uses *open focus* and looks at and speaks directly to the audience. During dialogue passages, use *closed focus* and character placement (if there is more than one character) and work to suggest that the characters are speaking to each other. The general audience, then, is sometimes directly addressed and is sometimes in the position of overhearing. *Inner-closed focus* may be used when characters are speaking their thoughts aloud. Epic mode literature is the most modally mixed; consequently, there may be epic, dramatic, and lyric mode moments, necessitating the use of open, closed, and inner-closed focus (and occasionally semi-closed focus) at various times.

Additional Performance Analogues With epic mode literature, the performer creates a sense of sharing with the audience. The narrator reaches out to the audience, becoming a sort of tour guide through the story. The narrator's perspective of the story dominates, so the audience sees the events, as well as the characters who

108

participated in those events, from the narrator's point of view. The performer creates the narrator and tells the story from that narrator's point of view.

Literary Examples Most short stories and novels are written in the epic speaker mode, as are epic poems and presentational plays (plays where a narrator or a character addresses the audience). Epic mode moments exist whenever a speaker in a short story, novel, play, or poem addresses the audience.

Class Exercise

Before we perform a modal analysis, find out how much you understand about modal voices. Read the poem below, and first decide in which speaker mode it is written. Then, perform an audience modal analysis—dividing the poem into lyric, dramatic, and epic mode moments. After you have done this, try to perform the poem using the suggestions just given to manifest each modal change.

WHAT RIDDLE ASKED THE SPHINX   Archibald MacLeish

In my stone eyes I see
The saint upon his knee
Delve in the desert for eternity.

In my stone ears I hear
The night-lost traveller
Cry *When?* to the earth's shadow: *When? Oh Where?*

Stone deaf and blind
I ponder in my mind
The bone that seeks, the flesh that cannot find.

Stone blind I see
The saint's eternity
Deep in the earth he digs in. Cannot he?

Stone deaf I hear
The night say *Then!* say *There!*
Why cries the traveller still to the night air?

The one is not content
With silence, the day spent;
With earth the other. More, they think, was meant.

Stone that I am, can stone
Perceive what flesh and bone
Are blind and deaf to?

Or has hermit known,
Has traveller divined,
Some questions there behind
I cannot come to, being stone and blind?

To all who ken or can
I ask, since time began,
What riddle is it has for answer, Man?

A Sample Modal Analysis of "Dover Beach"

Let us now perform a speaker and audience modal analysis of Matthew Arnold's "Dover Beach." Some preliminary research on Arnold, including the time he was writing, will help in performing a modal analysis of the poem. Since the speaker analysis tries to discover the relationship between the writer and the speaker, knowing as much as possible about the writer can be an excellent aid. In brief, Arnold was a Victorian writing during the same time as the two greatest Victorian writers—Robert Browning and Alfred, Lord Tennyson. Arnold was one of the few writers who was a working man (inspector of schools) as well as an intellectual and a scholar. His poem "Dover Beach" appeared in 1867, but was probably written in 1851. In this poem, Arnold speaks of the loss of self-identity and the melancholy he feels about his life and about life in general.

DOVER BEACH   Matthew Arnold

1   The sea is calm to-night.
2   The tide is full, the moon lies fair
3   Upon the straits;—on the French coast the light
4   Gleams and is gone; the cliffs of England stand,
5   Glimmering and vast, out in the tranquil bay.
6   Come to the window, sweet is the night-air!
7   Only, from the long line of spray
8   Where the sea meets the moon-blanch'd land,
9   Listen! You hear the grating roar
10   Of pebbles which the waves draw back, and fling,
11   At their return, up the high strand,
12   Begin, and cease, and then again begin,
13   With tremulous cadence slow, and bring
14   The eternal note of sadness in.

15   Sophocles long ago
16   Heard it on the Aegean, and it brought
17   Into his mind the turbid ebb and flow
18   Of human misery; we
19   Find also in the sound a thought,
20   Hearing it by this distant northern sea.
21   The Sea of Faith
22   Was once, too, at the full, and round earth's shore
23   Lay like the folds of a bright girdle furled.

24   But now I only hear
25   Its melancholy, long, withdrawing roar,
26   Retreating, to the breath
27   Of the night-wind, down the vast edges drear
28   And naked shingles of the world.

29   Ah, love, let us be true
30   To one another! for the world, which seems
31   To lie before us like a land of dreams,
32   So various, so beautiful, so new,
33   Hath really neither joy, nor love, nor light,
34   Nor certitude, nor peace, nor help for pain;
35   And we are here as on a darkling plain
36   Swept with confused alarms of struggle and flight,
37   Where ignorant armies clash by night.

A first reading of this poem seems to indicate that its speaker mode is lyric, since it seems to be the direct expression of Arnold's own thoughts and emotions. On second look, however, we see a dramatic situation—a lover addressing his beloved. The speaker mode, then, is dramatic, and the poet has created a defined character (a melancholy lover) to speak his thoughts for him.

The audience modal analysis of this poem yields a complex interweaving of speaker-audience situations. The melancholy lover begins with thoughtful reflections on the sight outside his Dover hotel window: the sea, the tide, the moon, the vast tranquil bay. Lines 1–5, then, seem to be lyric in mode as the speaker addresses himself. In line 6, the mode changes to dramatic as the speaker addresses his beloved, asking her to "come to the window." Lines 7 and 8 seem to move back into the lyric mode as the speaker reflects on the scene, until, perhaps, the "moon-blanch'd land" illuminates his lover and changes the mode back to dramatic. Although lines 9–14 seem to be directly spoken to his lover, they also give us the sense that the speaker is still meditating, metaphorically comparing the movement of the waves to the movements back and forth between his faithful past and his seemingly faithless present.

The "note of sadness" the speaker hears in line 14 brings him to the scene of "human misery" and back to the contemplative man who reflects on Sophocles and the similar reflections in *Antigone*.[3] In line 18, the speaker shifts out of the past and back to the present scene and to the character of the lover as the speaker sees, perhaps from her facial expression, that they share a thought—a thought motivated by the sounds from "this distant northern sea."

A shift back to lyric mode occurs in lines 21–28, as the speaker agonizes over his loss of faith. "The Sea of Faith" has ebbed for him, as the sea before him might, were the "tide" not "full." Arnold's personal loss of faith with the advent of Darwin's theory of evolution is the motivation for the next several lines in this stanza. These lines clearly switch to the lyric voice.

In the last stanza, the speaker addresses his lover and pleads that though the world is full of contradictions, upheavals, and disharmony, they, at least, should remain faithful to one another. But the lyric voice, though muted, is heard underneath this plea as the speaker brings to mind another image from the past—Greek historian Thucydides's account of the Battle of Epipolae, when the Greeks and their allies attacked Syracuse at night and in great confusion.

In the interpretation of the poem just offered, we see a constant shift between the lyric and dramatic audience modes. When performing this poem, the performer should work at making clear the shifts between the lyric, reflective meditations of the speaker and his dramatic communication with his companion. The interpreter must find the appropriate combination of facial expressions, gestures, body responses, and focuses to embody these modal shifts. The lyric lines provide clues for characterization: intense feelings, mental shifts back and forth in time and space, classical references, and tension between hope and hopelessness. Perform the lyric lines with inner-closed focus, softer volume, and triggering. When speaking the lines in the dramatic mode, the speaker should seem to be aware of his companion, observing her reactions to modify, when necessary, his delivery. When the speaker addresses his companion, the performer should use closed focus. (There is no need for character placement since only one character speaks.)

Most of this poem is lyric, so there really isn't the sense of interaction that you find in some other dramatic poems. Address to his lover is minimal, and most of the poem is made up of his musings and reflections. (Although we have continually referred to the speaker as "he," there is really no internal support for that assumption. It is conceivable that the speaker is female; however, the autobiographical nature of the poem seems to call for a masculine speaker.)

Both dramatistic and modal analysis should be performed on any selection you choose to perform, as both types of analysis help you make performance decisions as well as help you understand the literature. Once you feel comfortable working with these two types of initial literary analysis, you should then apply any additional type of analysis necessary to understand your selection.

Chapter 4 introduces and explains specific performance terminology. As you work through an analysis of your selection, you will need to know special terminology to translate your analysis into performance analogues. As you use these terms in class and in papers prepared for class, they will become part of your interpretation vocabulary.

SUMMARY

Though an abundance of literary theories exists—archetypal, biographical, deconstructionist, feminist, formalist, Marxist, new historical, psychoanalytic, reader-response, rhetorical, and structuralist—beginning solo performers often benefit when they begin by employing the modal and dramatistic analysis outlined in this book.

The dramatistic analysis asks you to view each literary work as a minidrama in order to discover who is speaking, to whom, about what, where, when, how, and why.

The speaker modal analysis investigates the relationship between the writer and speaker. The audience modal analysis examines the relationship between speaker and audience, and looks at literature in terms of lyric, dramatic, and epic voices.

Notes

1. See Wayne C. Booth's *The Rhetoric of Fiction* (Chicago: University of Chicago Press, 1961) for an excellent discussion of the difference between author and implied author—the writer's second self.
2. Wallace A. Bacon, *The Art of Interpretation*, 3rd ed. (New York: Holt, Rinehart & Winston, 1979), p. 418.
3. The second stanza, lines 15–20, could also be viewed as epic. The speaker tells a story, speaking to the audience with open focus.

4

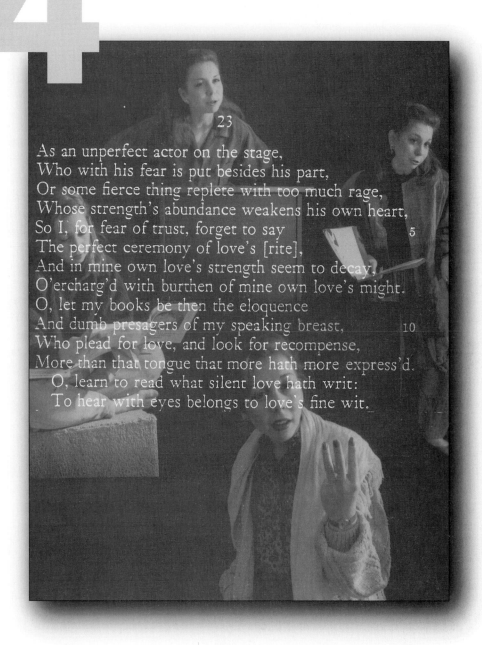

23

As an unperfect actor on the stage,
Who with his fear is put besides his part,
Or some fierce thing replete with too much rage,
Whose strength's abundance weakens his own heart,
So I, for fear of trust, forget to say   5
The perfect ceremony of love's [rite],
And in mine own love's strength seem to decay,
O'ercharg'd with burthen of mine own love's might.
O, let my books be then the eloquence
And dumb presagers of my speaking breast,   10
Who plead for love, and look for recompense,
More than that tongue that more hath more express'd.
    O, learn to read what silent love hath writ:
    To hear with eyes belongs to love's fine wit.

Scene: A dormitory room
Characters: Mary and Susan

Mary: (*Standing in her room practicing before a mirror.*)
"That's my last Duchess painted on the wall,
Looking as if she were alive; I call
That piece a wonder, now: Fra Pandolf's hands
Worked busily a day, and there she stands."

Susan: (*Standing outside Mary's room, watching and listening to her.*)
What on earth are you doing?

Mary: Practicing my performance for interpretation class next Tuesday.

Susan: Why do you have to practice? Anyone can read out loud. Isn't that what you're doing?

Mary: There's a bit more to it than that. Let me explain . . .

If this scenario does not sound familiar to you, it soon may. Many people think that anyone can "read aloud," and that no rehearsal time is necessary to do what you've been doing for years quite capably and naturally. Convincing others of the importance of rehearsal in preparation for performance is often difficult. But solo interpretation performance is as artistic an endeavor as opera singing, acting, piano playing, or any other art where practice is essential to achieve the desired effect. Interpretation, as we defined it in Chapter 1, is an artistic process that requires you to give as much time and attention as you would any other art form. A lengthy rehearsal period breeds comfort and self-confidence.

If you think of the rehearsal process (as well as the performance itself) as an additional way to study your text (in addition to the analytic approaches we discussed in Chapter 3), the experience will be more beneficial to you. After you have spent some time in preliminary silent reading, oral performance helps you come to a closer understanding of the text and may lead to insights that no silent analysis can provide. In other words, though the conventional process might be to find a selection, analyze the selection, rehearse the selection, and perform the selection, these processes are not mutually exclusive. Analysis, rehearsal, and performance are each ways to know a text, and you often work back and forth among them. The ultimate process may end up something like this: find a selection, read the selection silently, read the selection aloud, analyze the selection, rehearse the selection aloud, reanalyze the selection, rehearse, analyze, rehearse, perform, reanalyze, and so forth. The process continues until you think you have come to terms at this particular time with this particular text. Remember that repeated rehearsals and prior analysis are two ways of minimizing the effects of performance anxiety—or stage fright.

This chapter will help you get the most out of both the rehearsal process and the performance by defining and explaining the terminology and techniques available. Each term is explained, and literary selections are provided for practice.

THE INTRODUCTION

(The information on introductions that follows is for *class* presentations. Introductions for class would most likely be quite different from introductions you would give for paid or professional performances, where you would not necessarily tell the audience who you imagine them to be or what your intentions are. Introductions for class performances are primarily to prepare students to listen to texts with the performer's interpretation in mind and to facilitate postperformance discussions in a beginning performance studies class. The kind and amount of information included in introductions should be dependent upon the performance context.) Almost every interpretation performance is preceded by a well-planned introduction. You should include certain informational items in every introduction, but the order of the information is up to you. Your introduction should include most or all of the following:

1. Title of selection and author's name.
2. An attention-getting opening line, with a minimum of filler information—statements that could be used before any performance, such as "The piece I am going to present for you today . . ." or "I would now like to perform for you . . ."
3. A statement or two which carves out your interpretation of the text. (This both prepares the audience to listen and enables the audience to participate in the postperformance discussion on the basis of what you intend.)
4. Identification of the intended audience (necessary for epic-mode moments when open focus is employed).
5. A delivery that sets an appropriate mood for the selection (your introduction for the tragedy *King Lear*, for example, should set a different mood from an introduction for the comedy *Twelfth Night*).
6. Direct audience contact during delivery.
7. A natural delivery, in which you remain yourself.
8. Content designed to appeal to your expected audience.
9. Any biographical or critical information about the author or the selection that is interesting or important for the audience to know (the translation of foreign words, for example, or the identification of obscure allusions).
10. Background information about what has happened before your excerpt begins if you are not performing the entire work or if you are not performing the opening scene. (This is particularly relevant for the performance of prose fiction or drama, where many works are too long to perform in their entirety).

The introduction serves five distinct purposes: (1) it prepares the audience for the specific selection you are performing and your understanding of it, (2) it prepares you to perform for the audience, (3) it lets the audience see you as you are before you begin your performance, (4) it communicates your enthusiasm for the selection, which, it is hoped, will pique the audience's interest, and (5) it persuades the audience to attend to your performance.

On some occasions, an introduction might not be necessary or required to raise the curtain on your performance. Very little need be said, for example, if you can be assured that everyone in your audience has already read your selection. You might not want to give the audience an introduction in the hope that this will inspire their creative participation even more. If you want to challenge the audience's ability to perceive your selection with nothing but your performance to guide them, consider not giving an introduction (unless your assignment mitigates against this). Imagine before you decide, though, how an introduction, or the absence of one, might drastically change the overall impact of your presentation.

Styles of Delivery

Though you may choose from many styles of introduction delivery, four styles are most prevalent. These four delivery styles for introductions are manuscript, impromptu, memorized, and extemporaneous.

A manuscript delivery means that your introduction is written out ahead of time and read to the audience as a kind of prepared speech. However, two of the ingredients of a good introduction are frequent and direct eye contact with the audience and the ability to alter your introduction based on circumstance and audience feedback. Thus, manuscript delivery is not a recommended delivery style because you are restricted by having to read whatever you previously wrote. (If your introduction includes quoted material, however, it may be necessary to use a notecard to ensure accuracy.)

When the performer fails to plan what to say in advance, he or she must deliver an impromptu introduction. Often performers do not place enough importance on the introduction because they believe that they can successfully think on their feet and create one with no prior preparation. The problem with an impromptu introduction is that it is often unorganized and unfocused. If a performer seems uncomfortable, trying to make up an introduction as he or she goes along, natural communication is hampered. With the impromptu delivery, performers often seem to be concentrating more on what to say than on communicating openly with the audience.

Another type of delivery style is memorized. The memorized style is similar to the manuscript style in that your introduction is predetermined and cannot be affected by circumstance. Although many students use this style, it can be problematic if the performance situation affects your ability to remember. Often memory lapses occur because more time is spent remembering the selection than on memorizing the introduction. You must rehearse your introduction as often as you rehearse your selection so that memory lapses do not occur. The memorized style could alienate your audience if the introduction sounds canned or artificial. Just as you should work on "coining the language now" as you perform a selection, your introduction will be more effective in capturing your audience's attention if it sounds as though you are creating it now with this audience in mind.

An extemporaneous delivery style is best for those with some experience at public speaking who are able to work from a mental outline of what they would like to include in the introduction. The extemporaneous style requires that the performer prepare what he or she will say in advance but not memorize it word for word. The performer orders the main ideas and plans what to cover ahead of time but varies the exact wording each time the introduction is given. An extemporaneous delivery involves an element of spontaneity and allows the performer to relate the introduction specifically to this particular audience on this particular occasion. In an extemporaneous introduction, the performer maximizes communication with the audience. You can change things at the last minute, if necessary, with minimal worry or concern. Some beginning interpreters find the extemporaneous delivery style too difficult to master at first. If you feel this way, write out an introduction and memorize it, as we suggested earlier, but try to deliver it as if it were extemporaneous.

The presentation of your introduction requires much prior rehearsal before it can be delivered effectively. On performance day, use direct eye contact with your audience and try to have a natural, relaxed, appearance. Do not bring an outline or note cards with you unless you are quoting material and want to make sure you represent the source correctly. The essential purpose of an introduction is to make the curtain go up. Do not lower it before your performance has begun.

Content

Here are some helpful hints concerning the actual content of the introduction.

The length of the introduction should be adjusted for each performance and should be only a small proportion of the total assigned time for the performance. Thus, an introduction of one minute, while appropriate for a four-minute performance, might be too long if your total performance lasts for only two minutes. Be flexible, and consider the demands of your text and your audience's familiarity with it as you compose an appropriate introduction.

Your introduction should carve out your interpretation of the selection, including some of the major choices you have made. Your introduction should prepare your audience for what you are attempting to convey. If you were to perform the "closet scene" from *Hamlet* (Act III, scene iv), for example, you would want to suggest your interpretation of the scene in your introduction. You could say something such as, "In Act III, scene iv of Shakespeare's *Hamlet*, we see the true meaning of an Oedipal complex as Hamlet confronts his mother and inadvertently makes it clear that his love for her consumes him almost as much as his sorrow over the death of his father."

Another important aspect of your introduction is to identify your intended audience. As we stated earlier, there are four potential audiences in any given text: the speaker himself or herself; an inanimate object, a deceased or absent person, a muse, God, or some other mute listener; a character or characters created in the work; or the general public. Of these four possible audiences, the one that is the most vague is "the general public." Anytime you decide to look at this general public during a performance, you should decide who you think they *might* be based on cues in the text and share this information in the introduction. Deciding on this ahead of time helps you define your goals and objectives in terms of this audience and telling the audience in the room helps them understand the specific context of the piece by defining the speaker/audience relationship. You could speak to the general public as if they were a therapy group, a jury, a mob of protesting Romans, second-grade children, or high school seniors depending on your interpretation of the text.

Be very selective with details. Think carefully about the relevant information necessary. Include only that information which prepares the audience for the specific scene you have chosen to perform—not for the whole work. If, for example, you are going to perform the scene in *Medea* where Medea kills her children, you do not have to tell us that Jason, her former husband, obtained the Golden Fleece, or that he was living with another Princess, or that the Nurse told Medea what had happened. Following is a good opening for an introduction to this scene in *Medea:*

> In Euripides' *Medea,* we are confronted by the enchantress Medea, who is driven to revenge against her former husband, Jason, when he deserts her for another woman.

Sometimes a biographical detail proves useful or interesting to the audience. In this case, you will have to go to outside sources for information. Even then, be sure that you have selected information precisely suited to the particular audience and occasion. If you are performing Dylan Thomas's "Do Not Go Gentle into That Good Night," a poem about the struggle against death, it would be useful to tell the audience that Thomas was talking about his father's death. To provide the detail that Thomas died of alcoholism under a subway track in New York City, though it is true, does not prepare the audience for this particular poem.

Some students like to use critical comments in their introductions. Consider the following sample introduction:

> "The Jilting of Granny Weatherall" by Katherine Anne Porter is the story of a woman's final moments of life. As Granny lies on her deathbed, she moves back and forth in time—remembering her girlhood and the lover who jilted her. William Nance, in *Katherine Anne Porter and The Art of Rejection,* calls the story beautifully balanced. Says Nance: "The story refutes deathbed

sentimentality by showing the ironic discrepancy between the thoughts of a dying person and those of the mourners."[1] And now, the final scene from Katherine Anne Porter's "The Jilting of Granny Weatherall."

If you develop an introduction like this one, mention the critic's name and the source from which the quotation is taken. It is not necessary to have the whole citation within your introduction, although having all the specifics with you is helpful in case someone wants to read your source. The sample introduction for "Granny Weatherall" also exemplifies another useful technique—the frame. In this introduction, the title and author of the selection are stated both at the beginning and at the end, a technique that helps the audience in two ways. First, the most important information is stated and repeated to emphasize its importance. Second, by repeating the title and author, you signal to the audience that the introduction is over and the performance of the literature will now begin. If, however, you find this technique too formal, if you find that it interrupts a desired flow into the selection, or if it is obvious that the introduction is over and the selection is about to begin, avoid the frame technique.

One approach to the delivery of an introduction is to begin with lines from your selection (a "teaser"), break, and deliver the introduction, and then return to the selection again. If you try this kind of introduction, be sure that the lines you begin with are attention-getting, understandable out of context or intriguing enough that understandability does not matter, and significant to your cutting. Another technique you might want to try is to begin to suggest the speaker in your selection toward the end of your introduction. When experimenting with this technique, be sure that the audience is able to tell when the introduction is over and the selection begins.

The introduction for a drama performance is often the most difficult to compose because, unlike prose fiction, drama usually includes no narrator to provide essential background information and details, and unlike poetry, most plays are too long to be able to perform the entire selection. When delivering an introduction for a drama performance, you will want to supply enough information so that the audience will know exactly who will speak, where and when the scene takes place, and who speaks first, if it's not immediately apparent. You will also want to explain anything you cannot perform. You might, for example, want to mention that toward the middle of your scene, during a pause, twenty-seven men will arrive on horseback! An example of an occasion when an explanation might be required occurs in the following exchange taken from Tennessee Williams's play *The Glass Menagerie:*

Amanda:	No—No. I did not have the strength—to go to the D.A.R. In fact, I did not have the courage! I wanted to find a hole in the ground and hide myself in it forever.
Laura:	Why did you do that, Mother? Why are you—
Amanda:	Why? Why? How old are you, Laura?

If these lines were in a scene you were to perform, the audience would probably be curious as to what Amanda does to motivate Laura's question, "Why did you do that, Mother?" You should tell the audience in your introduction that Amanda rips up a typewriter keyboard diagram and a chart of the Gregg Alphabet (unless you can find a way to suggest this in performance) because this information is essential to the audience's understanding of that particular moment in the scene.

Were you to perform an entire poem, short story, or short play, your introduction need not be as lengthy, as you do not need to explain what has gone before; or, as stated above, you might decide not to give an introduction. If you do decide to give an introduction when performing a complete work, in addition to the title and author, talk of your intertextuality in terms of this text—how did you interpret it and why. In addition, you could mention something about the writer, something about why you chose this particular selection, or some interesting bit of research which may enhance the audience's enjoyment and/or understanding.

SAMPLE INTRODUCTIONS

Read the following two sample introductions for "Little Red Riding Hood" and see which one you think fulfills the criteria listed above.

Sample Introduction 1

The selection I would like to perform for you today is from "Little Red Riding Hood" by the Brothers Grimm. In this tale, Little Red is on her way to her ailing grandmother's house when she meets a wolf who asks her where she is going. She tells the wolf, and then when she gets to her grandmother's home, the wolf and not her grandmother is in bed. She and the wolf exchange dialogue, and eventually the wolf eats Little Red. At the end, a huntsman comes to the home, kills the wolf, cuts him open, and Little Red and her grandmother emerge unscathed.

Sample Introduction 2

According to child psychologist Bruno Bettelheim in *The Uses of Enchantment*, the woods in fairy tales like "Little Red Riding Hood" by the Brothers Grimm are places where inner darkness is confronted and uncertainty is resolved about who one is or who one wants to be. When Little Red meets the wolf in the woods there are subtextual overtones concerning young women and their budding sexuality. Little Red's encounter with this "wolf" is her initiation into the complications of the male/female relationship. The narrator warns young women that not everyone they meet on their path through life may be honest or have pure intentions. And now, Little Red meets the wolf.

The first introduction is primarily plot summary. It does not have a creative, attention-getting opening, does not carve out the performer's interpretation or define the speaker's audience, and does not state where the performer's cutting begins. The second introduction is much superior to the first; it is clear and succinct, includes outside research, carves out the performer's interpretation, and defines the intended audience.

USING THE SCRIPT/MEMORIZATION TECHNIQUES

One convention of interpretation is that the performer carries a script, holds it eye level, and uses it throughout the performance—glancing down at it periodically. A script has always been considered a necessity for the interpreter. Philosophically, the script represents a commitment to the author that the performer will be true to the literature and is also a symbol indicating the sharing of literature not composed by the performer. Physically, the script is used to prevent some audience members from feeling self-conscious because they are stared at too consistently. Also, performing without a script tends to shift the focus to the performer, rather than keep it on the literature. Although the use of the script is traditional, nowadays the script is not as often employed, and many teachers do not encourage the use of the "black folder." If the script is nothing more than a crutch for an unprepared performer, its conventional and symbolic uses are negligible. Performers who use scripts seem unprepared, and this impression can affect how the performance is received.

Although the script was a convention of interpretation, using one often causes beginning performers problems. Some do not spend enough rehearsal time because they know they will have their lines with them during the performance. Some are so tied to their scripts that they can make little or no contact with the audience. Some have the text memorized and consequently do not need to use the script at all. In this case, the performer has a script only because tradition expects it. When you bring a script with you and do not use it, the script often attracts more attention than if you were to use it too often. The audience members see the script and continually wonder if and when you will use it.

In some cases, the performer uses the script only when he or she has a memory lapse. This often desperate use of the script usually shifts the audience's attention (and compassion!) to the performer and away from the literature. Using the script in any of these ways defeats the purpose of having a script—to share the author's exact words with an audience. *We repeat, a script should never be used only to compensate for lack of preparation.*

There are two solutions to the conditions just described: (1) keeping the script eye level and referring to it periodically throughout the performance while maintaining as much eye contact with the audience and/or the imagined scene as possible or (2) using no script at all. If you use a script, hold it eye level at all times. Lifting the script up when you need it and then lowering it again when you don't is distracting. You can gesture with your free hand, but be careful of seeming to have only one arm! You may want to alternate your script from hand to hand so that you can use both for gesturing. Keep your glances at the script quick and minimal. Try to keep the flow of the performance going by quickly looking at your script for the next line *while* you are delivering the line before it. If you have certain things you want to remember to do in performance (slow down, increase volume, pause, and so on), you can mark them on the script. Find a way to make sure you can keep your place in the script—for example, by moving your hand down the page, keeping your thumb close to the line you are performing. Use the same script in rehearsal that you use in performance so that you will be able to look down and easily find the next line.

You can often use the script as a prop during your performance if this does not distract or pull the scene onstage. Scripts can be used to suggest fans, newspapers, trays, and hats, for example. One student interpreted the poem "The Unknown Citizen" by W. H. Auden as a prepared speech, and he used his script as though it were the text of the speech. Another student effectively used the script as the list of prepared questions that Lady Bracknell asks Mr. Worthing in *The Importance of Being Earnest.* Still another used the script symbolically to suggest the unknown soldier in a performance from Dos Passos's *U.S.A.;* the audience gasped when the performer threw the script to the ground and stepped on it at the end of the performance. If the speaker in your selection is reading, the script can be used to suggest the material being read. Here is a scene from T. H. White's novel *The Once and Future King* in which the script would work well as a prop.

From THE ONCE AND FUTURE KING   T. H. White

"I am writing a treatise just now," said the badger, coughing diffidently to show that he was absolutely set on explaining it, "which is to point out why Man has become the master of the animals. Perhaps you would like to hear it?

"It's for my doctor's degree, you know," he added hastily, before the Wart could protest. He got few chances of reading his treatises to anybody, so he could not bear to let the opportunity slip by.

"Thank you very much," said the Wart.

"It will be good for you, dear boy. It is just the thing to top off an education. Study birds and fish and animals: then finish off with Man. How fortunate that you came! Now where the devil did I put that manuscript?"

> The old gentleman scratched about with his great claws until he had turned up a dirty bundle of papers, one corner of which had been used for lighting something. Then he sat down in his leather armchair, which had a deep depression in the middle of it; put on his velvet smoking-cap with the tassel; and produced a pair of tarantula spectacles, which he balanced on the end of his nose.
>
> "Hem," said the badger.
>
> He immediately became paralyzed with shyness, and sat blushing at his papers, unable to begin.
>
> "Go on," said the Wart.
>
> "It is not very good," he explained coyly. "It is just a rough draft, you know. I shall alter a lot before I send it in."
>
> "I am sure it must be interesting."
>
> "Oh no, it is not a bit interesting. It is just an odd thing I threw off in an odd half-hour, just to pass the time. But still, this is how it begins.
>
> "Hem!" said the badger. Then he put on an impossibly high falsetto voice and began to read as fast as possible.
>
> "People often ask, as an idle question, whether the process of evolution began with the chicken or the egg. Was there an egg out of which the first chicken came, or did a chicken lay the first egg? I am in a position to say that the first thing created was the egg."

In this cutting, you could hold the script, but keep it closed until the badger finds the "dirty bundle of papers." Then you could open your script as the badger begins "to read as fast as possible." The script, then, becomes the dissertation, and the badger reads directly from it.

A script can also be used to indicate character differences. If, for example, a character in your scene is very self-conscious, shy, and withdrawn, you may want to use the script almost continually when projecting this character. If another character is more self-assured, use the script less when projecting this character. Using the script in this way underscores the psychological differences between the two characters. You might also try to turn the pages in character. If a character is angry, for example, turn the pages rapidly; if a character is in love, turn the pages slowly and dreamily.

If you do decide to use a script, keep certain practical suggestions in mind. Use double-spaced, typed pages placed in a folder or backed with construction paper during your performance. We recommend that you do not use the book in which you found your selection. There are five reasons for this. First, double-spaced, typed copy is easier to read during performance, and you will find it easier to keep your place. Second, the book can distract your audience, especially if writing or illustrations appear on the cover. Third, the book is usually bulky and awkward to hold. Fourth, using a folder or backing the script with construction paper minimizes distraction by preventing the audience from seeing through your paper and knowing how much you have performed and how much you have left to perform. Fifth, the use of a notebook or construction paper minimizes page rattling caused by nervousness. Use your typed script each time you rehearse so that you know where possible problem lines are. When you turn the pages of the script, be sure to do so without distracting the audience. If you turn a page without looking down at it, you could potentially distract the audience because there are two stimuli vying for their attention.

If you do not use a script, keep the following suggestions in mind. First and foremost, be sure that you know your material well enough that you can concentrate on sharing the literature rather than on trying to remember it. (Some professors allow performers to have an audience member "on book"—meaning the performer gives someone a copy of the selection to follow along during the performance. If the performer forgets a line, he or she says "line," and the person on book calls it out. Although this can relieve some performance apprehension, if "line" is called too often the flow of the selection is lost and the audience shifts in and out of scene along with the performer.) As is true of the performer who uses a script, the performer with no script tries, in most selections, to appear to be coining the language now—giving the audience the illusion of the first time. In other words, the lines sound spontaneous, as though they are being composed at the moment of utterance (as we mentioned above in relation to memorized introductions). Characters in literature like people in real life need time to think, to formulate their thoughts. Give the character time to formulate the words even though *you* know what they are. One additional precaution involves the audience's expectations. When you have no script, the audience usually expects fuller characterization and more physical involvement. Your hands are free for gesturing, and movement becomes easier. In general, your performance style varies considerably depending on whether you use a script. Be sure your decision is based on the necessities of your interpretation. What follows are some techniques to help you master the process of memorization.

Memorization Techniques

Some beginning performers find memorization the most troublesome aspect of performance. This is primarily because they have not discovered a method of memorization that helps them achieve their goals. Certainly there is no foolproof method of memorization (most professional performers will tell you that their method of memorization is simply a matter of repeating the lines over and over—a combination of time, effort, and concentration), but regardless of the technique you employ, memorization is a tool that must be mastered so that you are able to progress from rehearsal to performance.

Although you may believe that memorization is the last thing you do before performing, it really should be the first thing you do. If you rehearse your piece over and over, memorization may happen without much effort. Rehearsal happens before, during, and after your text is memorized. Not until you have learned your lines well, though, are you ready to concentrate on communicating them rather than merely remembering them. Only when the script is out of the hands can solo performers master techniques like physical embodiment, employing the appropriate focus, sensory showing, character placement, keeping the silent character alive, and attempting to coin the language now.

The best advice for you before beginning to memorize is to formulate your interpretation of the selection to ensure that you know what the words mean. There is a direct connection between having things make sense and remembering them. It is easier to remember lines when you know what you are saying and can imagine or visualize what is being related. It is easier, for example, to remember a story than a list of nonsense words! One performer puts it this way: "I strive to know what my text means first, then I learn my lines so well that they are second nature. This way, the lines become automatic responses and I can concentrate on communicating them." (Some performers find that they discover what the text means and formulate their interpretation during rehearsals rather than before—they try various approaches while rehearsing. If you have the luxury of an extended period of time to work on your selection, see if this technique will work for you.)

As we said above, memorization is the result of constant repetition. Most performers have to read their lines again and again, over a period of time, to feel really secure with them. Some have to read the lines aloud because then they can hear and feel the rhythm of the lines, which helps them remember them. Some use an index card to cover the lines as they repeat them and then check to see if they remembered them correctly. Often writing the text by hand several times can aid the memorization process. You could ask someone to hold the script while you say the lines aloud to be sure that you are not adding, omitting, or paraphrasing.

What follows are some specific techniques that have worked for professional performers. Try various ones until you find the one or the combination that works best for you.

Audio recorder

Many performers find an audio recorder helpful. They record all their lines on tape, and then listen to them while trying to sleep, while getting ready in the morning, while driving to work, etc. If you're performing a scene from a play with two characters, put the lines of one character on tape, and then leave a space for you to fill in the other character's lines. Once you have learned and "felt" one character's through lines, then record cues and work on the other character's lines.

Action verbs

Some performers learn their lines by imagining the action implied in the verbs. As Hamlet teaches, actors should always "suit the action to the word/The word to the action." They "see" the action and that helps them remember what happens next. If one were trying to remember, "She ran down the street, and kicked the can high in the air," one would concentrate on the action of "running" and then the action of "kicking."

Letter/sound cues

You may be able to make associations among the letters or sounds used. If words begin with the same letter of the alphabet, this may help you associate them. If a line ends with the "s" sound and the next line begins with an "s," this could help trigger the connection between the two lines. In the lines, "Then they went to mass. Soon after, they left church and headed home," notice that "mass" ends with an "s" sound, "Soon" begins with the "s" sound, and "headed home" employs the alliterative "h" sound.

Alphabetical order

If there is a particular combination of words that you have trouble remembering, try alphabetical association. If the line is "He thought about the pretty quail" and you have trouble remembering "pretty quail" remember that the two words begin with "p" and then "q"—alphabetical order. (This works if the words are in reverse alphabetical order as well.)

Block learning

Many performers talk about learning their lines in "blocks" or "chunks." They concentrate on one beat or main idea or stanza at a time. In the case of a prose fiction text, they might begin by learning only two or three paragraphs at a time. They go over and over those until secure before adding additional paragraphs. When learning a poem, they may learn one stanza at a time. Some performers break the script into thought sections or beats and go over each section several times before adding the next section. Memorization with this technique is cumulative. (One of the problems of using this technique is trying to remember which block comes next. Be sure you memorize the order of the blocks as well as the content of each block.)

Mnemonic devices

A mnemonic device is any technique you use to help you remember. In the case of a list or sequence, it may be useful to come up with a phrase to help you remember.

If, for example, you had to memorize the line, "She bought tuna, lemonade, and carrots," you could look at the first letter of each item on the list—"tlc"—and think of "tender, loving care" to help you remember the sequence order. If the line were "Bring the lectern tomorrow," you could think of "bacon, lettuce, tomato" to help you remember the key words "bring," "lectern," and "tomorrow."

Visualization

This technique may seem a bit silly but it has been very effective for many performers. Words often represent vivid pictures, and you can use these pictures to help you remember. Were you to try to remember the lines from *Hamlet*, "How all occasions do inform against me / And spur my dull revenge," for example, you could visualize a birthday party for "occasions" and the spur on the heel of a boot for "spur." Usually, this technique is used when first memorizing, then gives way to repetition, which gives way to emotional performance, which locks the lines in again.

Class Exercise

Try memorizing this passage by employing some of the techniques described above.

Mary Jane had never before thought of Bob, Tom, or Vince. She hurried to the grocery store trying to rid her memory of the three men. When she got to the store, she took out her list so she would buy only the items on it: bean soup, oatmeal, tuna, noodles, and triscuits.

When she arrived at her apartment, she put her groceries away, and noticed that her answering machine light was blinking. She played her messages. Tom and Vince had called. "How strange," she thought.

USING THE LECTERN

A lectern is sometimes mistakenly called a "podium." Performers stand on podiums and behind lecterns! If you have a lectern available for your performance, consider several advantages and disadvantages before you decide whether to use it. Practically speaking, the primary purpose of the lectern is to hold your script. By resting your script on the lip of the lectern, you free both hands for gesturing. (Of course, if you use no script, this reason for using the lectern is negated.)

If you want to communicate a relatively formal feeling, standing behind the lectern helps you create that feeling of formality. This position might be appropriate when you perform a selection in which the speaker is a preacher, a lawyer, or a teacher, for example.

The lectern, like the script, can also be used to show personality differences between characters. If you wanted to depict a character who is insecure and timid, you might want to use the lectern to stand or hide behind while projecting that character. You can then step away from the lectern to communicate a more secure, self-confident character. (This technique would probably not work well for passages of *stichomythia* or rapid-paced dialogue.) In addition, you can use the lectern symbolically to represent a tree, a bar, a pulpit, a table, or some other prop. Using the lectern in this way helps the audience visualize your projected scene.

If you decide not to use the lectern, you have the advantage of making your whole body visible to the audience. As we stated earlier, when you decide not to use a lectern (or a script), the audience has certain expectations of fuller characterization and freer movement and gesture. Symbolically speaking, you have a wider proscenium to fill when you decide not to use lectern or script.

Finally, let the demands of your particular interpretation determine whether to stand behind a lectern. Remember, everything you do in performance speaks. If you use a lectern, that in itself sends a message to the audience. If you decide not to use a lectern, that prepares the audience for a different kind of experience. Make your decisions with care.

CUTTING

Often, when you prepare a selection for class performance, especially when the selection is prose fiction or drama, you will have to delete words, lines, and even whole paragraphs or pages to fit time limits. Cutting literature is a very delicate art, because you want to make sure your excisions do not destroy the general flavor, tone, or theme of the original work. The best solution to the cutting problem is, in our opinion, not to cut at all, but to maintain the integrity of the material by beginning in the middle and then performing to the end. (For example, in the case of an assigned performance of three-to-five minutes, you would begin three to five minutes before the end of the selection and then perform to the end.) This way, your performance begins right before the climax—or high point of the action—and includes a sense of build-up and release, which is always desirable in a good performance. The introduction for a performance like this should bring the audience up-to-date, telling them the pertinent events leading up to the point where you begin. When you cut in this manner, the rest of the selection is kept intact, and the text need not be altered.

If this suggestion will not work for you because you want the audience to get the flavor of the whole work, you may need to make interior cuts. Before cutting anything, however, be sure to read and analyze the whole selection, decide what can be eliminated, and then begin to cut. Make sure to maintain the same verb tense, speaker(s), and style of language as the original selection. You should add words or lines only to provide a transition between sections where a great deal has been cut, and add nothing at all if the performance is clear without a transition. When cutting, keep the following suggestions in mind:

1. Expository passages (passages that set the scene in the beginnings of plays and prose fiction selections) may be cut. This information can easily be covered in the introduction.
2. Long descriptive passages may be cut.
3. A complete episode may be cut if the selection maintains its harmony and unity without that particular episode.
4. Minor characters may be cut as long as the scene makes sense without them.
5. Lines that provide stage directions—such as "laughing, she left the room"— may be cut if the action can be performed (shown) instead of spoken (told).
6. Unless otherwise instructed, do not cut anything from a poem. Select a poem that fits your time limit rather than cut a longer poem.

VOCAL AND PHYSICAL RESPONSIVENESS

Vocal Characteristics

Vocal characterizations in performance can be accomplished in a variety of ways. The devices of your voice that can be altered or changed to suggest a speaker's voice are (1) Pitch, (2) Quality, (3) Rate, (4) Volume, and (5) Dialect.

The following discussion of these devices is meant to offer possibilities for altering your normal vocal delivery to suggest speakers in texts whose voices may not be the same as yours. These are merely suggestions, not rules. The best way to project speakers is to work from the inside out—perform a dramatistic analysis so that you know who the speaker is, how he or she behaves, what motivates him or her, and so on, and rehearse the scene several times. As a result of analysis and rehearsal, certain vocal responses may occur naturally; if not, try out these various vocal devices, but be wary of imposing them artificially. In other words, do not alter your voice for the sake of being different—only use these devices when they seem inherently necessary to suggest speakers who are different from you.

The primary use of *pitch* is to communicate sarcasm or cynicism. Try saying "Don't you look nice" naturally, then try it altering your pitch to imply the opposite. In addition, you can raise or lower your normal pitch to suit the pitch level of the speakers in the text. Raising your pitch usually communicates youth or immaturity. Lowering your pitch usually communicates heaviness or sobriety. Beware, however, of changing pitch too much. Some beginning performers think they should drastically lower their pitch to suggest male speakers and drastically raise their pitch to suggest female speakers. Changing pitch too drastically low or high draws attention to the pitch and away from the scene. Very few people, and likewise very few speakers, have such exaggerated speaking voices. Slight differences in pitch are often sufficient.

There are many *vocal qualities* to choose from when you try to project a speaker whose vocal quality is different from yours: thin, strident, harsh, breathy, nasal, denasal, hoarse, and glottal fry. Since different vocal qualities communicate different emotions or different types of feelings, changing your vocal quality is often a very effective aid in characterization.

When you constrict the throat muscles, you get a thin or strident quality. A thin quality where you use very little effort when speaking can suggest youthfulness. A thin, weak voice often communicates nervousness or indecisiveness (Jennifer Tilly and Melanie Griffith are actresses who often produce a thin vocal quality). A strident voice (Roseanne comes to mind) sounds abrasive and can be used to communicate a nagging person or a constant complainer. A harsh quality (Roseanne often uses this vocal quality as well as strident) often communicates anger or hostility, and a breathy or whispery voice can communicate nostalgia or sexual allure (Marilyn Monroe exuded sexuality partly as a result of her breathy vocal quality). If you direct all your sound through your nose, you get a nasal quality which communicates a whiny or unpleasant character. (Fran Drescher used this type of quality in *The Nanny.*) A denasal quality is the opposite of a nasal quality. With a denasal quality, no sound comes through the nose, and your words sound muffled and often slurred. The denasal quality is useful to project someone who has a cold or someone who is not particularly intelligent. (The denasal quality was used by Lily Tomlin, for example, when she did her Edith Ann character on *Saturday Night Live* and is employed by some performers when portraying the role of the mentally challenged Lennie in *Of Mice and Men.*) A hoarse quality (such as the one employed by Marlon Brando when he portrayed the Godfather) is the type that laryngitis produces. This can be used to project a speaker who smokes too much or has strained his or her voice. Glottal fry is a vocal quality that suggests the sound of grease popping on a hot griddle or frying pan. The sound is often described as rattling, gravelly, gargling, cracking, or tickerlike. During glottal fry, the vocal folds become extremely tense and compressed and your pitch can drop as much as a full octave (Katherine Hepburn's voice in her later years exhibits glottal fry). Although glottal fry can be useful to suggest an older speaker, use it with caution as this is a vocal quality that usually suggests that you do not have adequate breath support. Using it too often can injure your vocal chords.

Changing the *rate* at which you normally speak to coincide with the rate of the speaker is another way to communicate vocal differences. No two people speak at the same speed, so changing rate is an effective means of differentiating speakers. When performing a scene from *Of Mice and Men*, for instance, a rate difference between Lennie and George is one way to suggest their intellectual differences.

Lennie, as stated above, is a slower thinker and speaker; consequently, he would have a slower rate of speech than would George. Pace is primarily determined by the amount of conflict or tension in a selection. Speed up slightly when the emotional tension is high, and slow down when the tension is eased. Pace also involves the use of pause. Beginning interpreters are often afraid to use pauses, but they are one of the most effective ways to build suspense, to let a point sink in, to show hesitation and uncertainty, and simply to give speakers time to think or ponder what to say next. Pauses, though, must always be filled. You must always stay in character using the pause for a particular reason. Pausing because you cannot find your place in the script, because you do not know your lines, or because the text says "pause" draws attention to you and away from the text. (One of the goals of the memorized performer is to learn your lines so well that you seem as though you do not know them and are constructing what you want to say as you go along.)

One special consideration when dealing with rate is *stichomythia*. Stichomythia is the rapid-paced dialogue commonly found in Greek plays and plays by William Shakespeare, but also found in contemporary plays. For a solo performer, stichomythia becomes a special problem because the dialogue exchanges are short and must be delivered very quickly. There must be no transition between lines; no dead space. Look at this dialogue exchange from Mark Hillenbrand's play *The Sea of Galilee:*

Samuel:	This is Frances. She's a nurse.
Fairchild:	Hello.
Samuel:	Hello.
Fairchild:	A nurse?
Samuel:	Yes.
Fairchild:	That's something.
Samuel:	Yes.
Fairchild:	Really now.
Samuel:	Yes.
Fairchild:	OK.

Practice this short exchange and see if you can capture the rapid pace of the stichomythia.

Volume is not a consistently useful device for differentiating between speakers by itself, but shifts in volume lend interest and variety to scenes. One mistake many beginning performers make is to substitute loudness for intensity when speakers argue. Sometimes it is more effective not to shout, but to pull back and speak very softly but intensely. Try saying "I hate you and I never want to see you again" by shouting the line. Now say the same line again and deliver it quietly but with intensity. Which seems more effective to you? Remember, less is often more!

Another element of vocal characterization is the use of *dialect*. Often playwrights (Tennessee Williams, for example) pick up the local color of a place by creating characters who speak in a dialect. Some poems, such as those by James Whitcomb Riley, require a southern Indiana dialect, and some prose fiction passages, like those in the stories of Georgian Flannery O'Connor, suggest a kind of vernacular narration—the speech of the natives. Dialects are often difficult for beginning performers because they take much time to master. Usually if you cannot do a dialect well or consistently, you should not choose a selection where the use of a dialect is mandatory. If you would like to try the challenge of a dialect performance, consult Jerry Blount's book *Stage Dialects* and become familiar with the International Phonetic Alphabet (see Chapter 8) which will enable you to transcribe the lines into phonetic equivalents.

Try employing some of these vocal techniques to differentiate the characters in this scene from Lorraine Hansberry's *A Raisin in the Sun*. How can pitch, quality, rate, volume, and dialect be used to differentiate these characters?

The situation in this scene involves the Younger family—Walter, Ruth, Mama, and Beneatha—a black family who just bought a home in an all-white neighborhood. Mr. Lindner, a white man, has arrived to try to convince the Youngers to cancel the deal.

From A RAISIN IN THE SUN   Lorraine Hansberry

Lindner: Well, I don't know how much you folks know about our organization. It is one of these community organizations set up to look after—oh, you know, things like block upkeep and special projects and we also have what we call our New York Neighbors Orientation Committee . . .

Beneatha: (*Drily*) Yes—and what do they do?

Lindner: Well—it's what you might call a sort of welcoming committee, I guess. I mean they, we, I'm the chairman of the committee—go around and see the new people who move into the neighborhood and sort of give them the lowdown on the way we do things out in Clybourne Park.

Beneatha: Uh-huh.

Lindner: And we also have the category of what the association calls—uh—special community problems . . .

Beneatha: Yes—and what are some of those?

Walter: Girl, let the man talk.

Lindner: Thank you. I would sort of like to explain this thing in my own way. I mean I want to explain to you in a certain way.

Walter: Go ahead.

Physical Characteristics

Speakers must be projected physically as well as vocally. You suggest a speaker's distinct body by transforming your physical appearance to suggest what you think the speaker looks and acts like. Since speakers must respond nonverbally, the body stances, gestures, facial expressions, and physical actions you employ become an essential part of suggesting the other. Beginning performers usually tend to under-characterize (especially physically) when performing drama scenes. They have difficulty projecting the physical dimension of characters, partly because of inhibition, partly because of the difficulty of having to suggest more than one character in a scene, but also because of convention. Interpretation was called *oral* interpretation for a long time, and performers were to suggest characters only from the neck up. The bodily involvement of the perfomer was not encouraged. This is no longer the case, and physical characterization can no longer be ignored. It is well known that actions often speak louder than words, a fact that is true in solo performances as well as in life. A performance is not as effective if only the voice of the performer is engaged, you cannot say to an audience, "Please, just hear me." The body must support what the voice is saying—there must be congruence between what is said and what is done—unless a purposely noncongruent moment is desired.

As was true for vocal responsiveness in projecting speakers, you should attempt to discover the appropriate bodily response by working from the inside out. Do not find an appropriate body type and then try to fit it to the speaker. Body traits come from analysis and rehearsal, from knowing who the speaker is and how he or she will move and respond. When you are performing drama scenes with more than one character, work on developing only one of the characters at a time. Once you have a physical feel for the individualizing qualities of each character, then try putting the scene back together. In general, men carry their weight higher in their bodies and women carry their weight lower. Stand up and see if you can feel where you carry the majority of your weight. By altering where you carry the weight in your body, you can suggest a character who is physically different from you. If, for example, you try to relocate the center of your weight in your knees and try to walk that way, you will suggest someone who is overweight or a pregnant woman. If you relocate all of your weight to the back of your neck, you suggest someone with very good posture, someone regal or snobbish. If you imagine all of your weight in your nose, you suggest a gossip. Experiment with weight relocation as a beginning to physical responsiveness.

Actor, director, author Robert L. Benedetti elaborates on this re-centering idea:

> I can suggest five primary character centers that, by bodily logic and by cultural tradition, are each associated with a different sort of person: head (the cerebral and/or sexually repressed person), chest (the sentimental, or even the "militaristic" person), stomach (the indulgent person), genitals (the libidinous,

or perhaps the naive person), and anus (the sexually withdrawn, "constipated" person). We have all known people who tend to relate to the world from one of these centers and who carry with them their own unique variations on the basic theme of their center; observe some of your acquaintances from this point of view.[2]

Though Benedetti is primarily talking about performing in plays, this same information relates to the performance of defined characters in any text.

Class Exercise

Review Benedetti's five primary character centers above and try to determine your center. Try experimenting with body center relocation by experimenting with how Willy Loman would move as compared to his son Biff. How would you physicalize Ariel, the fairy sprite, in *The Tempest* compared to the earth-bound creature, Caliban? What center might Porphyria's lover have in the poem by the same name by Robert Browning? How about the narrator in "The Tell-Tale Heart" or "The Use of Force"?

Employing gestures is one way to suggest the physical responsiveness of a speaker. People who normally gesture should have no difficulty gesturing during performance—as long as they concentrate on the differences between the way they gesture and the way the speaker in the text may gesture. Those who do not gesture normally must try to understand that gestures help us to be better understood by our audience. Gestures are related to the production of speech. *Gestural deictics* involves words like "this," "that," "those," and "there." These words imply or indicate action that you can use in performance. Certain gesturing is required, for example, when you say, "He was this tall" or "She stood right over there." If you were to say, "Look over there" without a gesture, the sentence would be meaningless. Gestures are necessary. Dramatists, for example, are writing for a world where the text is translated into gesture and a deictic word requires gestures. Recent experiments suggest that gesturing can prompt us to remember. Unconscious gesturing gives the brain time to download information and retrieve words from memory. Gestures are closely tied to thinking, and gesturing on purpose can improve your memory of your text.

Gestures and physical actions that are planned usually look planned and, consequently, the believability of the speaker may be lessened because the physical dimension is stilted and unnatural. As you work on creating a speaker in rehearsal, body characteristics, movement, and gestures should come naturally from your knowing the speaker and studying the language. Although we encourage you to incorporate movement and gesture into your performance, be wary of the kinds of movements and gestures you employ. In most interpretation performances, smaller movements and gestures communicate easily because of the interpreter's usual close proximity to the audience. Economy, therefore, is a key element in solo per-formances. As described in Chapter 3, economy simply means limiting the kinds and types of movements and gestures you use so that you suggest rather than lit-eralize actions. If, for example, a speaker is pacing back and forth from one end of a room to the other, you may want to narrow—economize—the movement, cover-ing a smaller area, or you may ask yourself what causes the speaker to pace and then decide if this cause may be communicated in a less distracting way. Remember, the stage directions that are usually included in plays, for example, are meant for the actors in a fully mounted production. You are free to translate these directions into what is right for a solo performance or perhaps ignore the direc-tions all together.

Consider, for example, the famous balcony scene in Shakespeare's *Romeo and Juliet.* How could this scene be done by a solo interpreter and still suggest the spa-tial relationship between Romeo and Juliet? How can you show that Romeo is on the ground and that Juliet is on the balcony? On the stage, of course, the set designer creates a balcony upon which Juliet stands. In the solo drama perfor-mance, however, this sort of construction is not possible, for the interpreter is Juliet only half of the time. Jumping on top of a desk to indicate Juliet on the balcony and jumping down to the floor to indicate Romeo below in the garden would be awkward, would lend an air of amusement not intended in the scene, and instead of minimizing the performer's intrusion in the scene would put the interpreter solidly between both characters. One way to solve the problem is to use economy in terms of focus changes. To project the illusion of the height difference, the inter-preter need only look slightly above eye level when speaking as Romeo, and then switch placements and lower the eye level when Juliet speaks. The audience's abil-ity to imagine and create the scene from the clues you provide and from the lan-guage in the text will enable them to see the garden and the balcony without the need for literalization.

If you were going to perform a scene from Edward Albee's "Zoo Story," you would be confronted with the challenge of having one hyperactive character (Jerry) and another character (Peter) who sits on a park bench throughout most of the play. How could you best suggest the physical activity of both men? One possible solution is to be physically active for Jerry and then remain still (though not seated) for Peter. If you were to sit each time Peter spoke and then stand up and move for Jerry, you would insert yourself in the middle of the scene since neither man is engaged in standing *and* sitting.

Economy is also involved when you project kisses, handshakes, slaps, or any other type of physical contact. Often beginning performers ignore these actions rather than trying to find a creative way to convey them. (These actions should be handled with care, though, to prevent serious moments from becoming comic.) The action is usually best performed with offstage focus and the employment of economy and suggestion, so that the audience understands what is happening. To suggest that one person is kissing another in a two-character scene, one character should look like he or she is kissing, and then the other should look as though he or she had already been kissed. For handshakes, one character can extend his or her right hand, and then you can switch to the other character whose right hand is already extended. For slaps, be sure you seem to make contact with the imaginary other before you, otherwise you will look like you are swatting flies! To hand someone something, for example, just extend your arm out and pretend to be giving the other character something. The other character's hand is already extended and he or she mimes taking the object in. (If you use a script, the script can suggest the something that is handed and received). You need not try to switch arms or hands between characters as this is something the performer not the character is doing.

IMAGERY AND SENSORY SHOWING

In many beginning acting classes, students sit in a circle and pass around foods to taste, spices to smell, cloth to feel, and so forth. The purpose behind this exercise is to help the student develop a sense memory. The idea behind sense memory is that once we have had a relationship with some object—once we have experienced it— we can later re-create it in our imaginations when the object is absent. Actors are often called upon to re-create a certain image or experience on stage. One may need to drink imaginary milk from an imaginary glass; another may have to react to tea as though it were whiskey; a third may have to attack an empty plate as though it contained a steak, mashed potatoes, and green beans!

Imagery

Literature is full of images created with language—images for you to react to, just as an actor reacts to imaginary props. Imagery is the writer's use of language symbols to reconstruct objects or experiences which stimulate sense impressions in the mind of the reader. If we have experienced the object or event either personally or vicariously, we can re-create these images in our minds. The images appeal to our senses, paint pictures in our minds, and help the writer's language seem clear and fresh.

When you see the word "automobile," for example, your mind translates this word symbol into a specific meaning. Once you have seen an automobile, your mind is able to re-create an image of it—you see the word "automobile," and you create one automobile or another in your imagination. You do not see exactly the same automobile the writer had in mind; you see your own constructed version of the image, based on clues in the text and your experiences with automobiles in general. (Of course, you cannot image anything you have never seen, heard of, or experienced. If a writer speaks of gefilte fish, and you have never seen, heard of, or tasted gefilte fish, you will have to do some research to reconstruct this image.) If the writer wants you to see a specific kind of automobile, he or she provides additional information to make the image more exact. The automobile could be described as "a brown and white 1994 four-door Oldsmobile 88," in which case we get a richer image. Look, for example, at how Katherine Mansfield creates an image of a doll's house by adding sensory appeals.

From THE DOLL'S HOUSE   Katherine Mansfield

When dear old Mrs. Hay went back to town after staying with the Burnells she sent the children a doll's house. It was so big that the carter and Pat carried it into the courtyard, and there it stayed, propped up on two wooden boxes beside the feed-room door. No harm could come to it; it was summer. And perhaps the smell of paint would have gone off by the time it had to be taken in. For, really, the smell of paint coming from that doll's house ("Sweet of old Mrs. Hay, of course; most sweet and generous!")—but the smell of paint was quite enough to make anyone seriously ill, in Aunt Beryl's opinion. Even the sacking was taken off. And when it was . . .

There stood the doll's house, a dark, oily spinach green, picked out with bright yellow. Its two solid little chimneys, glued on to the roof, were painted red and white, and the door, gleaming with yellow varnish, was like a slab of toffee. Four windows, real windows, were divided into panes by a broad streak of green. There was actually a tiny porch, too, painted yellow, with big lumps of congealed paint hanging along the edge.

But perfect, perfect little house! Who could possibly mind the smell? It was part of the joy, part of the newness.

Sensory Imagery

Highly imagistic literature, rich with descriptions, contains sensory appeals. There are many different kinds of sensory images.

Images that appeal to our sense of sight are *visual.*
Images that appeal to our sense of hearing are *auditory.*
Images that appeal to our sense of taste are *gustatory.*
Images that appeal to our sense of smell are *olfactory.*
Images that appeal to our sense of touch are *tactile.*

Images that appeal to our sense of temperature are *thermal.*
Images that appeal to our sense of overt action are *kinetic.*
Images that appeal to our internal body sensations—to our sense of body position, movement, or tension—are *kinesthetic.*

We may respond in other ways as well. We may feel a sense of loss, pain, pleasure, or relief, among others.

In the passage from "The Doll's House," we see the details of the house, we feel the heat of summer, we smell the paint, and we feel the muscular strain in our bodies (kinesthetic) when Pat and the carter carry the big doll's house into the courtyard. We also sense the joy the Burnell children feel when they receive the gift.

Sensory Showing

Whereas a silent reader may stop with just creating the image of that doll's house in his or her mind, an interpreter desires to share the image with an audience. The audience, then, is also able to reconstruct the image. Sharing these images with the audience is called *sensory showing.*

Sensory showing means feeling and making physical the sensory images in a literary text and projecting those images into the audience. Since impression precedes expression, you see, hear, or taste an image and then share it with the audience. Instead of looking only at the audience when speaking a line like, "The bird flew across the sky," you reconstruct the image in your mind (impression) and then project an imaginary bird out in an imaginary scene above the audience as you say the line (expression). Instead of just saying, "I hear the alarm bell," you actually try to hear the bell ringing (impression), and then you share the line with the audience (expression). If the line is, "I remember my stomach's reaction to the roller coaster ride," you try to re-create a kinesthetic response to this memory so that the audience is able to imagine what the ride may have been like.

You may use sensory showing in combination with any type of focus. If you are using open focus, then you share the image with the audience, as just indicated. If you are using closed focus, you respond to the image and then share it with another character in a specific literary setting. If you are using inner-closed focus, you are re-creating the image for your own benefit or need. With semi-closed focus, you attempt to share the image with a muse, some inanimate object, absent person, God, or other silent listener.

Although poetry is the most imagistic of the three genres, images do exist in prose fiction and drama as well. The passage cited from Mansfield's "The Doll's House" demands much sensory showing to enable the audience to participate in the creation of the scene. Allow your voice and body to respond to the imagery in the text.

Practice sensory showing as you perform the following poem by Chinese poet Tony Lin. Notice how he uses the seasons to underscore the sensual responses of the speaker. Try to show the thermal appeals as they underscore the emotional responses of the speaker.

WAITING FOR SPRING   Tony Lin

> When I meet her, you design spring;
> Everything is alive and smiles on us like new leaves born from the tree.
> When I fall in love with her, you design summer;
> Everything is burning hot and growing stronger.
> When I leave her, you design autumn;
> Everything is wistful and holding like the reluctant leaves almost
>   falling.
> When I miss her, you design winter;
> Everything is ruthlessly tested by frigid wind and snow like the
>   tree without leaves, swaying in the cold . . .
>   Waiting for spring

Reprinted by permission of the author.

AESTHETIC DISTANCE

Aesthetic distance deals with the emotional/psychological or physical distance between performer and text and between performer and audience. When performers are too close emotionally or psychologically to the text, either because the experience in the literature is too real or because they have had an experience similar to that in the literature, they often are not able to achieve enough objectivity to do justice to the text in performance. If, for example, you have just ended a long love affair and you choose a literary selection in which the same situation occurs, you may find yourself unable to differentiate between the speaker's attitude and your own. Performers must be able to separate themselves enough from the experience in the literature to be able to analyze it with some degree of objectivity. If the experience in the text is too real or too close to an experience you have had, ask yourself if you can view the literature objectively enough to achieve aesthetic distance.

The second aspect of aesthetic distance concerns the performer's relationship to the audience. Most art objects of any kind demand a certain amount of distance from spectators if they are to be aesthetically appreciated. Actors and dancers usually perform on a stage separated from the audience; paintings and sculptures require viewers to stand at a certain distance; opera and film all demand a certain distance between performer and audience. As you perform for an audience, make sure you are not standing too close to them. Be sure audience members do not have to look straight up to see you. Maintain enough distance so that all audience members have a clear view of you, and so that they are able to experience your performance from the best perspective.

There are exceptions, however, to this "keep-your-distance" dictum. The amount of distance maintained should be related to your specific intentions. Bertolt Brecht, for example, experimented with aesthetic distance (see the discussion on alienation in Chapter 10), attempting both to involve the audience emotionally, and then, at an opportune moment, to alienate them, or distance them, to encourage objective reflection. In the 1960s, the distance between performer and audience was eliminated in many productions as audience members often became participants in the action or as cast members appeared in the audience. Today's performance artists (see Chapter 9) also often want to diminish the degree of aesthetic distance and physically involve the audience. More or less aesthetic distance, then, is required depending on the nature of the text and your interpretation of it. Feel free to experiment.

EMPATHY AND SYMPATHY

Empathy and sympathy are related to aesthetic distance. *Empathy* literally means the ability to experience vicariously the feelings, thoughts, responses, and attitudes of another individual. When you empathize with someone, you maintain very little aesthetic distance. You project yourself imaginatively to such an extent that you actually feel what the other person is feeling, you identify with that person and think, respond, and act in a similar manner. In a 1999 interview with Dotson Rader in *Parade Magazine,* two-time Academy Award winner Kevin Spacey admitted, "All you have to do to have empathy for another human being . . . is to tap into his dreams, learn what his hopes are." When you *sympathize* with someone, you understand what the other person is feeling, but you maintain a bit more distance: instead of feeling *with* someone, you feel *for* someone. If, for example, you go to visit a friend in the hospital who has a broken leg, and you leave the hospital feeling bad and thinking, "What a shame," you are probably sympathizing. If, however, you walk out of that hospital and *your* leg hurts, you have empathized! When performing, you usually want to empathize with the characters. You want to convince the audience that you are creating the characters' physical appearances, as well as their feelings, emotions, beliefs, and so forth. When performing prose fiction, though, while you empathize with the narrator in the story, the narrator may empathize with some characters and sympathize with others. You will want to show this difference in performance.

The audience, too, empathizes and sympathizes, likes and dislikes, and this is also related to aesthetic distance. Often there is one character in a play, for instance, with whom the audience empathizes most—with whom the audience experiences the least emotional or psychological distance. This may be the most reasonable character—the *raisonneur*—or the touchstone character, a character who allows the audience to differentiate the good guys from the bad guys. Horatio in *Hamlet* might be considered the most reasonable character, a character whose point of view the audience often shares. The character Touchstone in *As You Like It* conveys a standard of comparison for our judgment of the worth of the other characters.

Empathy and sympathy are a consideration when dealing with the relationship between interpreter and text and between the speaker in the text and the other people with whom he or she relates. You, as interpreter, must empathize with the speaker regardless of whether you approve of his or her behavior or agree with his or her attitudes, feelings, or beliefs. Once you have accomplished this, you must deal with the relationship(s) between this speaker and the other characters in the text. Decide whom the speaker empathizes or identifies with, whom he or she sympathizes with, and whom the speaker keeps his or her distance from. In any prose fiction work, play, or poem, look closely at the language the author uses to help you determine the attitude of the speaker.

If the literary text you are performing were staged with a group of performers, one way to show the various relationships would be by the amount of physical distance maintained between the speaker and the other characters. In solo performance, however, this is not possible, so you must find a different way to show the speaker's feelings. You, as the speaker in a text, can soften your tone of voice, smile, and take on the behaviors, attitudes, and feelings of a character you identify with. For characters the speaker feels antipathy toward, you can clench your teeth, frown, and adopt a sarcastic tone of voice. If, for example, the speaker were to say, "Mary was feeling very ill as she put on her hat and coat," the speaker could suggest the ill feeling and the action of putting on the hat and coat—even suggest Mary's voice—if the speaker empathizes with Mary. If the speaker merely sympathizes with or even dislikes Mary and wants to convey distance between himself or herself and Mary, then the speaker observes rather than suggests Mary and maintains the speaker's attitude and voice, rather than adopting Mary's.

Read "When I Was One-and-Twenty" by A. E. Housman below. Which character do you empathize with? Which character do you sympathize with? How can you show the difference? Do your empathy and sympathy shift back and forth between the speaker and the wise man? If they do, try to find a way to show these shifts in your performance. To what extent does the young man empathize with the wise man? Do the young man's feelings for the wise man change? If they do, how can this change be communicated in performance?

WHEN I WAS ONE-AND-TWENTY   A. E. Housman

When I was one-and-twenty
I heard a wise man say,

"Give crowns and pounds and guineas
But not your heart away;
Give pearls away and rubies
But keep your fancy free."
But I was one-and-twenty,
No use to talk to me.

When I was one-and-twenty
I heard him say again,
"The heart out of the bosom
Was never given in vain;
'Tis paid with sighs a plenty
And sold for endless rue."
And I am two-and-twenty,
And oh, 'tis true, 'tis true.

FOCUS

Focus involves your decisions about the nature of the interaction in a text. Practically speaking, focus deals with where to direct your gaze during any moment of your selection. Focus involves the following:

1. Projecting the scene in the audience (offstage focus).
2. Shifts of audience mode (open focus, closed focus, inner-closed focus, semi-closed focus).
3. Location of characters in the imagined scene (character placement).
4. Shifts of time and place within a selection

Projection

As we pointed out in Chapter 1, the interpreter, like the public speaker, faces the audience. As you face the audience, the focus of your scene is *offstage*, created in the imaginations of the audience members. Facing your audience so that they get a full view of you at all times facilitates their participation in creating the imagined scene. Turning profile and looking *onstage* (as actors do), as though there were someone else with you, often distracts the audience. First, if you look as though you are speaking to someone onstage, the scene shifts onstage and consequently limits the audience's imaginative participation. Second, once you begin to shift to an onstage orientation, you may begin to literalize objects onstage (for example, pointing to the real door in the room to represent the imaginary door in the selection). This draws the attention of the audience to these literal objects and away from the literature. Third, when you do not face the audience, they miss much of the performance because they cannot see your full face. Your face (especially your eyes) is one of your most expressive features. When the audience misses facial expressions and responses, they lose much of the total effect of your performance.

The use of offstage focus enables you to perform even the most technically difficult or spectacle-oriented selections because the audience does much of the work themselves. As King Lear, you can summon the wind to "blow" and "crack its cheeks," and if you are responsive to the imaginative storm raging, the audience will create their own storm—sometimes more effectively than it could ever be literalized onstage. The first aspect of focus, then, is to project the scene out front or offstage as opposed to profile and onstage.

Shifts in Audience Mode

Another aspect of focus concerns where you will look as you perform any particular moment of your selection based on who is being addressed. As we stated earlier, during the performance of any piece of literature, speakers may address the general audience; another speaker or silent auditor; themselves; or inanimate objects, muses, God, and so forth. You will want to make these shifts clear in performance. These shifts in focus are caused by audience modal shifts , and a modal analysis will help you make focus decisions. You usually use *open focus* when speakers talk directly to the general audience, *closed focus* when characters speak dialogue to each other or when one speaker addresses a silent auditor, *inner-closed focus* when speakers speak their thoughts or feelings aloud to themselves, and *semi-closed focus* when speakers address inanimate objects, muses, God, or an absent or deceased person. Often a performer uses a combination of different focuses in one performance.

Figure 4.1 demonstrates how to employ each type of focus. The following outline indicates when each type of focus may be employed:

Open Focus	**Closed Focus**
Use for epic mode moments:	Use for dramatic mode moments:
Asides	Dialogue
Less private soliloquies	Dramatic monologues
Address to juries or large groups	
When narrator furthers the plot; expresses attitudes; describes objects, events, and so on	

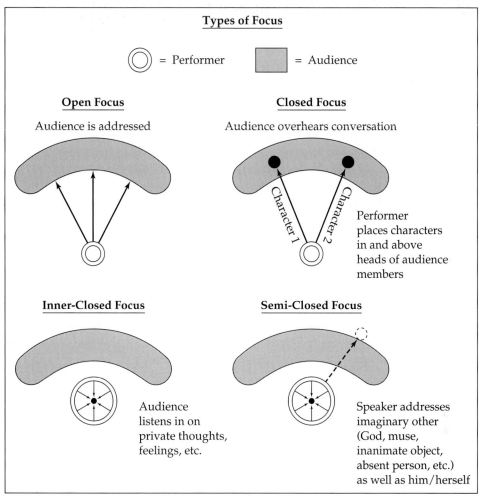

Figure 4.1

Inner-Closed Focus

Use for lyric mode moments:
Private, personal thoughts, feelings
Private soliloquies

Semi-Closed Focus

Use for lyric mode moments:
Address to muse, God, inanimate
    object, an absent or deceased person,
    and so on

Shifts in audience mode are particularly tricky when the speaker addresses the slippery "you"—slippery because the identification of this "you" is often vague.

This pronoun may refer to the speaker himself or herself (e.g., Joe, *you* are such an idiot), the general audience (e.g., *You* will now meet a fellow called Joe), an apostrophized other (e.g., I hope you can hear me?), or another character (e.g., "What do *you* want," asked Joe). Following is a more specific explanation of focus choices when a text uses the slippery pronoun "you" as the addressee:

Use *semi-closed focus* when the speaker is apostrophizing or addressing someone or something that is not present (implicit listener—for example, God, muse, or absent person, as in: Daddy, why did you have to die?). When this "you" is addressed, it must be obvious in the selection that this "you" is being only imaginatively addressed. You use semi-closed focus when specifically addressing "Daddy," and inner-closed focus for the rest.

When a character addresses "you" during a passage of dialogue, for example, the you is much less slippery. When Tom addresses Mary as "you," the performer employs *closed focus*. The "you" in this case is a clearly defined character who addresses another clearly defined character. In some cases, the "you" who is addressed is silent. This is the case when the Duke addresses the Count's envoy in "My Last Duchess," for example. If the performer decides that this "you" is present at the time of utterance, he or she must be sure to keep this silent auditor alive by imagining what the auditor may be doing and reacting to this when speaking.

Employ *open focus* when a speaker seems to be addressing a group of people who will in some way learn or benefit from what the speaker has to say. When a group "you" is addressed and the selection does not seem too personal or intimate, the speaker uses open focus and addresses the general audience. The performer must identify who this general audience might be by examining, for example, the language employed and the subject matter.

Use *inner-closed focus* when the speaker is addressing himself or herself as "you." If a "you" is referred to who is not the speaker and is not physically present (e.g., I think of you whenever it looks like rain), employ inner-closed focus if the performer decides that this "you" is not being apostrophized but merely thought of or remembered.

The lists which follow contain suggestions for using the four types of focus just discussed. Refer to them when you need help using any particular type of focus.

Suggestions for using open focus

1. If the speaker seems to be aware of a general audience and is consciously addressing them, be sure to look at everyone individually.
2. If the speaker seems aware of the audience but is concerned with a past memory or a self-assessment, use less direct eye contact with the audience.
3. Unless the speaker desires to create some discomfort, avoid prolonged eye contact with an audience member.
4. When using sensory showing, be sure to capture the image and share it with the audience.

Suggestions for using closed focus

1. When addressing another character, place him or her out front at eye level. Raise the level if the person is taller than the speaking character; lower it slightly if he or she is shorter or is seated.
2. When addressing another character, work on keeping that silent character alive through the responses of the speaking character.
3. When more than one character speaks, character placement is necessary to keep the speakers separated and to allow for the suggestion of movement and interaction.
4. When using sensory showing, be sure to capture the image and share it with the auditor (listener) created in the text.

Suggestions for using inner-closed focus

1. Look around the room, above the heads of audience members.
2. Avoid staring at the ground, as this directs energy to and establishes the scene on the floor.
3. Remember that even though the speaker may be unaware of a general or specific audience, the literature still must be heard and the performer still must be seen.
4. When using sensory showing, be sure to capture the image and allow the speaker to share it with himself or herself.

Suggestions for using semi-closed focus

1. Find a place for the apostrophized auditor to be. This should usually be some place directly out front, above the audience members' heads.
2. Do not stare too fixedly at the apostrophized auditor. Mediate between implied audience and self.
3. Analyze your text carefully to determine when the speaker is figuratively addressing the auditor and when the speaker is merely thinking aloud.
4. When using sensory showing, be sure to capture the image and then decide if the speaker is sharing it with himself or herself or with the apostrophized auditor.

Class Exercise

Work on the following four selections, concentrating on the type of focus or the combination of types of focus required. Which type of focus—open, closed, inner-closed, or semi-closed—do you think is best for each selection? Why do you think so? Is more than one type required? Why do you think so? How does the type of focus affect the way you communicate your interpretation of a text?

SOMETIMES WHEN IT RAINS   Gcina Mhlope

Sometimes when it rains
I smile to myself
And think of times when as a child
I'd sit by myself
And wonder why people need clothes

Sometimes when it rains
I think of times
when I'd run into the rain
Shouting "Nkce—nkce mlanjana
When will I grow?
I'll grow up tomorrow!"

Sometimes when it rains
I think of times
When I watched goats
running so fast from the rain
While sheep seemed to enjoy it

Sometimes when it rains
I think of times
When we had to undress
Carry the small bundles of uniforms and books
On our heads
And cross the river after school

Sometimes when it rains
I remember times
When it would rain for hours
And fill our drum
so we didn't have to fetch water
From the river for a day or two

Sometimes when it rains
Rains for many hours without break
I think of people
who have nowhere to go
No home of their own
And no food to eat
Only rain water to drink

Sometimes when it rains
Rains for days without break

I think of mothers
Who give birth in squatter camps
Under plastic shelters
At the mercy of cold angry winds

Sometimes when it rains
I think of "illegal" job seekers
in big cities
Dodging police vans in the rain
Hoping for darkness to come
So they can find some wet corner to hide in

Sometimes when it rains
Rains so hard hail joins in
I think of life prisoners
in all the jails of the world
And wonder if they still love
To see the rainbow at the end of the rain

Sometimes when it rains
With hail stones biting the grass
I can't help thinking they look like teeth
Many teeth of smiling friends
Then I wish that everyone else
Had something to smile about.

From THE ROCKING-HORSE WINNER   D. H. Lawrence

Although they lived in style, they felt always an anxiety in the house. There was never enough money. The mother had a small income, and the father had a small income, but not nearly enough for the social position which they had to keep up. The father went in to town to some office. But though he had good prospects, these prospects never materialized. There was always the grinding sense of the shortage of money, though the style was always kept up.

From A MIDSUMMER NIGHT'S DREAM   William Shakespeare

Hermia:	Why, get you gone. Who is't that hinders you?
Helena:	A foolish heart, that I leave here behind.
Hermia:	What, with Lysander?
Helena:	With Demetrius.
Lysander:	Be not afraid, she shall not harm thee, Helena.
Demetrius:	No, sir; she shall not, though you take her part.
Helena:	Oh, when she is angry, she is keen and shrewd!
	She was a vixen when she went to school;
	And though she be but little, she is fierce.

SONG   John Donne

Go, and catch a falling star,
   Get with child a mandrake root,
Tell me, where all past years are,
   Or who cleft the devil's foot,
Teach me to hear mermaids singing,
Or to keep off envy's stinging,
       And find
       What wind
Serves to advance an honest mind.

If thou be'st born to strange sights,
   Things invisible to see,
Ride ten thousand days and nights,
   Till age snow white hairs on thee,
Thou, when thou return'st, wilt tell me
All strange wonders that befell thee,
       And swear
       Nowhere
Lives a woman true, and fair.

If thou find'st one, let me know,
   Such a pilgrimage were sweet;
Yet do not, I would not go,
   Though at next door we might meet,
Though she were true, when you met her,
And last, till you write your letter,
       Yet she
       Will be
False, ere I come, to two, or three.

Remember, focus, or where to look, is based on who seems to be addressed. Is the information private? How does that affect the type of focus you use? Is the information public? Is it for the benefit of the speaker alone? Or for the benefit of another? Does the information further the action? In many instances (especially in modally mixed prose fiction), you may need to use a combination of focus. Experiment with shifts in focus by reading aloud the following from Stephen King's "Children of the Corn." All four types of focus are required to perform this passage.

From CHILDREN OF THE CORN   Stephen King

His eyes widened.

My God, there aren't any weeds!

Not a single one. Every foot and a half the corn plants rose from the earth. There was no witchgrass, jimson, pikeweed, whore's hair, or poke salad. Nothing.

Burt stared up, eyes wide. The light in the west was fading. The raftered clouds had drawn back together. Below them the golden light had faded to pink and ocher. It would be dark soon enough.

It was time to go down to the clearing in the corn and see what was there—hadn't that been the plan all along? All the time he had thought he was cutting back to the highway, hadn't he been being led to this place?

Dread in his belly, he went on down to the row and stood at the edge of the clearing. There was enough light left for him to see what was here. He couldn't scream. There didn't seem to be enough air left in his lungs. He tottered in on legs like slats of splintery wood. His eyes bulged from his sweaty face.

"Vicky," he whispered, "Oh, Vicky, my god—"

From "Children of the Corn," copyright 1977 by Stephen King, which appeared in *Nightshift* by Stephen King. Reprinted by permission of Doubleday & Company, Inc.

Character Placement

One additional aspect of focus (specifically closed focus) is *character placement*. This technique is employed when two or more characters speak dialogue, and it involves the projection of the characters out into an imagined scene in and directly above the audience. Character placement is a solo performance *convention* used to help keep the characters in a scene differentiated by supplying each of them with his or her own particular place in space. When a performer uses character placement, each character who speaks a line of dialogue receives a specific, permanent place from which to speak. This placement never changes, regardless of where characters move (unless they permanently exit) or to whom they speak. You place characters according to who is speaking, and the speaking character imagines those being addressed from his or her placement. When you use character placement, you will want to remember certain factors.

1. Place characters out in the audience, directly above audience members' heads. Do not place characters on the back wall, in each corner of the room, on the ceiling, on the floor, or onstage to your extreme left and right. If you place them on the wall, they will seem to be flat and one-dimensional. If you place them in each corner, timing and cue pickup will be affected by the need to turn your head to the extreme left and right. If you place them on the ceiling, they will seem like giants, and if you place them on the floor, they will seem like midgets! If you place them on stage, you will be forced to turn your complete body profile which neither character is doing and which means the audience only sees half your face. Raise or lower placement when characters are not on the same level and when you wish to show height differences. Vary the angle slightly to suggest speaking to a character who is slightly left or right of another character previously addressed.

2. In general, place the most important character (or the character with the most lines in your scene) in the center and the other characters to the left and right of the major character. If there are only two characters in the scene, place them left and right of center.

3. If you use a script, look down at it while a character is speaking but not during shifts between characters. There must be no dead space between speeches as you search to find the next line. Looking down at the script between lines of dialogue puts you in the middle of the scene!

4. Keep the silent characters alive by reflecting their responses in the voice and body of the speaking character. If the speaking character says, "Sit down and hand me the telephone," you can suggest the actions of the silent character by first lowering your focus as you "watch" the silent character sit and then reaching out as if to accept the telephone.

5. Do not consistently stare at one fixed spot. Establish the speaking character's placement as the line begins, then feel free to deviate from that fixed spot as people do in normal conversation. As long as it is clear exactly who is speaking and to whom, you need not maintain constant focus between speaker and audience.

6. Place characters who speak, and not those who are being addressed. If, for example, there are forty characters in your scene but only three characters speak, you need only three placements.

7. Do not give narrators a placement—unless they speak dialogue. Since narrators are usually speaking to the audience and not to characters, their focus is open, and they require no placement.

8. Once you have placed a character in a certain spot during a dialogue exchange, keep the character in that spot regardless of time or place shifts

and regardless of the character's audience. This does not mean that you cannot move during the performance. If movement is motivated, feel free to move. The placements may move slightly, but will remain in their relative position to each other—the character in the middle is still in the middle although this middle placement may have shifted slightly left or right.

9. Be careful not to catch the eyes of audience members. When you use closed focus, be sure that you keep the situation closed off from the audience.

10. Do not place the characters too far apart. Keep them close enough together so that there is no dead space as you move from one character's line of dialogue to another's. You may place characters with your eyes; you needn't use large, distracting movements of your head or body.

Dissolve Technique

Some experienced performers find the convention of character placement awkward and artificial. For more advanced students who have mastered the art of character differentiation, you might try the *dissolve* technique. With dissolve, one character simply begins speaking when the previous character finishes with no artificial shift of placement. In film, the dissolve is "a transition in which the old shot gradually fades as the new shot appears."[3] Nowadays, films such as *The Terminator* have used the idea of "morphing" as one character seems to become another before our eyes.

Translated into solo performance terminology, when you use the dissolve technique, one character appears as another character finishes speaking. There is no shift in placement or in focus; there is simply the transformation of one character into the other. If, for example, you are performing a scene with Bob and Mary, you need not worry about who is placed right of center and who is placed left of center—both are located center. Bob takes stage when he speaks. When he finishes speaking, Mary takes stage. As with the technique of character placement, one character begins to speak and act at the moment and place where the last character finished. If, for example, Bob finishes his line with his hands on his hips, when Mary speaks, she must begin from that position as she begins her line. Actor John Leguizamo employed this technique in his New York, one-man show *Freak*. Critic Ben Brantley described the actor's "sleight of character" in his 1998 *New York Times* review, "Mr. Leguizamo carries on four- and five-person dialogues without any noticeable clicks of transition. One moment he is clearly and unconditionally one person; one moment he's another."

This advanced technique works only if the characters in the scene are so clearly differentiated physically, vocally, and mentally that the audience can easily tell them apart without the need for artificial placements. Experiment with this technique after you have mastered character placement.

Class Exercise

Practice character placement by performing the following scene from Shakespeare's *Much Ado About Nothing.* You will need two placements, one for Beatrice and one for Benedick.

From MUCH ADO ABOUT NOTHING   William Shakespeare

Beatrice: Against my will I am sent to bid you come in to dinner.
Benedick: Fair Beatrice, I thank you for your pains.
Beatrice: I took no more pains for those thanks than you take pains to thank me. If it had been painful I would not have come.
Benedick: You take pleasure, then, in the message?
Beatrice: Yea, just so much as you may take upon a knife's point and choke a daw withal. You have no stomach, Signor? Fare you well.

If you feel that you have mastered characterization and do not need to use artificial placements, try employing the dissolve technique on the passage above.

Time and Place Changes

The last aspect of focus concerns shifts in time and place (for example, "The next morning," "We left the kitchen and entered the den"). In many pieces of literature, time passes, and speakers move from one place to another. These shifts are normally transitional moments during which the speaker takes us from one setting or time frame to another. To suggest these changes, try one or any combination of the following performance analogues: pause, change vocal inflection, move to your right or to your left (moving to one side usually suggests change or transition while moving forward, for example, usually adds emphasis). The type of focus you employ for these changes depends upon the speaker/audience situation. If it is an epic line, you address the shift to the audience using open focus. If it is a dramatic line, you address the shift to the character being addressed with closed focus and character placement. If the line is lyric, a time or place shift may indicate a shift in the speaker's thought process which could be indicated in performance by a shifting of your inner-closed or semi-closed focus.

Read this passage from William Faulkner's short story "Barn Burning." The italicized passages in this selection contain time and place changes. See if you can make these shifts clear in performance. The passage seem to be epic, which means that you will probably want to shift where you look within the open focus of the narrator. Try some of the performance analogues suggested above to make the shifts in time and place clear. On "Two hours later," for example, try moving to one side or the other while changing your vocal inflection to suggest that time has passed and that the boy is now in a different place. Take a pause before "and a moment later" to allow for a short passage of time. This passage also calls for much sensory showing to re-create the images of the noise of the horses, the "linen-clad man," the "fine sorrel mare," and so on. See if you can perform the passage using pause, vocal inflection, or physical movement to suggest time or place changes.

From BARN BURNING   William Faulkner

Two hours later the boy was chopping wood behind the house within which his mother and aunt and the two sisters . . . were setting up the stove to prepare a meal, when he heard the hooves and saw the linen-clad man on a fine sorrel mare, whom he recognized even before he saw the rolled rug in front of the Negro youth following on a fat bay carriage horse—a suffused, angry face vanishing, still at full gallop, beyond the corner of the house where his father and brother were sitting in the two tilted chairs; and *a moment later,* almost before he could have put the axe down, he heard the hooves again and watched the sorrel mare go back out of the yard, already galloping again. [Italics added]

From "Barn Burning" in *Collected Stories of William Faulkner,* by William Faulkner. Copyright 1939 and renewed 1967 by Estelle Faulkner and Jill Faulkner Summers. Reprinted by permission of Random House, Inc.

TENSIVENESS

Tensiveness, a term coined by Philip Wheelwright, refers to the elements within a literary text which give it life. According to Wheelwright, "The openness of language, so far as it exists, is valuable only potentially, only so far as it enables the language to be alive." Wheelwright continues, "In all organic life there is a ceaseless but varying struggle between opposite forces, and without such struggle the organism would go dead."[4] The contrasting rhythms, the movements in and out of characters' minds, the combination of different sounds and images, and the conflict situations within and between characters are examples of tensive elements. As you perform a text, you want to feel and project these tensive elements. When you are able to understand what in the literature causes its pulse to beat and its heart to pound, you are getting at the life of the text—its tensiveness. When you show this tensiveness in the literature during your performance, you are being responsive to the contrasting sounds, ideas, images, and rhythms in a text.

    As you study the speaker in your text, ask yourself what the tensive situation is.

According to renowned actor, teacher, and director Jeff Corey, in almost every literary text there is a problem to solve, and this problem helps further the action and keep the characters alive. The problem may be obvious or may be something a character is hiding. A religious man, for example, may be fighting the profane side of himself. A psychiatrist may be struggling against subjectivity. A sane woman might be fighting against the impulse to go mad.

Tensiveness arises in prose fiction as the narrator manipulates time. The narrator must decide how to recount the events of the story he or she relates. Narrators can re-create events exactly as they happened, hurry over seemingly unimportant details, or magnify certain details to give them added significance. These choices produce tensiveness to which the performer must respond. In drama, tensiveness arises when one character's needs or desires conflict with another character's needs or desires. This conflict is the lifeblood of drama, and the performer's response to it brings out the tensive situation. The surface rhythmic structure of a poem often produces tensiveness—the alternation of stressed and unstressed syllables (ta Da, ta Da, ta Da . . .). The performer's attention to rhythmic variations is, again, a response to tensiveness.

Immediately before actors walk onstage, they often feel a sense of anticipation, of conscious awareness and physical alertness, an adrenalin rush that lasts throughout the performance. The public speaker also experiences this sense of tautness, of readiness; solo performers, too, experience this sense of exhilaration. The performance situation itself causes this response in the performer—this feeling of being a live pin cushion! When you are responsive, you are physically, mentally, and emotionally prepared to perform—you have a "sense of performance." Every part of your body feels wired to some central circuit that keeps you charged up as adrenalin pumps through you. When you can match your exhilaration and sense of being alive with the rhythms and contrasts you sense in the text, you are being responsive to the tensiveness of the piece.

Do not confuse *tensiveness* with *tension.* Tensiveness is the lifeblood of a literary text—the existence of contrasts within it. Tension is caused by worry, fear, or anxiety and is *not* a necessary part of all performances. When you are unprepared, not in control of your nerves, tired, listless, or lack concentration, you might feel tension, and your ability to be responsive fails.

You show the tensiveness in a text when you are able to project the conflict situation in your selection. You show the tensiveness as you re-create the imagined scene out in the audience. You show the tensiveness when you respond completely to the language the author uses. Words like "joy," "sadness," "love," "slapped," "hopped," "wondered," and "kissed" have certain attendant responses. Try to show these responses (without being forced or literal) both in your voice and in your body. How does your voice sound and your body feel when you say "joy" as opposed to "sadness"? Reread the paragraph from Faulkner's "Barn Burning" and try to respond to the tensive language in the passage.

COPING WITH PERFORMANCE ANXIETY
OR STAGE FRIGHT

Everyone who performs experiences some form of stage fright as we discussed in Chapter 1. Even though stage fright is a common affliction, handling or coping with it is not easy. There is a reason why most people's biggest fear is public speaking—right up there with root canals. Our brains are telling our bodies that we are in a classic fight-or-flight situation. When we stand in front of an audience, our survival mechanism is trying to decide whether to wrestle them or run like mad out of the room.

Stage fright increases with uncertain expectations, novel situations, or unpredictability such as you might experience with your initial or early performances. This is why instructors often make these early performances ungraded. The formality of some solo performance situations where there seems little margin for deviation from performance conventions also may cause high levels of stage fright, because of public embarrassment or humiliation. Evaluation from peers and professor also increases stage fright. Frequent exposure to public speaking/performance situations helps to alleviate some stage fright.

Virginia P. Richmond and James C. McCrosky write much on this topic. They believe that communication apprehension (stage fright) involves a wide variety of personality characteristics including general anxiety, tolerance for ambiguity (uncertainty), emotional/psychological self-control, adventurousness (appreciation for diverse and new situations), emotional maturity, introversion versus extroversion, self-esteem, innovativeness (ability to accept change), tolerance for disagreement, and assertiveness.[5] Knowing how you react when meeting new people, when going on a job interview, when giving a presentation, as examples, can predict your level of communication apprehension.

> The lower the level of communication apprehension, the less the feeling of discomfort. People with low communication apprehension will still have physiological arousal about communicating, but their internal feeling is one of pleasure, not one of discomfort such as the high communication apprehension person experiences. The internal feeling the high communication apprehension individual experiences is one of discomfort, fright, being unable to cope, being inadequate, and possibly being dumb. Common physiological effects associated with this internal fear might be rapid beating of the heart, queasy stomach, increased perspiration, some shakiness, and dry mouth.[6]

The best solution for coping with stage fright is to be prepared, that is, to rehearse your selection often over an extended period of time. Some performers do not feel that they know their selections well enough unless they can perform them while listening to music. Performers have many different techniques for dealing with their performance anxiety. Some rehearse in front of close friends (one student then brought two of these friends to class because seeing them in the audience gave her comfort and confidence); some rehearse before strangers (to emulate more closely the situation in the classroom). Here are some suggestions for handling some of the more physiological problems you might experience. If your voice is quavering or shaky, try projecting it to the very back row of the audience. When you force that extra air out of your lungs, your voice wavers less. If your hands are shaky, try to move them, point, or employ natural gestures. If your legs or knees are shaking, move—walk around when the text calls for movement. If the speakers in your text are sitting, you could sit. If your heart is pounding, take a few deep breaths as your body requires more oxygen when you are nervous. If you are concerned about perspiring, use talcum powder on your hands and body. If you suffer from dry mouth, drink room-temperature water (a slice of lemon helps) and avoid caffeine, sugar, soda, alcohol, and milk products. A light coat of Vaseline on your teeth will keep them from sticking to your lips.

Students in a beginning performance studies class reported using the following techniques to help them control their stage fright:

> In the classroom setting, before a performance, my nerves get to me until I take a moment to think: hey, this isn't an audition. I'm not competing with these people—we are all in the same boat. This is about self-improvement and not about trying to be better than anyone else. That relaxes me.

> I try to put my performance into context by asking myself, What is the worst thing that could happen to me and how would I deal with that? That seems to work for me.

> I need time to prepare and know what I'm doing well in advance. Being prepared gets rid of a lot of my stage fright.

> The best way to overcome stage fright for me is to know my material—once I've got that down, the rest is all in my mind. I used to try to mentally run through the lines while others were performing, but that never worked. The best thing is to just sit back, relax, and enjoy everyone else's performances. Then, when you get up there, breathe, know that you've got the material down, and just relax! Enjoy your time up there and you'll do just fine.

> Before I go onstage to sing, speak, dance, whatever, I chew a piece of gum (usually [sugarfree] spearmint), and then right before I perform, I take a deep breath and spit out my gum (and my nerves) as hard as I can into the garbage.

If none of the above relieves your anxiety, you may need more extreme cures like hypnosis, meditation, biofeedback, prescription antianxiety drugs, or deep muscle relaxation techniques.

Remember that feeling some anxiety is normal; it is the body's means of preparing for a challenging situation. Channel that increased adrenaline flow into the energy necessary for performance. Without this, performances would be dull and lifeless.

MEETING THE AUDIENCE

The performance techniques we have articulated so far should be useful to you during both rehearsal and performance. There are, however, some specific adjustments that you must make during performance before an audience (an audience other than yourself). Your adjustment to the audience involves choice of selection, relation to the actual and implied audience, and specific performance adaptations.

In a classroom, your choice of selection is usually up to you and your particular tastes and interests. Your only restrictions are usually to select a text that you really want to perform, that you believe is good literature, that represents a prescribed genre, and that fits a certain time limit. Since, however, you will be performing before others, you might want to consider what would be of interest to your audience. If you pick a selection of potential interest to the other students in your class, you increase their attention and participation as audience members and evaluators.

If you perform for a group outside the classroom, other considerations may affect your choice. If you are asked to perform for a certain occasion (Thanksgiving, Christmas, or Mother's Day, for example), obviously your choice will have to adhere to the specific theme. If you are asked to perform for a club or organization, ask someone in charge to describe the nature of the audience. How many people will attend? What is the age range of the audience members? Why do these people meet together? Although it is dangerous to assume that a woman's club would prefer one type of literature, Boy Scouts another, and members of the Veterans of Foreign Wars yet another, it is useful to know as much as possible about your audience so you can choose material that at least the majority of your audience will appreciate.

You should also adjust your performance according to the actual audience (the people in the room who are listening to you perform) and the implied audience (the audience the speaker has in mind for this particular work). When you deliver the introduction, people watch you, trying to understand. Be aware of them. They may be sending you messages of comprehension or confusion. If it appears that something you are saying confuses them, reword or reexplain that aspect of your introduction so that it is clear. Are people craning their necks because they cannot see you; move so that everyone can see you. If you choose to sit, for example, be sure to place the chair where everyone can easily see you. You may have to ask everyone to move back or sit in a semicircle to enable adequate visibility.

If the delivery of your introduction is extemporaneous, you should be flexible enough to adjust to the actual audience's *feedback*—their verbal or nonverbal responses.

Once you get into the performance, your responsibility is to try to imagine the actual audience as the implied audience the speaker is addressing. This needs to be considered whenever the general audience is directly addressed as by the narrator in prose fiction, drama, or poetry. There is probably no text in which a speaker addresses an audience of performance studies students; consequently, just as you transform yourself into the speaker in the text, the audience appreciates knowing who you imagine them to be. In the short story, "Why I Live at the P.O.," for example, the narrator, Sister, addresses tourists who have come into the China Grove, Mississippi, post office to transact some business and are trapped into listening to Sister's tale of woe. When Che, the narrator in the musical *Evita,* addresses the audience, he does not think he is talking to a group of theatergoers. He addresses the people of Argentina—probably middle-class revolutionaries. The speaker in Shakespeare's sonnet "My Mistress' Eyes Are Nothing like the Sun" addresses an audience of people who hold the conventional view of beauty in that day (fair complected, with blonde hair and blue eyes) and tries to convince them that his mistress looks nothing like that, but is still beautiful in his eyes. Occasionally, the speaker refers to the audience directly, using the pronoun "you," as we stated earlier. The performer must decide who this "you" might be. How can you help the audience know who you imagine them to be? One way performers can do this is to make the audience's role clear in the introduction, and then relate to them during the performance with this particular audience in mind. More will be said about this in Chapters 6, 7, and 8.

The third adjustment the performer must make when he or she meets the audience involves performance techniques. When you rehearse your selection alone, you are usually in a small room, and one style of performance is called for. When you change environments and face an audience, your performance alters.

In general, keep the following in mind when you meet the audience. Your performance begins the moment you rise from your seat to give your presentation. If you have to tuck in your shirt or blouse or otherwise readjust your clothing or hair, do so before you stand up. Approach the front of the class with a confident step and a smile—even if you do not feel like smiling! Look at everyone freely and frankly, and deliver your introduction (should you decide to give an introduction). After doing so, pause, look down to check your script (if you use one), look up again, and begin the performance of the text. Make sure you know your selection well enough to establish the scene offstage. Make sure you adapt and adjust, where possible, to audience feedback. As you come to the end of your performance, it is usually a good idea to slow down the last line and pause again to indicate that the performance is over and to give the audience a sense of closure (if you desire to do so).

It is important to consider your responsibilities not only as a performer but also as the witness to other performers. Chapter 5 will explain your role as audience member and as an evaluator.

SUMMARY

One of the essential elements of the interpretation experience is the introduction. Introductions attempt to capture and intrigue the audience—to make them want to listen. An introduction should include the title of the selection and the name of the author and should carve out your interpretation. It should set an appropriate mood, relate any necessary biographical or critical information, define the audience if they are addressed, and explain what has happened before your scene takes place if you are not performing the entire work. The introduction prepares you to perform, prepares the audience for your selection, and allows the audience to see you as yourself before you create the speaker(s) in the work. Your delivery of the introduction should be or seem extemporaneous, and you should look directly at the audience as you deliver it trying to maintain a natural delivery style.

When you are deciding on a performance style, always rely on clues in the text to determine whether to use a script or a lectern and to determine what to cut. Vocal and physical responsiveness involves knowing how to alter your speaking voice and your body to suggest speakers in literary texts who in some large or small way are different from you. The text itself also gives you clues about whom to empathize or sympathize with as well as how much aesthetic distance to maintain, what focus to use, and the degree of tensiveness and sensory showing required. Rehearse often and over an extended period of time to minimize and control stage fright.

When you meet the audience, remember to be ready for performance from the moment you walk to the front of the room. Pause, deliver your introduction, pause again, and begin your selection, establishing the scene out front. As you perform, try to be conscious of audience feedback.

Notes

1. William L. Nance, *Katherine Anne Porter and The Art of Rejection* (Chapel Hill: University of North Carolina Press, 1964), pp. 43–44.
2. Robert L. Benedetti, *The Actor at Work,* 3rd ed. (Englewood Cliffs, NJ: Prentice Hall, 1981), p. 53.
3. Morris Beja, *Film & Literature: An Introduction* (New York: Longman, 1979), p. 46.
4. Philip Wheelwright, *Metaphor and Reality* (Bloomington: Indiana University Press, 1962), p. 45.
5. Virginia P. Richmond and James C. McCroskey, *Communication: Apprehension, Avoidance, and Effectiveness,* 2nd ed. (Scottsdale, AZ: Gorsuch Scarisbrick, 1989), pp. 47–52.
6. Ibid, p. 59.

se.] Damn it! It makes me nervous.

Christina. You have to make the most of it.

Smith [*looks all around again*]. Say, do you suppose—
mean, he hasn't stopped us from kissing—do you think
that——

    Christina. Right here on stage?

Smith. But it's the only way.

Christina. No.

Smith. Do you say that because of him?

Christina. No, it's just that——

Smith. You can be modest at a desperate time like this?

Christina. No, it's the censorship laws.

Smith. Ah! Damn the censors!

Christina. I'm sorry.

Smith. Look, why don't we just go offstage for
while——

    Christina. And leave the audience alone?

Smith [*looking out at the audience*]. They're not alone
They have plenty of company. [*To the audience.*] Look
why don't you talk to each other for a few minutes, or—
or go out for a smoke or something?

    Christina. The show must go on.

Smith. Rules! All these rules are killing me.

Christina. You make a beautiful martyr.

Smith. That's small compensation. I feel trapped on
this stage. I feel like I'm suffocating.

    Christina. It wouldn't work anyway. As soon as we step
off this stage, it's the end of our lives.

    Smith [*embracing her suddenly*]. My God, you're right
[*They look out together—two against the world, then h*

As we previously stated, the basic components of the interpretation process are a performer (you), a text, and an audience. The first four chapters of Part 1 focused on you and the text; this chapter focuses on the third aspect of the interpretation experience: the audience. In reality, you will probably spend more time in your class acting the roles of audience member and evaluator than the role of performer, so it is essential that these roles receive more than passing mention.

Although you are always your own audience in interpretation—listening to yourself, making discoveries, altering decisions, evaluating each rehearsal and performance—this chapter will focus on your role as audience for and evaluator of the performances of others. Much of what we say concerning your role as audience will be useful to you when you listen to and appraise your own performances.

YOUR RESPONSIBILITIES AS AN AUDIENCE MEMBER

Your responsibilities as an audience member are composed of four distinct but related functions: *to listen, to constitute, to accept,* and *to respond.* In other words, audience members must be prepared to listen attentively, to create their impression of what they see and hear, to be objective and open-minded, and to provide feedback. Let us analyze each of these related functions.

Your Role as Audience: To Listen

Listening is a skill which must be developed. Whereas *hearing* is a natural physiological process, listening is a psychological or mental process which demands practice and concentration. Although we spend 40 to 50 percent of our day engaged in listening activities, we know very little about the process. We hear sounds, but we must learn how to make sense of them. As an audience member, your first responsibility is to listen—to give the reader your full attention. This, however, is not as easy as it sounds.

We stress the importance of listening because the interpreter depends on, expects to have, and deserves a receptive audience. One of the reasons interpreters perform is to share their discovery of a text with an audience. We owe them our attention, but barriers often get in the way. The barriers are real and can prevent sharing from taking place; you must want to overcome the barriers and consciously work at surmounting them to be a good listener.

The barriers to good listening fall into three categories: *external* barriers, which are situational; *internal* barriers, which are audience centered; and *semantic* barriers, which are text or performance centered. What causes each of these barriers and how can each best be overcome?

External barriers

External barriers are disturbances that exist inside or outside the communication environment. External barriers also exist within a performer. The following are some situations which can cause external barriers:

1. The temperature in the room is too hot or too cold.
2. There is noise or disturbance outside the room.
3. The lights in the room are too bright, too dim, or flickering.
4. The performer speaks too fast or too slow, has a speech defect, moves around too much, jangles pocket change, is too loud or soft, cannot be seen, or wears distracting apparel.
5. A noise or disturbance occurs inside the room.

When any of these situations (or many others) occur, communication between interpreter and audience is inhibited.

Performers can anticipate and correct some external disturbances prior to the performance. They can select clothes with care (preferably with no writing on them), and they can check the lights, the seating arrangement, and the acoustics of the room ahead of time. The audience members can avoid some external barriers by adjusting to the temperature, closing the doors, ignoring outside stimuli, changing seats, or by doing anything that helps them to concentrate. Concentration is the key to improving communication and eliminating barriers. The performer can help by anticipating barriers; audience members can help by not causing disturbances and by not letting barriers distract them—by concentrating.

Internal barriers

Another kind of barrier that can occur during a performance results from an internal situation. An internal barrier exists within an audience member and can be just as harmful as an external barrier in preventing communication from occurring. The following are some situations that cause internal barriers:

1. The audience member has to perform the same day and is too nervous, upset, or scared to listen.
2. The audience member has just performed and is too relieved, excited, or anxious to listen.
3. The audience member stayed up too late and is too tired to listen.
4. The audience member has just experienced a major excitement or disturbance and is thinking of that instead of listening.

The best counter for internal barriers is the desire to listen. If you decide that the performer has something valuable and worthwhile to share and you might miss something important, your listening is sharpened. You must want to listen well. Once again, concentration is important. If your point of concentration is on the performance and not on yourself, your listening skills will improve. Of course, the performer, too, can eliminate internal barriers by motivating and maintaining audience interest.

Semantic barriers

The last kind of barrier that can occur is called a semantic barrier. Semantic barriers are text-centered or performance-centered barriers. The following are some situations causing semantic barriers:

1. The selection is too easy or too familiar, and the listener tunes it out.
2. The selection is too difficult or complex.
3. The selection is confusing because the performer did not adequately prepare the audience for it in the introduction.
4. The selection is one for which the listener has a conflicting interpretation that makes listening difficult.

To overcome these barriers, you may have to ask the performer for clarification before the performance begins, if this is possible. If it is not possible, you must try to objectify your response. If the text is too easy or too familiar, convince yourself that there may be something new in the selection or something that this performer may bring to the text that is different. If the selection seems too difficult or too complex, try even harder to listen. Remember, some texts—in fact, many texts— cannot be totally understood after only one hearing. Often we need to hear a selection again and again before we can begin to come to terms with it. If a selection is difficult, get what you can after one exposure. Then, read the selection yourself and spend some time analyzing it. A really good performance sends audience members to read the text for themselves.

In general, minimize semantic barriers by being objective and open-minded. Work with the performer as he or she performs; this brings us to your second responsibility as an audience member.

Your Role as Audience: To Constitute

In Chapter 1 we spoke of the empowerment the reader has been given in determining what a text has to say. Meaning forms in the reader, not in the black marks on the white page. If this is true of the reader, it is also true of the audience. Just as performers devise their understanding of texts and reveal that understanding through performance, each audience member devises his or her own understanding depending on background, past experiences, interests, preoccupations, and so forth. We call this *constituting* meaning. While the performer performs, the audience also performs by creating meaning.

To constitute meaning, the audience obviously must be paying close attention and must be willing to participate in the creation of the characters, setting, and other elements in their imaginations. The interpreter depends upon the involvement of the audience. In a play performance, for example, the playwright expects certain elements of spectacle to accompany the production: set, costumes, lights, make-up, and so on. The interpreter suggests the sense of more than one character, suggests the scenery and set pieces in the hope that audience members' natural ability to imagine will flesh out the suggested elements. Were a solo performer to do the balcony scene from *Romeo and Juliet,* the performer would hope that audience members would constitute their conceptions of the balcony, the appropriate make-up and costumes, the nighttime garden setting, and Romeo as well as Juliet. The audience, then, performs and creates, just as the performer does.

Your Role as Audience: To Accept

Your third responsibility is related to the points we made concerning the desire to listen. When you *accept* a performance, this means that you are giving the performer the chance to communicate his or her unique interpretation with you. Try to minimize barriers and eliminate all prejudices as you listen. You may not like the performer or the selection, you may not immediately understand the selection, or you may know the selection and have what you believe to be a better interpretation. Regardless of your relationship with the performer or with the selection, try to get as much as you can out of the performance by maintaining an open mind in regard to a literary selection that may not personally appeal to you or to an interpretation you do not agree with. It is from our ability to maintain an open mind, coupled with our desire to learn, that we gain new information and new insights as we empathize with the attitudes and beliefs of another. You get the experience of doing something by watching someone else do it.

Acceptance will make your evaluation of the performance more meaningful for the performer. Acceptance means that you are listening to the performer's interpretation with enough objectivity to be able to describe later what you heard and saw—not what you would have done or your negative reaction to the text being performed. Be receptive: this is the way you grow. As already stated many times, if a selection has universality, individuality, and suggestion, it can be interpreted in more than one way. Allow the performer to investigate alternatives with you.

Your Role as Audience: To Respond

Your last responsibility as an audience member is to be actively receptive, to *respond*. This means you give the performer *feedback* during a performance.

Feedback involves sending messages to the performer that indicate your reaction to the performance. There are two basic kinds of feedback that can be sent during a performance: situational feedback and text- or performance-centered feedback.

If, for example, you cannot see or hear the performer, what kind of nonverbal response can you send that will communicate this to the performer? Although you may think this action is potentially distracting, most performers would be grateful to receive such helpful information. This first kind of feedback is situational feedback.

The second kind of feedback is text- or performance-centered. In Chapter 4, we explained how the interpreter tries to transform the actual audience into the implied audience in the text. The speaker in a text usually has some specific listener(s) in mind. As you become this implied audience, you help the interpreter by giving the kind of feedback appropriate for the implied audience. Laughs, nods, sighs, applause—whatever you think is expected or you feel motivated to give—can be involved in this kind of feedback.

Some of your responsibilities, problems, and challenges as audience members are summarized here:

Responsibilities: To Listen   To Constitute   To Accept   To Respond
Problems: External Barriers   Internal Barriers   Semantic Barriers
Challenges: Concentrate   Be Objective   Participate

YOUR RESPONSIBILITIES AS AN EVALUATOR

Often you are given the opportunity to let performers know how well you think they interpreted the text. Although we would all probably prefer to be told we are wonderful and need no improvement, we can all benefit from honest, constructive criticism. Artists work constantly to express the fullest potential of their medium of expression. What better way can there be to determine at least a portion of that potential than by gaining thoughtful feedback from the audience? As your performance is evaluated, receive the evaluation in the spirit in which it is intended. We want to help you discover your potential, and our suggestions are aimed toward that end.

The role of evaluator is difficult for many beginning interpreters. They often do not believe they know enough to respond to another's performance, or they may be convinced that their contribution is not important. They sometimes worry that if they are too critical they will alienate the performer. The responsibility of evaluating is aided when the performer states in the introduction his or her interpretation of the text. When this is done, the evaluator should ask if the performance manifested the interpretation articulated in the introduction. Evaluators then need not feel compelled to say how they interpret selections, but instead can focus on what the performers intended and how well those intentions came through in performance. The following suggestions are meant to aid you in the evaluation process.

General Guidelines for Evaluation

As you participate in an evaluation session, keep in mind that the interpreter depends on your reactions to aid him or her in preparing additional presentations of the same selection and in preparing future performances. Even though you may be a beginning interpreter, you have something important to contribute. Audiences are very rarely composed of skilled interpreters! Audiences are primarily made up of people like you. Everyone is entitled to an opinion—especially if that opinion is supported. Critical comments are always useful to the interpreter if they are honest, constructive, tactfully given, and supported with reasons for making them. It is never enough merely to say "I liked it" or "I didn't like it." The interpreter needs to know *why*. You must verbalize your responses and explain your critical position carefully to be of maximum benefit to the performer. The most essential aspect of evaluation is to remember what the performer said in the introduction as to what he or she intended to do in the performance and relate your comments to that intention. In other words, your comments should focus on whether the performance demonstrated that intention. Let us examine some ways to make your role as evaluator the most beneficial.

One way to make your evaluations complete and specific is to take notes while the interpreter performs. If you are to hear a relatively few number of performances, these need be mental notes only. If, however, you are to hear many performances, you may actually want to write down your notes as unobtrusively as possible, keeping your attention on the performer. In an abbreviated form, write down what was effective and what was not as effective as specifically as you can. Write down specific lines from the text, if need be, to clarify your evaluation. The notes will help you remember what you want to say later and can be used to support your opinions.

As you prepare to participate in an evaluation session, one of the most important suggestions we can make is the following: *Analyze the performance techniques employed in terms of the interpretation.* For example, you might want to say, "I thought you spoke too rapidly," or "You were too loud," or "You were too soft," or "You stood too close to me," and so on. However, these bold statements evaluate the performance techniques without relating these techniques to the performer's particular interpretation of a text. The comment about a too-rapid pace might not be true if the interpreter were performing a scene from Eudora Welty's "Why I Live at the P.O." In this story, the narrator's (Sister's) pace is affected by the fact that she is probably speaking to an audience of impatient people who are not particularly interested in her story. The performer may feel that a rather fast pace and dramatic changes of pace are necessary to keep the audience's attention. Pace is affected by the emotional involvement of the speaker and by the situation, as well as by the performer's interpretation of the mood or atmosphere of the selection. Performance style depends on a performer's individual interpretation of a text. Good criticism relates performance choices to interpretation. Be sure that your comments specifically relate to the particular interpretation and not just to the performance techniques employed.

Keep five primary guidelines in mind when participating in an evaluation session:

1. Be objective.
2. Be specific.
3. Be constructive.
4. Be encouraging.
5. Be flexible in response styles.

If you listen to a performance with an open mind, you are being objective and are not allowing prejudices involving either the performer or the selection to get in your way. An objective evaluation focuses on the performer's unique interpretation and not on what you would have done were you to perform that same selection. Objectivity, then, is an important guideline to follow during an evaluation session.

Objectivity is related to the second guideline: be specific. Our first response to most things is subjective: either we like something, or we do not like it. The reasons behind our positive or negative response normally come after some reflection. As you observe a performance, ask yourself *why* you liked or disliked something. What did the performer do that worked? If you believe that a certain moment did not work, be specific in citing the line or lines that made up that moment. If you think a gesture was too literal, for example, tell the performer why. Work at being as descriptive as possible during the evaluation session. Comments that lack specificity are not particularly helpful to the performer.

When you evaluate, work on being constructive in your criticism. Any critical comment can be tactfully worded so that it sounds like a suggestion rather than a censure. You can say, "Your arms just remained at your sides throughout the entire performance," or you can be constructive and say, "If you had gestured more often, I might have seen the character's excitement more easily." Constructive comments suggest ways that a performance can be improved; they do not just tell a performer what he or she did "wrong." It may take a bit more time to be constructive, but your reward will be a more beneficial and appreciated evaluation.

It is always easier to say what is wrong with something, and we often tend to be too critical when we evaluate. Although it is good to be critical, it helps the performer if you can say something positive as well. There is some good in every interpretation performance. Be sure to encourage performers to keep trying by telling them not only what was wrong, but also what was right and why. Sometimes interpreters work even harder if they know there is something they do well.

Our last suggestion is to be flexible in your use of response styles. In everyday living, we are often confronted with situations in which our opinions are required. According to David W. Johnson in an interpersonal communication text entitled *Reaching Out*,[1] five types of response styles are used 80 percent of the time: Evaluative, Interpretive, Supportive, Probing, and Understanding. Let us describe each of these response styles, substituting interpretation terminology for the sender/receiver orientation Johnson employs.

Evaluative

A response that indicates that the audience member has made a judgment of relative goodness, appropriateness, effectiveness, or rightness of the performer's presentation. The audience member has in some way implied what the performer might or should do.

Interpretive

A response that indicates the audience member's intent is to teach, to tell the performer what his or her problem means, how the performer should really feel about the situation. The audience member has either obviously or subtly implied how the performer might have interpreted the text differently.

Supportive

A response that indicates the audience member's intent is to reassure, to pacify, to reduce the performer's intensity of feeling. The audience member has in some way implied that the performer should feel good about his or her performance. Use the supportive response when you want to convince performers that they did better than they may have thought. The supportive response can also be used to encourage someone to keep trying or to help alleviate future performance anxiety.

Probing

A response that indicates the audience member's intent is to seek further information, provide further discussion along a certain line, or question the performer. The audience member has in some way implied that the performer might profitably develop or discuss a point further. Use the probing response when you need more information from the performer before giving any other type of response. If the selection was particularly difficult or complex, you may want to ask questions before offering any reactions. A performer usually appreciates the opportunity to answer questions about a presentation. (Performers enjoy asking questions, too. They often want to know how what they intended was received.)

Understanding

A response that indicates the audience member's intent is to try to determine whether the audience member understood the performer's interpretation, as much as it is possible to do so. The understanding response is very valuable, but is the least employed response. With this response you do not attempt to criticize—instead you describe what you saw and heard. When you use this response, you try to paraphrase what you think the performer's interpretation was before giving any other kind of response.

Let us look at an example of how each response style might be used during a critique of a performance from Arthur Miller's *Death of a Salesman*.

Evaluative: While I thought your performance was good, I thought Willy needed to sound and look older, as he is over sixty years old.
Interpretive: I thought you needed to consider Willy's dependence on the past.
Supportive: I don't think you should feel bad about your performance. You certainly have shown improvement.
Probing: Why did Willy sit throughout the scene?
Understanding: What I saw was that you portrayed Willy as he saw himself and not as he really was.

The types of responses we normally give most often are the evaluative and the interpretive types—the kinds where we tell performers what they should have done or thought. Our general tendency, says David W. Johnson, is "to judge, evaluate, approve, or disapprove."[2] Although the evaluative and the interpretive types of responses are often necessary and useful, we should try to use all fives types of responses during an evaluation, depending on the situation and the performer. No one type of response is better than another, but a mixture of response styles can often produce the most complete kind of evaluation.

Specific Guidelines for Evaluation

The suggestions so far have been fairly general. Let us now discuss specific kinds of questions to ask if you are put in the position of leading or participating in a discussion.

Evaluating introductions

An evaluation should probably begin with a consideration of the introduction, if an introduction was given. Was it appropriate? Did it begin with an attention-getter? How well did it carve out the performer's interpretation? Did it offer enough or too much information? Did it set an appropriate mood? Was it delivered extemporaneously? If the introduction was memorized, did the performer know it well enough to concentrate on communicating and not on remembering? Did it make the audience want to listen? If an introduction was not given, was it missed? What impact did the lack of an introduction have on the performance?

Evaluating prose fiction performances

If the performance is a prose fiction selection, concentrate on questions about the narrator and his or her point of view. What was the narrator's point of view? Was the attitude of the narrator clear? Did the narrator's attitude change? Was that reflected in performance? With whom did the narrator empathize? sympathize? Was this clear? For whom did the narrator feel antipathy? Was this attitude clear? Was it clear that characters were projected through the narrator's perspective? Who was the narrator's audience? What did the narrator want or need from this audience?

Evaluating drama performances

If the performance is from a play, begin with questions involving the delineation of the characters in the scene. Were the characters vocally, physically, and emotionally distinct? What motivated the characters? How were performance techniques employed to keep the characters distinct? Could the characters performed in this scene fit back into the context of the whole play? What were the characters' goals, obstacles, and strategies?

Evaluating poetry performances

If the performance is a poem, consider first the type of poem: lyric, dramatic, or narrative (see Chapter 8) and whether the performance techniques helped to make the type of poem clear. If the poem is lyric, discuss the performer's emotional responsiveness. If the poem is dramatic, was the character(s) clearly defined? What was the conflict and how was it expressed? If the poem is a narrative, was the story line clear? Were the narrator's point of view and attitude easy to follow? Consider also how rhythm, sound, and image contributed to the aesthetic whole of the performance.

You should also consider the interpreter's "sense of performance." Did the performer communicate a desire to perform? Did he or she communicate a sense of confidence and readiness? Did the performer make you feel comfortable? Did the performer make his or her choices clear?

Discussion leaders should try to obtain copies of the selections they will evaluate and read them ahead of time. In addition, they should probably reserve their opinions for the end of the discussion since their prior preparation might lead others to believe that they are more qualified and prepared to comment on the performances than is anyone else, and this could limit discussion. Discussion leaders should try to maximize audience participation by calling on people, if necessary, and asking specific questions. Discussion leaders should think of themselves as "leaders" and not "givers" of evaluations.

Your roles as audience and evaluator are complex ones. The suggestions in this chapter should improve your participation in both situations. Remember, the purpose of having an audience is to have someone with whom to share your interpretation. The purpose of evaluation is to improve interpretation and performance skills. Your participation is appreciated when you respond honestly and sincerely as an audience member and as an evaluator.

You are now ready to delve into the specifics of performing prose fiction, drama, and poetry. As you prepare selections for performance, refer to the first five chapters to review your appreciation and analysis of literature and your roles as performer, audience member, and evaluator.

SUMMARY

Your role as audience member is as important as your role as performer. As an audience member, your responsibilities are to listen, to constitute, to imagine, and to respond. In other words, you give the performer your undivided attention, you create your impression of the text, you remain open-minded, and you show your reactions to the performance by sending feedback to the performer. As an audience member, try to prevent external, internal, and semantic barriers from getting in the way of the performance and your appreciation of it.

As an evaluator, work to give the performer an honest, constructive appraisal of the performance. Be sure you are evaluating the interpretation and not just the performance techniques employed. A good evaluator is objective, specific, constructive, encouraging, and flexible in the use of response styles.

Notes

1. David W. Johnson, *Reaching Out: Interpersonal Effectiveness and Self-Actualization* (Englewood Cliffs, NJ: Prentice Hall, 1972), chapter 7, especially p. 125.
2. Ibid., p. 130.

Part 2

Literary Roles

saying. Will you open it now by yourself or shall
to open it for you?

a move. Even her expression hadn't changed. Her
breaths however were coming faster and faster. Then the
battle began. I had to do it. I had to have a throat culture
for her own protection. But first I told the parents that it
was entirely up to them. I explained the danger but said
that I would not insist on a throat examination so long as
they would take the responsibility.

If you don't do what the doctor says you'll have to go to
the hospital, the mother admonished her severely.

Oh yeah? I had to smile to myself. After all, I had already
fallen in love with the savage brat, the parents were contemptible to me. In the ensuing struggle they grew more and
more abject, crushed, exhausted while she surely rose to
magnificent heights of insane fury of effort bred of her terror of me.

The father tried his best, and he was a big man but the
fact that she was his daughter, his shame at her behavior
and his dread of hurting her made him release her just at the
critical moment several times when I had almost achieved
success, till I wanted to kill him. But his dread also that
she might have diphtheria made him tell me to go on, go
on though he himself was almost fainting, while the mother
moved back and forth behind us raising and lowering her
hands in an agony of apprehension.

Put her in front of you on your lap, I ordered, and hold
both her wrists.

But as soon as he did the child let out a scream. Don't,
you're hurting me. Let go of my hands. Let them go I tell
you. Then she shrieked terrifyingly, hysterically. Stop it!
Stop it! You're killing me!

Do you think she can stand it, doctor! said the mother.

You get out, said the husband to his wife. Do you want
her to die of diphtheria?

Come on now, hold her, I said.

Then I grasped the child's head with my left hand and
tried to get the wooden tongue depressor between her teeth.
She fought, with clenched teeth, desperately! But now I also
had grown furious—at a child. I tried to hold myself down

Storytelling is one of the oldest art forms and at one time was the primary form of entertainment. In early days, people gathered from miles around to hear solo performers sing narrative songs. As children, you may have been told stories by parents or teachers, and you may still enjoy hearing and telling stories today. Of the three literary genres—prose, drama, and poetry—you are probably most familiar with prose, not only because of its emphasis on storytelling but also because you have been speaking prose ever since you were able to speak. For these reasons, we begin Part 2 of this text with prose and specifically with prose fiction—an introduction to the short story and the novel (see Chapter 9 for a discussion of other prose forms).

To become a good storyteller, you should familiarize yourself with the distinguishing characteristics of prose fiction. To facilitate your study, we will discuss prose fiction (and drama and poetry in subsequent chapters) in relation to the questions posed by the dramatistic analysis of literature explained in Chapter 3. We will examine prose fiction in terms of several questions: Who is speaking? Who is being addressed? About what? Where? When? How? and Why? We then will discuss how prose fiction can be analyzed modally. It is difficult, however, to make generalizations about any literary genre that apply in all cases. We, therefore, relate the pertinent terminology necessary for learning to analyze prose fiction and then show the various ways these terms can be applied.

A SAMPLE ANALYSIS OF "THE OPEN WINDOW"

First, read the story, "The Open Window," by Saki (H. H. Munro). As we explore the dimensions of prose fiction, we will apply the terminology to this story.

THE OPEN WINDOW   Saki (H. H. Munro)

"My aunt will be down presently, Mr. Nuttel," said a very self-possessed young lady of fifteen; "in the meantime you must try and put up with me."

Framton Nuttel endeavoured to say the correct something which should duly flatter the niece of the moment without unduly discounting the aunt that was to come. Privately he doubted more than ever whether these formal visits on a succession of total strangers would do much towards helping the nerve cure which he was supposed to be undergoing.

"I know how it will be," his sister had said when he was preparing to migrate to this rural retreat; "you will bury yourself down there and not speak to a living soul, and your nerves will be worse than ever from moping. I shall give you letters of introduction to all the people I know there. Some of them, as far as I can remember, were quite nice."

Framton wondered whether Mrs. Sappleton, the lady to whom he was presenting one of the letters of introduction, came into the nice division.

"Do you know many of the people round here?" asked the niece, when she judged that they had had sufficient silent communion.

"Hardly a soul," said Framton. "My sister was staying here, at the rectory, you know, some four years ago, and she gave me letters of introduction to some of the people here."

He made the last statement in a tone of distinct regret.

"Then you know practically nothing about my aunt?" pursued the self-possessed young lady.

"Only her name and address," admitted the caller. He was wondering whether Mrs. Sappleton was in the married or widowed state. An undefinable something about the room seemed to suggest masculine habitation.

"Her great tragedy happened just three years ago," said the child; "that would be since your sister's time."

"Her tragedy?" asked Framton; somehow in this restful country spot tragedies seemed out of place.

"You may wonder why we keep that window wide open on an October afternoon," said the niece, indicating a large French window that opened on to a lawn.

"It is quite warm for the time of the year," said Framton; "but has that window anything to do with the tragedy?"

"Out through that window, three years ago to a day, her husband and her two young brothers went off for their day's shooting. They never came back. In crossing the moor to their favorite snipe-shooting ground they were all three engulfed in a treacherous piece of bog. It had been that dreadful wet summer, you know, and places that were safe in other years gave way suddenly without warning. Their bodies were never recovered. That was the dreadful part of it." Here the child's voice lost its self-possessed note and became falteringly human. "Poor aunt always thinks that they will come back some day, they and the little brown spaniel that was lost with them, and walk in at that window just as they used to do. That is why the window is kept open every evening till it is quite dusk. Poor dear aunt, she has often told me how they went out, her husband with his white waterproof coat over his arm, and Ronnie, her youngest brother, singing 'Bertie, why do you bound?' as he always did to tease her, because she said it got on her nerves. Do you know, sometimes on still, quiet evenings like this, I almost get a creepy feeling that they will all walk through that window—"

She broke off with a little shudder. It was a relief to Framton when the aunt bustled into the room with a whirl of apologies for being late in making her appearance.

"I hope Vera has been amusing you?" she said.

"She has been very interesting," said Framton.

"I hope you don't mind the open window," said Mrs. Sappleton briskly; "my husband and brothers will be home directly from shooting, and they always come in this way. They've been out for snipe in the marshes today, so they'll make a fine mess over my poor carpets. So like you men-folk, isn't it?"

She rattled on cheerfully about the shooting and the scarcity of birds, and the prospects for duck in the winter. To Framton it was all purely horrible. He made a desperate but only partially successful effort to turn the talk on to a less ghastly topic; he was conscious that his hostess was giving him only a fragment of her attention, and her eyes were constantly straying past him to the open window and the lawn beyond. It was certainly an unfortunate coincidence that he should have paid his visit on this tragic anniversary.

"The doctors agree in ordering me complete rest, an absence of mental excitement, and avoidance of anything in the nature of violent physical exercise," announced Framton, who laboured under the tolerably wide-spread delusion that total strangers and chance acquaintances are hungry for the least detail of one's ailments and infirmities, their cause and cure. "On the matter of diet they are not so much in agreement," he continued.

"No?" said Mrs. Sappleton, in a voice which only replaced a yawn at the last moment. Then she suddenly brightened into alert attention—but not to what Framton was saying.

"Here they are at last!" she cried. "Just in time for tea, and don't they look as if they were muddy up to the eyes!"

Framton shivered slightly and turned towards the niece with a look intended to convey sympathetic comprehension. The child was staring out through the open window with dazed horror in her eyes. In a chill shock of nameless fear Framton swung round in his seat and looked in the same direction.

In the deepening twilight three figures were walking across the lawn towards the window; they all carried guns under their arms, and one of them was additionally burdened with a white coat hung over his shoulders. A tired brown spaniel kept close at their heels. Noiselessly they neared the house, and then a hoarse young voice chanted out of the dusk: "I said, Bertie, why do you bound?"

Framton grabbed wildly at his stick and hat; the hall-door, the gravel-drive, and the front gate were dimly noted stages in his headlong retreat. A cyclist coming along the road had to run into the hedge to avoid imminent collision.

"Here we are, my dear," said the bearer of the white mackintosh, coming in through the window; "fairly muddy, but most of it's dry. Who was that who bolted out as we came up?"

"A most extraordinary man, a Mr. Nuttel," said Mrs. Sappleton; "could only talk about his illness, and dashed off without a word of good-bye or apology when you arrived. One would think he had seen a ghost."

"I expect it was the spaniel," said the niece calmly; "he told me he had a horror of dogs. He was once hunted into a cemetery somewhere on the banks of the Ganges by a pack of pariah dogs, and had to spend the night in a newly dug grave with the creatures snarling and grinning and foaming just above him. Enough to make any one lose their nerve."

Romance at short notice was her speciality.

WHO IS SPEAKING?

The most important speaker in any prose fiction text is the narrator. The narrator is the central and controlling voice in any story or novel. Without the narrator, there would be no story. Since most prose fiction works are written in the past tense (e.g., "Once upon a time . . .") and relate events that have already occurred, the narrator is the only one who exists in the present to relate these events. If you were to tell someone what you did last night, you would be a narrator re-creating past events. You would decide which events to tell and in which order, and you could imitate what others as well as you said in the past. Narrators in prose fiction function in the same way. As you prepare a prose fiction selection for performance, your responsibility is to study and create the narrator.

As you begin to analyze a text to discover who the narrator is, you can immediately eliminate one choice. As we already stated, the author of the work is never the speaker in it. Although you may think the narrator and the author are one and the same, there is always a difference between the writer, who creates a literary work and has a life apart from it, and the created, fictive speaker who inhabits it. If the narrator were the author, speaking of and from personal experience only, every story would seem to be autobiographical. Prose fiction, however, is by definition fictive—a made-up story, a created series of events. There may be some similarities between the events in the story and the events in the writer's life, but they are usually altered, exaggerated, or severely distorted to give the story a sense of universality. The writer creates the narrator; the narrator tells the story. The writer is the speaker OF the work; the narrator is the speaker IN it. For the purposes of performance, you create the narrator. Since the narrator (as well as the fictive series of events which comprise the story) is a creation and not "real," you are free to determine from your own personal dealings with a text what the narrator looks like, sounds like, acts like, and so on, whereas an impersonation of the writer would limit your creative involvement. You may be able to make certain assumptions about writers after reading all of their works, but no single work will give you a total impression of a writer.

The personality and attitude of the narrator are the most important aspects of prose fiction to convey in performance. The narrator's personality and attitude toward the events and the characters who participate in those events are ultimately what you convey in performance. The process is complicated because no two narrators are the same. Think of the people who tell you stories every day. Do you tend to take some people's stories more seriously than others? Are some better at telling stories than others? Do some people have a dramatic flair for storytelling? Do some people tend to leave things out or exaggerate some things? All these considerations and more are involved when you analyze the narrator.

The narrator, too, is a person who exhibits a certain style of storytelling. In fact, if you can describe the narrator's style (somber, stuffy, humorous, sarcastic, formal, ironic, or exaggerated), you are on your way toward describing the narrator. Narrators may be male or female, subjective or objective, dramatized (a defined character) or undramatized (an undefined speaker), inside or outside the story, conscious or unaware of self, reliable or unreliable. The combination of elements the author chooses for any particular narrator should be examined and communicated in performance. Since your responsibility is to create the narrator, you will want to know as much as possible about this person and his or her *point of view*.

Point of View

Point of view involves the relationship between the narrator and the story. Point of view not only involves how the narrator chooses to tell the story—from what perspective—but also the distance involved both in time and space between the narrator and the events. Point of view involves how, when, and where the narrator tells the story and also relates to the narrator's degree of personal involvement. The narrator often exhibits the same control and serves the same function as a television or movie camera—determining what we will see, how we will see it, and what we will not see.

The point of view of a narrator is affected by many things. His or her attitude is certainly affected by personal involvement. A narrator who was a participant in the action (dramatized narrator) has a different perspective from an outside observer (undramatized narrator). The perspective is also affected by his or her motive or reason for telling the story. In addition, the narrator's attitude is often affected by time. Since the narrator usually tells about past events, he or she may have had second thoughts, memory loss, or new experiences which may affect the way the story is told. The narrator's attitude is also conditioned by the intended narratees or the audience—the audience the narrator speaks to affects how he or she speaks.

The various points of view from which most stories are seen or told are outlined in Figure 6.1.

The arrows across the top and down the left side of the chart show a continuum for the degree of unreliability or reliability (how trustworthy and credible the narrator is), subjectivity or objectivity (how opinionated or biased this narrator is),

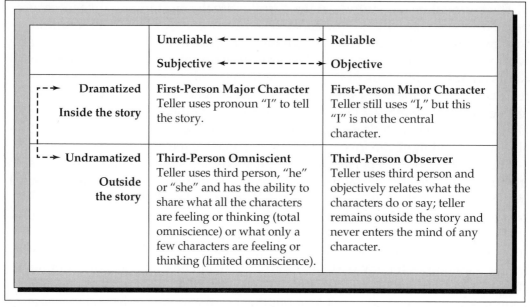

Figure 6.1

and dramatization or lack thereof (how characterized this narrator is). Though every narrator is unique and is privileged with more or less information about the story and the characters in it, most narrators are either *first-person major character, first-person minor character, third-person omniscient,* or *third-person observer.* With this information in mind, let us analyze the point of view of the narrator of "The Open Window."

Point of View and "The Open Window"

The point of view of the narrator of "The Open Window" is third-person limited omniscient. The narrator uses the third person (e.g., "he," "she") to tell the story, and he (we'll assume a masculine narrator since author and major character are male—if the author and major character are women, then the narrator is probably a woman) is omniscient (all-knowing) because he knows more than he relates and because he knows things about Framton (and Vera) that would not be discernible through mere observation. The narrator is primarily omniscient with Framton Nuttel and secondarily with Vera. Some of the lines or phrases that show that the narrator is omniscient with Framton are:

> *Privately he doubted* more than ever . . .
> Framton *wondered* whether Mrs. Sappleton . . .
> . . . he *was conscious* that his hostess. . . .

The italicized words or phrases are signals that the narrator enters Framton's mind and knows what he is thinking. The narrator in this story is also omniscient with Vera, the niece. The narrator shows his omniscience with Vera when he says: "she judged that they had had sufficient silent communion" and "Romance at short notice was her speciality." In both statements, the narrator exhibits an omniscient or all-knowing relationship with Vera because he knows what she is thinking and what she always does. The narrator, however, withholds information about Vera, cleverly hiding his omniscience with her to keep the ending of the story a surprise. If the narrator were more overtly omniscient with Vera, we might hear Vera thinking: "This guy knows no one around here and seems really nervous and gullible; lying to him will be easy and provide me with a good laugh."

We say that this narrator manifests *limited* omniscience because he reveals what only two of the characters are thinking or feeling. If he told us what Mrs. Sappleton and the men who return through the window were thinking, then the narrator would reveal *total* omniscience.

The narrator is subjective for two reasons. First, he goes into characters' minds and tells us what they are thinking and feeling. Second, like most narrators, he is opinionated and has a certain bias. He tells us that the niece is a "very self-possessed young lady," and that Mrs. Sappleton's response to Framton "replaced a yawn at the last moment." The narrator is slightly unreliable because of his super-human ability to read minds, and because he knows Vera is lying, but does not let us know until the end. The narrator is undramatized (not a defined character) and relatively unobtrusive. He is not a character in the story, and he rarely takes focus away from the characters.

Let us now examine passages from four different prose fiction works and analyze the point of view of each.

First-Person Point of View

From THE REUNION   Maya Anjelou

Some of the guys went out to turn on and a couple went to tables where they had ladies waiting for them. But I went to the back of the dark smoky bar where even the occasional sunlight from the front door made no difference. My blood was still fluttering in my fingertips, throbbing. If she was listed in the phone directory I would call her. Hello Miss Beth . . . this is Philomena . . . who was your maid, whose whole family worked for you. Or could I say, Hello Beth. Is this Beth? Well, this is Miss Jenkins. I saw you yesterday at the Blue Palm Cafe. I used to know your parents. In fact your mother said my mother was a gem, and my father was a treasure. I used to laugh 'cause your mother drank so much whiskey, but my Momma said, "Judge not, that ye be not judged." Then I found out that your father had three children down in our part of town and they all looked just like you, only prettier. Oh Beth, now . . . now . . . shouldn't have a chip . . . mustn't be bitter . . . She of course would hang up.

From "The Reunion" by Maya Anjelou. Reprinted by permission of the author.

From THE GREAT GATSBY   F. Scott Fitzgerald

And as I sat there brooding on the old, unknown world, I thought of Gatsby's wonder when he first picked out the green light at the end of Daisy's dock. He had come a long way to this blue lawn, and his dream must have seemed so close that he could hardly fail to grasp it. He did not know that it was already behind him, somewhere back in that vast obscurity beyond the city, where the dark fields of the republic rolled on under the night.

These two examples are both told from the first-person point of view. The narrator in the short story "The Reunion" is a female, and the narrator in the novel *The Great Gatsby* is male. Both refer to themselves as "I." What are the differences between them? Certainly you would not read both passages in the same way, nor do the narrators project similar attitudes or personalities.

In the passage from Anjelou's "The Reunion" the narrator is a major character inside her own story. We call this first-person major point of view. She is a black musician named Philomena Jenkins from Baker, Georgia, who now lives and works on the South Side of Chicago playing the piano. During one performance, she notices Miss Beth Ann Baker—the daughter of the white family Philomena and her family used to work for in Georgia—seated in the bar with a black man. Philomena talks about her jealousy of and resentment toward Beth, and she fantasizes about what she would like to say to Beth should she get the opportunity. She is dramatized—a defined character in a defined place and time (you would, of course, know more about her from reading the entire story)—and subjective and unreliable simply because she is central to the action and does not have the aesthetic distance to be honest about an event that affected her so personally. We are uncertain as to whether we can believe all that Philomena tells us about Beth. Though there is no such thing as a pure perception, first-person major character narrators, more than any other type of narrator, allow their biases and prejudices to color and/or exaggerate their telling of personal experiences—much like anglers when they tell about the fish that got away! First-person major character narrators are in a sense "confessing," and because they have something to confess, they may also have something to conceal. Although Philomena's mother has told her not to "judge," and though Philomena feels free now and has her music, she still seems to be in bondage to her past. When Beth confronts Philomena at the end to tell her that she is engaged to that black man, much to the chagrin of her parents, all Philomena can say is, "Good-bye Beth. Tell your parents I said go to hell and take you with them, just for company."

The passage from *The Great Gatsby*, however, seems to be told from a more objective and reliable point of view. The narrator in this passage, Nick Carraway, is a first-person minor character narrator. He is, like Philomena, a character in the story he tells, but he is not the central character; Jay Gatsby is. Unlike Philomena, Nick is believable—we can rely on what he tells us of Gatsby. As this narrator speaks, he directs our thought and attention to Gatsby. Nick is still a dramatized narrator who interests us, still a character in the story, but because the events he recounts do not specifically center around him, we call him a minor character narrator. Nick is a kind of touchstone character, reasonable and honest (ironically his father, like Philomena's mother, has told him not to judge, but he seems to have taken the advice more to heart than Philomena has), who helps us differentiate the sympathetic characters from the unsympathetic characters by his relationship with them. He can look at events more objectively and more reliably than can Philomena, the narrator in "The Reunion."

Third-Person Point of View

Look now at these selections, which are told from the third-person point of view.

From PARKER'S BACK   Flannery O'Connor

Parker had never before felt the least motion of wonder in himself. Until he saw the man at the fair, it did not enter his head that there was anything out of the ordinary about the fact that he existed. Even then it did not enter his head, but a peculiar unease settled in him. It was as if a blind boy had been turned so gently in a different direction that he did not know his destination had been changed.

Excerpt from "Parker's Back" from *Everything That Rises Must Converge* by Flannery O'Connor. Copyright © 1961, 1965 by the Estate of Mary Flannery O'Connor. Reprinted by permission of Farrar, Straus, and Giroux, Inc.

From HERE WE ARE   Dorothy Parker

"Well!" the young man said.

"Well!" she said.

"Well, here we are," he said.

"Here we are," she said, "Aren't we?"

"I should say we were," he said. "Eeyop. Here we are."

"Well!" she said.

The narrators in both of these selections speak from what is called a third-person, outside-the-story point of view. (While "third-person" is used to describe these narrators, the label is really a misnomer. First-person narrators are called first-person because they tell their story from an "I" perspective—they are actual participants in the stories they tell. Third-person narrators, however, are not participants in the stories they tell, but they are still, in a sense, first-person narrators, in that they tell their stories from a personal perspective—even though they do not refer to themselves as "I." The real difference between these two types of narrators is that the first-person narrator was a participant and is characterized in the story, and the third-person narrator was not a participant in the action and is not characterized. Because third-person narrators do not refer to themselves—are not "confessing"—but speak of others, they usually seem more credible than first-person narrators.)

In the example from "Parker's Back," the narrator is omniscient with Parker. An omniscient narrator has the ability to reveal character thoughts and feelings. When the narrator says that "Parker had never before felt the least motion of wonder in himself" and that he "did not know his destination had been changed," the narrator manifests omniscience. Each time the narrator goes inside Parker's head to tell us what he thinks or feels, he shows omniscience. The omniscient narrator in "Parker's Back" is subjective, because throughout the story he uses language that helps us know how to feel about Parker—language, moreover, which is frequently beyond Parker's usage or comprehension. The narrator is undramatized because he is not himself a character in the story he tells. The narrator does not seem self-conscious—his emphasis is on Parker's new sense of self.

In the example from "Here We Are," the narrator also speaks from the third-person point of view, but this narrator is very different from the narrator in "Parker's Back." The narrator in this passage does not enter a character's mind; she remains more objective and reliable in her retelling. In this passage, it is only the *tag lines*—the "he saids" and "she saids"—that remind us that the selection is prose fiction and that there is a narrator. The narrator, in this passage, has decided to let the characters take center stage and she shows the story more than she tells it. In fact, this passage resembles a play in that it is predominantly dialogue with little direct narrative comment. We call the narrator in "Here We Are" a third-person observer.

Second-Person Point of View

Although earlier we stated that there are primarily four points of view from which a story may be seen and told, we now must add one additional point of view. The second-person point of view is rare, but is becoming more and more prevalent, especially in contemporary, postmodern literature. In second-person stories, the narrator uses the pronoun "you," and seems to address the reader directly. We are apparently invited to become part of the work, to become more actively involved in the creation of the events than in first- or third-person texts. In fact, the technique creates an odd, almost intoxicating sense of intimacy. But who is the "you"? The difficulty and complexity offered by these stories involves the identification of this slippery "you." As we stated in Chapter 4, the pronoun "you" has many referents. Is the "you" the reader? Could the "you" be the narrator? Could the "you" be the author? Is the "you" some character in the story? The answer varies depending on the work. These texts present interesting problems to solve when they're performed, but they may not be especially good texts with which to begin your study of prose fiction.

Performance and Point of View

When performing either of the passages told from the first-person point of view, your job of creating the narrator is facilitated somewhat because the narrator is dramatized, and information about his or her character is provided within the story. This information is extremely useful to you in preparing a selection for performance. Although translating this information into performance is up to each individual's interpretation of the entire story, here are some questions and suggestions to consider.

In the story "The Reunion," you create your impression of Philomena, the black piano player from Georgia, as well as her impression of Beth, the daughter of the family Philomena and her parents once worked for. Find out what you can about the name "Philomena." How can that information help you in performance? Although warned by her mother not to judge others, Philomena does her share of that throughout the story. Is she suggesting that Beth's father was her father as well? Why does she mention Beth's mother's drinking problem? How would you characterize Philomena when she fantasizes about what she would like to say to Beth? How do you rationalize her relative silence when Beth finally does confront her? How honest is Philomena with herself? Do you think she really believes she is free of the pain of her past, as she tells us at the end of the story? There is a sense of spontaneity in this story as Philomena's thoughts are revealed in the present tense. How does that affect performance?

In performing the scene from *The Great Gatsby* your responsibility is to create your conception of Nick Carraway. You should ask yourself questions not only about Nick and his feelings about himself, but also about Nick's changing attitude toward Jay Gatsby. Since Nick is a first-person minor character narrator, his focus of attention is often on the major character—Gatsby. In this novel, for example, Nick feels very differently about Jay Gatsby in the present than he did when the story first took place. Ask yourself this: Do I perform Nick as he is now when I recount past events, or do I let Nick express the feelings and attitudes he had then, or do I attempt to convey Nick's attitude both then and now? Remember that all narrators color our perspective of events and of other characters. We never really see Gatsby, for example; we see only Nick Carraway's remembrance of him.

Some beginning students find it more difficult to perform prose fiction selections told from the third-person point of view than from the first-person point of view because third-person narrators are not dramatized in the story. Often there is little information provided to help create third-person narrators. This need not become a problem if it is remembered that third-person narrators are NOT characters in the work, and you need not try to dramatize them. Writers have the option of creating defined or undefined narrators. If an author decides to create an undefined narrator, the student need not try to do the writer's work and create a character anyway.

One of the most important aspects of third-person narrators to project in performance is their *attitude* toward the events and the characters in the story. To determine narrative attitude, look closely at the narrator's word choice, style of language, and syntax. For example, a narrator may say, "Mary walked delicately through the door" or "Mary lumbered through the door." Each sentence contains clues to narrative attitude and indicates a different narrative view of Mary. Narrators are free to choose any words to tell their stories, and the particular words they choose become keys to the narrator's personality and attitude.

If you were to read all of "Parker's Back" (which you would have to do before preparing a selection for performance), you would see that the narrator is sympathetic with Parker—although not entirely in agreement with Parker's behavior or attitudes. The narrator is, however, able to see Parker quite objectively at times. The interpreter must be able to show the narrator's attitude toward Parker, as well as the narrator's attitude toward the other characters in the story.

In "Here We Are" the narrator's personality is revealed in her description of the husband and wife. The narrator has a minor role. She is not self-conscious, nor does she take focus away from the major characters through long passages of exposition or description. She merely tells us what we need to know to understand what the characters are doing and supplies tag lines (e.g., he said, she said) so that we know exactly who is speaking. What assumptions can you make about this narrator in regard to her minimal intrusion? What clues to understanding the narrator are provided by her repetitive use of "he saids" and "she saids"? Although this narrator is a third-person observer, she still has an attitude toward the characters. She is not entirely objective, as this opening description from "Here We Are" indicates:

> He sat down, leaning back against bristled green plush, in the seat opposite the girl in beige. She looked as new as a peeled egg. Her hat, her frock, her gloves were glossy and stiff with novelty. On the arc of the thin, slippery sole of one beige shoe was gummed a tiny oblong of white paper, printed with the price set and paid for that slipper and its fellow, and the name of the shop that had dispensed them.

The narrator here shows a slightly sarcastic, mocking attitude toward these two innocent newlyweds. The language the narrator uses pokes fun at the wife, who looks like a "peeled egg." The narrator heightens our amusement by noticing that the girl still has the price tag on her "slipper and its fellow." The performer should project the narrator's amusement and also suggest the characters from a more objective stance when the narrator's voice is submerged.

As stated earlier, when you perform a prose fiction selection, the most essential elements to communicate are the vocal, physical, and emotional characteristics of the narrator. Each narrator will have a unique voice, body, psychology, and emotional makeup. Analyzing the narrator's point of view and particular attitude toward the story and the characters in it is the first step toward developing a voice, body, and emotional response for the narrator. Get your clues from the text. Let the language the narrator uses determine how that narrator will look, sound, and feel. Work from the inside out; let the actions, voice, and feel of the narrator come as a result of your natural response to the language in the text. If, for example, the narrator says, "She was the most gorgeous of old maids," you must decide how the line should be intoned. Is the narrator serious? If so, how would that line be delivered? Is the narrator sarcastic? comic? As you attempt to suggest the narrator's attitude in performance, you must work on vocal flexibility to be able to convey any shifts in perspective. Sometimes the narrator projects a line from his or her point of view, sometimes the narrator suggests a line as one of the characters might say it, and sometimes the narrator imitates characters and satirizes or parodies them. Although your clues for projecting the narrator must come from the whole story, try practicing the set of sentences that follow to help you attain the flexibility you need to project narrative attitude.

Frank and Sally walked through the door together.

1. Say the line suggesting that you like Frank, but dislike Sally.
2. Say the line suggesting that you dislike Frank and Sally.
3. Say the line suggesting that you envy Frank and Sally's relationship.
4. Say the line suggesting that they looked ridiculous walking through the door.

I love you more than words can say.

1. Say the line and mean it.
2. Say the line and do not mean it.
3. Say the line suggesting that you really feel hate, not love.

The beautiful woman was standing on the beach alone.

1. Say the line as a jealous woman might say it.
2. Say the line as an admiring man might say it.
3. Say the line suggesting that the woman was anything but beautiful.

The boys kicked the old man in the leg and ran off howling with laughter.

1. Say the line as though the situation were comic.
2. Say the line as though it were sadly dramatic.
3. Say the line approving of the boys' actions.
4. Say the line as one of the boys might say it.

The girl loved her dog, Randy, better than anything else in the world.

1. Say the line as though you approved of the girl's behavior.
2. Say the line as though the girl's behavior were ridiculous.

Christmas is my favorite holiday.

1. Say the line as an old woman might who knows she will be alone for Christmas.
2. Say the line as a young child might.
3. Say the line suggesting that you do not like Christmas.

Class Exercise

Look at the following two longer passages from John Gardner's *Grendel* and O. Henry's "The Furnished Room." See if you can determine the nature of the narrator and the particular point of view from which each selection is told. Try reading the passages aloud, giving a personality and an attitude to each narrator. Then see if you can rewrite the opening paragraphs of each selection, employing the point of view of the other. For example, try rewriting the opening paragraph of *Grendel* from the third-person point of view, and try rewriting the opening paragraph of "The Furnished Room" from the point of view of the man searching for the room. How does each story alter depending on the point of view from which the story is seen and told?

From GRENDEL   John Gardner

The old ram stands looking down over rockslides, stupidly triumphant. I blink. I stare in horror. "Scat!" I hiss. "Go back to your cave, go back to your cowshed—whatever." He cocks his head like an elderly, slow-witted king, considers the angles, decides to ignore me. I stamp. I hammer the ground with my fists. I hurl a skull-size stone at him. He will not budge. I shake my two hairy fists at the sky and I let out a howl so unspeakable that the water at my feet turns sudden ice and even I myself am left uneasy. But the ram stays; the season is upon us. And so begins the twelfth year of my idiotic war.

The pain of it! The stupidity!

"Ah, well," I sigh, and shrug, trudge back to the trees.

Do not think my brains are squeezed shut, like the ram's, by the roots of horns. Flanks atremble, eyes like stones, he stares at as much of the world as he can see and feels it surging in him, filling his chest as the melting snow fills dried-out creek-beds, tickling his gross, lopsided balls and charging his brains with the same unrest that made him suffer last year at this time, and the year before, and the year before that. (He's forgotten them all.) His hindparts shiver with the usual joyful, mindless ache to mount whatever happens near—the storm piling up black towers to the west, some rotting, docile stump, some spraddle-legged ewe. I cannot bear to look. "Why can't these creatures discover a little dignity?" I ask the sky. The sky says nothing, pre-dictably. I make a face, uplift a defiant middle finger, and give an obscene little kick. The sky ignores me, forever unimpressed. Him too I hate, the same as I hate these brainless budding trees, these brattling birds.

Not, of course, that I fool myself with thoughts that I'm more noble. Pointless, ridiculous monster crouched in the shadows, stinking of dead men, murdered chil-dren, martyred cows. (I am neither proud nor ashamed, understand. One more dull victim, leering at seasons that never were meant to be observed.) "Ah, sad one, poor old freak!" I cry, and hug myself, and laugh, letting out salt tears, he he! till I fall down gasping and sobbing. (It's mostly fake.) The sun spins mindlessly overhead, the shadows lengthen and shorten as if by plan. Small birds, with a high-pitched yelp, lay eggs. The tender grasses peek up, innocent yellow, through the ground: the children of the dead. (It was just there, this shocking green, that once when the moon was tombed in clouds I tore off sly old Athelgard's head. Here, where the startling tiny jaws of crocuses snap at the late-winter sun like the heads of baby watersnakes, here I killed the old woman with the irongray hair. She tasted of urine and spleen, which made me spit. Sweet mulch for yellow blooms. Such are the tiresome memories of a shadow-shooter, earthrim-roamer, walker of the world's weird wall.) "Waaah!" I cry, with another quick, nasty face at the sky, mournfully observing the way it is, bitterly remembering the way it was, and idiotically casting tomorrow's nets. "Aargh! Yaww!" I reel, smash trees. Disfigured son of lunatics. The big-boled oaks gaze down at me yellow with morning, beneath complexity. "No offense," I say, with a terrible, sycophantish smile, and tip an imaginary hat.

It was not always like this, of course. On occasion it's been worse.

From THE FURNISHED ROOM   O. Henry (William Sydney Porter)

Restless, shifting, fugacious as time itself is a certain vast bulk of the population of the red brick district of the lower West Side. Homeless, they have a hundred homes. They flit from furnished room to furnished room, transients forever—transients in abode, transients in heart and mind. They sing "Home, Sweet Home" in ragtime; they carry their *lares et penates* in a bandbox; their vine is entwined about a picture hat; a rubber plant is their fig tree.

Hence the houses of this district, having had a thousand dwellers, should have a thousand tales to tell, mostly dull ones, no doubt; but it would be strange if there could not be found a ghost or two in the wake of all these vagrant guests.

One evening after dark a young man prowled among these crumbling red mansions, ringing their bells. At the twelfth he rested his lean handbaggage upon the step and wiped the dust from his hatband and forehead. The bell sounded faint and far away in some remote, hollow depths.

To the door of this, the twelfth house whose bell he had rung, came a housekeeper who made him think of an unwholesome, surfeited worm that had eaten its nut to a hollow shell and now sought to fill the vacancy with edible lodgers.

He asked if there was a room to let.

"Come in," said the housekeeper. Her voice came from her throat; her throat seemed lined with fur. "I have the third-floor back, vacant since a week back. Should you wish to look at it?"

The young man followed her up the stairs. A faint light from no particular source mitigated the shadows of the halls. They trod noiselessly upon a stair carpet that its own loom would have forsworn. It seemed to have become vegetable; to have degenerated in that rank, sunless air to lush lichen or spreading moss that grew in patches to the staircase and was viscid under the foot like organic matter. At each turn of the stairs were vacant niches in the wall. Perhaps plants had once been set within them. If so they had died in that foul and tainted air. It may be that statues of the saints had stood there, but it was not difficult to conceive that imps and devils had dragged them forth in the darkness and down to the unholy depths of some furnished pit below.

Use these questions to help you analyze the characteristics of the narrator in any short story or novel.

1. Is the narrator telling the story from a position inside or outside the story?
2. Is the narrator dramatized or undramatized?
3. How reliable or credible is the narrator? Can we believe what the narrator says? What is his or her motive or intention in telling the story?
4. With how much information is the narrator privileged? Is the narrator omniscient or an observer?
5. How much information does the narrator reveal about himself or herself? How self-conscious or self-aware is the narrator as the story is being told? Is the narrator aware that she or he is telling a story?
6. How has the passage of time affected the narrator?
7. How do I relate my analysis to performance? How does the information I learn from answering these questions provide me with clues to devising my own interpretation and performing this particular narrator?

Telling and showing

The narrator in most prose fiction works is the only speaker who exists in the present to tell the story which took place in the past. Most stories and novels also have dialogue which characters once spoke. When narrators speak, they are *telling* the story. When the characters speak, the narrator is *showing* or illustrating the story with lines of dialogue. When you analyze a prose fiction work, you decide how to convey the narrator, and then decide how the narrator will convey the characters in the story.

Characters in prose fiction texts

The characters, then, are also the *who* in the story, and they, as impersonated and communicated by the narrator's attitude, may be either *round* or *flat, static* or *dynamic*. Flat, static characters have only one predominant characteristic (flat) and never undergo change (static). Cartoon characters are considered flat and static because they usually have only one dimension and remain the same regardless of circumstance. The Road Runner will always out distance Wile E. Coyote, and Bugs Bunny will always outwit Elmer Fudd! Characters in most short stories are also flat and static as the short story format usually does not permit deep characterization. The husband and wife in "Here We Are" are flat, static characters. Round, dynamic characters, on the other hand, have more depth and are more complex. Round characters are multidimensional and show different sides of their personalities. Dynamic characters, as the word implies, change and exhibit various moods and emotional responses. Philomena Jenkins (the narrator as well as the character) in "The Reunion," Nick Carraway (the narrator as well as the character) in *The Great Gatsby*, and Parker in "Parker's Back" seem to be round, dynamic characters. The major characters in most full-length novels are often round and dynamic.

All of the characters in "The Open Window" seem to be flat and static. Framton, the central character, has one prevailing trait: he is nervous and anxious throughout the story. He is especially nervous to be making visits to a "succession of total strangers." He is nervous and anxious when he arrives at the Sappleton home, and he is even more nervous and anxious when he makes his hasty exit. Vera, as is obvious from the last line of the story, is a liar. She lies to Framton about the death of the hunters, and she lies to the hunters and to her aunt at the end when she tells them why Framton left so quickly. Consequently, the niece does not change; she is a liar at the beginning and she is a liar at the end. Mrs. Sappleton and the three men who return through the open window are all flat, static characters. We do not learn enough about them to make them either round or dynamic. They are peripheral to the story's central action: the relationship between Framton and the niece. Saki probably made all the characters in this story purposely flat and static to make the story line more significant than the characters themselves. We are to get caught up in the plot of the story and not get too involved with any of the characters. We are in the same ignorant position as poor Framton; we believe the niece and are fooled until the end.

When you are analyzing the characters, always remember that they are being re-created by the narrator who may be more or less reliable in how he or she makes the characters sound, look, and think. The narrator is responsible for re-creating the entire story, including the characters. How the narrator feels about the characters is an essential aspect to convey in performance. The narrator's attitude is sometimes blatantly expressed (for example, "Tom was not to be trusted"), sometimes suggested in the language the narrator chooses to describe a character's behavior ("Tom deliberately caused Mary to drop the cake"), and sometimes implied in the events the narrator chooses to relate ("Tom sat for hours attempting to balance a spoon on the end of his nose"). Sometimes a narrator uses all three devices, as well as many more, to make his or her attitude clear. As you study the narrator, ask yourself what kind of relationship the narrator has with each character physically, emotionally, psychologically, and morally. If you decide that the narrator likes a character and wants the audience to feel the same way, you would want to convey that in performance (e.g., smiling, saying the character's dialogue kindly, talking about the character with obvious pleasure, etc.). If you decide that the narrator dislikes a character and wants the audience to feel similarly, then the narrator could sound gruff, or angry, or use sarcasm when portraying or discussing the character. In essence, narrators are free to decide how the characters are to sound and look. Unlike a play where the characters seem to live and breathe before our eyes, in prose fiction texts, only the narrator lives and breathes before us.

In "The Open Window" the narrator seems to be physically and psychologically close to Framton. The narrator is physically close to Framton since he often tends to see the story through Framton's eyes. The narrator is psychologically close enough to hear Framton's thoughts (for example, "Framton wondered whether Mrs. Sappleton . . . came into the nice division."). The narrator is not emotionally close to Framton because he knows that Vera is not telling the truth and yet he does nothing to save Framton from falling victim to her "romance." The narrator's relationship with Vera is more complex. He seems to know more about Vera than he reveals to us. The last line tells us that Vera's speciality is "romance at short notice." What, then, is the narrator's moral relationship with Vera? The narrator does seem eager to surprise us as well as Framton, so he would probably not show any negative reaction while describing Vera's behavior. He might have a gleam in his eye as he knows he's fooled Framton as well as us.

In performance, the use of different types of focus can help to make the relationship between the narrator and the audience and between the narrator and the characters clear. Focus involves two separate considerations. First, in a prose fiction performance (as in most interpretation performances), you project the scene offstage. The narrator faces front, establishing the scene in the audience so that they can participate in its creation.

Second, when prose fiction is performed, open, closed, and inner-closed (and occasionally semi-closed) focuses are often employed. Focus choices are based on internal modal analysis. (Look again at Figure 4.1 in Chapter 4 to review your focus choices.) Epic mode moments (narrator describing or summarizing) are usually performed with open focus. Dramatic mode moments (lines of dialogue or direct address of characters) are usually performed using closed focus and character placement. Lyric mode moments (thought revelations of narrator or characters) are usually performed using inner-closed focus. If the narrator or characters address a God, muse, an absent person, or a deceased person, these are also lyric-mode moments and semi-closed focus would be employed.

WHOM IS THE NARRATOR SPEAKING TO?

The nature of the audience, the narratees, is an important element to consider when you analyze a prose fiction selection for performance. When you deliver your introduction, the audience you speak to is that audience present in the classroom—or wherever you are performing. The audience during the introduction remain themselves.

Once you begin your selection, you address the present audience as if they have been transformed into an audience appropriate for your selection. As we stated in Chapter 4 in relation to meeting the audience, your goal is to make that audience as particular for the narrator as it is for the characters who address each other during dialogue passages. Ideally, you want to define who the narrator's intended, or imagined audience might be and address the general audience with this particular group in mind. (If you cannot suggest the audience's identity in the introduction, you must simply tell the audience whom you imagine them to be.) In Chapter 7, we discuss that characters in plays have goals, obstacles that prevent them from achieving those goals, and strategies to try to overcome the obstacles. This is true for the dialogue exchanges in prose fiction passages as well and is also true concerning the narrator's relationship with the audience. The narrator must play goals and objectives with the general audience just as characters do with each other, but a narrator cannot play a goal or an objective if the narrator has no idea whom he or she is addressing. Ask yourself, What does the narrator want or need from the audience? and How will he or she go about getting it?

Defining who the general audience *might* be is often a very difficult task. You must often deduce from how the narrator speaks who his or her audience might be—friends, enemies, supporters, children, or others. Just as we change our delivery style to accommodate various audiences (we would speak differently to the president of the United States than we would to members of our family), narrators use different styles, depending on the nature of their audiences and what they want or need from them. An effective audience choice for some texts is a group that does not already agree with the narrator's position. If you were performing a pro-war story, for example, how would your performance be affected if you imagined an audience of anti-war protesters?

There are three aspects of a text to examine to help you identify who the implied or imagined audience might be: the location of the first-person narrator at the end of the story, the type of language the narrator uses, and the subject matter of the text.

First, if the point of view is first person, ask yourself where the narrator is at the end of the story. In Eudora Welty's short story, "Why I Live at the P.O.," for example, the title tells us that currently the narrator, Sister, is living at the P.O. (post office)—so who could be in that post office to hear her story? Since China Grove is a small town, we could assume that Sister is not talking to members of the town because they probably already know the story. Sister might be addressing an audience of tourists who have come into the China Grove, Mississippi, post office to buy stamps or mail a postcard and are trapped into listening to Sister's tale of woe as she attempts to convince them of the veracity of her version of the events. How would this decision affect your performance? In Poe's "The Tell-Tale Heart" we know that the narrator is arrested at the end of the story, so as he retells it he could be talking to police officers, psychiatrists, or other prisoners to justify his reasons for committing murder. Holden Caulfield in *The Catcher in the Rye* is in a mental institution at the end of the novel; consequently, one possible audience for him could be other patients in the institution.

Second, examine very closely the language the narrator uses as it can provide strong hints as to whom the audience might be. Is the language fairly simple, written in the active voice, informal, with normal, syntax (subject-verb-object) or is it complex, written in the passive voice, formal with inverted syntax? (See the discussion of style at the end of this chapter for more information about language.) The type of language used is often an indication of whether the narrator is addressing children or adults, for example. Is there a lot of clarification, explanation, description? Then the narrator might be talking to people whom he or she does not know well. Is there less detail? Are things assumed to be understood? Then the narrator might be addressing close friends.

Third, look at the subject matter of the text. Who might be an appropriate audience for a story about an impending marriage? death in battle? growing old? dealing with adolescence? Who would benefit from hearing a pro-war story or a story that stresses that crime doesn't pay? Looking at what the story is about, then, helps you to determine who might be the best audience for that story.

Once you have decided who the implied audience is, think of ways this information will affect your performance. You will want to talk and relate to the audience as though they are the audience you have selected. If, for example, you are telling a children's story and you want your adult audience to become children, you must first prepare them for this transformation in the introduction. You then address them as if they were children, making sure to stress those parts of the story that convey the moral you want the children to learn and exaggerating the characters so that the children can imagine what they look and sound like. If you can convey the identity of the audience through performance, you need not explain their identity in the introduction.

In "The Open Window," the audience seems to be strangers, in a position similar to that of Framton Nuttel. Since one of the narrator's goals seems to be to shock or surprise the audience, he would show tremendous sympathy for poor Framton so that the audience would identify with him. The narrator would withhold all knowledge of the ending so that both Framton and the audience are surprised by what happens.

WHAT DOES THE NARRATOR SPEAK ABOUT?

The *what* of the story is called the *plot,* or the sequence of events involving articulated actions and a certain amount of conflict. There are many different kinds of plot structures, but they can be categorized into two general groups: *causal* and *contingent.* When a narrator chooses to tell a story causally, one event happens as a result of another event that has previously occurred. The events need not be in chronological order—related in the order in which they occurred—but each event that happens is directly related to another event with an implied "because." That is, B happened because A happened, C happened because B happened, and so forth. E. M. Forster's comment on the difference between a sequence of events and a plot makes the causality of some plot structures clear: "'The king died and then the queen died,' is a story. 'The king died and then the queen died of grief,' is a plot."[1] In causal plots, then, the motivations or reasons behind events or actions are stated in the story. Fairy tales are based on causal plot structures. Everything that happens happens for a cause, with some overall moral order, and everything usually turns out happily.

"The Open Window" is based on a causal plot structure. Framton goes to the Sappleton home *because* his sister recommended meeting the Sappletons during his stay in the quiet place he had gone to for a needed rest. Vera tells Framton a lie *because* she has been conveniently left alone with Framton and *because* she determines that he knows nothing about the area, seems gullible, and *because* in his nervous condition, his reaction might bring her a chuckle or two! Framton makes a hasty exit *because* he thinks the returning men are ghosts. When plots are based on a causal structure, the narrator explains events in terms of their relationship to each other. Give the narrator time to make the necessary cause-effect connections when you perform causal stories.

As stated earlier, many causal plots are not told in chronological order. Some stories, for example, may begin with the climax and then go back in time to relate what caused that climax to happen. Some stories shift back and forth in time, relating, for example, flashback incidents that occurred in one character's life. Since different parts of causal plots have more tensiveness—contrary pulls—than others, such as the climax, be aware of the ordering of events so that you can be responsive to these pulls in performance.

In many stories, particularly some modern and many contemporary stories, the causal plot structure is not employed. In causal stories, the good are rewarded; the bad are punished. Causality is not the pattern in real life, however. In real life, good things occasionally happen to bad people and bad things occasionally happen to good people. Things are not so neatly realized. Stories that mirror this quality of real life have what is known as contingent plot structures, in which events happen seemingly without any logical relationship or causal link: A happens and then Q happens! Events seem to happen at random or by accident: a clock strikes thirteen, an eagle scout is hit by a bus, a nun suddenly decides to steal for no apparent reason.

Often writers use contingent plots to reveal the absurdity of life, to satirize commonplace events, or to comment on the haphazard nature of life. In stories by contemporary writers like Alain Robbe-Grillet, John Barth, and Thomas Pynchon, it is often difficult to tell exactly what happened or to whom. Some writers have been very much influenced by electronic media. Robert Coover, for example, wrote a short story called "The Babysitter," which is based on contingency and reads like a screenplay for a postmodern movie. When performing stories based on contingency, avoid making the narrator seem to be logically or causally connecting phenomena. Things should seem to be occurring to the narrator almost spontaneously, without much prior deliberation. This quality is heightened in some stories that are written in the present tense.

Within some causal and contingent plots are *associative* moments. In other words, narrators may be relating one incident when something triggers their minds, and the story goes off in another direction. *Triggering* is the stimulation of thoughts during moments of free association. "The Secret Life of Walter Mitty," for example, has a causal framework centering on Mitty and his overbearing wife. The rest of the story, however, deals with Mitty's associative fantasizing. Mitty walks down the street and hears a noise, and suddenly he imagines himself a war hero or a great surgeon. These triggering stimuli are associative moments within a basically casual plot. In *stream-of-consciousness* novels, like those of Virginia Woolf and James Joyce, all events are triggered by the mental associations of the narrator or of a character. These novels read like recordings of thought revelations—often not even interrupted by punctuation. Show this triggering of associations in performance.

Studying the plot of a story helps to discover the logical, illogical, or associative thought patterns of the narrator. Does the narrator follow a causal pattern in relating the story? Does the narrator seem to be relating events as they occur in a sort of mental association or stream-of-consciousness fashion? These considerations provide valuable information to help characterize the narrator during performance.

WHERE DOES THE NARRATOR TELL THE STORY FROM?

When the *where* of the story is analyzed, two considerations should be made. First, where does the story take place? What is the setting or locale of the past events? The setting, for example, of "The Open Window" is Mrs. Sappleton's sitting room or living room. As you tell this story, you would want to be sure the audience is able to visualize the place, and especially the open window itself, which is the most important aspect of the setting.

The second aspect of setting involves the locale of the narrator as he or she retells this story in the present. Since there is usually a time differential between the narrator's telling the story and the time the events actually occurred, the narrator is often in a different setting. In "Why I Live at the P.O.," for example, the events of the story took place in Sister's home. As Sister tells her story in the present, the setting is the China Grove, Mississippi, post office where Sister currently lives.

The setting in the present is often difficult to define, as in "The Open Window." If it is not clear where the narrator is as he or she tells the story, you could assume that the present setting is not as significant as the past environment to establish in performance. Again, the language the narrator uses can help determine which setting is significant at any given moment and whether the narrator feels comfortable, and is thus in a friendly environment, or whether uncomfortable and possibly in a hostile environment. This passage from Wilkie Collins's short story "The Traveler's Story of a Terribly Strange Bed" demonstrates the kinds of spaces interpreters must create.

From THE TRAVELER'S STORY OF A TERRIBLY STRANGE BED   Wilkie Collins

Shortly after my education at college was finished, I happened to be staying at Paris with an English friend. We were both young men then, and lived, I am afraid, rather a wild life, in the delightful city of our sojourn. One night we were idling about the neighborhood of the Palais Royal, doubtful to what amusement we should next betake ourselves. My friend proposed a visit to Frascati's; but his suggestion was not to my taste. I knew Frascati's, as the French saying is, by heart; had lost and won plenty of five-franc pieces there, merely for amusement's sake, until it was amusement no longer, and was thoroughly tired, in fact, of all the ghastly respectabilities of such a social anomaly as a respectable gambling-house. "For Heaven's sake," said I to my friend, "let us go somewhere where we can see a little genuine, blackguard, poverty-stricken gaming, with no false gingerbread glitter thrown over it at all. Let us get away from fashionable Frascati's, to a house where they don't mind letting in a man with a ragged coat, or a man with no coat, ragged or otherwise." "Very well," said my friend, "we needn't go out of the Palais Royal to find the sort of company you want. Here's the place just before us; as blackguard a place, by all report, as you could possibly wish to see." In another minute we arrived at the door, and entered the house, the back of which you have drawn in your sketch.

The story centers around Mr. Faulkner, the narrator. As the narrator tells the story, he is in the home of an artist friend. The artist has shown Mr. Faulkner a sketch of the back of the Palais Royal, which reminds the narrator of an adventure he now recounts to the artist. All the narrative lines are addressed to the artist in the present. The scenes which he recounts from the past take place in the Palais Royal. The dialogue lines, then, take place in the Palais Royal in the past. As you perform the story, you can imagine the audience as the artist to whom the narrator is speaking. You will use open focus and speak directly to them, imagining that they are artist friends. When you re-create the dialogue, do not look at the audience, but at the imagined scene in the Palais Royal.

The different locales in which the narrator and characters exist are important to project in performance. If the lines in your scene do not make the spatial environments clear, then prepare the audience for the spatial shifts in the introduction.

WHEN DOES THE NARRATOR TELL THE STORY?

Time is one of the most fascinating aspects of prose fiction. As stated earlier, most prose fiction stories—though not all—are written in the past tense. The once-upon-a-time opening of many children's stories signifies that the events of the story have already taken place. The narrator is responsible for manipulating time and for determining the ordering of the events. Since the narrator already knows the ending of the story before retelling it, the narrator has the option of eliminating some details that may not seem important, maintaining the story time frame in which an event occurred, or stretching out some events to give them added significance. Time, then, plays an important part in the way the narrator tells the story. Time analysis is divided into two essential elements: (1) rhythm of action and (2) actual time and virtual time.

Rhythm of Action

When a play is read aloud, the rhythm of action is primarily determined by the amount of conflict within a scene. In poetry, the rhythm of action is felt in the meter—the alternation of stressed and unstressed syllables within a line or phrase. In prose fiction, the rhythm is primarily determined by the narrator's manipulation of time in terms of *scene, summary,* and *description*. Phyllis Bentley writes that the narrator's use of scene, summary, and description in a narrative determines the movement and rhythm of action.[2] Because the events of the story have already taken place, the narrator decides how to retell them, which elements to stress, and which elements to minimize or eliminate in accordance with his or her point of view.

The narrator's responsibility is to decide how much time to take verbalizing past events. The narrator verbalizes the events in *discourse time; story time* is the time it actually took for those events to occur. What happened to you yesterday is your "story"; how you choose to tell someone about what happened is "discourse." Scene, summary, and description involve the relationship between story time and discourse time.

Scene occurs when discourse time is equal to story time. Scene exists when the narrator's use of time in telling the story is equal to the actual amount of time needed for the events to occur. Since it would take the narrator as long to repeat a line of direct discourse or dialogue ("'I am staying home,' Mary said") or indirect discourse ("Mary said that she was staying home") in the present as it would for the character to have said the line in the past, direct discourse and indirect discourse are scenic. Scene may also occur within the narrative line, however, when the narrator's retelling of an action takes as long to say as it did to enact, as in, "She took two steps forward" or "She picked up the bottle of wine." Dramatic mode moments, then, are usually scenic.

When narrators shorten events or capsulize long sequences of time, they use *summary,* and discourse time is shorter than story time. If the narrator says, "He woke up early, went to work, got fired, drove to the bar, had two drinks, and went home," the narrator is using summary. Summary lines are usually epic in mode.

When narrators elaborate on the narrative line, making events take longer and seem more detailed than they actually were, the narrator is using *description,* and discourse time is slower than story time. An example of a descriptive line is, "Her hair was long and blond, tied back with an ornamental barrette, which glimmered in the sunlight like an oriental doll." The example just cited is a descriptive line in the epic mode.

When a narrator goes into the mind of a character and tells us what he or she is thinking or feeling (often lyric mode moments), these mental narratives may also be told in scene, summary, or description. If the narrator were to say, "She thought about the man she saw on the beach," it would be lyric scene. Lyric summary would sound like this: "She thought about the man on the beach, the groceries she needed to buy, the house that needed cleaning, and the deposit she needed to make at the bank." If the narrator were to say, "She thought about the man in the white trousers, blue shirt, brown sandals, and metal-framed glasses who had smiled at her so alluringly that sunny, Monday morning," it would be lyric description.

Occasionally, these categories interrelate. Description or summary, for example, may occur within scene. In the following dialogue from "The Open Window," summary exists within scene.

> "Out through that window, three years ago to a day, her husband and her two young brothers went off for their day's shooting. They never came back. In crossing the moor to their favorite snipe-shooting ground they were all three engulfed in a treacherous piece of bog. It had been that dreadful wet summer, you know, and places that were safe in other years gave way suddenly without warning. Their bodies were never recovered."

Figure 6.2 reviews the basic definitions of scene, description, and summary.

Scene	Description	Summary
Discourse time is equal to story time.	Discourse time is slower than story time.	Discourse time is faster than story time.

Figure 6.2

Read the three passages that follow to see if you can hear how scene, summary, and description sound and feel. In general, scene would go at a normal (whatever "normal" would be for this narrator in this situation) pace, summary would be a bit faster to suggest time capsulized, and description would be slowed down to allow the audience time to re-create the images the narrator describes.

Scene

From EVERYTHING THAT RISES MUST CONVERGE   Flannery O'Connor

"I see yoooooo!" she said and put her hand in front of her face and peeped at him. The woman slapped his hand down. "Quit yo' foolishness," she said, "before I knock the living Jesus out of you!"

From "Everything That Rises Must Converge" from *Everything That Rises Must Converge* by Flannery O'Connor. Copyright © 1961, 1965 by the Estate of Mary Flannery O'Connor. Reprinted by permission of Farrar, Straus, and Giroux, Inc.

Description

From PAUL'S CASE   Willa Cather

It would be difficult to put it strongly enough how convincingly the stage entrance of that theatre was for Paul the actual portal of Romance. Certainly none of the company ever suspected it, least of all Charley Edwards. It was very like the old stories that used to float about London of fabulously rich Jews, who had subterranean halls, with palms, fountains, and soft lamps and richly apparelled women who never saw the disenchanting light of London day. So, in the midst of that smoke-palled city, enamored of figures and grimy toil, Paul had his secret temple, his wishing-carpet, his bit of blue-and-white Mediterranean shore bathed in perpetual sunshine.

From "Paul's Case" in *Youth and the Bright Medusa* by Willa Cather. Copyright 1933 by Willa Cather. Reprinted by permission of Alfred A. Knopf, Inc.

Summary

From THE ASSISTANT   Bernard Malamud

Morris went back to waiting. In twenty-one years the store had changed little. Twice he had painted all over, once added new shelving. The old-fashioned double windows at the front a carpenter had made into a large single one. Ten years ago the sign hanging outside fell to the ground but he had never replaced it. Once, when business hit a long good spell, he had had the wooden icebox ripped out and a new white refrigerated showcase put in.

Let us now examine a passage from "The Open Window" to see how the narrator manipulates time.

1. She rattled on cheerfully about the shooting and the scarcity of birds, and the prospects for duck in the winter.
2. To Framton it was all purely horrible.
3. He made a desperate but only partially successful effort to turn the talk on to a less ghastly topic;
4. he was conscious that his hostess was giving him only a fragment of her attention, and her eyes were constantly straying past him to the open window and the lawn beyond.
5. It was certainly an unfortunate coincidence that he should have paid his visit on this tragic anniversary.
6. "The doctors agree in ordering me complete rest, an absence of mental excitement, and avoidance of anything in the nature of violent physical exercise,"
7. announced Framton, who laboured under the tolerably wide-spread delusion that total strangers and chance acquaintances are hungry for the least detail of one's ailments and infirmities, their cause and cure.

Line 1 is written in summary—time is capsulized. The narrator does not seem to want to trouble the audience by detailing Mrs. Sappleton's cheerful rattling on, so he summarizes what she said for us. When performing this line, you could use a slightly rapid pace. Line 2 capsulizes Framton's feelings and is an example of summary. This line is an example of lyric summary, as forward action is stopped when the narrator enters Framton's mind to tell us what he is thinking. Line 3 is an example of narrative summary. Framton made attempts to change the subject but rather than show us this, the narrator summarizes his attempts. Line 4 shows us Framton's mind at work again. Here, the narrator uses lyric scene as Framton's thoughts narrate what was happening—from Framton's point of view. Line 5 is an example of lyric summary. We hear Framton's capsulized reaction to his visit. Line 6 is scenic—a line of dialogue as the narrator quotes Framton's exact words. Line 7 shifts back to the narrator, and he addresses the audience. This line shifts back to description and the pace could be slowed.

This one passage shows how complex the narrator's manipulation of time can be in prose fiction. You must pay attention to the use of time and to the shifts in voice, body, and attitude that are necessary when performing prose fiction.

Actual Time and Virtual Time

In addition to scene, summary, and description, you also deal with *actual time* and *virtual time*. In telling the story, the narrator exists in what is known as the virtual present; "virtual" in that the narrator is an imaginary, fictive character, and "present" because the narrator is speaking now. The characters, however, about whom the narrator speaks, exist in the virtual past; "virtual" in that this past is illusionary or intangible, and "past" because the events have already occurred. As Suzanne Langer puts it, "The events in a novel are purely virtual events, 'known' only to equally virtual people."[3] Narrators offer us their remembrances of each character, so at no time do we actually see or hear the characters in the virtual present. (This is not the case in present-tense stories where there is no virtual past.)

When you deliver your introduction to a selection, you exist in the *actual present* in relation to your audience. As soon as you begin the performance, you shift from the actual present to the *virtual present* as you create the narrator. When you suggest the dialogue of characters through this narrator, you shift to the *virtual past*. Often narrators seem to project themselves back into the remembered scenes—reliving them once again—but the projection is never complete. The narrator will always exist in the virtual present; the scenes the narrator recounts always exist in the virtual past. (Again exceptions are stories written in the present tense. See the present-tense passage from *Grendel* we looked at earlier in this chapter.) When the story itself seems dominant, the narrator seems to take us back in time to the virtual past, as in "The Open Window." When the narrator seems to be the center of our attention, the narrator keeps us in the virtual present most of the time.

It is often necessary to determine the amount of time that elapses between the virtual past and the virtual present—between the time the events occurred (the then) and the time they are recounted (the now). Occasionally, a narrator will say "a long time ago," or "years passed," or "five days later," which helps you calculate the passage of time, but it is just as customary for there to be no clear indication of the passage of time and other elements of the text must be examined. One aspect of the text to examine is the amount of detail in the narration. If there is much detail, chances are the events remembered are fairly recent. If there is little detail, this could signal that the events happened long ago.

Always ask yourselves—especially for first-person texts—Has time changed the narrator? Experiment with this by remembering a story about something horrible that happened to you in the past. How do you feel now about the events that happened then? Has time mellowed you or has the passage of time caused the events to be more painful? In the story "My Oedipus Complex," for example, the narrator recounts an experience he had when he was a young boy. The language in the story tells us that he is a man now no longer afflicted with the "complex" he suffered as a young boy. When the narrator impersonates himself as a young boy during dialogue passages, he would want to suggest the pain and the humiliation of that time. But when the narrator speaks to the general audience now, he just may find some humor in his past.

HOW IS THE STORY TOLD?

Tone and Style

The *how* of the story involves the overall effect of the storytelling. There are two primary considerations when analyzing the how of a story:

1. The author's tone.
2. The narrator's manner or style of telling the story.

Tone is the author's attitude toward the work. The tone can be described as ironic, sarcastic, sympathetic, or humorous. The tone is really not something that you can locate specifically in the text or project directly in performance. You create the narrator, not the author, and unless the narrator's tone is the same as the author's (which is often the case), the author's tone is not directly heard. The author's tone *is* received, but indirectly. After we have heard or read a story (or read many works by the same writer), we sit back and begin to understand what the author's attitude may have been. In Jonathan Swift's essay, "A Modest Proposal" (see Chapter 9), for example, Swift's persona suggests that to solve the overpopulation and hunger problems in Ireland we should roast and eat all the newborn babies. Certainly Swift does not intend us to take this suggestion seriously. After we read the essay (or, in this case, as we read the essay, since Swift's persona's solution is so exaggeratedly absurd), we realize that the tone is hyperbolic and sarcastic.

The tone of "The Open Window" is humorous and ironic. Saki is well aware that the niece is lying. After all, Saki created Vera and her lies. Saki does not mourn the death of the men. He is secretly laughing behind our backs because he has trapped us into sympathizing with Framton and believing Vera.

The narrator's manner of telling the story is called *style*. As we stated earlier, if you can describe the narrator's style, you can begin to describe the narrator. Style involves the narrator's choice of language, syntax (way of linking words and sentences together), and overall manner of storytelling. Style is called "formal" if the narrator uses the passive voice (e.g., The ball was thrown by John), inverted syntax (e.g., In the wake of the disaster, the captain sounded the alarm), does not employ the slippery pronoun "you," avoids contractions, and employs long, complex sentences or metered language. Conversely, style is informal if the narrator uses active voice verbs (e.g., John threw the ball), normal syntax (e.g., The captain sounded the alarm in the wake of the disaster), uses the pronoun "you" and contractions, employs fragments and run-on sentences, and nonmetered language. Style is a manifestation of the narrator's personality. Style may be described as terse, poetic, gothic, convoluted, sentimental, or bathetic, among others. The narrator's style in "The Open Window" could be described as concealing and tricky. He forces the audience to be concerned with Framton's well-being and identify with him only so he can reverse things and surprise us at the end. Throughout the story, the narrator knows more than he reveals.

Mood

Style is related to *mood*. Mood is the atmosphere the narrator creates when telling the story. The mood may be described as eerie, suspenseful, somber, or joyous, etc. The mood of "The Open Window" is somewhat somber, suspenseful, and mysterious, but is also affected by a humorous, ironic tone. Since we believe Vera's story about the death of the three men, we are caught up in the tragedy and the seeming senility of Mrs. Sappleton, just as Framton is. The irony and humor seep through when Vera tells her second lie—after Framton has bolted. By this time, we realize the joke and can share in it. The narrator's style of letting the audience make discoveries along with the characters is effective in this story.

A performer can discover the clues for capturing the mood of the total work, as well as the mood at any given moment, by studying the narrator's style of speaking. Look carefully at the kinds of words narrators use and at their manipulation of different sounds. Look at the sensory images the narrator uses and show your response to them in your voice and body. Read this passage from "The Open Window" aloud, and show your response to the sensory images.

> In the deepening twilight three figures were walking across the lawn towards the window; they all carried guns under their arms, and one of them was additionally burdened with a white coat hung over his shoulders. A tired brown spaniel kept close at their heels. Noiselessly they neared the house, and then a hoarse young voice chanted out of the dusk: "I said, Bertie, why do you bound?"

Direct and Indirect Discourse

As narrators tell stories, they have the choice of speaking to us directly in their own voice and body or of suggesting the voice and body of the characters in the virtual past. As stated earlier, narrators can give opinions or describe characters and events, speaking directly to us as themselves. A narrator interested in suggesting what a character once said or thought has the choice of using either:

1. Direct discourse.
2. Indirect discourse.

Direct discourse is dialogue, or the recorded speech of characters—the exact duplication by the narrator of what characters once said. Direct discourse is usually set off by quotation marks (the direct discourse in "The Use of Force" at the end of Chapter 1 is an exception) and is relatively easy to recognize. "I want to be alone" is a line of direct discourse.

Indirect discourse is the narrator reporting what a character said. "She said that she wanted to be alone." Or it is the narrator reporting what someone once felt or thought or hoped. "She thought that she wanted to be alone."

When you are performing direct discourse, use closed focus (unless, as in rare cases, the character is speaking to the audience; in this case, use open focus), shift to that character's placement, and alter your voice and body to suggest the character speaking. Remember, however, that the narrator is really the only "character" who speaks in a prose fiction selection so during moments of direct discourse, the narrator is suggesting what a character said through the narrator's voice and body. The narrator's point of view, style of speaking, and ability to suggest other characters will condition the reproduction of the direct discourse.

The performance of indirect discourse is a bit more complex and was discussed earlier in relation to lyric scene, summary, and description. Whether the indirect discourse involves what a character once said or what a character once felt or thought, you must decide:

1. If the narrator should take the line, maintaining his or her own voice, body and attitude (open focus).
2. If the narrator should imitate the character, suggesting the character's voice, body, and attitude (closed focus or inner-closed focus).
3. If the narrator should imitate the character's voice and body, but maintain the narrator's attitude (open focus).

Since the narrator had the option of employing direct discourse and chose instead to use indirect, your first consideration should be whether the narrator should take the line. If the vocabulary, style of speaking, and point of view seem to be the narrator's, let him or her take the line and speak directly to the audience. If the line incorporates the vocabulary and style of the character, the narrator imitates the character saying the line (even though the character would be talking about himself or herself in the past tense and in the third person). If, for example, a story centers around a six-year-old boy who has to take a test the following day and the narrator says, "Bill wondered about the test," the narrator could imitate Bill saying this line if it is Bill's vocabulary and style of speaking throughout the story. If the line is, "William contemplated the ensuing examination," it might be more in keeping with the narrator's style of speech, and the narrator should take the line. If the narrator imitates the character, decide whether closed or inner-closed focus is more appropriate. If the line seems to be the narrator's comment on the character—a moment of ridicule or humor, for example—let the narrator imitate the character by suggesting the character's voice and body, but use open focus. If, for example, a line of indirect discourse were, "She said it was none of his bidness," the narrator could imitate the character's vernacular here, but speak directly to the audience to make a kind of ironic comment.

Tag Lines

One additional consideration of the narrator's manner of storytelling concerns tag lines.[4] Tag lines are the "he saids" and "she saids" normally associated with lines of direct discourse. In general, since tag lines are usually meant for the eye—so silent readers will know who is speaking—the tags may be cut when prose fiction selections are performed. This practice should not, however, be followed in all cases. It is true that many tag lines may be cut once the personality and placement of a character are established; however, some tag lines should be retained even after a character's personality and placement have been clarified.

Tag lines should be retained if the action included within the lines cannot be suggested, if the rhythm of the narrative is dependent on the tags, if they seem to be the only contribution the narrator makes (thus reminding us that this is indeed prose fiction narrated by someone and told from a past-tense perspective), if they provide valuable information for audience comprehension, or if they include information difficult for the performer to enact.

Sometimes the tag lines, in conjunction with the dialogue, form the basis of the rhythmic flow of the selection. If this is the case, you will not want to cut the tag lines. Look at this passage from Ray Bradbury's *The Martian Chronicles.*

> From THE MARTIAN CHRONICLES   Ray Bradbury
>
> Dad looked at it. His voice was deep and quiet.
>
> "Just like war. War swims along, sees food, contracts. A moment later—Earth is gone."
>
> "William," said Mom.
>
> "Sorry," said Dad.
>
> They sat still and felt the canal water rush cool, swift, and glassy. The only sound was the motor hum, the glide of water, the sun expanding the air.

"When do we see the Martians?" cried Michael.

"Quite soon, perhaps," said Father. "Maybe tonight."

"Oh, but the Martians are a dead race now," said Mom.

"No, they're not. I'll show you some Martians, all right," Dad said presently.

In addition to helping us identify the speaker, the tag lines in this passage contribute to our information about how something was said and have a rhythmic feel which adds to the story.

Sometimes, too, tag lines are the only contribution the narrator seems to make. Such was the case in the first passage cited earlier from "Here We Are." This condition occurs most often in prose fiction written from the third-person observer point of view. If the tag lines were cut in this situation, the story would begin to resemble a play and the narrative voice would be eliminated. The tag lines help the reader remember that a past-tense story is being narrated.

Often the tag lines tell us substantial things about the narrator. In the short story, "The Third Prize," by A. E. Coppard, for example, the narrator (a third-person observer) uses tag lines like "retorted" and "intimated" to describe the rather simplistic and unsophisticated speech of Cockney children. The tags in this story help the narrator create a formality and a distance and help him communicate the superior self-impression that he wishes to project.

Keep the tag lines when they seem to serve a purpose beyond helping the silent reader know who is speaking. If the tag lines seem only for the eye, or if the action they describe can be effectively enacted, then they may be cut.

As with indirect discourse, the performance of tags offers some choices. The narrator may say a tag such as "Mary replied softly" by communicating his or her attitude toward Mary and what she said, or Mary may say it as though it were a continuation or extension of her direct discourse, among other possibilities.

WHY IS THE STORY TOLD?

Narrators have different reasons for telling stories. They may want to amuse, shock, entertain, share, impress, or fool. Knowing the narrator's reason for telling the story and what he or she wants or needs from the audience affects all performance choices. The narrator in "The Open Window," for example, wants to surprise or shock us; consequently, he would not want to give the ending away by smiling during seemingly serious or shocking moments—like the men returning home through the open window.

The "why" of the story is also related to the story's *theme*. Theme is the basic idea or moral the writer tries to convey. Being able to state the theme of a story usually brings you closer to understanding why the story was written. Like the author's tone, the theme is usually not directly stated in the story. The theme is something you understand after reading the entire story and asking yourself whether the author had, for example, a moral in mind. The theme can usually be stated in a short aphorism such as "Art will outlive the life span of humanity" or "Judge not, lest ye be judged."

The theme of "The Open Window" might be, "Don't believe everything you hear" or "Beware of people who let their vivid imaginations get the best of them." The theme involves both a liar and a gullible person, a romancer and a person who assumes that fiction is fact. Saki, in addition to entertaining us, may be saying that those who are too easily fooled deserve to be fooled. In this case, Saki is talking about both Framton Nuttel and the reader.

MODAL ANALYSIS OF PROSE FICTION

A speaker modal analysis categorizes a prose fiction text according to who is speaking. The speaker mode of "The Open Window" is epic because both a narrator and defined characters speak. An audience modal analysis involves deciding who is being addressed at any given time. Often one selection shifts from one audience mode to another audience mode many times, and your performance should make these shifts clear.

The audience mode shifts to correspond with the various communicative interactions and intentions in a text. The epic voice is heard when the narrator speaks to the audience directly and furthers the story line, gives opinions, or describes characters, objects, or events for the benefit of the general audience. Examples of lines in the epic mode are "John was Sara's husband and was never on time," "Tim had been editor of the newspaper for three years and was now retired," "Mary walked to the store to get her usual assortment of TV dinners," "The girl was a sharp-tongued shrew," and "The house was a brilliant yellow." In each of these examples, the narrator's intention is to provide needed information to help make the narrator's personal view of character and event clear to the audience.

The dramatic voice is heard when the narrator suggests characters. If the narrator reproduces either the exact words of the character (direct discourse) or retells what a character said (indirect discourse), it is in the dramatic mode. (If the narrator speaks a character's indirect discourse in the narrator's voice, however, and addresses the audience, it is the epic mode.) Examples include, "'I want to go to the store,' said Mary" and "Mary said that she wanted to go to the store."

When the narrator is psychologically close to a character, able to tell us what that character is thinking or feeling, it is lyric. Examples would be, "Ken felt doom approaching" and "Heather thought about the man she saw at the circus." When performing lines in the lyric mode, consider closely the language the narrator uses. If the line incorporates the vocabulary and style of the character, let the narrator imitate the character saying the line—even though the character may be talking about himself or herself in the past tense and in the third person. If the line seems to be in the narrator's language style and vocabulary, as well as the narrator's version of what the character thought or felt from the narrator's perspective alone, then let the narrator say the line.

Let us look again at the passage from "The Open Window" analyzed earlier. This time we will locate the modal shifts and provide possible performance analogues.

1. She rattled on cheerfully about the shooting and the scarcity of birds, and the prospects for duck in the winter.
2. To Framton it was all purely horrible.
3. He made a desperate but only partially successful effort to turn the talk on to a less ghastly topic;
4. he was conscious that his hostess was giving him only a fragment of her attention, and her eyes were constantly straying past him to the open window and the lawn beyond.
5. It was certainly an unfortunate coincidence that he should have paid his visit on this tragic anniversary.
6. "The doctors agree in ordering me complete rest, an absence of mental excitement, and avoidance of anything in the nature of violent physical exercise,"
7. announced Framton, who laboured under the tolerably wide-spread delusion that total strangers and chance acquaintances are hungry for the least detail of one's ailments and infirmities, their cause and cure.

Let us now perform one possible modal analysis of these lines. Line 1 of this passage is in the epic mode. The narrator furthers the plot line by summarizing what Mrs. Sappleton did. In performance, you would speak directly to the audience and use open focus. As you read this line, you can show the narrator remembering what Mrs. Sappleton sounded like as she "rattled on" and suggest the narrator's rather patronizing attitude toward her. Line 2 shows what Framton is thinking. You have at least two choices when delivering this line. You could allow the narrator to deliver the line to the audience, maintaining the narrator's attitude, or the narrator could suggest Framton thinking this aloud. If you choose the latter option, you should have a slight shift in muscle tone as you move from addressing the audience to an identification with Framton. If the narrator imitates Framton— speaking of himself in the third person and in the past tense—the audience would be put into the position of overhearing a private moment of reflection. Framton would speak aloud as though no audience were present. Line 3 again shifts to the epic voice, and the narrator again uses open focus. The narrator's attitude toward Framton is suggested with the words "desperate" and "partially successful." Line 4 seems to be a lyric line—Framton's description of what he sees. Either the narrator could take the line as himself or the narrator could imitate Framton, depending on whose vocabulary and syntax you felt were represented. If you feel the line represents the narrator's vocabulary and syntax, let the narrator deliver the line with open focus. If you decide that the line is representative of Framton's language and syntax, let the narrator imitate Framton, and use inner-closed focus. Line 5 could be Framton's assessment of his situation or the narrator's commentary. There are at least three options for the performance of this line. Since the narrator uses the stuffy kind of language peculiar to Framton, the narrator may imitate Framton and deliver the line very seriously using inner-closed focus. Another possibility would be to have the narrator take the line and—with tongue firmly in cheek—imitate Framton, using open focus. A third option would be to have the narrator deliver the line seriously, in order to hide his superior knowledge of this "tragic anniversary." Again, the decision is up to you within your modal analysis. Line 6 is a line of dialogue—direct discourse—and shifts to the dramatic mode. For this scenic line, the narrator suggests Framton's voice and body as well as his nervousness and discomfort. When projecting the dramatic voice, the performer usually uses closed focus. When using closed focus, you create the character and imagine the character(s) to whom you are speaking above and in the middle of the audience. Framton speaks this line to Mrs. Sappleton, whom he sees out in the imagined scene. The second half of this line, labeled line 7, shifts again to the epic voice. The narrator probably says this line and speaks directly to the audience. The focus is open for the tag line and for the rest of the description, which is the narrator's opinion of Framton.

The audience mode constantly shifts in this passage, depending on who is speaking and to whom. If it will help you, mark your script (if you use a script) for changes in mode so that you will know where to look, what character to suggest, and what attitude or feeling to convey.

PUTTING IT ALL TOGETHER

See if you can answer each question below in relation to the story you have selected to perform. (We suggest you rehearse the selection several times before attempting to answer these questions.)

1. How would you describe the narrator? Is the narrator male or female? What does he or she look like? sound like? act like? If you were a Hollywood casting director, whom would you cast to play the narrator?

2. What is the narrator's point of view? With whom does the narrator seem to identify? Is he or she inside or outside the story? objective or subjective? dramatized or undramatized? reliable or unreliable?

3. To whom might the narrator be speaking? Who is the narratee—the implied audience?

4. Are the characters in the story round or flat? static or dynamic?

5. What is the relationship between the narrator and the characters physically? emotionally? psychologically? morally?

6. Does the plot have a definite beginning, middle, and end? Does the story follow a causal pattern or do events seem to happen at random?

7. Where does the story take place? What is the setting? Where are the characters in the virtual past? Where is the narrator in the virtual present? At any given moment, which environment is more important to suggest—the virtual present or the virtual past?

8. Which parts of the story are written in scene? which in summary? which in description? How does knowing this affect your performance?

9. How much time elapsed between the virtual present and the virtual past? How can you tell?

10. What is the tone? What does the author's attitude seem to be? How is this conditioned by the author's gender and by the time or era in which the author was writing?

11. What is the narrator's style? How does his/her style help to characterize personality? How does style affect the story?

12. What is the mood? How is it created? How does the story make you feel?

13. What would you do with the tag lines when you perform this story?

14. What seems to be the narrator's purpose in telling the story? Is the narrator's purpose the same as the author's? What is the "theme"?

15. What is the speaker mode of this story?

16. Which parts of the story are in the lyric audience mode? which dramatic? which epic? What does knowing this tell you about performance?

17. What kinds of focus are necessary? open focus? closed focus? inner-closed focus? semi-closed focus? How many character placements do you need for dialogue moments?

18. How much sensory showing will you need while performing?

19. Through what other "texts" did you read the story? How did your past experiences, interests, and preoccupations influence your understanding of the story?

20. How would you introduce the story if you were going to perform it for class? If you are able to read the entire story, must an introduction be delivered? What must the audience know to understand only one section of the story?

SELECTED PROSE FICTION TEXTS APPROPRIATE FOR PERFORMANCE

The following titles represent short stories and novels that are appropriate for performance. These are meant only as suggestions! There are hundreds of other prose fiction works that you may choose, and there are other titles by the authors listed below that would be fine for performance. (The starred [*] selections are short-short stories which because of their abbreviated length are appropriate for performance.) Consult this list if you need a starting point.

Conrad Aiken	"Impulse," "Silent Snow, Secret Snow"
Mahshid Amir-Shahy	"Brother's New Family"
Sherwood Anderson	"The Egg"
Margaret Atwood	*Cat's Eye, The Handmaid's Tale,* "Significant Moments in the Life of My Mother"
Isaac Babel	"The Death of Dolgushov"*
Donald Barthelme	"me and miss mandible"
Heinrich Boll	*The Clown, Billiards at Half-Past Nine, Group Portrait with Lady,* "The Laughter"*
Jorge Luis Borges	"The Dead Man"*
Ray Bradbury	"And the Rock Cried Out," "The Veldt," "And There Will Come Soft Rain"
Italo Calvino	*If on a Winter's Night a Traveler, Cosmic Comics*
Caleb Carr	*Alienist*
Denise Chávez	"Willow Game"
Frank Chin	"Food for All His Dead"
A. E. Coppard	"The Third Prize"
Stephen Crane	"The Open Boat," "The Bride Comes to Yellow Sky"
Don DeLillo	*White Noise*
Isak Dinesen	"The Sailor-Boy's Tale"
James Ellroy	*White Jazz*
Shusaku Endo	"Old Friends"
Louise Erdrich	"The Red Convertible"
William Faulkner	"Barn Burning," "A Rose for Emily"
Richard Ford	*Independence Day*
N. V. M. Gonzalez	"The Bread of Salt"

Ernest Hemingway	"Soldier's Home," "The Killers," "A Clean Well-Lighted Place"
Zora Neal Hurston	"The Gilded Six-Bits"
Kazuo Ishiguro	*Remains of the Day*
Shirley Jackson	"Charles," "The Lottery," "The Witch"
James Joyce	"Eveline," "The Boarding House," "The Dead"
Maria Luise Kaschnitz	"Going to Jerusalem"*
D. H. Lawrence	"The Horse Dealer's Daughter"
Doris Lessing	"Homage for Isaac Babel"*
Catherine Lim	"Monster"
Katherine Mansfield	"The Doll's House," "Marriage à la Mode"
Gabriel Garcia Marquez	*One Hundred Years of Solitude, The Autumn of the Patriarch,* "A Very Old Man with Enormous Wings," "Tuesday Siesta," "Bitterness for Three Sleepwalkers"*
Yukio Mishima	*Confessions of a Mask, Sun and Steel,* "Swaddling Clothes,"* "Patriotism"
Augusto Monerroso	"The Eclipse"*
Toshio Mori	"Slant-Eyed Americans"
Toni Morrison	*Beloved*
Daniel Moyano	"The Rescue"
Aziz Nesin	"Dog Tails"
Flannery O'Connor	"Good Country People," "A Good Man Is Hard to Find," "The River"
Frank O'Connor	"My Oedipus Complex"
Grace Paley	*The Little Disturbances of Man, Enormous Changes at the Last Minute,* "Wants"*
Octavio Paz	"The Blue Bouquet"*
Katherine Anne Porter	"Flowering Judas"
Varlam Shalamov	"In the Night"*
Moshe Shamir	"Next of Kin"
Irwin Shaw	"The Girls in their Summer Dresses"
Leslie Silko	"Yellow Woman"
Isaac Bashevis Singer	"Gimpel the Fool"
James Thurber	"The Catbird Seat," "University Days"
Kurt Vonnegut, Jr.	"Long Walk to Forever," "Harrison Bergeron," "Welcome to the Monkey House"

Alice Walker	*The Color Purple,* "Everyday Use," "The Hell with Dying," "Really, Doesn't Crime Pay," *The Temple of My Familiar*
Eudora Welty	"Why I Live at the P.O.," "Lily Daw and the Three Ladies"
William Carlos Williams	"The Use of Force"
Mikhail Zoschenko	"The Bathhouse"*

SUMMARY

When you are studying prose fiction for performance, ask yourself these questions: Who is the narrator? What is the narrator's point of view (first-person major character, first-person minor character, third-person omniscient, third-person observer)? How does the narrator choose to tell the story? from what perspective? Ask yourself also, What does the narrator look like, act like, and feel like? How can I project these qualities in performance? What is the narrator's attitude toward the events and the characters in them? Consider also the narrator's audience (to whom the narrator speaks), where and when the story is being told, where and when the story takes place, how the story is being told (tone, style, language), and why the story is being told (intention, theme).

As you analyze selections for performance, decide when the lyric, dramatic, and epic voices are heard. If it is lyric, speakers address themselves; if it is dramatic, speakers address other characters in the imagined scene; if it is epic, speakers address the audience.

Notes

1. E. M. Forster, *Aspects of the Novel* (New York: Harcourt, Brace & World, 1927), p. 130.
2. Phyllis Bentley, *Some Observations on the Art of the Narrative* (New York: Macmillan, 1947), especially pp. 28–39.
3. Suzanne Langer, *Feeling and Form: A Theory of Art* (New York: Charles Scribner's Sons, 1953), p. 295.
4. See Lilla Heston, "A Note on Prose Fiction: The Performance of Dialogue Tags," *Speech Teacher* 22 (January 1973): 69–72.

really tight. It makes all the difference. Like this. Then
you won't wobble so much.

                              RUTHANNE
Okay. Thanks. Will you teach me?

                              FRANCES
Yes. You'll skate like Peggy Flemming.

                              RUTHANNE
Who?

                              FRANCES
Dorthy Hammill.

                              RUTHANNE
I know her, I think.

                              SAMUEL
Okay, now.

        (Lights down on set. Lights up on Ruthanne.)

What you should know is that I love cows. Some people love
cats. Some people love dogs. A boy in my class loves grain
elevators--draws them all over his notebook all day long.
But I love cows. After Moss was born I decided that I was
going to be a veterinarian. I found out that there are
thirty-five schools of vet med in America. The real students
call it "vet med." Neat. So, I typed up thirty-five letters
asking for information, a huge stack of them, and mailed
them off. Guess what? About a month later all this stuff
came back. These huge, thick packets, and college
catalogues, and application forms. My dad wasn't real happy.
But he let me keep all of it. I started studying for the
MCAT test a month ago. I'm going to specialize in cows, like
a doctor specializes in ear-nose-and-throat. Doctor Ruthanne
Creighton, cow vet. A doctor of bovinity. Neat. Something I
found out. It's harder to become a vet than it is to be a
regular people doctor. It's true. You need better grades and
they accept fewer people. And I think that's right. Animals
can't tell you what is wrong. You just have to know. I think
I know.

        (Lights up on set.)

In the second act of *Hamlet,* the title character speaks the following words: "The play's the thing/Wherein I'll catch the conscience of the king." Hamlet is convinced that a dramatic presentation has the power to move or "catch" up an audience.

If you have ever read a play (play as literature) or seen a play performed (play as theatre), you may be able to testify to drama's effectiveness in stimulating mental, emotional, and psychological responses. Many of our great tragedies have the power to invoke in us pity or fear—feelings which are purged when the play ends and the tragic hero meets his or her inevitable demise. Comedies, which usually have a happy ending, can motivate our laughter or our scorn. In addition to providing valuable vicarious experiences, reading, viewing, and performing in plays can teach us something about ourselves as well as about others who may be quite different from us.

Reading plays silently, as well as performing them as actors, actresses, or interpreters, is an often difficult but always rewarding experience. Reading plays is challenging because of the degree of participation required of the reader. As you read, your mind must be very active, visualizing the scenes and the costumed characters moving about in them. This imaginative participation provides you with information necessary when you ultimately perform the play.

Imagining is especially important to interpreters, who usually do not have other performers, costumes, sets, makeup, or props to help them in their performances. Interpreters use their own inner resources, past experiences, and imaginations to create the scenes as well as each of the characters in them. Knowing how to be an informed silent reader and performer of plays increases your appreciation of a play as a piece of literature and as a vehicle for performance. Although plays were written to be enacted on a stage usually with a number of performers and costumes, lights, set, and props, etc., the solo performer can suggest these elements by calling upon performance conventions and the audience's willingness to believe and use their imaginations. The advantage of a solo performance of a dramatic scene is that it provides the audience with a unified perspective with no distractions. The text of the play is what is important. The audience participates in the creation of a scene by fleshing out aspects suggested by the performer. In this way, the audience becomes an active (if silent) participant in the creation of a scene. In this chapter, you will find the information you need to become a more informed reader and performer of plays. Before we begin, let us first examine the differences between drama and prose fiction.

DRAMA AND PROSE FICTION

Drama differs from prose fiction in three essential ways. First, most plays are written in the present tense as though the action were occurring right now, as opposed to the past-tense action of most prose fiction works. In addition, the rhythm of prose fiction is primarily created by the alternation of scene, summary, and description, while drama is written almost exclusively in scene—lines of dialogue. This scenic rhythm gives drama its spontaneity and vitality. Summary and description may exist in plays, but usually only within scene. The most apparent difference between prose fiction and drama concerns the presence of a narrator. The narrator, as we have said, is the primary and central speaker in a short story or novel. Plays rarely have narrators, but when they do, as in *Our Town, The Glass Menagerie, A View from the Bridge,* or *Equus,* the narrator is usually a character in the play, not "third-person observer" or "third-person omniscient," and the narrative role is one of many roles and may not be the central or major role in the play. In plays with narrators, there is a sense of vicarious experience, as there is with prose fiction. The audience learns what has already happened from the point of view of a first-person narrator/character.

WHAT ARE THE BASIC CHARACTERISTICS OF DRAMA?

Just as specific terms relate to the analysis of prose fiction, particular terms also relate to the study and analysis of dramatic literature, and you should master them. Many of the traditional terms for the study of drama will seem familiar to you, since we also discussed them in relation to the analysis of prose fiction. When these terms are used in the study of drama, however, they often have a slightly different meaning or emphasis.

Aristotle's *Poetics* was primarily responsible for establishing the traditional terminology common to dramatic analysis, and although Aristotle wrote in the fourth century B.C., his terms are still useful today. The terms most often associated with the study of dramatic literature (listed in their order of importance as far as Aristotle was concerned) are *plot, character, thought, diction, music,* and *spectacle.* Let us examine each of these terms individually as they apply in dramatistic analysis.

WHO IS SPEAKING?

Character

One of the essential materials of all plays is *character.* It is through characterization that the playwright differentiates one dramatic speaker from another. Since dramatic purpose is different for each play, playwrights may stress characterization and thus develop totally round, dynamic characters or they may wish to create flat, static characters to shift emphasis to another element of the play. Although there are exceptions, you will normally find round, dynamic characters in full-length plays and flat, static characters in the shorter one-act play. In any case, you will want to spend much time studying each character and the role he or she plays. You accomplish this by studying what characters say and do, what characters may be thinking that they are not saying, what other characters say about them, and what the playwright may supply in notes or stage directions. You could also consult outside research books and reviews of productions of the play, such as in *The New York Times*. Use all available information in determining your interpretation of how each character looks, sounds, thinks, and behaves.

There are primarily four levels of characterization: *physical, social, psychological, and moral*.[1] When analyzing the physical behavior of characters, you examine such external characteristics as age, gender, height, weight, race, and so forth. Although playwrights may not always specifically supply this information, usually clues within the context of the play help you to describe the characters physically. While physical depiction is the simplest level of character analysis, it is still essential to begin with the physical level to give concrete form to the characters in performance.

The social level of analysis examines a character's circumstances with regard to family, religion, and business, for example. How this character functions with others in the environment comprises the social level of analysis. This information is necessary to depict character interrelationships within scenes.

The psychological level of analysis is of extreme importance to performers, for it gets at the inner workings of a character's mind. The psychological level of analysis examines the attitudes, beliefs, desires, likes and dislikes, and especially the motivations and intentions of a character. The psychological level of analysis helps to get at why characters say what they say and do what they do. Characters may laugh or cry; the psychological analysis helps us to discover what triggers those reactions.

The *subtext*—the implied message communicated either consciously or unconsciously underneath or between the lines of dialogue—can also be ascertained through psychological character analysis. Subtext was used by Stanislavski, Russian actor, producer, and director, to mean the inwardly felt expression of a human being which can be felt beneath the words of the text. No analysis of character is complete until one analyzes the subtext as well as the text. Speech, it is sometimes said, was given to humans so they could hide their thoughts. If, for example, one character tells another, "You've never looked better," you must decide from your understanding of the context whether the line should be read sincerely or whether the character is really thinking "You've never looked worse." Just because a character tells another character, "I love you," does not necessarily make it true. The subtext is developed by careful reading of the text to discover the hidden or disguised motivations or intentions of characters. As in real life, characters do not always say what they really think or feel. You communicate the subtext in a scene through movement, gesture, facial expression, and vocal inflection. If, for example, the line is "I truly care about you" and you say it with a frown and a sarcastic tone while walking away, the opposite sentiment is suggested!

Look, for example, at this scene from Arthur Miller's Pulitzer Prize-winning play *Death of a Salesman*. Miller has described the play as a tragedy about a commonplace salesman (Willy Loman) who sacrifices his life to secure one thing—a sense of personal dignity. Willy is an aging traveling salesman who has had difficulties keeping up with his road business. Willy pressures his children (especially his son Biff) into fulfilling his expectations. Willy wants his children to have a better life than he did, but Willy exists in an illusory world where he sees things as he would like them to be rather than the way they are. Willy feels like a failure because he has run out of resources to support his family. Unfortunately, Willy is convinced that his desire for personal dignity can only be fulfilled by committing suicide.

In this scene, Willy demeans himself by coming to his young boss, Howard, and asking to be taken off the road and given a desk job. Read the scene aloud, and see if you can analyze the physical, social, and psychological dimensions of each character. Can you determine when Willy and Howard are sincere and when they are disguising their real intentions?

From DEATH OF A SALESMAN   Arthur Miller

Willy:	Pst! Pst!
Howard:	Hello, Will, come in.
Willy:	Like to have a little talk with you, Howard.
Howard:	Sorry to keep you waiting. I'll be with you in a minute.
Willy:	What's that, Howard?
Howard:	Didn't you ever see one of these? Wire recorder.
Willy:	Oh. Can we talk a minute?
Howard:	Records things. Just got delivery yesterday. Been driving me crazy, the most terrific machine I ever saw in my life. I was up all night with it.
Willy:	What do you do with it?
Howard:	I bought it for dictation, but you can do anything with it. Listen to this. I had it home last night. Listen to what I picked up. The first one is my daughter. Get this. (*He flicks the switch and "Roll Out the Barrel" is heard being whistled.*) Listen to that kid whistle.
Willy:	That is lifelike, isn't it?
Howard:	Seven years old. Get that tone.
Willy:	Ts Ts. Like to ask a little favor of you. . . . (*The whistling breaks off, and the voice of Howard's daughter is heard.*)
His Daughter:	"Now you, Daddy."

Howard:	She's crazy for me! (*Again the same song is whistled.*) That's me! (*He winks.*)
Willy:	You're very good! (*Whistling breaks off again. Machine runs silent.*)
Howard:	Sh! Get this now, this is my son.
His Son:	"The capital of Alabama is Montgomery; the capital of Arizona is Phoenix; the capital of Arkansas is Little Rock; the capital of California is Sacramento . . ." (*and on, and on*).
Howard:	(*Holding up five fingers*) Five years old, Willy!
Willy:	He'll make an announcer some day!
His Son:	(*Continuing*) "The capital . . ."
Howard:	Get that—alphabetical order! (*The machine breaks off suddenly.*) Wait a minute. The maid kicked the plug out.
Willy:	It certainly is a—
Howard:	Sh, for God's sake!
His Son:	"It's nine o'clock, Bulova watch time. So I have to go to sleep."
Willy:	That really is—
Howard:	Wait a minute! The next is my wife. (*They wait.*)
Howard's Voice:	"Go on, say something." (*Pause*) "Well, you gonna talk?"
His Wife:	"I can't think of anything."
Howard's Voice:	"Well, talk—it's turning."
His Wife:	(*Shyly, beaten*) "Hello." (*Silence.*) "Oh, Howard, I can't talk into this . . ."
Howard:	(*Snapping the machine off*) That was my wife.
Willy:	That is a wonderful machine. Can we—
Howard:	I tell you, Willy, I'm gonna take my camera, and my bandsaw, and all my hobbies, and out they go. This is the most fascinating relaxation I ever found.
Willy:	I think I'll get one myself.
Howard:	Sure they're only a hundred and a half. You can't do without it. Supposing you wanna hear Jack Benny, see? But you can't be at home at that hour. So you tell the maid to turn the radio on when Jack Benny comes on, and this automatically goes on with the radio.
Willy:	And when you come home . . .
Howard:	You can come home twelve o'clock, one o'clock, any time you like, and get yourself a Coke and sit yourself down, throw the switch, and there's Jack Benny's program in the middle of the night.
Willy:	I'm definitely going to get one. Because lots of times I'm on the road, and I think to myself, what I must be missing on the radio.
Howard:	Don't you have a radio in the car?

Willy:	Well, yeah, but who ever thinks of turning it on?
Howard:	Say, aren't you supposed to be in Boston?
Willy:	That's what I want to talk to you about, Howard. You got a minute? *(He draws a chair in from the wing)*
Howard:	What happened? What're you doing here?
Willy:	Well . . .
Howard:	You didn't crack up again, did you?
Willy:	Oh, no. No . . .
Howard:	Geez, you had me worried there for a minute. What's the trouble?
Willy:	Well, tell you the truth, Howard. I've come to the decision that I'd rather not travel any more.
Howard:	Not travel! Well, what'll you do?
Willy:	Remember, Christmas time, when you had the party here? You said you'd try to think of some spot for me here in town.
Howard:	With us?
Willy:	Well, sure.
Howard:	Oh, yeah, yeah. I remember. Well, I couldn't think of anything for you, Willy.
Willy:	I tell ya, Howard. The kids are all grown up, y'know. I don't need much any more. If I could take home—well sixty-five dollars a week, I could swing it.
Howard:	Yeah, but Willy, see I—
Willy:	I tell ya, Howard. Speaking frankly and between the two of us, y'know—I'm just a little tired.
Howard:	Oh, I could understand that, Willy. But you're a road man, Willy, and we do a road business. We've only got a half-dozen salesmen on the floor here.
Willy:	God knows, Howard, I never asked a favor of any man. But I was with the firm when your father used to carry you in here in his arms.
Howard:	I know that, Willy, but—
Willy:	Your father came to me the day you were born and asked me what I thought of the name of Howard, may he rest in peace.
Howard:	I appreciate that, Willy, but there just is no spot here for you. If I had a spot I'd slam you right in, but I just don't have a single solitary spot. *(He looks for his lighter. Willy has picked it up and gives it to him. Pause.)*
Willy:	*(With increasing anger)* Howard, all I need to set my table is fifty dollars a week.
Howard:	But where am I going to put you, kid?
Willy:	Look, it isn't a question of whether I can sell merchandise, is it?

Howard:	No, but it's a business, kid, and everybody's gotta pull his own weight.
Willy:	(*Desperately*) Just let me tell you a story, Howard—
Howard:	'Cause you gotta admit, business is business.

From *Death of a Salesman* by Arthur Miller. Copyright 1949, renewed 1977 by Arthur Miller. Reprinted by permission of Viking Penguin, Inc.

In this scene, we are dealing with two male characters: Willy Loman and Howard Wagner. Willy is an aging salesman working for a company for which Howard is now the boss. Howard is younger than Willy, and Willy is uncomfortable having to be subservient to him. Willy has been with the company much longer and even worked for Howard's father. Their social relationship is worker-boss. Willy seems to be overtly interested in Howard's wire recorder; he even tells Howard that he plans to buy a recorder. We know (from earlier scenes in the play) that Willy cannot afford to buy a wire recorder, and that he has no intention of buying one. While Willy is making polite conversation, he is really hoping for an opportunity to tell Howard the reason for his visit. Howard, on the other hand, is sincerely interested in his new toy. During the first half of the scene, then, Howard does not seem to be withholding anything while Willy conceals his true intentions. At the midpoint of the scene, when Howard consciously realizes to whom he is speaking ("Say, aren't you supposed to be in Boston?"), a reversal occurs. Willy slowly reveals the reason for his visit, and Howard becomes uncomfortable and evasive. He begins to patronize Willy, calling him "kid" and using Willy's name over and over (as some salesmen do), and he hides his previously made decision to fire Willy. As Willy gets angrier at Howard's dismissal of his request to be taken off the road, Howard finally does euphemistically let Willy go, claiming Willy needs a long rest. When you perform this scene, work on conveying your understanding of both the text and the subtext.

The last level of characterization is moral. This aspect of character usually determines whether the audience views a character sympathetically, unsympathetically, or objectively. When analyzing the moral dimension, one examines the kinds of choices characters make and the way in which they live their lives. The ethical or nonethical behavior of characters is more likely to be a consideration in serious plays than in comic plays, where actions are likely to be the result of expediency rather than of moral decisions. The moral dimension is often controversial because everyone may not share the same moral values. At the end of *Death of a Salesman,* Willy commits suicide. How does Willy's choice affect your consideration of his moral character?

As you develop these four levels of characterization, keep in mind that your real goal in the solo performance of drama is to make the characters seem real and believable. This is the goal, regardless of whether the play is a comedy, tragedy, farce, or melodrama. (Comic George Burns once quipped that acting is all about honesty. If you can fake that you've got it made.) It is a classic trap in comedy for performers to fall into the belief that the characters they are playing are somehow less real than those in a serious play or tragedy. This lessens the impact of the comedy. An audience does not want to laugh at cartoon caricatures of people; they want to laugh at representations of people they know and recognize: the fool, the bully, the eccentric. If the performer does not believe in the character, then neither will the audience. Characters can be absurd, but they must be *real*.

When performing scenes from plays, ask yourself the five questions below, and examine the possibilities listed under each question (many other possibilities exist):

1. What is the general nature of each character's personality?
   A. Flat or round?
   B. Static or dynamic?
   C. Simple or complex?
2. What are each character's life history and habits?
   A. What was each character doing before the play began?
   B. What will each character do when the play is over?
   C. Where has each character been, and what has each character been doing before he or she enters a scene?
   D. What is each character's family background? religion? education? social class?
3. What is each character's attitude toward life?
   A. Accepting?
   B. Hostile?
   C. Trusting?
   D. Fatalistic?
   E. Optimistic?
   F. Pessimistic?
4. How does each character behave?
   A. Carefree?
   B. Rigid?
   C. Conventionally?
   D. Impulsively?
   E. Compulsively?
   F. Stoically?
   G. Eccentrically?
5. How does each character's behavior make us respond?
   A. Sympathetically?
   B. Unsympathetically?
   C. Objectively?
   D. Compassionately?
   E. Coldly?

Body Fact and Body Act

When you translate your analysis of character into performance analogues, you are interested in how to transform *body fact* (what you are physically, socially, and so on) into *body act* (what you will do in performance to project the physical, social, psychological, and moral dimensions of each character in a scene).

Body fact comprises all the qualities that make you uniquely you: your gender, height, weight, race, and so forth. In drama performances, more than in the performance of poetry or prose fiction, you usually deal with more than one character. When performing a scene, it is essential, therefore, that you work on the individualizing characteristics of each character who speaks. Your responsibility in a solo drama performance is to create your impression of each character in the scene you have chosen to perform. The end result of this process is called body act.

Laurence Olivier's body fact is well known, but his body act as Shylock is different from his body act as Hamlet, which is different from his body act as Richard III. This process could be summarized as follows:

You {Your Body Fact} Study the {Character's Body Fact} to Create the {Body Act of the Character} which is a {Product of your Unique Interpretation}.

Students often wonder how to project an elderly person, or how to suggest a child, as though there were only one voice and one body for all elderly people and all children. Remember, no two characters are alike and no character is exactly like you. In addition, there is no such thing as a "typical" or "average" character. What is a "typical mother," "typical college student," or "average old lady"? Each character in a play has his or her own unique feel and personality. Find out what you have in common with each character in your scene, and use these qualities to help you. In addition, find out how each character is different from you and from the other characters, and use this information as well. Even though Pulitzer-prize- and Tony-award-winning playwright Marsha Norman is speaking about creating characters in the following excerpt from a speech delivered in March of 1998 at Ball State University, her advice applies to performing characters as well:

> If you are a man and you write a woman central character, check her out with a woman friend of yours. Does she seem real? Will she pass? As though you were an alien designing a human life form. Same with women. Don't just assume that because you've known some men that you can write one. Check him out. Test-drive a character. Watch how his real life models respond to him. Pay attention.

When you are performing characters in plays then, keep these general considerations in mind. Try to learn all the relevant facts (learned by applying a dramatistic analysis) that influence a character's behavior and then use these facts to place yourself inside his or her life perspective. Ask yourself what the character wants most in life and analyze his or her range of lesser but still important goals, both conscious and unconscious. How does this character deal with obstacles and setbacks? What is the character thinking that he or she is not speaking about? In other words, be concerned with what goes on *inside* the character as he or she behaves in relation to other characters and in each new situation. It is not important, though, to have experienced the same emotions or similar feelings as the characters you are portraying. Imagination and observation are often more vital. Observe carefully the behavior of people who do resemble the characters and determine whether this information can be incorporated into your scene. (Watching other people closely and listening to them speak are valuable habits that provide useful information as you seek to create different types of characters.) Remember, however, to adapt all your observations to your understanding of the specific characters in the specific scene under consideration.

WHO IS BEING ADDRESSED: AUDIENCE MODE

Four potential audiences are involved in the performance of drama. The nature of the audience is essential in determining focus but is also a consideration of character. The type of language a character uses is a key to characterization and often helps you determine who is being addressed. Characters may speak to themselves (lyric moment); to other characters (dramatic moment); to a god, inanimate object, or muse (lyric moment); or to the general audience (epic moment).

Occasionally, there are moments in plays when a character thinks aloud. In Eugene O'Neill's play, *Strange Interlude,* for example, characters speak interior thoughts as well as direct discourse. When you find a line that suggests private musings, ask yourself whether open focus or inner-closed focus is more appropriate. Your decision should be based on how private or public the utterance is.

Most often, characters speak to each other, establishing scenes onstage behind the fourth wall—the imaginary wall between the audience and the performers. The performers address lines to each other, apparently unaware that an audience is present. When a solo interpreter performs a scene from a play, the performer establishes the scene offstage, uses closed focus to suggest that one character is speaking to another, and uses character placement to help keep the characters physically differentiated and to help project the illusion of movement.

In some plays, characters break the fourth wall and speak directly to the audience. This action occurs during an *aside* or a *soliloquy,* or when a narrator or a chorus is present.

Asides are lines meant to be addressed directly to the audience. The conventional aside allows a character to speak to the audience and not be heard by the other characters on stage. The soliloquy, famous in plays by Shakespeare, is usually a longer speech than the aside and the character is usually alone on stage. (The word "soliloquy" comes from the Latin *solus,* alone, and *loqui,* to speak.) Traditionally, the Shakespearean soliloquy was addressed directly to the audience (open focus). Today, less private soliloquies may be delivered to the audience with open focus, and more private soliloquies may be delivered with inner-closed focus, if a more intimate mood is desired, or semi-closed focus if a god, a muse, or some other silent listener is addressed.

Narrators in plays like those by Brecht and Wilder and the chorus in Greek dramas traditionally speak directly to the audience. When this happens, you will want to choose who this audience is as part of your interpretation—the same way you identified the audience when performing the narrator in a prose fiction selection. Che in *Evita* is not talking to a generalized theatre audience when he says, "It's our funeral, too," for example. He seems to be addressing Argentinean revolutionaries, and when you create Che you want to address the audience with this in mind. At the end of the play *Agnes of God,* the narrator, Dr. Livingstone, a lapsed Catholic, tells the audience that as a result of her experience with Agnes, she has gone to confession once again. From the very beginning of the play, then, the Doctor—who tells us about an experience that has already happened—could address the audience as if they were the priest in that confessional.

One scene from a play may necessitate the use of all four types of focus, depending on the nature of the audience being addressed at any given moment. Be aware of the four potential audiences as you practice the following scene from *Mother Hicks* by Suzan Zeder and the two scenes from *Do Black Patent Leather Shoes Really Reflect Up?* by John R. Powers.

In *Mother Hicks,* the central character is Tuc, who is mute and deaf. As he signs the narration, various members of the cast speak his words. See if you can decide whom Tuc may be addressing. (An additional consideration when performing this scene is how the solo performer presents a chorus. Read the whole play to see how the chorus lines may be distributed.)

From MOTHER HICKS   Suzan Zeder

> (*TUC signs in silence for a beat or two, then the CHORUS speaks his words.*)
>
> **Chorus:** Mother Hicks is a witch, people say.
> And she lives all alone at the top of Dug Hill
> And she works her magic on the town below.
>
> When cracks is seen in the dry creek bed
> When the corn burns up
> When a calf's born dead
> Mother Hicks is a witch, people say.

When a child falls sick
And there ain't no cause
And there ain't no cure
Then everybody knows that it's witched for sure.
Mother Hicks is a witch . . . people say.

(During the following, CHORUS members come forward, speak a few lines, take an article of clothing from the wagon, and exit. TUC continues signing.)

Chorus: This time is Spring in 1935
A year of fear in the Great Depression.
This place is Ware. W. A. R. E.
The Mississippi River's over there.
This is southern Illinois.
But we call it Egypt.

(A single CHORUS member remains; comes forward and shares the edge of the spotlight with TUC. All subsequent translations of sign language will be handled this way: the interpreter shares the light, but gives focus to the sign.)

Chorus: My name is Tuc.
I cannot speak. I cannot hear.
I use my hands and the words appear.
I hang these words in the air for you
To tell a story that I know is true;
'Cause I heard every word with my eyes.

It is deep in the early,
Just before dawn.

(Lights fade to blackout, a low throbbing electrical hum pulsates in the darkness. The sound is pierced by the shrill sound of a whistle. Lights come up on GIRL at the top of the telephone pole.)

Girl: A dare is a dare and done. Dare and double dare, to sneak over the fence at the power station and fetch the quarter that Ricky threw there. Up and over the fence and then drop down into the cool wet grass. *(She drops down a rung.)* Then I heard it, that stinging, singing sound; racing through them wires, and round them coils and cables; like the electricity wanted to be out like lightning bolts. It's true fact, that I do dares of mortal danger. Things that no one else in town would dare to do, or dare to tell they'd done 'em. A dare is a dare and done!

(From out of the darkness, a voice is heard offstage. It is RICKY RICKS, a boy about GIRL's age.)

Ricky: Girl! Hey . . . You here, Girl?

(*GIRL ducks behind the pole and hoots like an owl. RICKY enters.*)
Ricky: Dang it, Girl, come out! If my Ma finds out I'm not in bed . . .

(*GIRL jumps out of the tree and startles him.*)
Ricky: You just made me jump to Jesus!
Girl: You should have guessed, Ricky, them hoot owls live in trees.
Ricky: It's five o'clock in the morning, and I don't exactly feel like guessing!

Excerpts from *Mother Hicks* by Susan Zeder. Reprinted by permission of the author.

Now let us examine the two scenes from *Do Black Patent Leather Shoes Really Reflect Up?* In both scenes, try to chart the modal shifts. On every line, ask yourself who is being addressed, and adjust your performance accordingly.

From DO BLACK PATENT LEATHER SHOES REALLY REFLECT UP?
John R. Powers

This is the first scene in the play. Eddie Ryan, the play's "hero" and central character, is addressing a secretary at his old Catholic high school.

Secretary: May I help you?
Eddie: Yes, I'd like to see the Principal, please.
Secretary: I'm her secretary. Perhaps I can be of assistance.
Eddie: Well, you see. I graduated from here a number of years ago and . . .
Secretary: All grades are final.
Eddie: Yes, yes, I know that. I would just like to talk to her about something.
Secretary: Sister is quite busy right now, but if you can come back in awhile . . .
Eddie: Oh, sure, that's fine. No problem.
Secretary: I'll inform Sister of the situation. Now what is your name?
Eddie: Edward A. Ryan.
Secretary: You better not fail to be here when Sister is ready to see you.
(*She exits through the office door.*)
Eddie: Oh no. I won't fail (*The door slams into his face*) to be here. (*Crosses downstage.*) I did a lot of failing when I was around here. All the empty workbook pages. F's on the homework I did do. Report card day. Yeah Ma, I gotta try harder. This is the world that Rebecca and I shared together. A world she never left. I still can't figure out why, after all these years, I can't forget her. I've looked everywhere else for the answer. I might as well look here.

(*In a dream light, children of Eddie's past enter, playing such games as tag, hopscotch, patty cake, and ball. After awhile, the children notice Eddie.*)
Becky: Eddie, did you remember your mission money?

Eddie:	Rebecca?
Louie:	Eddie. Hey guys, look!
Nancy:	Eddie.
Mike:	Ryan?
Nancy:	Come on.
Mike:	Ole, ole, ocean free!

This scene is the last one in the play, and Eddie returns to the high school.

Eddie:	*(To the audience.)* On my graduation day, I saw hundreds of people for the last time. Becky was one of them. As I walked home that day, I presumed that we'd get back together again just as we always had. So what, I said. I'm young, there will be plenty of other girls. And there were, but I was never that young again. *(Eddie crosses stage left as the lights fade up to the principal's office. He is obviously getting impatient as he glances at his watch. The door opens and out hobbles Sister Lee.)*
Eddie:	Sister Lee!
Sister Lee:	Disappointed I'm still around, huh?
Eddie:	Oh, no, Str.
Sister Lee:	Yeah, I bet. Well, what do you want?
Eddie:	Ah . . . Sister, I understand, that Rebecca Wright left your order a few months ago . . .
Sister Lee:	For you?
Eddie:	No, Str. But I was wondering if you might know where I could get in touch with her.
Sister Lee:	I can only give out that kind of info to relatives.
Eddie:	Sister, I would very much like to become one.
Sister Lee:	Okay. Becky's teaching at a small school in Indiana. *(As she hands him a small piece of paper.)* Here is the address.
Eddie:	Thank you, Sister.
	(Sister Lee opens the folder she has been holding and smiles warmly.)
Sister Lee:	Did you know, Eddie, that you were the only boy in the history of this school to buy his own pagan baby?
Eddie:	I guess I did a lot of dumb things when I was a kid.
Sister Lee:	Dumb! It's the only good thing on your permanent records. Good day, Mr. Ryan! *(She exits through the door.)*
Eddie:	Good day, Sister Lee. *(He steps downstage.)* No, I will never be that young again, thank God.

From *Do Black Patent Leather Shoes Really Reflect Up?* by John R. Powers. Reprinted by permission of the author.

WHAT DO THE CHARACTERS SPEAK ABOUT?

Plot

Plays are normally structured into acts and scenes. A play may have one act (a currently popular form with condensed action, limited scope, and usually limited characterization), two acts (many contemporary dramas), three acts (probably the most common structure), four acts (plays by Chekhov, Shaw, Ibsen), or five acts (plays by Shakespeare and Molière). The division of a play into acts automatically supplies a kind of structure. The "what" of the play is its *plot*—the sequence of events articulated to yield a beginning, a middle, and an end. Aristotle identified plot as the essential or primary element of drama. The plot involves the characters in action, and the action frequently follows the traditional pattern shown in Figure 7.1.

This pattern has been metaphorically compared to the flight and crash of an airplane. The ride down the runway is the exposition, the liftoff is the rising action,

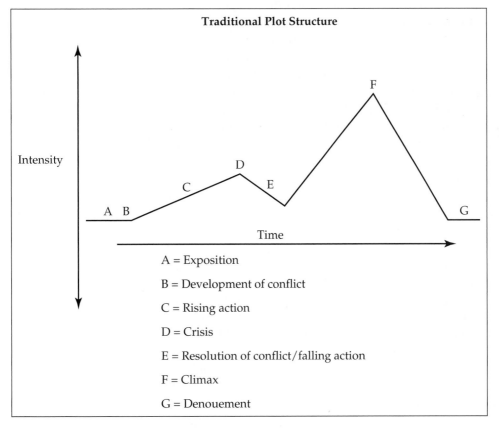

Traditional Plot Structure

A = Exposition

B = Development of conflict

C = Rising action

D = Crisis

E = Resolution of conflict/falling action

F = Climax

G = Denouement

Figure 7.1

the plane running out of gas is the crisis, the fall of the plane is the falling action, the crash is the climax, and the cleanup is the denouement!

The exposition usually establishes the time frame, introduces the characters, and sets the scene. Often the exposition is delivered by relatively minor characters who discuss past events or the current state of affairs to prepare the audience for what is to come and to build anticipation as the audience waits to meet the major characters. In *Hamlet*, for example, the exposition involves two sentinels: Barnardo and Francisco, who are later joined by Horatio, Hamlet's friend, and Marcellus, an officer. Francisco exits, and then Barnardo, Marcellus, and Horatio discuss what has gone on in Denmark prior to this moment: a ghost (King Hamlet, the ghost of Hamlet's dead father) has walked (and he catches the men and the audience off guard by appearing twice during the exposition). Horatio has been summoned to try to communicate with the ghost but is unable to convince the ghost to speak to him. Then a long scene ensues where we learn that Denmark is preparing for war and where we hear of the struggles between old Fortinbras of Norway and the now deceased King Hamlet. The exposition ends with Horatio deciding to tell young Hamlet what the men have seen that night.

Conflict is the element in plot that creates suspense and keeps the audience interested and attentive. The conflict in this play is established when *Hamlet* confronts the ghost of his dead father. This conflict leads to the rising action. The ghost tells Hamlet that he was murdered by Claudius (Hamlet's uncle, who is now the usurping King of Denmark). The ghost wants Hamlet to seek revenge for his murder, but warns Hamlet not to harm Gertrude (Hamlet's mother). The ghost tells Hamlet "to leave her [Gertrude] to heaven." Hamlet must now decide what to do about the information the ghost has given him. Should he believe the ghost? What will happen to Hamlet if he carries out the ghost's demands? How can he revenge his father's murder? How should he feel about his mother?

Conflict is established in three ways. There may be conflict within a character. There may be conflict between or among characters. There may be conflict between a character and the environment. In the case of *Hamlet*, all three types of conflict exist. Hamlet is torn between believing the ghost and not believing the ghost. Hamlet also is in conflict with his uncle and his mother. He resents his uncle for taking his father's place both in Denmark and with his mother. He is angry with his mother because she has remarried so hastily. If Hamlet were to follow the ghost's demands "to revenge his foul and most unnatural murder," he would surely be in conflict with the state—for he would have to kill the king. If *Hamlet* kills the king, what will happen to his immortal soul?

The crisis is the turning point of the play—that point in the action where the directions the plot line can take are limited. One way to discover the crisis is to determine the climax—the highest point of action—and look back to see what event occurred to make the climax inevitable. The better the play, the more obvious is the crisis. *Hamlet* is an early Shakespearean tragedy with structural ambiguity.

Because of this, there are three possible crisis moments in this play. Any one of these moments could lead to the inevitable death of Hamlet at the climax of the play. The crisis could be during the play-within-a-play, "The Mousetrap," when Hamlet seems finally convinced of Claudius's guilt, and Claudius suspects Hamlet knows his crime. The crisis could also be that moment when Hamlet sees Claudius alone, seemingly praying, and decides not to kill him, for Hamlet does not want Claudius to die after "the purging of his soul,/When he is fit and season'd for his passage." Hamlet wants to be sure that when Claudius dies, his soul "may be as damn'd, and black,/As hell, whereto it goes." The crisis could also be the Gertrude closet scene (Act III, Scene iv). In this scene, Hamlet kills a man, speaks his mind to his mother, and receives an admonition from the ghost. To determine which of these scenes is the crisis, ask, In which of these scenes does Hamlet seal his doom?

In the fourth act, the action begins to fall. Claudius sends Hamlet to England and surreptitiously plans to have him killed. Hamlet escapes, however, by jumping onto a pirate ship and returns to Denmark only to discover that Ophelia, once Hamlet's lady, has drowned herself and that her brother, Laertes, has returned from France seeking revenge.

The climax occurs in the fifth act. Here the action peaks and conflicts are resolved. In the climax of *Hamlet*, many of the characters die, including Claudius, Laertes, Gertrude, and Hamlet.

The denouement is the section of the plot which ties up loose ends and often projects the action into the future. In *Hamlet*, the denouement involves the arrival of young Fortinbras, Hamlet's successor, who will ultimately restore order.

We have provided only a skeleton outline of the sequence of events in *Hamlet*. More intensive isolation and analysis of each section of a play are aids to understanding the play's structure. It is important for you to be able to divide a plot into its component parts to facilitate understanding of the flow of action and to help you select a scene appropriate for performance. Although we have been talking of the play as a whole, rising and falling actions also occur within acts and often within scenes. You will want to make sure the scene you choose has a sense of build and release as well as some conflict—as these scenes are easier to pace in performance and hold more interest for the audience. A scene, for example, from the exposition or denouement sections of a play might not work well in performance.

WHERE AND WHEN DOES THE PLAY TAKE PLACE?

If it is essential, the playwright usually provides information about where and when a play takes place in the notes at the beginning of a play. Playwrights may include such information as "an apartment in Brooklyn" and "a summer's day, 1955" to indicate where and when a play takes place. This information should affect your performance in terms of the characters' relationships to their environment (comfortable, uneasy, and so on) and in terms of the definition of your projected scene (see the discussion in this chapter of spectacle fact and spectacle act). Remember, however, that the scene in an interpretation performance is created in the audience's imagination; consequently, it is unnecessary to literalize. If the playwright does not want a definite place and time, aiming, perhaps, for a universal anywhere and anytime, a specific locale and time need not be established. If there is a definite scene location and time period, include this information in your introduction.

HOW DO THE CHARACTERS SPEAK?

Diction and Music

When analyzing the language in a play, we are concerned with Aristotle's terms *diction* and *music*.

Diction is the language of the play. The play may be written either in prose—which is what we use in speaking—or in verse (condensed, poetic, metered language). The language in a play is the primary determinant of character, because what characters say is one of the primary ways of understanding their personalities, determining what ego state dominates at any given moment, and analyzing the types of transactions being exchanged. Analyzing the language in a play is also essential in determining the nature and type of action required from a character at any given moment. Lines such as "It was about this high off the ground" and "He was that close to me" imply a certain type of gesture. Lines such as "I never want to see you again" and "I always want to be near you" imply a certain type of bodily response. The action implied might also be more subtle than these examples indicate, demanding a certain kind of internal response, as in the line, "Whenever I think about her, a strange feeling overcomes me."

Analyzing the style of language a character uses is another method of determining characterization, especially the social level of characterization. Martin Joos delineates five styles of language we use daily and which are commonly found in the dialogue of characters. These five styles are *frozen, formal, consultative, casual,* and *intimate.*[2]

The frozen style of speaking is reserved for all literature in general. Although playwrights ostensibly purport to write as people speak, the language in a play is usually a bit more elaborate and more fluent than dialogue in everyday life. In a play, characters often wait for each other to finish speaking before they speak, but in real life, people often speak at the same time. Characters in plays always seem to know what to say and how to say it well, without hesitation, without using vocalized pauses (such as "um" and "ah"), and without unnecessary filler words ("you know," "OK"). Frozen style, then, is characteristic of the print medium, where language is frozen on the page and unchangeable as written.

The formal style of speaking is characteristic of dialogue between two characters who either do not know each other well or who have a relationship in which one feels or is superior to the other because of position, age, or reputation. In this case, a character uses formal language to convey a feeling of respect or awe, or to convey an air of propriety. The formal style is characterized by a careful, deliberate type of speech that is free of grammatical errors and uses a well-chosen vocabulary. The formal speaker probably has erect posture and excellent diction. An example of formal language would be King Claudius's speech to his people in Act I, Scene ii of *Hamlet*.

The consultative style of speaking is the norm of spoken English—the common style we use when speaking to people we know but not extremely well. It is the style usually used with people we feel relatively comfortable with. Consultative speech tends to be a bit more colloquial than formal speech and is characterized by hesitancies and shortened speech phrases. An example of consultative speech would be found in many plays by Agatha Christie, where a group of people are forced to spend time together and gradually get to know each other.

The casual style of speech is used by people who know each other very well and by people who have a special kind of relationship. Characters use casual speech, for example, with family members and with people with whom they share common interests, hobbies, or social involvements. This style of speaking is usually characterized by some sort of jargon understood only by the participants—a special vocabulary only this particular group of people uses. The dialogue between Felix Unger and Oscar Madison in *The Odd Couple* would be classified as casual.

The last speaking style delineated by Joos is intimate. The intimate style of speaking is reserved for lovers and for characters who spend much close, private time together and need to say very little to communicate messages. Intimate language is characterized by hesitancies, ungrammatical speech, colloquialism, slang, and even shorter speech phrases than in either consultative or casual speech. Hal Carter and Madge Owens use intimate language in William Inge's play *Picnic*.

In the following four dialogue exchanges, notice how the style of language changes, depending on whether the characters are engaged in a formal, consultative, casual, or intimate relationship. (We assume that *all* dialogue in print is frozen. In terms of performance, this means that despite the fact that the language is frozen on the page and is unchangeable, your responsibility is to make each character appear not to know what a line is beforehand.)

Formal Language

Man: Excuse me, please. I am sorry to bother you, but have you by any chance the correct time?

Woman: No trouble at all, sir. It is precisely four o'clock.

Consultative Language

Man: Do you have the correct time, please?
Woman: Sure. It's four o'clock.

Casual Language

Man: Got the time?
Woman: Yeah. It's four.

Intimate Language

Man: Time?
Woman: Four.

When you are reading a play, look at the type of language the characters use. See whether you can analyze how each one's style of speech helps define them and underscore the kind of relationships the characters share. Be aware, also, of when (or if) the language style within one character changes.

In addition to examining the style of language, examine also the rhythm of a character's speech. All language has rhythm, and all characters have a certain rhythmic speech pattern—some more pronounced than others. When a play is written in verse, the pattern is more apparent than when a play is written in prose. However, even nonverse plays have a rhythmic quality. Look, for example, at this prose exchange from *As You Like It*. Notice how rhythmic the language is, primarily as a result of syntactical repetition (similar sentence construction).

From AS YOU LIKE IT   William Shakespeare

Phebe: Good shepherd, tell this youth what 'tis to love.
Silvius: It is to be all made of sighs and tears;
And so am I for Phebe.
Phebe: And I for Ganymede.
Orlando: And I for Rosalind.
Rosalind: And I for no woman.
Silvius: It is to be all made of faith and service;
And so am I for Phebe.
Phebe: And I for Ganymede.
Orlando: And I for Rosalind.
Rosalind: And I for no woman.

When studying a character's vocal characteristics, ask yourself how the character's rhythm of speaking is different from your own. Since no two people have exactly the same rhythm, capturing the character's rhythmic style is an aid in characterization.

Related to the rhythm of speech is Aristotle's element of *music*. Although not all plays have the elements of song and dance common to musical theatre and some melodramas, the language of many plays has a musical, rhythmic quality of its own. Verse plays, for example, are highly musical in tone. The blank verse (unrhyming iambic pentameter) plays of Shakespeare and the freer verse plays of Maxwell Anderson and T. S. Eliot, to name just three, have a high degree of musicality.

Notice the different musicality in the following verse passage from Shakespeare's *Romeo and Juliet*.

From ROMEO AND JULIET   William Shakespeare

Romeo: Why, such is love's transgression.
Griefs of mine own lie heavy in my breast,
Which thou wilt propagate, to have it prest
With more of thine. This love that thou hast shown
Doth add more grief to too much of mine own.
Love is a smoke rais'd with the fume of sighs;
Being purg'd, a fire sparkling in lovers' eyes;
Being vex'd, a sea nourish'd with lovers' tears.
Why is it else? A madness most discreet,
A choking gall, and a preserving sweet.

Here the rhythm and the rhyme project Romeo's melancholy mood. As you prepare a selection for performance, pay close attention to the style, the rhythm, and the musicality of the language. Each element provides information as to the type of character speaking.

WHY ARE THE CHARACTERS SPEAKING?

Goals, Obstacles, and Strategies [GOS]

When you watch a basketball game, you are aware that the general goal of each team is to win the game. Specific goals throughout the game include trying to defend (when on defense) or score (when on offense). The obstacle to these specific goals is the behavior of the players on the opposing team. When you are trying to defend, they are trying to score; when you are trying to score, they are trying to defend. Time-outs are called so that coaches may use Xs and Os to map out strategies to foil the opposing team's goals.

Ironically enough, this same principle is involved in performing a scene from a play. Each character in the play has a general *goal* (also known as a "super objective") as well as many specific goals (other terms for "goal" include "intention" and "objective," among others), *obstacles* that prevent those goals from being fulfilled, and *strategies* or tactics by which to achieve those goals—for this type of study we use the acronym GOS. When analyzing the psychological level of characterization an important consideration is the analysis of character motivation at any given time.

All characters—like all people, although we may be less aware of our intentions—have agendas. Characters do not merely speak to be heard; they want or need something. The search for motivation in any character is a necessary step to understanding the behavior of that character. Always ask what motivates characters to behave as they do, and state their goals using verbs that imply action. What do they need and want? What stands in their way? How have they decided to go about getting what they need or want? Some possible goals are to make an impression, to be admired and loved, to act without causing suspicion, to gain respect, or to get revenge, among others. When Hamlet, for example, says he is going to put on an "antic disposition," what motivates him to decide this? What does he intend with this action? When Linda Loman tells her sons, Biff and Happy, that "attention must be paid" to their father, Willy, what does she intend?

This process is made more challenging in the solo performance of a play when a performer plays more than one role. You must analyze the GOS for each character at any given time, and work on playing both actions and reactions. Look, for example, at this scene from Beth Henley's play *Crimes of the Heart.* The play surrounds the three Magrath sisters: Lenny, the oldest; Meg, the middle sister; and Babe, the youngest. Before the play begins, Babe shot her husband, senator Zachery Botrelle, in the stomach when he discovered that she was having an affair with a young black boy named Willie Jay. The three sisters have united because of this crisis. In this scene from Act Two, Barnette Lloyd, a lawyer, meets with Babe to try to figure out how best to defend her. The scene takes place late in the evening in the Magrath kitchen in Hazelhurst, Mississippi, a small southern town. The time is five years after Hurricane Camille. See if you can determine each character's GOS— goals/obstacles/strategies.

From CRIMES OF THE HEART   Beth Henley

Barnette:	(*To himself.*) Mmm-huh! Yes! I see, I see! Well, we can work on that! And of course, this is mere conjecture! Difficult, if not impossible to prove. Ha! Yes. Yes, indeed. Indeed—
Babe:	Sure you don't want any oatmeal?
Barnette:	What? Oh, no. No, thank you. Let's see, ah, where were we?
Babe:	I just shot Zachery.
Barnette:	(*Looking at his notes.*) Right. Correct. You've just pulled the trigger.
Babe:	Tell me, do you think Willie Jay can stay out of all this?
Barnette:	Believe me, it is in our interest to keep him as far out of this as possible.

Babe:	Good.
Barnette:	(*Throughout the following, Barnette stays glued to Babe's every word.*) All right, you've just shot one Zachery Botrelle, as a result of his continual physical and mental abuse—what happens now?
Babe:	Well, after I shot him, I put the gun down on the piano bench and then I went out into the kitchen and made up a pitcher of lemonade.
Barnette:	Lemonade?
Babe:	Yes, I was dying of thirst. My mouth was just as dry as a bone.
Barnette:	So in order to quench this raging thirst that was choking you dry and preventing any possibility of you uttering intelligible sounds or phrases, you went out to the kitchen and made up a pitcher of lemonade?
Babe:	Right. I made it just the way I like it with lots of sugar and lots of lemon—about ten lemons in all. Then I added two trays of ice and stirred it up with my wooden stirring spoon.
Barnette:	Then what?
Babe:	I drank three glasses, one right after the other. They were large glasses, about this tall. Then suddenly, my stomach kind of swoll up. I guess what caused it was all that sour lemon.
Barnette:	Could be.
Babe:	Then what I did was . . . I wiped my mouth off with the back of my hand, like this . . . (*She demonstrates.*)
Barnette:	Hmmm.
Babe:	I did it to clear off all those little beads of water that had settled there.
Barnette:	I see.
Babe:	Then I called out to Zachery. I said, "Zachery, I've made some lemonade. Can you use a glass?"
Barnette:	Did he answer? Did you hear an answer?
Babe:	No. He didn't answer.
Barnette:	So, what'd you do?
Babe:	I poured him a glass anyway and took it out to him.
Barnette:	You took it out to the living room?
Babe:	I did. And there he was; lying on the rug. He was looking up at me trying to speak words. I said, "What? . . . Lemonade? . . . You don't want it? Would you like a Coke instead?" Then I got the idea, he was telling me to call on the phone for medical help. So I got on the phone and called up the hospital. I gave my name and address and I told them my husband was shot and he was lying on the rug and there was plenty of blood. (*Babe pauses a minute, as Barnette works frantically on his notes.*) I guess that's gonna look kinda bad.
Barnette:	What?
Babe:	Me fixing that lemonade, before I called the hospital.
Barnette:	Well, not . . . necessarily.

Babe:	I tell you, I think the reason I made up the lemonade, I mean besides the fact that my mouth was bone dry, was that I was afraid to call the authorities. I was afraid. I—I really think I was afraid they would see that I had tried to shoot Zachery, in fact, that I had shot him, and they would accuse me of possible murder and send me away to jail.
Barnette:	Well, that's understandable.
Babe:	I think so. I mean, in fact, that's what did happen. That's what is happening—'cause here I am just about ready to go right off to the Parchment Prison Farm. Yes, here I am just practically on the brink of utter doom. Why, I feel so all alone.
Barnette:	Now, now, look—Why, there's no reason for you to get yourself so all upset and worried. Please, don't. Please. (*They look at each other for a moment.*) You just keep filling in as much detailed information as you can about those incidents on the medical reports. That's all you need to think about. Don't you worry, Mrs. Botrelle, we're going to have a solid defense.
Babe:	Please, don't call me Mrs. Botrelle.
Barnette:	All right.
Babe:	My name's Becky. People in the family call me Babe; but my real name's Becky.
Barnette:	All right, Becky. (*Barnette and Babe stare at each other for a long moment.*)

From *Crimes of the Heart* by Beth Henley. Reprinted by permission of the author.

This scene may be interpreted as a kind of comic love scene. While Barnette's general or super objective is to find a legal defense for Babe, he does seem to fall victim to her quirky southern charm. Babe's general or super objective is to provide Barnette with the facts of the case, but she seems—whether subconsciously or consciously—to be attempting to use her feminine wiles to win Barnette over. She offers to fix him some oatmeal, she wipes her lips, she asks him to call her Becky, and they engage in long stares. Babe's obstacles include Barnette's attempts to remain impersonal and professional as well as his knowledge that Babe is married. Her strategies seem to be to try to get Barnette to feel sorry for her (e.g., "I am just about ready to go right off to the Parchment Prison Farm" and "I feel so all alone") and to convince him to see her as the victim. Barnette's goal to provide Babe with a winning defense is often prevented by Babe's rather eccentric behavior both when she shot her husband and now as she recounts the events to Barnette. His strategies are to concentrate on the facts of the case and remain focused on his notes.

Often actors *indicate* how they feel: they scowl, or look confused, or cry real tears to show their emotions. These performers are often being self-indulgent rather than focusing on goals—on playing what do I want, what obstacles stand in my way, and how do I overcome them. Concentrate, then, on what each character wants and needs from the other; if scowls or tears are called for, they will come naturally as a result of fulfilling goals and intentions. Remember, your analysis should be done in conjunction with rehearsals. We learn about GOS as a result of analysis, rehearsal, and even during performance.

Thought

Aristotle's term *thought* may be interpreted as the play's meaning or *theme*. The theme involves why the playwright wrote the play as well as the motivations or intentions of the characters. Being able to articulate the theme of the play supports your performance by helping you determine the playwright's purpose, which may be to amuse, to shock, to inform, to persuade, to convince, or something else. Some plays, like many by Neil Simon, were written for our entertainment and enjoyment, while others, like those of G. B. Shaw, Harvey Fierstein, Joshua Sobol, Václav Havel, and Athol Fugard, provide social commentary, evoke controversial issues, or pose racial questions.

Although there can be no one agreed-upon meaning in a play which all readers must somehow discover, there are often repeated motifs or ideas to help readers arrive at their own concepts of what the playwright is trying to say. Playwrights often use various devices in addition to the exchange of dialogue between characters to convey their meanings, for instance, asides, soliloquies, and other forms of direct statement (as in the plays of Bertolt Brecht and Thornton Wilder) in which characters may speak directly to the audience. Or playwrights convey their philosophical position through a special character referred to as the *raisonneur*—the reasoner—whose statements we take as the playwright's disguised attitudes, beliefs, and opinions. Horatio in *Hamlet* is the raisonneur—the character who seems the most reasonable and clear-thinking. The raisonneur often serves as a touchstone of reliability, helping the audience know whom to believe and whom not to believe.

Regardless of these devices that help communicate the playwright's thought, it is dangerous to assume that any one character actually *represents* the playwright. We must examine characters within the context of the play as dramatic embodiments created by the playwright and not as puppets through whom the playwright proffers personal philosophies. While it is true that playwrights infuse part of themselves into each character they create, a character (even the raisonneur) is usually more than simply a mirror image of the playwright, just as the narrator is not the author in a prose fiction work.

The point of view in drama is usually thought to be objective, in that no character in the play determines how we are to view the events and the other characters. Occasionally, however, there is a character who controls how the audience thinks and feels because we see things mostly through this character's point of view or personal perspective (as is the case with Willy Loman in *Death of a Salesman*); because the character is the narrator who speaks to us, sharing his or her impressions as well as point of view (Dr. Dysart in *Equus,* Tom Wingfield in *The Glass Menagerie*, Dr.

Livingstone in *Agnes of God*); because we tend to agree with a character's view of others (we tend to agree with Hamlet's assessment of the other characters in the play, though we see Hamlet from Horatio's point of view); or because a character observes others, and we view things with him or her (Oberon in *A Midsummer Night's Dream*, Prospero in *The Tempest*). When you try to discover the theme of a play, consider point of view as a contributing factor to what we know and how we know it.

Like the tone in a prose fiction selection, the theme is often not explicitly stated in a play. The theme is something you understand after reading and studying the play, and your understanding of the theme may change with time.

SPECTACLE: THE VISUAL AND AUDITORY DIMENSIONS

Spectacle Fact and Spectacle Act

Aristotle's last element is *spectacle*. Since spectacle includes all the visual and auditory elements of a play—set, props, costumes, makeup, music, sound, lighting, and so forth—it is probably more important to the production of a play than to the play as literature. Although the playwright often inserts ideas for adding spectacle to a play in production, the fulfillment of spectacle for the silent reader of a play comes from imaginative creation of the playwright's suggestions. As we stated earlier, when you read a play silently, your mind becomes the stage on which the play is performed. You see the characters in costume and makeup, you imagine the lighted set lavish with props and set pieces, and you hear the music playing. In this way, you, as silent reader, provide the play's spectacle.

When the play is translated from a literary piece to a performed piece, the director needs the assistance of a lighting designer, a makeup coordinator, a costumer, and the like to provide the spectacle suggested or implied by the playwright. The director is usually free to translate the playwright's suggestions to comply with his or her interpretation of the text. The actor, then, has spectacle provided; the interpreter—performing without the aid of others—must find a way to suggest the spectacle elements. As you perform drama scenes, you will find that incorporating the spectacle aspect of the text is an exciting and creative challenge. This challenge involves translating the *spectacle fact* into *spectacle act*.

The spectacle fact of a play includes all the visual and auditory accoutrements the playwright intended to accompany the play in production. The spectacle act, on the other hand, is what the solo performer does to project the play's spectacle fact. Solo performers, because they work without props, costumes, sets, and so on, often find projecting the spectacle fact difficult. Interpreters must depend quite a bit on performance conventions like character placement and the economical use of movement and gesture, as well as the audience's ability to imagine, to help them suggest the spectacle in the scene. The audience sees four characters when the interpreter performs a scene from Albee's *Who's Afraid of Virginia Woolf?* because the interpreter changes voice, placement, and emotional and body responses for each character who speaks. The audience members complete the picture and see a high-necked, floor-length gown on Anne Boleyn in *Anne of the Thousand Days* because the interpreter suggests Anne's stance and her manner of walking and holding her head. The audience members create the blinding of Gloucester in *King Lear* by imagining the gouging described in the language. The interpreter can show that Elizabeth is jumping rope in Wishengrad's *The Rope Dancers* by pretending to hold the handles of the rope and perhaps rocking slightly forward and back to suggest jumping without literally jumping. The lines themselves often help the audience to imagine the action without the necessity for literalization. Hand props must be mimed since literalizing one prop for one character means, of course, that all characters will have the same prop. Also, literalizing tends to pull the scene onstage.

The solo interpreter, then, endeavors to incorporate into a performance the spectacle fact the playwright intended. Although Aristotle listed spectacle last in his *Poetics*, it still remains the highlight of a theatrical experience for many audience members. The solo performer wants to involve the audience by stimulating their sensory responses in as many ways as possible. If you are not going to do a disservice to the play, you must work to suggest the spectacle elements. As Timothy J. Gura states:

> Plays may and do require spectacle, but not always the theatre's "spectacle fact" nor concrete, literal facts. For the solo performance of drama, the pleasures and rewards of spectacle are those available to the physically aware mind *and* body of a solo performer who, together with the play, persuades an audience to join in creating actions, costumes, settings, lightings, and stagings that do not pretend to exist in fact, but frequently, exist in act.[3]

A SAMPLE ANALYSIS OF "CONSTANTINOPLE SMITH"

Let us now look at a modern play by Charles L. Mee entitled "Constantinople Smith" and analyze it using the terminology just described.

CONSTANTINOPLE SMITH   Charles L. Mee, Jr.

A Play in One Scene

Characters: Constantinople Smith
Christina
Reality

The lights come up on a street of a city, a street lined with garbage cans, all of which are marked in large white letters: RUBBISH. A man in his forties, youthful, lithe, with easy careless steps, relaxed, letting his hands fall to his sides after each gesture as though there were no ligaments in his arms, backs on to the stage shouting into the wings. He wears a flowing black cape with crimson lining. (The part was once played by a large actor acting thin and lithe, to good effect.)

Smith: Let it be known, sir, that I consider your proposition an affront, an insult to my character, a slanderous attack upon my dignity. *(He pauses for a moment, steps farther to the center of the stage, allowing the audience to see the long, bright red scarf that distinguishes his otherwise shabby clothing, then turns back and raises a finger to emphasize another point in his hackneyed British accent.)* Let it further be known, sir, that any more overtures on your part will be considered calumnious assault, subject to fine, imprisonment, or both, and that, in addition, I shall find it necessary to sue you for full damages if you persist in these repugnant schemes. *(Raising his voice to a near scream.)* Let it finally be known, sirrah, that I, Constantinople Smith, am the grandson of an American aristocrat, a titan of business, a mogul of the late nineteenth century—a gentleman who would have had titles had there been any— and that I, the ne'er do-well grandson, still have sufficient influence to show you the innards of a dungeon, do you hear? I, Constantinople Smith, will have no truck with pimps! Do you hear? *(A pause.)* I say, do you hear? *(Without the accent.)* Gone—poor beggar. So beset with the vicissitudes of life that he can no longer separate fact from fantasy and still goes on trying to peddle a fifty-dollar trollop that never existed. I wish you luck, pimp. Perhaps you will find a man who wants your fantasy slut to satisfy his fantasy love. *(Sings.)* "A wandering minstrel I—" *(A beer can is lobbed in from the wings—or from the audience—narrowly missing him.)* Let them eat cake! What this city needs is a good old-fashioned revival meeting—or at least a solid goose. *(Moving upstage.)* Look around you! What do you see? *(Picks up the lid on one of the trash cans.)* Garbage! Let's be realistic about it. What do you find at every turn? *(Turns and lifts another lid.)* Trash! How do you expect the poets to write of heroes and heroines, when all around them they see—(He lifts another lid with a flourish and Christina, an attractive girl, stands up.)* Mirages! *(He reaches out and pinches her.)*

Christina: Ouch!

Smith: Very clever mirages! Mirages with flesh! *(He begins poking her and she retreats from him, giggling.)* What do you take me for, Diana? What sort of fool do you think I am, Helen? What kind of nincompoop would you make of modern man, Venus? I know you're not real! *(He kisses her.)* Ah!

Christina: My name is Christina.

Smith: Christina?

Christina: Accent on the antepenult.

Smith: The resurrection, is that it? Birth from death, is that what you mean? Miracle out of the muck, eh?

Christina: Yes.

Smith: Ha! *(Pause)* He-ha-ha-ha-ha-ha! Hum! Ha-ha!—Rrrrubbish! Pure, unadulterated garbage. Do you expect me to swallow that? I am a modern man! I laugh at the idea. Ha-ha. I sneer at the thought. Humph! I swear, I bluster, I mock, I rave—but, most of all, I wonder what your real name is.

Christina: But we've only just met.

Smith: Damn it, don't complicate it. What do you want to do—get to know each other? Uhhh! I have no doubt that you'd be disgusting if I knew the truth—Gertrude! I shudder to think of it. Why do I always find Gertrudes? *(He goes back and looks in another trash can.)* Mott's apple sauce! Not even a Gertrude. Life is an empty jar of Mott's apple sauce—slightly cracked.

Christina: Life is an overstuffed jelly bean.

Smith: *(Turning to her.)* Ah-ha! *(He walks around her slowly, trying to comprehend her.)* Then you do have a philosophical turn of mind! An overstuffed jelly bean. Yes. Yes! Naive perhaps, but good! Fresh!

Christina: I'm beginning to love you, but I didn't want to.

Smith: That's understandable, of course, but then you've only seen my bad side. How will you feel when I shine my shoes and publish a story in the *New Yorker?*

Christina: *(Laughs)* Well, I am innocent, but I'm not a virgin!!

Smith: Oh, Christina, do you see that beam of light?

Christina: Yes.

Smith: I would cup it in my hands and give it to you to drink.

Christina: *(Taking his hands and kissing them.)* You are silly.

Smith: There isn't a subway ride I wouldn't brave to see you!

Christina: Now you've spoiled it.

Smith: Didn't I tell you? It always happens when I get to know someone. They find out that I'm Gertrude.

Christina: I didn't say that. But you mustn't torture yourself so. You have the makings of a genuine—yes, even a marvelous—martyr.

Smith: Thank you. There! Did you see how I said that? Without a blush, with no resentment at all. I am learning aren't I? I am Constantinople Smith. Do you see what you've done?

Christina: Yes. I do love you now. And I'm not at all sorry. *(Thunderous, threatening music accompanies the entrance of Reality. He stands, casually glowering.)*

Smith: Who are you?

Reality: I am Reality.

Smith:	*(Laughs.)* Come on now, cut it out. You'll destroy the illusion.
Reality:	I can't help it. That's my line.
Smith:	It is not! You're ad-libbing.
Reality:	It's in the script.
Smith:	The hell it is!
	(Reality reaches into his pocket, unfolds a piece of paper, shows it to Smith, and reads.)
Reality:	I am Reality.
Smith:	God damn it!! What did he put that in there for?
Christina:	Some people can't resist temptation.
Smith:	*(Turning to her.)* Did he write that line, too?
Christina:	Well, what do you think? He wrote them all—this one too—that one I'm saying right now—these words coming out of my mouth—right here—*(Trying to catch them in her hands.)* These.
Smith:	You mean this whole beautiful love affair is going to fold up before we can even sleep together?
Christina:	You didn't think they'd allow that on stage, did you?
Smith:	But we could have gone off for a few minutes while someone else did a scene.
Christina:	You are silly.
Smith:	I won't stand for it!
Reality:	Hell, it was all an illusion, anyhow. Even this is, what we're doing now. It just throws over one illusion for another.
Smith:	I don't care. I don't care if it is an illusion. I don't know about you, but, for Christ's sake, I was enjoying myself. *(To the audience.)* Weren't you? Don't you hate to see this happen? This goddam modern theatre. No one can have any fun any more. It all has to be about reality and all like Pirandello, and all very intellectual. Can't we have any fun anymore? My God, it's the Decline and Fall, it's the Crumbling of Civilization when you can't have any fun anymore.
Reality:	Sorry, I just say what—
Smith:	I know. The line was there, so you said it. You parrot. You goat. It's actors like you who can't bear to cut a single line—always have to be in front of the audience—*(Pause.)* Look, will you do me a favor?
Reality:	It depends.
Smith:	Will you stay out here for a while and do a monologue or something while Christina and I just slip out for a couple of minutes and—
Reality:	Sorry, but I couldn't do that.
Smith:	Come on, don't be a spoil sport. It would just take a minute to create the illusion.
Reality:	So then what would you have?
Smith:	An illusion?

Reality: You see? What good is it?

Smith: But a beautiful illusion! Look at her!

Reality: I know. Listen, I sympathize with you, but there's nothing I can do about it.

Smith: You could if you wanted to.

Reality: No, honest to God. I don't have a speech to give.

Smith: I'll write one for you!

Reality: Oh—O.K., then.

Smith: Let's see now—let me see—Oh, I have it right on the tip of my tongue—You could say—you could say—Damn you! Will you write a speech for me?

Reality: Sorry, old boy. He is being rather arbitrary, isn't he? Fact is, I have an exit now. *(Reality leaves.)*

Smith: Spoilsports—all of them! Damn Pirandello! No one will believe anything anymore. No more heroes. No more poetry. No more beauty. This avant-garde is a real bore. It takes the life out of everything.

Christina: Well, let's enjoy it while we can. *(Smith goes to her and kisses her.)*

Smith: There! Do you see? He let me kiss you. He's just trying to tease me!— Kiss me again. *(They kiss.)*

Christina: I love you. *(They kiss and cling to each other.)*

Smith: My God, you're beautiful! And so tender—so wonderfully tender, it makes me want to scream. *(They kiss. Smith begins to look around; looks up into the grid.)* He isn't stopping us, is he? *(They kiss again, then Smith backs away abruptly.)* What the hell is he trying to do?

Christina: Don't let it unnerve you. Just relax and enjoy yourself.

Smith: I can't. He thinks he's God, that's what. Just like God, keeping us hanging like this—wondering when it's going to end, wondering what happens when it does end. *(Pause.)* Damn it! It makes me nervous.

Christina: You have to make the most of it.

Smith: *(Looks all around again.)* Say, do you suppose—I mean, he hasn't stopped us from kissing—do you think that—

Christina: Right here on stage?

Smith: But it's the only way.

Christina: No.

Smith: Do you say that because of him?

Christina: No, it's just that—

Smith: You can be modest at a desperate time like this?

Christina: No, it's the censorship laws.

Smith: Ah! Damn the censors!

Christina: I'm sorry.

Smith: Look, why don't we just go offstage for a while—

Christina: And leave the audience alone?

Smith:	*(Looking out at the audience.)* They're not alone. They have plenty of company. *(To the audience.)* Look, why don't you talk to each other for a few minutes, or—go out for a smoke or something.
Christina:	The show must go on.
Smith:	Rules! All these rules are killing me.
Christina:	You make a beautiful martyr.
Smith:	That's small compensation. I feel trapped on this stage. I feel like I'm suffocating.
Christina:	It wouldn't work anyway. As soon as we step off this stage, it's the end of our lives.
Smith:	*(Embracing her suddenly.)* My God, you're right! *(They look out together—two against the world, then he breaks from her.)* Hold that curtain, you bastards, I'll think of something yet. *(Reality enters.)*
Reality:	How are you coming?
Smith:	Not very well.
Reality:	I have an idea for you if you want to try.
Smith:	Let's have it.
Reality:	You could do it symbolically.
Smith:	Symbolically?
Reality:	Yes, like a dance, for instance.
Smith:	You mean a ballet?
Reality:	No, I mean the dirty jag or something like that—the twist.
Smith:	Christina?
Christina:	Why not?
Smith:	Terrific. Go and get us some music, will you?
Reality:	I'll see what I can do. *(Reality leaves.)*
Smith:	Symbolic! Not bad for him. He's learning. *(The music comes up, possibly the tune of "It's Istanbul not Constantinople." But, if significance will be read into that tune, then anything along the same lines will do. The dance is highly stylized, broadly farcical mambo, or whatever, of the cheek-to-cheek-taking-a-long-walk-at-Hernando's-Hideaway variety.)*
Christina:	They're playing our song. *(They dance.)*
Smith:	*(Stopping mid-step, a pause; speaks to the audience.)* This doesn't embarrass you, does it? *(Turn, pause.)* We're trying to do it with tasteful restraint. *(They resume the dance.)* Oh, this is wonderful!
Christina:	I love you!
Smith:	Say, this is the real thing—better even! I'm getting to like art.
Christina:	You wouldn't be able to believe it any other way. It's too beautiful.
Smith:	You mean life isn't like this?
Christina:	Don't you call this living? *(Christina continues dancing, a wild, ludicrous half shimmy, half rumba, and*

the additional fifty percent pure invention, as Smith breaks out of the dance and speaks to the audience.)

Smith: I take it all back, all my cursing. Thank you, Mr. Playwright. Thank you, Christina, you've opened my eyes. Now I am really alive. I am Constantinople Smith! I strut and fret my hour upon the stage, living many parts—exulting in life! Give me a moment, I say to the world, give me but an instant of feeling the blood in my veins and the tingling in my spine. You may have your afterlife, just let me have my life!

Voice from
Offstage: Curtain! *(The music stops, and Christina stops with it.)*

Smith: What's that?

Christina: It's time to go.

Smith: No, wait: Hold the curtain. I have so much more to say! I have so much more to do. There is so much more life left in me. Cue up the music. This time a ballet, or a modern dance if you must. Anything! But don't let it end now. *(Calls out.)* Reality! Come out here. Save us. *(Calling again.)* Isn't there someone back there who will do something? *(Runs to one side of the stage.)* Keep your hand off that curtain rope. *(Running toward the other side.)* Keep your hands off that light board. *(Running upstage.)* Is there an actor back there who wants a chance to appear? Come out here. This may be your big break. Come out here, will you? *(Looks up at grid.)* Can't you write in another role, another speech? Can't you have any more complications in this plot against me? Why not make it a full-length play? *(A long pause, then he goes to Christina, kneels in front of her, and embraces her.)* I can't face it. My God, I can't face it. Why? Why must it be like this?

Christina: *(Holding his head against herself.)* Don't be sad, darling. We had a moment or two.

Smith: Yes, beautiful moments!

Christina *(Smiling.)* Then don't despair. Those moments made it all worthwhile.

Smith: But will they die now?

Christina: I don't know.

Smith: Perhaps the audience will remember. Will you remember? Please remember. They were so very real for us.

Christina: They will remember, darling. They've had them, too. *(She holds his head against her. Reality enters, drawing the curtain closed.)*

Reality: Last scene of all in this strange, eventful history is second childishness and mere oblivion. *Sans* eyes, *sans* teeth, *sans* taste, *sans* everything. *(Lights out slowly and curtain.)*

Let us now perform one possible dramatistic analysis of "Constantinople Smith." Although the play is classified absurdist—not based on a conventional view of reality—there is some logic to the sequence of events. The pattern is fairly traditional: boy meets girl, boy loves girl, boy loses girl. The plot has a very definite beginning, middle, and end, framed by Smith's opening soliloquy and by Reality's final speech.

The characters in this play are difficult to classify traditionally. Mee is borrowing from early morality plays in which characters were often given names like Beauty, Strength, and Greed. The playwright makes no attempt to flesh out these characters, nor does the one-scene structure allow for much fleshing out. The characters are actors on a stage—representatives of types of people rather than round, dynamic characters in and of themselves. (You still have to believe in their "reality" in performance, however!) Let us apply the four levels of characterization mentioned earlier to these three characters.

Analysis of Constantinople Smith

Physical characteristics

The playwright supplies the following physical description of Smith: "A man in his forties, youthful, lithe, with easy careless steps, relaxed, letting his hands fall to his sides after each gesture as though there were no ligaments in his arms . . . He wears a flowing black cape with crimson lining."

Social characteristics

Rather brusque; not easy to get along with. He maintains a fairly formal or consultative style of speech, until the end of the play when he uses an intimate style.

Psychological characteristics

Intent on convincing others of his intelligence and supposed nobility, though he demonstrates little of either. He is not easily swayed to accept reality. He prefers to change the inevitable to satisfy his own needs and desires.

Moral characteristics

Not what we might consider moralistic. Smith's decisions are not ethically motivated: his major motivation is fulfilling his desires, which seem primarily sexual. However, the fact that the characters are meant to be stereotypical allows us to judge him less harshly. We feel rather sympathetic toward Smith, despite his behavior.

Analysis of Christina

Physical characteristics

Female; early twenties; physically attractive.

Social characteristics

Rather simple and naive, but better able to understand the situation she is in than is Smith. She is fairly easy to get along with. She uses consultative speech, but at times she uses intimate speech with Smith. When she sticks too closely to "her lines," there is conflict. When she responds to his compliments and complies with his wishes, the conflict lessens.

Psychological characteristics

Fairly uncomplicated; accepts reality; uninterested in changing the inevitable. She is fairly romantic, responds to compliments, and falls in love rather easily. Like Smith, she tends to say what she really thinks and feels. She seems to be psychologically healthier than Smith.

Moral characteristics

Fairly moral; she humors Smith, but does not give in to him because of the limitations of "the stage" and "the censorship laws." We view her sympathetically, perhaps because of the religious overtones implicit in her name (she tells Smith that the accent is on the first syllable of her name: CHRIST-i-na), and because she attempts to please Smith—*symbolically*—without sacrificing her own view of right and wrong.

Analysis of Reality

Physical characteristics

Male; old enough to have acquired quite a bit of experience; of indeterminate height and weight. Since Reality is a generalized figure, the role is open for interpretation on a physical level. What does "reality" look like?

Social characteristics

Uncompromising; faces "reality" with little hesitation or deviation. He has a job to do and he does it. He uses formal, consultative, and casual language at various times to meet the occasion. He is clever and flippant at times. Because Smith, in particular, is unable to face Reality squarely, there is conflict between them. His first entrance is heralded with "thunderous, threatening music" and he is described as "casually glowering."

Psychological characteristics

Uncomplicated psychologically—a realist. There is no subtext for Reality's character. He says exactly what he has been scripted to say. He presents the situation to Smith and helps him, when possible, to make the situation better.

Moral characteristics

Although Reality has been scripted to behave a certain way, he does volunteer a suggestion to help Smith and Christina consummate their relationship. We tend to judge Reality sympathetically because of his wit and *savoir-faire*.

Performance Suggestions for "Constantinople Smith"

As you prepare this play for performance, work on developing a voice, body, and emotional feel for each character. Use the foregoing information as well as the playwright's notes and stage directions to help you decide how the characters should sound, look, feel, and behave.

Economy of gesture and movement are necessary during a performance of this play. Smith can pantomime opening the garbage can lids, finding Christina, and poking her out front. You project the scene out and directly above the audience, so that when Smith finds Christina, he seems to see her above the heads of the audience members, making them feel part of the scene. The appearance of Reality necessitates a fanfare of some kind to highlight his entrance, since the text indicates that his entrance is to be significant. Economy is essential, also, when Smith and Christina dance. You might suggest one character facing front and dancing and then shift placement to the other character who is also facing front and dancing. There is, of course, no way in a solo drama performance to show both dancing at the same time!

The kisses and embraces in this play take special consideration. For the kiss, you might show Smith pursing his lips to kiss Christina and then switch to her placement and show her reaction to having been kissed. This technique might work well in this play, but may seem too comic for more serious plays. The same technique can be applied to project the embraces. When one character embraces another, show one character reaching out and the second character reacting to the embrace. This action economically allows the required time to pass between the action and reception of the action.

As characters describe objects or surroundings, be sure they are showing through focus or inner responsiveness what they see, hear, taste, smell, touch, and so forth. When Smith speaks his opening soliloquy, for example, let him react to the imaginary objects (garbage cans, beer can, and so on) in the imaginary street you project in the audience. If you do not use real music, you will want to show Smith and Christina hearing imaginary music. Showing images through a responsive body is an additional way to allow the audience to participate in the creation of the imagined scene.

The characters in this play address three different audiences. Most often, the characters speak to each other, and occasionally Smith addresses various unseen offstage characters. These moments all necessitate the use of closed focus and projection out front, with the characters seeing the characters they speak to in the imaginary scene in and directly above the audience. Each character receives his or her own placement, and the placement changes when a different character speaks. There are also various times when Smith addresses himself, as when he opens a trash can and says, "Mott's apple sauce! Not even a Gertrude." These moments could be performed with open or inner-closed focus depending on your interpretation. Often Smith addresses the audience. Most of these moments are indicated by the playwright in notes such as "Speaks to the Audience" and "To the Audience." Often the language in the play implies direct audience contact, as when Smith says to Christina, "Perhaps the audience will remember" and then he turns to the audience and says, "Will you remember? Please remember. They were so very real for us." Open focus would be useful for these moments and for Reality's closing speech. Who might Smith's audience be? Since this is a play about a play—the audience could very well be defined as a theatre audience.

The plot structure loosely fits the traditional structure—in a condensed fashion. The exposition section includes the opening soliloquy, in which we are introduced to the title character. He establishes his personality and prepares us for what is to come. As a result of his speech, we know what Smith is like, where the scene takes place, and the kind of mood and tone to expect. Christina's rise out of the garbage can and subsequent confrontation with Smith creates the conflict and begins the rising action. This new character and the transformation of the garbage-can-lined street into a theatrical stage complicate Smith's life. The crisis point is reached when Reality appears and dispels Smith's wonderful illusion of a love affair with Christina. Reality convinces Smith that he is a character in a play, as is Christina, and even Reality himself. The illusion-versus-reality theme is established. When the crisis point is reached, the direction the plot can take is limited. Smith can either accept the transience of his relationship with Christina or continue to strive to maintain the illusion. After Reality makes his appearance, the falling action begins. The falling action continues until the climax is reached—when the "curtain" is announced by an offstage voice. Smith's realization that his relationship with Christina must end, as a play ends when the curtain falls, constitutes the high point of the action. The denouement is Reality's closing speech to the audience, borrowed from Shakespeare's *As You Like It*, which adds a bit of the sublime to the ridiculousness which preceded it.

When you perform "Constantinople Smith" your voice and body must show the tensiveness in the text. Whereas the tensiveness in prose fiction arises primarily out of the manipulation of scene, summary, and description, the tensiveness in drama arises out of the internal conflicts within characters as well as the conflicts between characters and between characters and their environments. The conflict in "Constantinople Smith" involves all three of these conditions. Smith is in conflict with both Reality and Christina. He is frustrated and bewildered by the situation in which he finds himself, and he continually struggles against accepting the reality of his situation. The amount of tensiveness in the play increases as Smith's illusion of a love affair with Christina begins to wane. You can project the tensiveness by suggesting the body act of each character, by speeding up your pace to show characters in emotionally charged confrontations, by feeling a taut aliveness in your body, and by always staying in character.

The where of this play is specified by the playwright: "a street of a city, a street lined with garbage cans." As the play develops, however, we discover that the street is a mere illusion and that Smith and Christina are really actors on a stage. The interpreter, then, need do nothing to suggest a real street. The when of the play can be any time, although the dances that Reality suggests do seem to date the play as taking place in the sixties.

As charted earlier in relation to the characters, the diction—style of language—used in the play changes as the play progresses. The play is written in prose, though Reality's last speech is highly poetic. Looking at each line in the play gives a good indication of the kind of action appropriate to accompany the language. In the opening soliloquy, for example, the language indicates the kind of volume to use (as in "I, Constantinople Smith, will have no truck with pimps! Do you hear? [said loudly with closed focus] Gone—poor beggar" [said more softly with inner-closed or open focus]), as well as the type of gesture and body movement (as in "Look around you! What do you see?").

The language style of the two major characters traverses through the four language styles, beginning with formal diction (Smith's "hackneyed British accent") and then moving to a more intimate style as their "love" grows. Try softening your volume and tone when the characters speak in more intimate language. This will suggest that Christina and Smith are physically closer together as well. Reality's language style adjusts to conform to the situation at any given time. He moves from formal, to consultative, to casual. His style of speech is terse, laconic, and occasionally, colloquial.

Live music is called for in this play. The music is used as a symbolic representation for the consummation of Smith and Christina's relationship. Threatening music is also called for to highlight or emphasize Reality's first entrance. The interpreter can tape music and have Reality turn on the recorder, prearrange with someone in the audience to turn on the tape recorder, or have someone play music live. Alternatively, the music can be imaginary, in which case the characters have to react as though music really is playing. The addition of music heightens the auditory interest and adds to the humor.

The thought or theme of the play centers around Smith's inability to differentiate reality from illusion, thus, the numerous references to the playwright Pirandello who also deals with this theme in plays such as *Six Characters in Search of an Author*. The metaphor Mee has chosen is the stage, where actors with lines try to convince an audience that what is happening on stage is real—is reality. The reason for the appearance of Reality as a character on stage is to help dispel the illusion of reality—to destroy any possibility of the characters' lives continuing after the play ends. To heighten his use of the "all the world's a stage" metaphor, Mee borrows lines from Jacques's famous speech from *As You Like It*, in which he describes the roles men and women play through the "seven ages of man." Mee seems to be making a statement about the impact the theatre has on the audience as well as on the characters—its power to move, to inspire, to transcend fantasy and make us believe that illusion is reality. Mee seems to be saying, however, that reality often dispels the illusion.

SPEAKER AND AUDIENCE MODE AND DRAMA

Although plays are normally classified generically, according to type (comedy, tragedy, melodrama, farce, tragicomedy, and so on), they may also be classified according to their speaker modality: lyric, epic, or dramatic. Lyric plays are rare, but are increasing in number as a result of the resurgence of one-man and one-woman shows. Plays written in the lyric mode usually explore the inner workings of the mind or the life experiences of one character only. You live with this person for the length of the play and share his or her personal feelings and reflections. When you perform plays or scenes from plays written in the lyric mode, concentrate on the total match of your voice, body, and mind with the voice, body, and mind of the character in the play. You would probably use a combination of open focus and inner-closed focus, unless there is a specific implied auditor (as is the case several times in *The Belle of Amherst*, for example) when semi-closed focus is appropriate. Lyric mode plays are often, though not always, pensive and introspective. Make sure you give yourself the time in performance to suggest the appropriate tone and mood. Some plays written in the lyric mode are *The Search for Signs of Intelligent Life in the Universe* by Jane Wagner, "Krapp's Last Tape" and "Happy Days" by Samuel Beckett, "Tongues" and "Savage/Love" by Sam Shepard and Joseph Chaikin, "A Lovely Light" by Dorothy Stickney, "Mr. Happiness" by David Mamet, "Doctor Gallery" by Conrad Bromberg, "Laughs, Etc." by James Leo Herlihy, "Rupert's Birthday" by Ken Jenkins, *The Belle of Amherst* by William Luce, *Miss Margarida's Way* by Roberto Athayde, *Gertrude Stein, Gertrude Stein, Gertrude Stein* by Marty Martin, *Tru* by Jay Presson Allen, and *Rose* by Martin Sherman.

Plays written in the epic mode are immediately recognizable because they always have a character who plays the role of narrator or who makes contact with the audience in addition to characters who address each other. In modally epic plays, at lease one character speaks directly to the audience, furthering or commenting on the action. Performing scenes from modally epic plays is similar to performing prose fiction selections (except that in modally epic plays, the narrator is usually a defined character, whereas in prose fiction the narrator is often undefined). You must discover the nature of the narrator and what his or her attitude is toward the play and toward the characters in it. You might also consider if and in what way time has changed the narrator, since in most epic plays the narrator presents events that have already happened. Since the modally epic play, like the modally epic prose fiction selection, has a sense of past tenseness uncharacteristic of most drama, give the narrator time to think and remember, if your play calls for this kind of reflective narrative voice. You would primarily use open focus for the narrator when he or she addresses the audience and closed focus if the narrator is also a character and speaks dialogue. Some plays written in the epic mode are *Our Town, The Skin of Our Teeth,* and *The Matchmaker* by Thornton Wilder; *A View from the Bridge* by Arthur Miller; *Mother Courage* and *The Caucasian Chalk Circle* by Bertolt Brecht; *Agnes of God* by John Pielmeier; and *Equus* and *Amadeus* by Peter Shaffer.

Plays written in the dramatic mode, which comprise the largest category, are written totally in dialogue between characters with no narrative intervention. When performing plays in this mode, you normally use closed focus. Inner-closed focus might also be used for a lyric moment when a character appears to be thinking aloud and not addressing anyone particularly.

As we stated earlier under Who Is Being Addressed, the audience mode involves your awareness of the nature of the audience for each line and how that awareness affects your performance. Ask yourself how the speaker is affected when there is a shift in audience. We speak differently, use different syntax, choose words with more or less care, use prose or poetry, say more or less, partially based on who it is to whom we speak. Characters at any given time may address themselves (Hamlet's "To be or not to be"), a muse, a god, an inanimate object, etc. (the Chorus in *Lysistrata* complains, "Oh Zeus, what's the use of this constant abuse?"), another character (dialogue), or the general audience as does the Stage Manager/Narrator in *Our Town* when he tells the general audience that "This is Grovers Corners." The general audience may be addressed by narrators, during asides, and during some less personal soliloquies. As we have said, whenever you address the general audience, you should define who this general audience might be. This choice is part of your interpretation and should influence the way the narrator addresses the audience. Always decide how the nature of the audience affects the communicative transaction.

PUTTING IT ALL TOGETHER

See how much you understand about the analysis and performance of drama by answering the following questions in relation to the scene you have selected to perform. Be sure you have read the entire play. (We suggest you rehearse the selection several times before attempting to answer these questions.)

1. What is necessary to tell an audience in the introduction to this scene?
2. Describe the physical, social, psychological, and moral aspects of each character in your scene. Are the characters flat or round? static or dynamic? simple or complex?

3. Analyze each character's subtext. Are characters thinking thoughts that they are not saying? Are subtextual intentions conscious or unconscious? How will subtext be communicated in performance?

4. What is each character's attitude toward life? toward himself or herself? toward the other characters? toward the situation he or she is in?

5. How can you project the body fact of each character (body act) and the spectacle fact the playwright intends (spectacle act)?

6. What type of vocal and physical responses do you need? Are dialects required? What centering adjustments will you have to make to suggest each character's physicality?

7. How would you describe each character's diction or style of language? formal? consultative? casual? intimate?

8. Do the characters always address each other or are there times when they address themselves, an imaginary other, or the audience?

9. When you perform, what kinds of focuses are necessary? open focus? closed focus? inner-closed focus? semi-closed focus?

10. Where is sensory showing required?

11. How many placements do you need? Where will each character be placed?

12. What is the plot structure? causal? contingent? Are there any associate moments? Where in the plot does your scene occur? Describe the conflict. Who is involved in the conflict?

13. Where is the crisis moment in your scene? Where is the climax? How can the significance of these moments be projected in performance?

14. Where and when does the scene take place?

15. Why do the characters speak? What are their goals or intentions? obstacles that prevent them from obtaining their goals? strategies or tactics for overcoming the obstacles and accomplishing their goals?

16. What do you believe the thought or theme of the entire play is? How does your scene contribute to the development of the theme?

17. Is there a character whose point of view we share in the scene or do we view the action objectively?

18. Through what other "texts" did you interpret this scene? How did your past experiences, interests, and preoccupations influence your understanding of this play?

SELECTED PLAYS APPROPRIATE FOR PERFORMANCE

Here is a list of plays and playwrights from which you may find a good scene for performance. This is just a list of suggestions. Many other plays are possible choices.

Edward Albee	*Who's Afraid of Virginia Woolf? "Zoo Story," The American Dream*
Aristophanes	*Lysistrata, The Birds*
Samuel Beckett	*All That Fall, Waiting for Godot, Endgame*
Anton Chekhov	*The Three Sisters, The Cherry Orchard, The Sea Gull, Uncle Vanya*
Caryl Churchill	*Top Girls, Cloud 9, Mad Forest*
Brian Friel	*Lovers, Philadelphia, Here I Come!, Dancing at Lughnasa, The Faith Healer*
Athol Fugard	*A Lesson from Aloes, My Children!* My *Africa, The Road to Mecca*
Janusz Glowacki	*Cinders, Hunting Cockroaches*
John Guare	*The House of Blue Leaves, Six Degrees of Separation*
Lorraine Hansberry	*A Raisin in the Sun*
Václav Havel	*Temptation, Memorandum*
Beth Henley	*Crimes of the Heart, The Miss Firecracker Contest, Impossible Marriage*
Tina Howe	*Painting Churches, Approaching Zanzibar*
Henrik Ibsen	*An Enemy of the People, A Doll's House, Ghosts*
William Inge	*Come Back, Little Sheba; Picnic; Bus Stop*
Eugene Ionesco	*The Bald Soprano, The Chairs*
John Logan	*Never the Sinner*
Craig Lucas	*Blue Window, Reckless*
David Mamet	*American Buffalo, Speed the Plow*
Jane Martin	*Talking With, Keely and Du*
Arthur Miller	*Death of a Salesman, All My Sons, The Crucible*
Molière	*Tartuffe, The Misanthrope*
Marsha Norman	*Getting Out, 'night Mother*
Eugene O'Neill	*Desire Under the Elms; Ah, Wilderness!*
Harold Pinter	*The Homecoming, The Dumb Waiter*
Shakespeare	Any Play
George Bernard Shaw	*Major Barbara, Pygmalion*
Sam Shepard	*Buried Child, Fool for Love, A Lie of the Mind, True West*
Neil Simon	*Brighton Beach Memoirs, Biloxi Blues, Broadway Bound, Lost in Yonkers*
Antonio Skarmeta	*Burning Patience*
August Strindberg	*"Miss Julie," The Ghost Sonata*

Michel Tremblay	*Les Belles Soeurs*
Wendy Wasserstein	*The Heidi Chronicles, Isn't it Romantic, The Sisters Rosensweig*
Oscar Wilde	*The Importance of Being Earnest*
Tennessee Williams	*A Streetcar Named Desire, The Glass Menagerie, Cat on a Hot Tin Roof*
August Wilson	*Ma Rainey's Black Bottom, Fences, The Piano Lesson, Joe Turner's Come and Gone*
Lanford Wilson	*5th of July, Balm in Gilead, Talley's Folly, Burn This, Redwood Curtain*

SUMMARY

Reading plays silently is a challenging experience, for you are asked to create characters and scenes in your imagination. Interpreters can use this imaginative information (as well as past and projected experiences) when performing scenes from plays.

Drama differs from prose fiction in three ways. Most plays are written in the present tense, in contrast to the past-tense action of most prose fiction works. Most plays are written in scene, while most prose fiction works include moments of scene, summary, and description. In addition, prose fiction has a narrator as the central character, but not every play has or features a narrator.

When performing plays, study the physical, social, psychological, and moral dimensions of each character to facilitate your transformation of body fact into body act. Consider the intended audience for every line. At any given time, does a character speak to himself or herself (lyric), to another character (dramatic), or to the audience (epic)? Analyze the plot structure (exposition, development of conflict, rising action, crisis, falling action, climax, denouement); where and when the play takes place; how diction and music are used; the goals, obstacles, and strategies of each character; why the playwright wrote the play; and how you can translate spectacle fact into spectacle act.

Notes

1. Hubert Heffner, Samuel Selden, and H. D. Sellman, *Modern Theatre Practice*, 5th ed. (New York: Appleton-Century-Crofts, 1973), especially pp. 81–83.
2. Martin Joos, *The Five Clocks* (Bloomington, IN: Indiana University Research Center in Anthropology, Folklore, and Linguistics, 1962), especially pp. 13, 17–26.
3. Timothy J. Gura, "The Solo Performer and Drama," *Speech Teacher* 24 (September 1975): 278–81.

The End of the World

Quite unexpectedly as Vasserot
The armless ambidextrian was lighting
A match between his great and second toe
And Ralph the lion was engaged in biting
The neck of Madame Sossman while the drum
Pointed, and Teeny was about to cough
In waltz-time swinging Jocko by the thumb—
Quite unexpectedly the top blew off:

And there, there overhead, there, there, hung over
Those thousands of white faces, those dazed eyes,
There in the starless dark the poise, the hover,
There with vast wings across the canceled skies,
There in the sudden blackness the black pall
Of nothing, nothing, nothing—nothing at all.

He who reads a poem well is also a poet

Ralph Waldo Emerson

Nature never set forth the earth in so rich tapestry as divers poets have done; neither with so pleasant rivers, fruitful trees, sweet-smelling flowers, nor whatsoever else may make the too much loved earth more lovely.

Sir Philip Sidney, The Defence of Poesy, 1595

There is a special intimacy to poetry because the medium is not the expert's body, as when one goes to the ballet: in poetry, the medium is the audience's body. When I say to myself a poem by Emily Dickinson . . . the artist's medium is my breath . . . This makes the art physical, intimate, vocal and individual.

Robert Pinsky, U. S. poet laureate

In the unlikely event that a young person who mistook maturity for wisdom were to approach me at a gathering and ask me for my most valuable piece of advice, I wouldn't quote the usual precepts . . . My advice would be . . . the four words that have served me well for many years and in more ways than one. I'd say, Memorize your favorite poems.

William Walden, freelance writer

As the four writers above suggest, performing poetry—reading it well—does make you as much an artist as the poet, and memorizing your favorite poems, as Walden suggests, makes them readily available to share. As we've stated several times in this book, the reader is empowered to create and contribute to what a poem means. Poetry is a beautiful, delicately crafted art as Sidney suggests: your performance gives voice and body to that art. There is power in the spoken word, and your performance can evoke that power. At a recent appearance at Ball State University, Russian poet Yevgeny Yevtushenko explained that many Russian poets were shot, hanged, or committed suicide. Russian writer Alexander Pushkin gave him some advice, "Never write about a tragic end because poetry has magic power." Yevtushenko followed his advice and became famous as a poet about love, then later a political poet penning lines against Leninism and Stalinism.

Although poetry has never been as popular or mainstream as prose and drama, poetry today is enjoying a resurgence of popularity. Poets are engaging in poetry Slams where they perform their own poetry competing for prizes. Rhino Records recently released *Our Souls Have Grown Deep Like the Rivers*, a collection of African-

American poets reading their works. It stood at Number 1,300 on amazon.com's sales list. This is impressive considering that the list includes hundreds of thousands of books, CDs, and other titles.

Despite its recent popularity, many students confront poetry with fear and trepidation. "I do not like poetry" and "I can never understand what it means" are common reactions. Often these reactions are a result of either little exposure to poetry or poor guidance in studying poetry in the past. If you give poetry a chance, however, you will be amply rewarded. Studying poetry can increase your sensitivity to sounds and words and to the intricacies of rhythm, and you may be amazed at how much can be implied with so few words. When you perform poetry aloud, you increase your understanding of it. Silent reading does not permit you to hear the sounds or to feel the rhythm. Performance offers you the opportunity to get inside the poem—to hear the sound patterns, to feel the rhythmic movement, and to embody the speaker's experience.

There is no mystique or formula for understanding poetry, any more than there is for prose or drama. If you think there is, you probably have an overreverent feeling about poetry, or you have been convinced that only one interpretation is possible. As we have stated more than once, literary texts have more than one possible meaning. The creation of your personal interpretation is all that is expected of you. You do not have to try to find that one definitive reading that will make your interpretation "right." You need not worry that your experience with poetry is minimal. Use whatever experience you have, read more poetry, and study what the critics have to say. The more you study poetry, and the more you expose yourself to poetry performances, the more your confidence will grow. Your reward is discovering those truths which poets express so well. You, too, can go from disliking poetry to appreciating its "genuine" place, as did the speaker in Marianne Moore's poem, "Poetry":

> I, too, dislike it: there are things that are important beyond all this fiddle. Reading it, however, with a perfect contempt for it, one discovers in it after all, a place for the genuine.

> From "Poetry." Reprinted with permission of Macmillan Publishing Co., Inc. from *Collected Poems* by Marianne Moore. Copyright 1935 by Marianne Moore, renewed 1963 by Marianne Moore and T. S. Eliot.

There are elements in poetry (which this chapter will help you to recognize) that will aid in your understanding and appreciation. When you know what to look for, your analysis can begin. In this chapter, we will examine poetry dramatistically, paying attention to its sense, sound, and rhythm. Though we realize the inseparability of these elements, for the purposes of explication we examine each element independently. The skill is being able to put the parts back together into an aesthetic whole after the examination.

BEGIN ANALYSIS WITH THE POEM'S TITLE

Before beginning your dramatistic analysis of a poem, consider the poem's title. Since poets do not speak in their poems, the title of a poem is one clear way for poets to signal what they feel is important. Often the title will help you begin your analysis of who is speaking and who is being addressed. The title of Gwendolyn Brooks's poem, "The Mother," for example, is very significant. The title clearly indicates who is speaking. The title also helps to point up the irony in the poem, for the mother speaking in this poem is childless—a woman who has had more than one abortion. In another Brooks poem, "the preacher: ruminates behind his sermon," the speaker is a preacher who, while delivering or writing a sermon, is thinking about how lonely it must be to be God. The title suggests the tensiveness in the situation, which the interpreter must handle in performance. How can the performer suggest that the preacher is simultaneously delivering or writing a sermon while thinking to himself? The titles of the majority of poems in Edgar Lee Masters's *Spoon River Anthology* are the names of the characters who speak in the poems.

In the lyric odes of Keats and Shelley, for example, the titles help the reader understand who is being addressed, as well as the direction of utterance, in addition to telling us what kind of poems they are. Shelley's "Ode *to* the West Wind," for example, calls for a different kind of performance than does Keats's "Ode *on* a Grecian Urn."

In addition to helping you know who is speaking and who is being addressed, the title of a poem also supplies other valuable information. In some instances, the title may give you an indication of the speaker's locale (for example, "Dover Beach" by Matthew Arnold, "Fern Hill" by Dylan Thomas, and "Lying in a Hammock at William Duff's Farm in Pine Island, Minnesota" by James Wright) or when the poem takes place ("After Great Pain" by Emily Dickinson and "After Apple Picking" by Robert Frost). Often, as we saw previously, the title tells you what kind of poem it is (for example, "The Ballad of Rudolph Reed" by Gwendolyn Brooks, "Elegy Written in a Country Churchyard" by Thomas Gray, and "Ode to a Nightingale" by Shelley). The title can also be a key to the poem's "theme" or to its primary image or motif (for example, "God's Grandeur" by Gerard Manley Hopkins and "Wanting to Die" by Anne Sexton). Let the title of the poem, then, be your first consideration when beginning your analysis of a literary selection.

Let us now begin our dramatistic exploration of poetry. We introduce you to some of the specialized terminology involved in understanding poetry and relate this information to performance.

WHO IS SPEAKING? AND WHO IS BEING ADDRESSED?

Mode

When we categorize poetry in terms of its speaker mode, we find that a persona speaks in lyric poetry, a character(s) speaks in dramatic poetry, and both a narrator and character(s) speak in epic poetry. When we look at poetry according to its audience modality, we find that a lyric line is when the speaker addresses himself or herself or apostrophizes someone or something who is not present, a dramatic line is when a defined character is addressed, and an epic line is when the general audience is addressed. Understanding the modality of a poem reveals valuable information, especially when this information is combined with knowledge of the poem's genre—the type or kind of poem it is. Though being able to classify a poem into a certain category will not supply you all the answers about the nature of the experience in the text, you will be able to begin asking the right questions. Our objective in discussing the poetry types that follow is to show how categorizing a poem, along with a modal analysis of it, helps determine who is speaking and who is being addressed, as well as other performance considerations.

Genres of Poetry

There are three genres (types) of poetry: lyric, dramatic, and narrative. We now examine the specific characteristics of each of these types.

Lyric poetry

Lyric poetry features an emotional experience to be shared and is often highly personal and contemplative. The speaker in lyric poetry is called a persona. The persona is often remembering or creating a capsulized experience, often for personal benefit or purgation. When you perform lyric poetry, you usually try to maintain a high degree of emotional responsiveness as you become involved in the persona's pain or elation. It is the feeling or experience of the persona that you want to embody and project, for the personality of the speaker is characterized only in terms of those feelings and experiences. In the performance of lyric poetry, inner-closed focus is used if the sentiment in the poem is highly personal and private;

semi-closed focus is used if the speaker addresses a muse, God, or absent person. If the sentiment seems less personal, you may use open focus and address the general audience directly.

Descriptions of the most common types of lyric poems follow.

Sonnet   A sonnet is a poem of fourteen lines with a prescribed rhyme scheme. Sonnets are written in iambic pentameter—a type of meter based on the repetition of an unstressed syllable, followed by a stressed syllable (˘´) with five feet to the line. This is the opening line of a sonnet by John Keats and is written in iambic pentameter:

$$\text{Whĕn Í}\mid \text{hăve feárs}\mid \text{thăt Í}\mid \text{măy ceáse}\mid \text{tŏ bé}$$
$$\quad 1 \qquad\quad 2 \qquad\quad 3 \qquad\quad 4 \qquad\quad 5$$

We have divided the line into metrical feet by marking the unstressed and stressed syllables and inserting the bar lines. Each foot is composed of one unstressed syllable followed by a stressed syllable, and the five feet are demarcated by the bar lines and numbered. There are two basic kinds of sonnets: Petrarchan (Italian) and Shakespearean (English). These two sonnet types are defined primarily by their rhyme scheme. The Petrarchan sonnet rhymes as follows: ABBAABBA CDCCDC or CDCDCD (other variations are possible), which means that the last word in the first line rhymes with the last words in the fourth, fifth, and eighth lines; the last word in the second line rhymes with the last words in the third, sixth, and seventh lines; and so forth. The Shakespearean sonnet rhymes as follows: ABAB CDCD EFEF GG. Sonnets are highly personal lyric poems in which the persona reflects on or relives an experience or describes an object or event. When performing a sonnet, the most important thing is the realization of its prescribed structure.

Examples: Milton's "When I Consider How My Light Is Spent" and Elizabeth Barrett Browning's "How Do I Love Thee?"

Elegy   An elegy is a serious lyric poem written in memory of someone—often someone famous—who has died. It is an eulogy in verse.

Examples: "In Memory of W. B. Yeats" by W. H. Auden and "Elegy Written in a Country Churchyard" by Thomas Gray.

Ode   An ode is a relatively long lyric poem, often celebrating a specific occasion or praising an object or idea. The ode is very serious and is written in a very elevated, sophisticated style of language.

Examples: "Ode on Melancholy" by Keats and "Ode: Intimations of Immortality from Recollections of Early Childhood" by Wordsworth.

Descriptive Lyric Poetry   A descriptive lyric poem is a general type of lyric written in the present tense which, unlike the sonnet, has no specifically defined form. The persona in a descriptive lyric poem is describing an object, an event, or a private experience as if it were present or happening now. (Other types of lyrics written in the present tense may also be labeled descriptive, such as a descriptive sonnet.)

Examples: "The Eagle" by Alfred, Lord Tennyson and "Poetry" by Marianne Moore.

Reflective Lyric Poetry   A reflective lyric poem is also a general type of lyric, except that reflective lyrics are written in the past tense and the persona is remembering or reliving an experience or event. (Other types of lyrics written in the past tense may also be labeled reflective, such as a reflective ode.)

Examples: "Poem in October" and "Fern Hill" by Dylan Thomas and "Daffodils" by William Wordsworth.

Confessional Lyric Poetry   Confessional poetry is a relatively recent phenomenon. A confessional poem is a special category of lyric poetry. A confessional lyric poem may be written in any of the forms just described and reads like an autobiography in verse. Although someone like the poet *seems* to be speaking in all lyric poems, there is usually a certain amount of distance between the experience in the poem and the poet's life. In confessional poems, the distance is much less. Often, though, the events are altered, exaggerated, or underplayed to give the confessional poem more universal appeal. To know if a poem is a confessional lyric, research into the life of the writer is often mandatory. This research will also help you get a flavor of the poet's personality in preparation for performance. Confessional poets include Sylvia Plath and Anne Sexton, among others.

Examples: "Daddy" by Sylvia Plath and "Ringing the Bells" by Anne Sexton.

Class Exercise

Read the following poems aloud. What kinds of lyric poems are they? Can you tell who is speaking and who is being addressed? What kind of focus would you use when performing these poems?

THE END OF THE WORLD   Archibald MacLeish

Quite unexpectedly as Vasserot
The armless ambidextrian was lighting
A match between his great and second toe
And Ralph the lion was engaged in biting
The neck of Madame Sossman while the drum
Pointed, and Teeny was about to cough
In waltz-time swinging Jocko by the thumb—
Quite unexpectedly the top blew off:

And there, there overhead, there, there, hung over
Those thousands of white faces, those dazed eyes
There in the starless dark the poise, the hover
There with vast wings across the canceled skies,
There in the sudden blackness, the black pall
Of nothing, nothing, nothing—nothing at all.

MY BLACK SKIN   Warren Jackson

My Black skin flows
from head
        to toe.
It stops and starts
        only to show
the milk-chocolate smoothness,
a beige tinted glow.
Creases and crevasses, lines and scars,
the years have taken their toll,
but time still moves slow.
Strands of black bend and blow,
curl and curve to fit brown features.

I look in the mirror at my tan skin,
arched brows, a round nose,
chiseled cheeks
        with a chin sloped low;
delightfully dark eyes
        below a smooth forehead,
two ears too small
for my apple-shaped head.

I stared in the mirror,
at my Black skin,
        and wondered
how could they hate it . . .,
why do they want it to end?

Dramatic poetry

Generically speaking, dramatic poetry features a character(s) in a conflict situation. Like most lyric mode poems, dramatic mode poems are often told from the first-person point of view. In lyric mode poems, however, the "I" perspective is that of the poet-surrogate, and in dramatic mode poems the "I" signifies a dramatic character who is distinctly not the poet. The speaker may be solving a problem or explaining motivation for behavior, for example. Dramatic poems are usually, though not always, in the present tense, and the speaker is in a particular place and time. When dramatic poetry is performed, characterization of the speaker(s) is of ultimate importance. Begin by asking yourself, Who is this character? and How can I best project this character's voice, body, and mind?

As traditionally classified, there are primarily five types of dramatic poetry.

Dramatic Lyric   A dramatic lyric poem features a clearly defined character speaking the sympathies, values, or attitudes of the poet. To discover if a poem is a dramatic lyric, some research on the poet is essential. When you perform dramatic lyrics, use open focus if the speaker seems to be addressing the general audience (be sure to define who they might be) and inner-closed focus if the speaker is addressing himself or herself.
Example: "The Love Song of J. Alfred Prufrock" by T. S. Eliot.

Dramatic Monologue   In a dramatic monologue, one (monologue) character (dramatic) directly addresses another person or group whose nonverbal responses or gestures are often suggested by the words of the dramatized speaker. When dramatic monologues are performed, closed (for one silent auditor) or open (for a group of auditors) focus is usually required. The emphasis in performance is on portraying the personality of the character speaking as well as on keeping the silent auditor(s) alive.
Example: "Ulysses" by Alfred, Lord Tennyson.

Dramatic Narrative   In a dramatic narrative poem, a character (dramatic) tells a story (narrative). The character telling the story speaks from a first-person perspective and recounts a personal experience. Usually both narration and dialogue are used in dramatic narratives. Use open focus for the narration and closed focus for the dialogue.
Example: "Wild Grapes" by Robert Frost.

Dramatic Soliloquy   In a dramatic soliloquy a clearly defined character speaks to himself or herself. The character is alone—no one but the speaker is responding or reacting to the words being spoken. When you perform a highly personal dramatic soliloquy, use inner-closed focus. If the poem is less personal, you may use open focus.
Example: "Porphyria's Lover" by Robert Browning.

Dramatic Dialogue   Dramatic dialogues are written in the form of a conversation: a defined character addresses another defined character. When performing dramatic dialogues you will need to embody both characters vocally, physically, and psycho-logically, use closed focus and character placement.

Examples: "Ah, Are You Digging On My Grave" and "Is My Team Plowing" by Thomas Hardy.

Class Exercise

Read the following poem aloud. What kind of dramatic poem is it? How can the nature of the dramatic situation in this poem be projected in performance?

MY LAST DUCHESS   Robert Browning

Ferrara

That's my last Duchess painted on the wall,
Looking as if she were alive. I call
That piece a wonder, now: Frà Pandolf's hands
Worked busily a day, and there she stands.
Will't please you sit and look at her? I said
"Frà Pandolf" by design, for never read
Strangers like you that pictured countenance,
The depth and passion of its earnest glance,
But to myself they turned (since none puts by
The curtain I have drawn for you, but I)
And seemed as they would ask me, if they durst,
How such a glance came there: so, not the first
Are you to turn and ask thus. Sir, 'twas not
Her husband's presence only, called that spot
Of joy into the Duchess' cheek; perhaps
Frà Pandolf chanced to say, "Her mantle laps
Over my lady's wrist too much," or "Paint
Must never hope to reproduce the faint
Half-flush that dies along her throat": such stuff
Was courtesy, she thought, and cause enough
For calling up that spot of joy. She had
A heart—how shall I say?—too soon made glad,
Too easily impressed: she liked whate'er
She looked on, and her looks went everywhere.
Sir, 'twas all one! My favor at her breast,
The dropping of the daylight in the West,
The bough of cherries some officious fool
Broke in the orchard for her, the white mule

She rode with round the terrace—all and each
Would draw from her alike the approving speech,
Or blush, at least. She thanked men,—good! but thanked
Somehow—I know not how—as if she ranked
My gift of a nine-hundred-years-old name
With anybody's gift. Who'd stoop to blame
This sort of trifling? Even had you skill
In speech—(which I have not)—to make your will
Quite clear to such an one, and say "Just this
Or that in you disgusts me; here you miss,
Or there exceed the mark"—and if she let
Herself be lessoned so, nor plainly set
Her wits to yours, forsooth, and made excuse,
—E'en then would be some stooping; and I choose
Never to stoop. Oh sir, she smiled, no doubt,
Whene'er I passed her; but who passed without
Much the same smile? This grew; I gave commands;
Then all smiles stopped together. There she stands
As if alive. Will't please you rise? We'll meet
The company below, then. I repeat,
The Count your master's known munificence
Is ample warrant that no just pretense
Of mine for dowry will be disallowed;
Though his fair daughter's self, as I avowed
At starting is my object. Nay, we'll go
Together down, sir. Notice Neptune, though,
Taming a sea-horse, thought a rarity
Which Claus of Innsbruck cast in bronze for me!

Narrative poetry

The central feature in all narrative poetry is the story being told. This story reveals a chronology of events spanning a certain period of time. Narrative poems are usually relatively long with a clear beginning, middle, and end. The speakers in narrative poems are undefined. (If the speaker in a narrative poem is defined, then the poem is a dramatic narrative.) The narrator tells the story in the third person and in the past tense. The characters speak the dialogue lines in the past-tense story. When you perform narrative poetry, use open focus with sensory showing when the narrator speaks and closed focus when the characters speak. The sequence of events and the impact of these events on the narrator are the most important elements to capture in performance.

There are three kinds of narrative poetry: ballads, metrical tales, and epics.

Ballad   A ballad is a tightly metered poem which tells a story. Usually you can feel a very rhythmic beat when a ballad is read aloud. Ballads are usually written in short stanzas (a poem's equivalent to the paragraph) and in simple language. Ballads are often characterized by stark images and repetitive words and phrases, and they often have refrains. One of the oldest of poetic forms, many ballads were passed down orally and are, therefore, of unknown authorship. Ballad themes include disappointment in love, revenge, supernatural beings and events, and physical strength or agility. One difficulty in performing ballads is to communicate the story line within a very pronounced rhythm.

Examples: "Sir Patrick Spens" and "Lord Randall."

Metrical Tale   The metrical tale is a relatively long poem which tells a completely developed story in verse. Metrical tales can be the length of a short story or of a complete novel.

Examples: "The Death of the Hired Man" and "Home Burial" by Robert Frost and *The Canterbury Tales* by Chaucer.

Epic Poem   An epic poem is a very long narrative poem which centers on the accomplishments of a traditional or historical hero who faces and meets trials in order to aid a race or a nation.

Examples: *The Illiad* and *The Odyssey* by Homer, *Beowulf,* and *Paradise Lost* by Milton.

Class Exercise

The following poem fits into two different genres. The title tells us it is a ballad, but the speaker in the poem is a defined character, Pearl May Lee. This poem, consequently, is both a ballad and a dramatic narrative. As you perform this poem, try to embody the character and work on keeping the story line clear as well as the ballad rhythm. Pay close attention to the lines of the refrain. How should they be sounded? Will you read these lines the same way each time, or will you read them differently? What is your decision based on?

BALLAD OF PEARL MAY LEE   Gwendolyn Brooks

Then off they took you, off to the jail,
A hundred hooting after.
And you should have heard me at my house.
I cut my lungs with my laughter,
  Laughter,

Laughter.
I cut my lungs with my laughter.

They dragged you into a dusty cell.
And a rat was in the corner.
And what was I doing? Laughing still.
Though never was a poor gal lorner,
    Lorner,
    Lorner.
Though never was a poor gal lorner.

The sheriff, he peeped in through the bars,
And (the red old thing) he told you.
"You son of a bitch, you're going to hell!"
'Cause you wanted white arms to enfold you.
    Enfold you,
    Enfold you.
'Cause you wanted white arms to enfold you.

But you paid for your white arms, Sammy boy,
And you didn't pay with money.
You paid with your hide and my heart, Sammy boy,
For your taste of pink and white honey,
    Honey,
    Honey.
For your taste of pink and white honey.

Oh, dig me out of my don't-despair.
Pull me out of my poor-me.
Get me a garment of red to wear.
You had it coming surely,
    Surely,
    Surely.
You had it coming surely.

At school, your girls were the bright little girls.
You couldn't abide dark meat.
Yellow was for to look at,
Black for the famished to eat.
Yellow was for to look at,
Black for the famished to eat.

You grew up with bright skins on the brain,
And me in your black folks bed.
Often and often you cut me cold,

And often I wished you dead.
Often and often you cut me cold.
Often I wished you dead.

Then a white girl passed you by one day,
And, the vixen, she gave you the wink.
And your stomach got sick and your legs liquefied.
And you thought till you couldn't think.
    You thought,
    You thought,
You thought till you couldn't think.

I fancy you out on the fringe of town,
The moon an owl's eye minding;
The sweet and thick of the cricket-belled dark,
The fire within you winding. . . .
    Winding,
    Winding. . . .
The fire within you winding.

Say, she was white like milk, though, wasn't she?
And her breasts were cups of cream.
In the back of her Buick you drank your fill.
Then she roused you out of your dream.
In the back of her Buick you drank your fill.
Then she roused you out of your dream.

"You raped me, nigger," she softly said.
(The shame was threading through.)
"You raped me, nigger, and what the hell
Do you think I'm going to do?
    What the hell,
    What the hell
Do you think I'm going to do?"

"I'll tell every white man in this town.
I'll tell them all of my sorrow.
You got my body tonight, nigger boy.
I'll get your body tomorrow.
    Tomorrow.
    Tomorrow.
I'll get your body tomorrow."

And my glory but Sammy she did! She did!
And they stole you out of the jail.

They wrapped you around a cottonwood tree.
And they laughed when they heard you wail.
 Laughed,
 Laughed.
They laughed when they heard you wail.

And I was laughing, down at my house.
Laughing fit to kill.
You got what you wanted for dinner,
But brother you paid the bill.
 Brother,
 Brother,
Brother you paid the bill.

You paid for your dinner, Sammy boy,
And you didn't pay with money.
You paid with your hide and my heart, Sammy boy,
For your taste of pink and white honey,
 Honey,
 Honey.
For your taste of pink and white honey.

Oh, dig me out of my don't-despair.
Oh, pull me out of my poor-me.
Oh, get me a garment of red to wear.
You had it coming surely.
 Surely.
 Surely.
You had it coming surely.

"Ballad of Pearl May Lee" from *Blacks*. Copyright 1987 by Gwendolyn Brooks Blakely. Reprinted by permission of the author.

Class Exercise

Read the following poem aloud. What is the significance of the title? What is the genre of this poem? Lyric? Dramatic? Narrative? Now, try to perform a speaker and audience modal analysis. What is the speaker mode of this poem? Is a persona speaking? a character? a narrator? Now focus on who is addressed on each line. Can you decide when the lyric voice is heard? when the dramatic voice is heard? when the epic voice is heard? Lastly, see whether you can translate your understanding into performance analogues.

FEBRUARY EVENING IN NEW YORK   Denise Levertov

1   As the stores close, a winter light
2   opens air to iris blue
3   glint of frost through the smoke,
4   grains of mica, salt of the sidewalk.
5   As the buildings close, released autonomous
6   feet pattern the streets
7   in hurry and stroll; balloon heads
8   drift and dive above them; the bodies
9   aren't really there.
10   As the lights brighten, as the sky darkens,
11   a woman with crooked heels says to another woman
12   while they step along at a fair pace,
13   *"You know, I'm telling you, what I love best*
14   *is life. I love life! Even if I ever get*
15   *to be old and wheezy—or limp! You know?*
16   *Limping along?—I'd still . . . "* Out of hearing.
17   To the multiple disordered tones
18   of gears changing, a dance
19   to the compass points, out, four-way river.
20   Prospect of sky
21   wedged into avenues, left at the ends of streets,
22   west sky, east sky: more life tonight! A range
23   of open time at winter's outskirts.

WHAT IS THE SPEAKER SPEAKING ABOUT?

The action of a poem varies according to the nature of the speaker and the type of experience he or she undergoes. Speakers can be contemplating, reflecting, emoting, intellectualizing, describing, and so forth. They can be involved in a dialogue with other characters or can be relating a story. Depending on the type of poem, the action can be analyzed as we analyzed the action in prose fiction or drama. Ask yourself whether the action is causal or contingent. Are there any associative moments? What motivates the speaker's thoughts? Ask yourself, also, whether the action is revealed literally or figuratively. In poetry, ideas are often expressed either directly or indirectly according to the speaker's purpose. A direct statement is usually less abstract and invites less misunderstanding and misinterpretation. This poem by Elizabeth Barrett Browning is a fairly literal, direct statement of the speaker's love.

HOW DO I LOVE THEE?   Elizabeth Barrett Browning

How do I love thee? Let me count the ways.
I love thee to the depth and breadth and height
My soul can reach, when feeling out of sight
For the ends of Being and ideal Grace.
I love thee to the level of everyday's
Most quiet need, by sun and candle-light.
I love thee freely, as men strive for Right;
I love thee purely, as they turn from Praise.
I love thee with the passion put to use
In my old griefs, and with my childhood's faith.
I love thee with a love I seemed to lose
With my lost saints—I love thee with the breath,
Smiles, tears, of all my life!—and, if God choose,
I shall but love thee better after death.

Many poems do not say exactly what they mean or are not about what they seem to be about. They communicate metaphorically—by indirection, double meaning, or innuendo. In the following poem by Rupert Brooke, the poet talks indirectly and invites many possible interpretations. Though on a literal level the poem seems to be about fish, what concept is figuratively implied?

HEAVEN   Rupert Brooke

Fish (fly-replete, in depth of June
Dawdling away their wat'ry noon)
Ponder deep wisdom, dark or clear,
Each secret fishy hope or fear.
Fish say, they have their Stream and Pond;
But is there anything Beyond?
This life cannot be All, they swear,
For how unpleasant, if it were!
One may not doubt that, somehow, good
Shall come of Water and of Mud;
And, sure, the reverent eye must see
A Purpose in Liquidity.

We darkly know, by Faith we cry,
The future is not Wholly Dry.
Mud unto Mud!—Death eddies near—
Not here the appointed End, not here!
But somewhere, beyond Space and Time,
Is wetter water, slimier slime!
And there (they trust) there swimmeth One
Who swam ere rivers were begun,
Immense, of fishy form and mind,
Squamous, omnipotent and kind;
And under that Almighty Fin
The littlest fish may enter in.
Oh! never fly conceals a hook,
Fish say, in the Eternal Brook,
But more than mundane weeds are there,
And mud, celestially fair;
Fat caterpillars drift around,
And Paradisal grubs are found;
Unfading moths, immortal flies,
And the worm that never dies.
And in that Heaven of all their wish,
There shall be no more land, say fish.

When you are examining the what of your poem, look at the organization of its parts and determine whether the action is directly or indirectly expressed. This provides valuable information about the speaker which can be translated into performance. A speaker who is fairly straightforward sounds and looks different from a speaker who takes a more circuitous approach. Is your speaker openly communicating, or is this speaker slyly or wittily ironic, satirical, or symbolic?

Poetry often communicates by indirection. While it seems to be about one topic, it may be about something quite different. Although poets may seem to be talking about lambs or tigers or fish, for example, they may be using these images to represent certain qualities in human beings or they may be symbolically using them to suggest something else. In poetry, you must consider a figurative (nonliteral) meaning.

The action in a poem often contains conflicting pulls. Examine your poem to discover whether your speaker is in some sort of conflict situation. Is the speaker trying to make a decision? Is the speaker attempting to make something clear? Is the speaker concerned about a past deed, a present condition, or a future possibility?

This conflict causes the tensiveness in the poem as the speaker tries to express himself or herself. In some poems, speakers use repetition, self-examination, or self-amendment while struggling to communicate or to understand. Look at the following two examples. In each case, the speaker is involved in a tensive situation.

THE MAN HE KILLED   Thomas Hardy

1   'Had he and I but met
2   By some old ancient inn,
3   We should have sat us down to wet
4   Right many a nipperkin!

5   'But ranged as infantry,
6   And staring face to face,
7   I shot at him and he at me,
8   And killed him in his place.

9   'I shot him dead because—
10   Because he was my foe,
11   Just so: my foe of course he was;
12   That's clear enough; although

13   'He thought he'd 'list, perhaps,
14   Offhand like—just as I—
15   Was out of work—had sold his traps—
16   No other reason why.

17   'Yes; quaint and curious war is!
18   You shoot a fellow down
19   You'd treat if met where any bar is,
20   Or help to half a crown.'

"The Man He Killed" from *Complete Poems of Thomas Hardy*, copyright 1925 Thomas Hardy, edited by James Gibson, Macmillan Publishing Co., New York, 1978, and Macmillan London Ltd., London and Basingstoke, 1976.

In this poem, the speaker is quoting another—the "He" of the title. This "He" is relating an experience he had during war time (World War I) when he was forced to kill another man. There is a tensive feel as he tries to explain, using rationalization and a sort of self-argumentation about the situation in which he found himself. There is a sense, especially in lines 9–12, that he is thinking aloud—trying to define his feelings. The speaker repeats "my foe" in an attempt, perhaps, to convince himself that the man was indeed his "foe," despite the commonalities he sees between this foe and himself. Be responsive to this in performance. The man the speaker is quoting seems to realize the irony of his situation. Give him time to think and to show his confusion and uncertainty.

CARRION COMFORT   Gerard Manley Hopkins

1   Not, I'll not, carrion comfort, Despair, not feast on thee;
2   Not untwist—slack they may be—these last strands of man
3   In me ór, most weary, cry *I can no more.* I can;
4   Can something, hope, wish day come, not choose not to be.
5   But ah, but O thou terrible, why wouldst thou rude on me
6   Thy wring-world right foot rock? lay a lionlimb against me? scan
7   With darksome devouring eyes my bruisèd bones? and fan,
8   O in turns of tempest, me heaped there; me frantic to avoid thee and flee?
9   Why? That my chaff might fly; my grain lie, sheer and clear.
10   Nay in all that toil, that coil, since (seems) I kissed the rod,
11   Hand rather, my heart lo! lapped strength, stole joy, would laugh, chéer.
12   Cheer whom though? the hero whose heaven-handling flung me, foót tród
13   Me? or me that fought him? O which one? is it each one? That night, that year
14   Of now done darkness I wretch lay wrestling with (my God!) my God.

In this sonnet variant, Hopkins creates a persona who seems to be editing himself as he speaks. Look at lines 10 and 11, for example. In line 10, he says, "I kissed the rod," and in line 11, he changes "rod" to "hand." The persona's indecisiveness is shown throughout the poem as he is in a constant state of self-reflection—asking questions, answering them, and then posing new ones.

Give the speaker time for this editing and questioning process. Feel the speaker's indecisiveness, ask yourself what ultimate conclusion the speaker comes to when he repeats "(my God!) my God."

WHEN AND WHERE DOES THE SPEAKER SPEAK?

Time and place are important considerations in the performance of most literary works. In some poems, time and place are literalized and in some there is no definite indication of either. As you perform a poem, ask yourself whether the when and the where of the action are significant. Is there a progression of time within the poem, or does everything seem to be happening during a timeless present? Does the speaker speak in the immediate present, the remembered past, or the projected future? In general, lyric poems seem to encompass a short period of time—a flash of illumination. Dramatic poems take place now—in the present—and often the time covered in the poem is the same amount of time it would take to perform the poem. Narrative poems are usually the longest and involve a progression of events in time. If the poem is written in the past tense, how much difference, if any, is there between the speaker's attitude in the virtual present as opposed to the virtual past? If the speaker is remembering, how can this fact be shown in performance?

Take a moment to remember a past incident that happened to you. Begin to verbalize your memory. What happens to you? Use this information when you perform a poem in which the speaker is reflecting. Now try to describe an object in the room you are in. Speak aloud and relate directly to the object. How is this feeling different from the reflection you just did? Now try to anticipate what your future will be. Orally describe where you think you will be in ten years, in twenty years. As you go through these exercises, remain very conscious of what happens to your voice and body, so that you can use this information when projecting the time element in your selection.

In addition to considering the movement of time within a selection, consider also the moment before the poem begins. Some poems, for example, give the impression that the beginning occurred before the first line. The opening line in T. S. Eliot's "The Love Song of J. Alfred Prufrock," for example, is "Let us go then, you and I." The word "then" in this line implies that something has gone on before the poem begins. In "My Last Duchess," the Duke tells the envoy, ". . . since none puts by/The curtain I have drawn for you, but I." This, too, implies that some action has been accomplished before the Duke begins speaking. How can these "moments before" be suggested in performance?

The where of a poem is, of course, the location of the action. Is there a specific setting? Is there more than one setting? Is the speaker in the scene he or she describes (as in "The Applicant" by Sylvia Plath) close to the scene ("Home Burial" by Robert Frost), or is he or she separated from it in some way ("Daffodils" by William Wordsworth)? How can place be clarified in performance? Remember to define your scene. Where are people and objects located? Be sure your audience members are able to create the imagined scene in their minds.

Dylan Thomas was capable of depicting vivid locales and of capturing the ephemeral nature of time. Read his poem "Fern Hill" and consider how time and place are depicted.

FERN HILL   Dylan Thomas

Now as I was young and easy under the apple boughs
About the lilting house and happy as the grass was green,
   The night above the dingle starry,
    Time let me hail and climb
   Golden in the heydays of his eyes,
And honored among wagons I was prince of the apple towns

And once below a time I lordly had the trees and leaves
    Trail with daisies and barley
  Down the rivers of the windfall light.

And as I was green and carefree, famous among the barns
About the happy yard and singing as the farm was home,
    In the sun that is young once only,
      Time let me play and be
    Golden in the mercy of his means,
And green and golden I was huntsman and herdsman, the calves
Sang to my horn, the foxes on the hills barked clear and cold,
      And the sabbath rang slowly
    In the pebbles of the holy streams.

All the sun long it was running, it was lovely, the hay
Fields high as the house, the tunes from the chimneys, it was air
    And playing, lovely and watery
      And fire green as grass.
    And nightly under the simple stars
As I rode to sleep the owls were bearing the farm away,
All the moon long I heard, blessed among stables, the nightjars
    Flying with the ricks, and the horses
      Flashing into the dark

And then to awake, and the farm, like a wanderer white
With the dew, come back, the cock on his shoulder: it was all
    Shining, it was Adam and maiden,
      The sky gathered again
    And the sun grew round that very day.
So it must have been after the birth of the simple light
In the first, spinning place, the spellbound horses walking warm
    Out of the whinnying green stable
      On to the fields of praise.

And honored among foxes and pheasants by the gay house
Under the new made clouds and happy as the heart was long,
    In the sun born over and over,
      I ran my heedless way,
    My wishes raced through the house high hay
And nothing I cared, at my sky blue trades, that time allows
In all his tuneful turning so few and such morning songs
    Before the children green and golden
      Follow him out of grace,

Nothing I cared, in the lamb white days, that time would take me

Up to the swallow thronged loft by the shadow of my hand,
    In the moon that is always rising,
        Nor that riding to sleep
    I should hear him fly with the high fields
And wake to the farm forever fled from the childless land.
Oh as I was young and easy in the mercy of his means,
    Time held me green and dying
    Though I sang in my chains like the sea.

HOW DOES THE SPEAKER SPEAK?

How poets make their vision clear is a complicated matter. *Prosody* is the art of patterning in poetry, and when analyzing poetry, you seek to discover the poet's use of these patterns. These patterns may be based on the repetition of sensory images (appeals to the senses), literary images (figures of speech), tone color (sound repetitions), or meter (rhythmic patterns). Discovering and understanding these patterns helps you to devise your own interpretation. In addition, the type of pattern—the choice of sensory appeals, the originality or triteness of the literary images, the complexity or simplicity of the sound and meter—tells you much about the speaker and his or her attitudes and emotional responses. Discovering the how of a poem is one way to determine the location of the *fulcrum*—that moment of silence that marks a major change in image, sound, meter, thought, point of view, tone, or mood, for example, within a poem. Let us now examine each of these patterns and discover the changes to see how the speaker in a poem manipulates language to communicate.

Sensory Imagery

Sensory images are images that appeal to the senses. Sensory imagery exists in most literary texts but is more obvious in the more condensed poem. As we stated in Chapter 4, when studying sensory imagery you put yourself in the place of the speaker and try to re-create all of the sensory images. Ask yourself what the speaker is seeing, hearing, tasting, and so forth, and try to suggest these images in your performance. As described earlier, there are primarily eight kinds of sensory images: visual (sight), auditory (hearing), olfactory (smell), gustatory (taste), tactile (touch), kinetic (physical movement), kinesthetic (muscular involvement, awareness of body position and tension), and thermal (hot and cold).

You respond to the sensory images in a poem through sensory showing. Sensory showing involves the re-creation of sensory images and may be employed within lyric, dramatic, or epic mode moments. Try saying the line "I saw the dog" using each type of focus. Can you re-create the visual image of the dog with each type of focus?

Remember, though, that not all speakers respond to sensory images in the same way. We all react differently to things we see and hear, taste and touch, and so forth, and the intensity of our reaction is different also. Be sure you respond as you think the speaker would. For example, people who grew up on farms react differently to the smell of new hay than city people do—this is related to the idea of intertextuality, the idea that we all read texts through our accumulated experiences. A speaker who is consciously aware of the surroundings, who provides us with a great deal of description, is much more involved in sensory showing than is a speaker who is unconscious of or uninterested in the environment.

One line of verse may have many different sensory appeals. The line "I threw the coins and they landed on the piece of fruit baking on the sidewalk in the hot sun" has images which appeal to all of the eight senses just listed. "Threw" is an appeal to the kinetic sense. "Coins" can be seen, heard, smelled, tasted, and touched. "Piece of fruit" is a visual, a gustatory, and an olfactory image. "Baking" has a thermal appeal, "sidewalk" has a visual appeal, and "hot sun" has thermal and visual appeals. Although it is probably impossible to respond to all these different appeals, you will want to read the line slowly enough and with enough vocal, physical, and emotional responsiveness, as well as enough sensory showing, to enable the audience to sense those images you feel are significant to your interpretation.

Class Exercise

Read the following poem aloud, noting how the poet has used a variety of sensory appeals to express a particular mood.

A LADY   Amy Lowell

You are beautiful and faded
Like an old opera tune
Played upon a harpsichord;
Or like the sun-flooded silks
Of an eighteenth century boudoir.
In your eyes
Smolder the fallen roses of outlived minutes,
And the perfume of your soul

Is vague and suffusing,
With the pungence of sealed spice-jars.
Your half-tones delight me,
And I grow mad with gazing
At your blent colors.

My vigor is a new-minted penny;
Which I cast at your feet.
Gather it up from the dust,
That its sparkle may amuse you.

From *The Complete Poetical Works of Amy Lowell* by Amy Lowell. Copyright © 1955 by Houghton Mifflin Company. Copyright © 1983 by Houghton Mifflin Company, Brinton P. Roberts, Esquire, and G. D'Andelot Belin, Esquire. Reprinted by permission of Houghton Mifflin Company.

Literary Imagery

Literary imagery, like sensory imagery, exists in many literary texts but again is more often employed in poetry. Whereas the purpose of sensory imagery is to heighten or expand our response to a poem by involving as many of our senses as possible, literary imagery (or figurative language) helps to make a poem clearer, fresher, or more vital, usually through some means of comparison or by relating to something outside the poem. Being able to identify a literary image is one talent; being able to translate what the use of a certain type of image tells you about the nature of the persona and the situation in the poem is another talent essential to performance. Let us discuss the major kinds of literary images.

Allusion

An allusion is a reference to a person, place, or thing outside the confines of the poem. Poets usually allude to characters or events in mythology and the Bible, to another literary work, or to a contemporary or historical event. The use of allusion in a poem widens its dimensions. The kinds of allusions used provide valuable information about the speaker. "The couple went to Adam's grocery store and stole an apple" is an allusion to the book of Genesis in the Bible.

Apostrophe

An apostrophe is an address to an inanimate object, a muse, God, or an absent or deceased person. Usually a degree of tensiveness is present in poems that contain or are apostrophes. In an apostrophe, the speaker is reaching out, trying to communicate with someone or something who is not physically present and will not respond. In John Donne's "Death Be Not Proud," the speaker addresses "Death" in a valiant struggle to vanquish the enemy.

> Death, be not proud though some have called thee
> Mighty and dreadful, for thou art not so,

Hyperbole

A hyperbole is an exaggerated statement employing inflated language. A speaker who uses many hyperbolic statements is prone to overstatement. What do you know about people who use exaggeration when relating an incident or describing an object or a person? How can this information influence your performance of a hyperbolic character? "She was the most talented and beautiful girl in the world" is a hyperbolic statement.

Litotes

A litotes is an understatement in which the affirmative is implied by denying its opposite. Litotes are used by characters who are a bit uncertain or unsure of themselves and who hesitate to commit themselves too vehemently. Characters who do not want to reveal their true feelings may also use litotes. "She wasn't bad looking" is an example of a litotes if the speaker really thought she was gorgeous.

Metaphor

A metaphor is a comparison that suggests a likeness between two apparently unlike things. A speaker might use a metaphor to make an image stronger and clearer, to relate something not so easily seen or understood to something that is more tangible and concrete. The use of metaphor, then, is usually a conscious attempt by the speaker to communicate more effectively, often on many different levels. In a popular song, Paul Simon says he would rather be "a sparrow" than "a snail." This is metaphoric use of language. Ask yourself what links sparrows and snails together, and why the speaker prefers to be one rather than the other. Often entire poems function as metaphors. The poem "The End of the World" by Archibald MacLeish, cited earlier, is a metaphor. It is implied that life is a circus, and death (the end of the world) occurs when the big top explodes.

Metonymy

In metonymy one word or image is used to represent another with which it is closely associated. When we say, "I have read all of Shakespeare," we use Shakespeare's name to stand for his works. Calling a detective "a gumshoe" is also an example of metonymy. In a recent *Newsweek* article, singer Celine Dion was metonymically referred to as a "Canadian megaphone." In the Eagles' song "Hotel California," "California" seems to be metonymical for the entire United States. A very common metonymic saying is "the pen is mightier than the sword" which implies that writing is more powerful than warfare. There is usually more tensiveness in the metonym than in the metaphor. Whereas the metaphor establishes relationships of similarity, metonymy establishes relationships of close proximity (see Chapter 9 for a discussion of how this relates to performance).

Oxymoron

An oxymoron is a contradiction that seemingly cannot be resolved. "Parting is such sweet sorrow" is an oxymoron. Other everyday-life examples include friendly fire, freezer burn, pretty ugly, jumbo shrimp, science fiction, original copy, and tax return. An oxymoron usually implies a tensive quality and adds to the conflict the speaker may be undergoing.

Paradox

A paradox is a seemingly contradictory statement that turns out to be true in some sense. A paradox implies a less tensive quality than an oxymoron. Here are the last two lines of the Eagles' song "Hotel California" just mentioned:

> You can check out any time you like,
> But you can never leave.
>
> The Eagles. From "Hotel California," words and music by Don Felder, Don Henley, and Glenn Frey. Copyright 1976, 1977, and 1979 Cass Country Music and Red Cloud Music and Fingers Music. Reprinted by permission.

There is a seeming contradiction in these lines, but there is also a resolution. "Checking out" seems to imply death. Consequently, you have permanently "checked out," and you may "never leave."

Personification

Personification occurs when the poet bestows human characteristics on inanimate objects, abstract qualities, and animals. Wordsworth uses personification in the following lines from "Ode: Intimations of Immortality from Recollections of Early Childhood":

> The moon doth with delight
> Look round her when the heavens are bare

By using personification, the speaker helps us to identify with nonhuman elements by giving them human emotions or characteristics.

Simile

Simile, which is similar to metaphor, is a comparison using the words *like, as,* or *as if.* A simile, then, usually implies a less exact comparison than a metaphor: two qualities, objects, persons, and so forth, are similar rather than identical. "O my love is like a red red rose" is a simile. Look closely at the type of similes the speaker uses. What specific images are used to compare the unknown to the known? The types of comparisons the speaker makes are important clues to personality.

Synecdoche

Synecdoche is closely related to metonymy. In synecdoche, a part is used to suggest the whole. "Hotel California," for example, is both synecdoche and metonymy. "California" is a part of the United States and is used to represent the whole nation. A speaker uses synecdoche when wanting to create vivid imagery that needs the audience's participation for completion. In Coleridge's "The Rime of the Ancient Mariner," he substitutes "wave" for "sea" in the following line:

The western wave was all aflame.

When analyzing poetry, be sure to analyze the kinds of literary images used and how these images contribute to your understanding of the speaker. Some literary images, like the simile, are obvious because they include key words, but some are very subtle, such as the synecdoche and the allusion. Spend time studying each line of your poem. Look up words that seem unfamiliar to you, look for comparisons, look for images that imply a contradiction. The more aware you are of where the literary images are and what they signify, the more you will be able to communicate the images in performance.

The number and kind of literary images employed in a poem are clues to the nature of the speaker. A speaker who uses many sophisticated kinds of literary images is telling you something about his or her intelligence or educational level. Another type of speaker may be using literary images in an attempt to make the experience in the poem clearer or to communicate more effectively.

One last consideration of imagery is the *motif*. A motif is any image repeated often enough to become significant. A poem might contain light motifs, death motifs, animal motifs, or religious motifs. If the speaker uses images like "blowing sand," "parched throat," "oasis in sight," and "hot sun," he or she is creating a desert motif. Motifs are clues to the speaker's preoccupations.

Class Exercise

Read the following Shakespeare sonnet aloud, paying special attention to the literary images. How does the nature and use of each image contribute to your understanding of the persona? (The poem "A Lady" cited earlier also contains many literary images. Reread that poem to see how literary images are used there as well.)

WHEN IN DISGRACE WITH FORTUNE AND MEN'S EYES   William Shakespeare

When in disgrace with fortune and men's eyes
I all alone beweep my outcast state,
And trouble deaf heaven with my bootless cries,
And look upon myself, and curse my fate,
Wishing me like to one more rich in hope,
Featured like him, like him with friends possessed,
Desiring this man's art, and that man's scope,
With what I most enjoy contented least;
Yet in these thoughts myself almost despising,
Haply I think on thee, and then my state,
Like to the lark at break of day arising
From sullen earth, sings hymns at heaven's gate;
For thy sweet love remembered such wealth brings
That then I scorn to change my state with kings.

Tone Color

Tone color is the repetition of like sounds (not letters) throughout a poem. When you examine the tone color in a poem, use the signs in the International Phonetic Alphabet (Figure 8.1) to represent the repetitive sounds. These sounds become significant if they are repeated often enough to show a pattern. Tone color appeals to our auditory sense. When you are looking for patterns of tone color, do not depend on your eyes alone. Sound each word so you can hear the way the poet has manipulated sounds. There are five primary kinds of tone color which a poet may employ: alliteration, assonance, consonance, rhyme, and onomatopoeia.

Alliteration

Alliteration is the repetition of identical consonant sounds, usually at the beginning of words in close proximity, throughout a poem. Alliteration occurs on stressed syllables or words—those syllables or words which receive the most emphasis when read aloud. In the following line, the repetition of the /f/ and /d/ sounds is an example of alliteration:

I wake and *feel* the *fell* of *dark*, not *day*.

INTERNATIONAL PHONETIC SIGNS

Phonetic Symbol*	Example	Phonetic Transcription
i	eat	it
ɪ	sit	sɪt
ɛ	bet	bɛt
æ	sat	sæt
ɑ	pop	pɑp
ɔ	tall	tɔl
ou	slow	slou
eɪ	day	deɪ
aɪ	my	maɪ
au	cow	kau
ɔɪ	toy	tɔɪ
ʌ	up	ʌp
u	flute	flut
ʊ	foot	fʊt
ɝ	bird	bɝd
ŋ	sing	sɪŋ
ʃ	ship	ʃip
ʒ	treasure	trɛʒur
ð	this	ðɪs
θ	thin	θɪn
dʒ	jump	dʒʌmp
tʃ	church	tʃɝtʃ
j	yes	jɛs
ɚ (in unaccented syllables)	after	æftɚ
ɝ (in accented syllables)	urge	ɝdʒ
ə (in unaccented syllables)	sofa	soufə
ʌ (in accented syllables)	cut	kʌt

*Source: Edward S. Strother and Alan Huckelberry. *The Effective Speaker* (New York: Houghton Mifflin Co., 1968), pp. 373–85.

Figure 8.1

Assonance

Assonance is the repetition of identical vowel sounds in words in close proximity throughout a poem. The repetition of the /ir/ sound in the following line is an example of assonance:

And all is s*ea*red with trade; bl*ea*red, sm*ea*red with toil

Consonance

Consonance is the repetition of identical consonant sounds that are preceded by different vowel sounds, for example, *struts, frets*. Note the consonance in the repeated /d/ sound in the following line:

The col*d*, har*d* diamon*d* was hel*d* in her han*d*.

Rhyme

Rhyme is an element of poetry which helps to unify a poem by keeping thought groups together. Rhyme exists when words have the same vowel and succeeding sounds with different preceding sounds, for example, *sang-rang, high-dry, sailing-failing*. Rhyme is a useful device, but is not an essential element of poetry in general. Rhyme should never be used for its own sake; it must be used to underline and reinforce the sense of the poem. Russian poet Yeutushenko admitted that much of his early poetry was bad because he played with rhyme and didn't care about content. Ask yourself why the speaker uses rhyme and what effect is created by its use. Decide also how sophisticated or trite the rhyming words are. Rhyme can be discussed in terms of where it occurs in a line (at the end of the line or within the line) and by how closely the sounds approximate each other (full rhyme, half rhyme, eye rhyme).

End Rhyme   End rhyme is a commonly used type of rhyme in which the rhyming words occur at the ends of lines. By charting these end rhymes, you discover the poem's *rhyme scheme.* To chart the rhyme scheme, you look at the last word of the first line of the poem and give it an A. If the word at the end of the second line rhymes with the word at the end of the first line, it, too, gets an A; if it does not, it gets a B. Let's look again at "The End of the World" and chart its rhyme scheme.

THE END OF THE WORLD   Archibald MacLeish

Quite unexpectedly as Vasserot	A
The armless ambidextrian was lighting	B
A match between his great and second toe	A
And Ralph the lion was engaged in biting	B
The neck of Madame Sossman while the drum	C
Pointed, and Teeny was about to cough	D
In waltz-time swinging Jocko by the thumb—	C
Quite unexpectedly the top blew off:	D
And there, there overhead, there, there, hung over	E
Those thousands of white faces, those dazed eyes	F
There in the starless dark the poise, the hover,	E

There with vast wings across the canceled skies,	F
There in the sudden blackness, the black pall	G
Of nothing, nothing, nothing—nothing at all.	G

From *New and Collected Poems 1917–1976* by Archibald MacLeish. Copyright © 1976 by Archibald MacLeish. Reprinted by permission of Houghton Mifflin Company.

The rhyme scheme in this poem is ABABCDCDEFEFGG; thus, the poem is a Shakespearean sonnet. "Vasserot" at the end of line 1 rhymes with "toe" at the end of line 3, so they are given the same letter—A. When you come to a new sound, as here "lighting," that gets a B, and since "biting" rhymes with it, that gets a B, as well. You work through the entire poem giving the same sounds the same letter. Since "drum" does not rhyme with any sounds so far, it receives a new letter—C, and so on. The poem concludes with the tightest kind of rhyme—a rhymed couplet—GG.

Internal Rhyme   Internal rhyme occurs within lines. In the following line, "beams" and "dreams" are an example of internal rhyme:

For the moon never dreams without bringing me beams

Full Rhyme   Full rhyme can also be referred to as *exact, perfect,* and *true* rhyme. Full rhyme is the rhyme already discussed in which the initial consonants of the words differ, while the vowel and succeeding consonants are the same, as in *drum-thumb, cough-off, eyes-skies.*

Half Rhyme   Half rhyme is a type of approximate rhyme where one of the three conditions for full rhyme (same vowel sound, different preceding consonant sounds, same succeeding consonant sounds) is not met. Usually the vowel sound is slightly different, as in *comes* and *tombs.* Were you to chart the rhyme scheme, you would give half rhymes the same letter.

Eye Rhyme   Eye rhyme is less common than the other types just described. In eye rhyme, the poet uses two words that at one time rhymed and look as if they still do. But the words no longer rhyme because over time the pronunciation of one of the words has changed. In this category are words like *love* and *prove* and *daughter* and *laughter.* For this reason, eye rhyme resembles half rhyme. Were you to chart the rhyme scheme, you would give eye rhymes the same letter.

Onomatopoeia

Onomatopoeia, the last aspect of tone color, involves words that sound like their meanings—that imitate actual sounds. In Emily Dickinson's poem "I Heard a Fly Buzz When I Died," the word "buzz" is an example of onomatopoeia because "buzz" is the noise flies actually make. Other words used in poetry can be made to sound like their meanings if the sound closely approximates what the word represents and if you color the word in performance. Say the words *quick, hot, icy, groan, murmuring, thud,* and *break.* Now say the words again, trying to make the sounds approximate their meanings. Can you hear the difference?

When a poet uses tone color, he or she is trying to underline the sense of a line with sound. Although most poets do not consciously say, "I think an /a/ sound would be useful here," they are all aware of sound qualities on a less conscious level. Poets develop an inner ear—the ability to know which sounds are right in a given place, often without conscious deliberation. Your awareness of which sounds are used can be valuable in knowing how a poem is to be interpreted.

Certain sounds communicate certain feelings and moods, and certain other sounds accelerate or impede the progress of a line. Some sounds, for example, are difficult to say and cause "friction" when they are produced: a forced sensation against the lips, tongue, teeth, or palate. These *fricatives* include the /k/, /f/, /s/, /z/, /th/, and /sh/ sounds. If a poem has many repeated fricatives, and if the speaker is in some sort of conflict situation, the sounds of the words can be used to underscore the tension. The fricatives /s/ and /z/ are prominent in the poem "Out, Out—" by Robert Frost. In this poem, a young boy's hand is severed by a buzz-saw; the repeated /s/ and /z/ sounds suggest the hum of the saw.

> From OUT, OUT—   Robert Frost
>
> The buzz-saw snarled and rattled in the yard.
> And made dust and dropped stove-length sticks of wood,
> Sweet-scented stuff when the breeze drew across it.
>
> From "Out, Out—" from *The Poetry of Robert Frost* edited by Edward Connery Lathem. Copyright 1916, 1969 by Holt, Rinehart and Winston. Copyright 1944 by Robert Frost. Reprinted by permission of Holt, Rinehart and Winston, Publishers.

Some sounds are caused by a temporary block and then release of the sound and are therefore called *plosives.* If a poem has repeated /p/ and /b/ sounds, the sounds may signal that an explosive effect is to be created in performance, as in this line from "The End of the World":

Quite unexpectedly the top blew off:

The plosives in this line help to underscore both the tension and the explosion.

The *nasal* sounds—/n/, /m/, and /ng/—are produced almost entirely through the nose. Nasal sounds can be emphasized when you want to project a character with a reedy or whiny vocal quality.

The *dental* sounds (/t/, /d/) are easily produced because they flip quickly off the tongue. A succession of dental sounds may suggest that the speaker is rushing or in a hurry.

The liquid /l/ sound is pleasant to the ear and easily produced. Look, for example, how Gwendolyn Brooks uses the liquid /l/ sound in this poem to highlight the sensual mood of the persona:

> From WHEN YOU HAVE FORGOTTEN SUNDAY: THE LOVE STORY
> Gwendolyn Brooks
>
> And how we finally undressed and whipped out the light and flowed into bed,
> And lay loose-limbed for a moment in the week-end
> Bright bedclothes,
> Then gently folded into each other.
>
> From "when you have forgotten Sunday: the love story" from *Blacks.* Copyright 1987 by Gwendolyn Brooks Blakely. Reprinted by permission of the author.

Sounds and their placement affect the pacing of a line. If the poet has used /b/, /p/, /k/, /t/, and /d/ sounds, a line will usually move along fairly quickly. Short vowel sounds also move a line along. Long vowel sounds and diphthongs (two sounds combined in one vowel, as with the "y" in "my") often slow down a line, as they take longer to produce. The following sounds often slow down the tempo of a line: /sh/, /s/, /z/, /m/, /n/, /ng/, /f/, and /v/.

As you analyze the sounds, ask yourself how they underline the sense of the poem and help characterize the speaker. Remember, though, that your attention to tone color must be consistent with the nature of the speaker. Do not exaggerate the tonal qualities of a poem simply to hear what beautiful sounds you can make! Your response to the tone color in a poem should support your interpretation of what the poem means.

Meter

Poetry is heightened language, crystallized experience. Because it is so condensed, its rhythm is more pronounced than the rhythm in prose or most dramas. When you read poetry aloud, therefore, discovering the metrical or rhythmical base is essential. The kind of metrical prosody we will discuss is called *foot prosody.* Foot prosody is a type of metrical prosody based on a combination of metrical feet and the number of syllables per line. We are concerned both with the type of feet used (e.g., iambic—an unstressed syllable followed by a stressed syllable) and the number of feet in each line (e.g., pentameter—five feet). Foot prosody is the most common type of prosody and the type most often representative of *conventional verse—*

poems that have a discernible metrical pattern. Poems written in *free verse*—characteristic of much contemporary poetry—have a rhythmic base but it is usually not regular and not as easily discernible. There are many other types of metrical prosody, including stress, syllabic, and visual, but since foot prosody reveals the most useful information for performance, we will only discuss this kind of prosodic structure.

In the English language, we give more emphasis to certain syllables than to others when we speak. Some words receive more emphasis than others. When we discover this pattern of emphasis, we are finding the poem's *meter*—the pattern of stressed and unstressed syllables.[1] Look at the line below:

> The day is cold, and dark, and dreary;

In this line, the words "day," "cold," "dark," and the first syllable of "dreary"—"drear"—receive the emphasis and determine the line's meter. This line can then be divided into smaller units, each with an accented or stressed syllable and at least one unaccented or unstressed syllable. Such units are called *feet* and are isolated from each other by bar lines. If we divide the same line into metrical feet, it would look like this:

> Thĕ dáy | ĭs cóld | ănd dárk | ănd dréarў;

When we mark a line in this way—indicating its stressed and unstressed syllables and putting in the bar lines—we are scanning the line. Determining the metrical pattern in poetry is called *scansion*.

Poetic lines are labeled according to the type of foot which predominates and by the length of the line. There are eight common types of metrical feet: iamb, trochee, anapest, dactyl, spondee, pyrrhic, amphibrach, and amphimacer (also called cretic). Of these types, the iamb is found the most often in conventional poetry. Line length is determined by the number of feet in a line. The following terms are used to represent the number of feet in a line of poetry:

One foot: monometer	Five feet: pentameter
Two feet: dimeter	Six feet: hexameter
Three feet: trimeter	Seven feet: heptameter or septameter
Four feet: tetrameter	Eight feet: octameter

Trimeter, tetrameter, and pentameter are the most common line lengths in conventional English verse.

Here are descriptions of the eight common types of metrical feet.

Iamb (iambic) (˘´)

An iamb is a foot of two syllables, an unstressed syllable followed by a stressed syllable. If a line of verse has all iambs or a majority of iambs, the line is called *iambic.* Because iambic feet move to the stressed syllable, a *rising rhythm* results. Rising rhythm underlines poems with uplifting or optimistic themes, though exceptions exist. Look at the line below:

> I wake to sleep and take my waking slow.

This line is an example of *iambic pentameter:* iambic because the line is composed entirely of iambs and pentameter because there are five feet in the line. When you scan a poem, begin by marking the words of more than one syllable. You begin scanning this line by looking at the word "waking." In a dictionary, the accent in this word is on the syllable "wak," so this syllable receives the stress. Now mark the rest of the line, stressing those words or syllables that carry the meaning: "wake," "sleep," "take," and "slow." Once you have marked the line for its stressed and unstressed syllables, you then must put in the bar lines. You look for the first recognizable foot and place the bar line after it, and so on, through the whole line. The scanned line looks like this:

> Ĭ wáke | tŏ sleép | ănd take | mў wak | ĭng slów.

Only by scanning do you find the one irregularity in this line. Lee and Galati refer to this irregularity as an *override.*[2] An override results when a bar line splits a word and the rhythm is altered as the reader maintains the integrity of the word, despite the foot break. In this case, the iambic rhythm changes to a trochaic feel on the word "waking." If you read this line paying attention to the override, the trochaic feel of "waking" slows you down and prepares you for the word "slow." Consequently, the rhythm underscores the sense of the line. Overrides are important in poetry performance because they often signal a moment where the poet wants a change of emphasis and because they provide rhythmic variety in a regularly metered line.

Trochee (trochaic) (´˘)

A trochee is a foot of two syllables, a stressed syllable followed by an unstressed syllable. A line of verse which has a predominance of trochees is called *trochaic.* Because in a trochaic foot there is a fall from the stressed syllable, a *falling rhythm* results. Falling rhythm underscores poems with pessimistic or depressing themes, though again this is not always the case. Look at the following line:

> sómewhĕre | Í havĕ | névĕr | travélled, | gládlỹ | bĕyónd

The first five feet are trochees, and the last foot is an iamb. Because the trochees outnumber the iambs, the line is called trochaic. Because there are six feet, the line is an example of *trochaic hexameter*.

Anapest (anapestic) (˘˘´)

An anapest is a foot of three syllables, two unstressed syllables followed by a stressed syllable. A whole line of anapests is called *anapestic*. An anapest speeds up the pace of a line and produces a running feel. Anapests also fit into the category of rising rhythms. Look at this line:

Ŏf mў dár | lĭng, mў dár | lĭng, mў life | and mў bride

In this line, each foot is an anapest. Since there are four feet, the line is an example of *anapestic tetrameter*. What effect do the overrides have in this line?

Dactyl (dactyllic) (´˘˘)

A dactyl is a foot of three syllables, a stressed syllable followed by two unstressed syllables. A line composed predominately of dactyls is called dactyllic. A line of dactyls has a falling rhythm, as in this line:

Cánnŏns tŏ | right ŏf thĕm,

Both feet are dactyls, and the line is an example of *dactyllic dimeter*.

The four remaining feet are primarily used to substitute for the four more commonly employed feet just described. Rarely, if ever, are any of these feet the only type of foot in a line.

Spondee (´´)

A spondaic foot contains two stressed syllables. When a spondee is used, the pace is temporarily slowed as the poet attempts to add more emphasis to certain words. The third foot in the following line is a spondee:

Ănd soón | ĕst oŭr | best mén | with thĕe | dŏ gó.

Pyrrhic (˘˘)

Pyrrhic describes a foot of two syllables, both of which are unstressed. Again, a pyrrhic is never the predominant foot in a line, but is used only as a substitute to vary the basic meter. The pyrrhic foot usually precedes or follows a foot that receives more emphasis, as in the following line. In this line, the second foot is pyrrhic:

And soon | est our | best men | with thee | do go.

Amphibrach (˘ ˊ ˘)

An amphibrach is a foot of three syllables; an unstressed syllable, followed by a stressed syllable, followed by an unstressed syllable. A line that contains many amphibrachs has a sort of rocking, rhythmic feel. The last foot in the following line is an amphribach.

That looks | on tem | pests and | is nev | er shaken.

Amphimacer (ˊ ˘ ˊ)

An amphimacer is a foot of three syllables; a stressed syllable, followed by an unstressed syllable, followed by a stressed syllable. In the following line, the first foot is an amphimacer; the second, fourth, and fifth are iambs; and the third is a spondee:

Thou art slave | to fate, | chance, kings, | and des | perate men,

Figure 8.2 illustrates each of the eight types of metrical feet just described.

When you scan a poem, keep the following guidelines in mind:

1. Read the whole poem aloud first. Listen to the rhythm. Try to feel which syllables or words receive the stress. Scanning a poem is done with the ear; it is difficult to scan a poem by reading it silently. The rhythm truly becomes apparent only when the poem is heard.
2. Scan for sense. Stress those words or syllables which seem to carry the meaning. *To be* verbs, prepositions, articles, and conjunctions are rarely stressed. Nouns, action verbs, and most adverbs and adjectives are usually stressed.
3. Begin your scansion by marking the words of more than one syllable first. Mark the words of more than one syllable exactly as indicated in a dictionary.
4. Do not force your lines to conform to one metrical type. Although most conventional poems are written in one prevailing meter, poets often include other types of feet to provide variety, gain attention, or underscore a change of emphasis essential to the meaning.
5. When putting in the bar lines, place them where the word naturally breaks into syllables. Bar lines often go where there is a punctuation mark in a line.

THE MOST COMMON TYPES OF METRICAL FEET

Meter	Characteristics	Marking	Example
Iamb	An unstressed syllable followed by a stressed syllable. Rising feel. The most common type of foot.	[˘ˊ]	bĕlieˊve
Trochee	A stressed syllable followed by an unstressed syllable. Falling feel. A common substitute for an iamb.	[ˊ˘]	suˊmmĕr
Anapest	Two unstressed syllables followed by a stressed syllable. Gives a line a running rhythmic or rising feel. Quickens pace.	[˘˘ˊ]	ŭnĕxceˊlled
Dactyl	A stressed syllable followed by two unstressed syllables. Falling feel. Slows pace.	[ˊ˘˘]	Aˊnnăbĕl
Spondee	Two stressed syllables. Adds emphasis. Slows pace.	[ˊˊ]	Noˊ, stoˊp!
Pyrrhic	Two unstressed syllables. Used to deemphasize. Quickens pace.	[˘˘]	ănd thĕ
Amphibrach	Three syllables: one unstressed, one stressed, and one unstressed.	[˘ˊ˘]	văcaˊtiŏn
Amphimacer	Three syllables: one stresed, one unstressed, and one stressed	[ˊ˘ˊ]	diˊvĭng boaˊrd

Figure 8.2

6. If a poem is in free verse, placement of bar lines can be difficult because an overall metrical pattern may not be apparent. There may, however, be patterns apparent in individual lines. Look for these patterns and try to discover how the particular metrical pattern underscores the sense of that particular line.

Rhythmic Variety

When applying to your performance what you learned from scanning your poem, be very conscious of the prevailing meter. This is your first clue to how the poet wishes to underline the sense rhythmically. Many conventional poems have a very regular rhythm, and you may find yourself locked into a "ta tum, ta tum, ta tum, ta tum, ta tum" which you do not know how to vary. There are, however, at least four possible sources of variety.

Caesura

A caesura is a pause *within* a line, usually marked by punctuation. In terms of internal pauses, the most important questions to ask are Where should I pause? and How long should I pause? You pause within a line whenever the line contains a mark of punctuation. Some poets, like e. e. cummings, do not use punctuation conventionally. Many of cummings's poems have no punctuation at all, but the configuration of the lines on the page often suggests where you are to pause and for how long. If there is a long space between two words, take a long pause; if less space, take a shorter pause. If words are pushed together with no space between them, that means no pause.

   The length of pause is dependent on two conditions: the type of punctuation mark employed and the pace at which the speaker is speaking (which, of course, depends on the situation, amount of tension, and emotional state of the speaker). Relatively speaking, commas receive a shorter pause than do periods, exclamation points, and question marks, which indicate the completion of a *primary cadence*—a complete sentence. The general tendency of many beginning interpreters is to rush through the performance. Poetry is often difficult to understand on the first reading. Keep your audience in mind. Reading poems too rapidly—especially short poems, such as sonnets—may mean that your audience cannot understand half of what you would like them to understand. Audiences do not have the luxury of time and repeated readings, as the silent reader does.

Substitute foot

Substitution is the use of a metrical foot other than the prevailing meter. If the prevailing meter is, for example, iambic, it is common for a poet to use a different type of foot on occasion to provide variety or to point up something of greater or lesser importance. If a poem is primarily iambic, a poet may use any type of foot as a substitute. Shakespeare, for example, who wrote primarily in iambic pentameter, often began a line with a trochaic foot to grab attention because the trochee, unlike the iamb, begins with a stressed syllable. A poet may substitute a spondee when more emphasis is wanted or a pyrrhic when less emphasis is needed. The spondee tends to slow down the pace, and the pyrrhic tends to speed up the pace. The anapest, for example, has a running feel and tends to speed the pace, while the dactyl tends to impede the progress of a line. Attention to the variety of metrical feet prevents a too regular-sounding rhythm and aids the reader in knowing where the poet is indicating a change in thought or feeling.

End-line variation

Another source of variety in the performance of poetry is achieved by paying attention to the presence or absence of punctuation at the end of the lines. You may have been taught to pause at the end of every line when reading poetry aloud, or you may have been taught never to pause until you came to a primary cadence—a complete sentence. *Our suggestion, however, is to maintain the integrity of the line as written, regardless of whether there is a punctuation mark at the end of the line.*

There are two kinds of line ends: *enjambed* (run-on lines with no punctuation at the end and where the thought carries over to the next line) and *end-stopped* (lines which end with some kind of punctuation mark). The following list suggests the length of pause that should be taken at line ends:

Type of Punctuation		Length of Pause
1. No punctuation (enjambed line)	End-stopped lines	1. Half-comma pause (half-beat)
2. Comma (,) and dash (—)		2. Long pause (about one beat)
3. Semicolon (;) or colon (:)		3. Longer pause (about two beats)
4. Period (.), exclamation mark (!) and question mark (?)		4. Longest pause (about three beats)

Of course, the length of the pause varies according to the pace at which you read the poem (primarily determined by the meter), but this information should help you translate the poet's use of punctuation into performance cues. You may ask, Why should I pause at the end of every line, especially if the intellectual thought or rhetorical meaning of one line carries over into the next line? There are five primary reasons why you should maintain the integrity of the line as a unit of sound and sense.

1. You help the audience to *see* as well as to *hear* each line of the poem.
2. The pause at line ends gives the speaker time to conceive of what to say next, and often this can be a surprise for both speaker and audience.
3. The pause helps to underscore the rhythm of the line and contributes to the variety of a poem's rhythm in general. The line ends add to the total rhythmic effect.
4. You help to differentiate images. For example, look at these lines from Dylan Thomas's "Poem in October":

My birthday began with the water—
Birds and the birds of the winged trees flying my name

In these lines, a pause at the end of the first line creates in the audience's mind three images rather than just one image. Pausing after the word "water" gives the audience time to image "water" first and possibly to get the connotations of birth, baptism, and beginning. Then when the persona adds "Birds," we get the bird image, along with its possible religious connotations. The audience then puts the two words together and gets the specific kind of bird evoked. Pausing at line ends, then, provides the audience with a richer experience.

5. Last, pausing at line ends is ultimately what makes poetry sound like poetry and not like prose. If you read poetry by continuing the sound until you come to a final punctuation mark, you might as well be reading prose. Look, for example, at this poem by Gwendolyn Brooks.

WE REAL COOL   Gwendolyn Brooks

The Pool Players.
Seven at the Golden Shovel.

We real cool. We
Left school. We

Lurk late. We
Strike straight. We

Sing sin. We
Thin gin. We

Jazz June. We
Die Soon.

If this poem were written the way most people perform it, it would look like this:

We real cool.
We left school.

We lurk late.
We strike straight.

We sing sin.
We thin gin.

> We jazz June.
> We die soon.

Why do you think Brooks wrote the poem with the word "We" at the end of each line? Read the poem aloud twice, with the "We" at the end of each line and then at the beginning of the next line. If you read the poem as written, the accent or stress falls on the rhyming words: "cool" and "school," "late" and "straight," and so forth. If you read the poem as if it were prose, pausing only at end punctuation marks, the stress falls on the "We's." Brooks has written that "the ending 'We's' in 'We Real Cool' are tiny, wispy, weakly argumentative 'Kilroy-is-here' announcements. The boys have no accented sense of themselves. . . . Say the 'We' softly."[3] Although you are free to interpret this poem as you perceive it, consider that Brooks—a good performer of her own poems—indicates the effect she wishes to create. In addition to the pause at the end of every line, think, too, about vocal inflection. You should try to effect a rise in inflection at the ends of lines unless they are primary cadences. You want to suggest that there is more to come. Do not read every line with a downward inflection that indicates the end of a sentence unless the line is a primary cadence. (A question mark at the end of the line really does not call for a downward inflection either.)

Override

When a bar line divides a word, an override results. As stated earlier, an override changes the overriding rhythm as the reader maintains the integrity of the word and, thus, provides variety in the meter. In this line "stillness" is an override:

$$\text{Thĕ stíll | nĕss ín | thĕ roóm}$$

After scanning your poem, look for the overrides. Do the overrides seem to occur in a pattern? How do they signal a change in rhythm? How does this change underscore sense? Be aware of these four elements—caesura, substitute foot, end-line variation, and override—to help give your performance variety and prevent it from sounding mechanical.

Before we conclude our discussion of scansion and meter, we need to make one additional point. Beginning readers often have difficulty knowing what to stress when they perform poetry. True, scansion will help you, but not all the stressed syllables are equal in importance. The English language is a bit more complex in terms of emphasis than just unstressed or stressed; there are many relative degrees of stress. Remember, when you scan a poem, you are only marking stress in terms of the words or syllables that seem to get more emphasis compared to the words or syllables surrounding them. However, though there may be four stressed words or syllables in a line, some words or syllables are ultimately more important than others in terms of the meaning of the line. Look at each line, decide which words carry the meaning, and give them more emphasis. Then look at each stanza (grouping of lines). Are all the lines of equal importance? If they are not, give the line or lines that carry the most meaning more importance in performance. Finally, look at the poem as a whole, and see whether you can subordinate stressed words or syllables so that what is ultimately most important sounds that way.

Class Exercise

Try scanning the following lines to determine the rhythm and the variations of rhythm. See whether you can discover the prevailing meter and line length.

1. I heard a fly buzz when I died;
2. Beautiful Warren Gamaliel Harding
3. Once upon a midnight dreary, while I pondered, weak and weary,
4. A simple declarative sentence with seven grammatical
5. There in the starless dark the poise, the hover,

> "I heard a fly buzz when I died" by Emily Dickinson. Reprinted by permission of the publishers and the Trustees of Amherst College from *The Poems of Emily Dickinson,* edited by Thomas H. Johnson, Cambridge, MA: The Belknap Press of Harvard University Press. Copyright 1951, © 1955, 1979, 1983 by the President and Fellows of Harvard College.
> The lines from "the first president to be loved by his" from *Viva,* Poems by e. e. cummings, is reprinted by permission of Liveright Publishing Corporation. Copyright 1931, 1959 by e. e. cummings. Copyright © 1973, 1979 by Nancy T. Andrews. Copyright © 1973, 1979 by George James Firmage.
> The line from "The End of the World" from *New and Collected Poems 1917–1976* by Archibald MacLeish. Copyright © 1976 by Archibald MacLeish. Reprinted by permission of Houghton Mifflin Company.

Conventional Verse and Free Verse

You will find that traditional or conventional poetry is much more highly patterned than free-verse poetry. Conventional poetry usually has a discernible metrical pattern, a consistent line length or line length pattern, and approximately the same number of lines in each stanza.[4]

Free-verse poetry has patterns, but they are not always easy to recognize. Free-verse poetry does not scan easily, and sometimes it does not scan at all into any regular type of meter. Free-verse poetry has a rhythmical pulse, but that pulse is not regular and may not always be a result of the alternation of stressed and unstressed syllables. Free verse is characterized by a variety of metrical feet and a variety of line lengths. If it is divided into stanzas, the stanzas rarely contain a consistent number of lines. Free-verse poems may or may not rhyme. If they do contain rhyme, it is often internal rhyme and is rarely as patterned as in conventional verse. Free-verse poems tend to sound a bit more conversational and often less formal than conventional-verse poems.

Fulcrum

When performing the how of your poem, pay close attention to the changes in image, sound, and meter. As stated earlier, when the speaker changes attitude, thought direction, emphasis, or mood, there is an attendant change in image, sound, or meter. There may be many minor changes in a poem, but often only one major change. This change is called the *fulcrum*, and it exists before the line where the change occurs. The fulcrum, then, is the silence before the change. As John Ciardi says in *How Does a Poem Mean?* "A poem is one part against another across a silence."[5] Knowing where the fulcrum occurs is an important consideration in performing a poem, since its location determines whether the poem is balanced or unbalanced. If the fulcrum occurs approximately in the middle of a poem, the parts are balanced, and the poem is said to be *symmetrical*. If the fulcrum is off-center, the poem is unbalanced, or *asymmetrical*.

See if you can detect the location of the fulcrum in the following poem.

LOST KEYS. AGAIN   Cara Osborne

```
1   It's been one of those days.
2   One of those days in which
3   eight glasses of whiskey
4   would beat out the water
5   they say I need.
6   One of those days that I have had
7   to back track my own damn tracks
8   just to get my keys that I left
9   on some slimy counter somewhere.
10  A day where people want eye contact
11  because it's sunny outside and they
12  feel like living.
13  But, I've got junk to do.
14  No space for eye-contact, whiskey,
15  or lost keys.
16  And wouldn't you know,
17  I'm sitting here squandering more time
18  writing poetry about it.
```

Reprinted by permission of the author.

In this self-reflexive poem, the fulcrum is indicated by the word "but" (a word that often conveys opposition to what has gone before) in line 13—an unlucky number consistent with "one of those [bad] days." The poem changes in thought here from a description of the speaker's day to the realization that she or he has no time or space to sit around and reflect anymore because there is "junk to do." The poem changes then in the silence before the line "But I've got junk to do." In performance, you might want to take a pause during that silence, reflect on what you've been doing, and show more frustration because you have wasted time writing about the incidents of the day instead of getting "junk" done.

Changes in sound can also indicate the location of the fulcrum in a poem. A change in rhyme scheme is often a good indicator. Earlier we discussed the rhyme scheme of two kinds of sonnets. Close examination of the rhyme scheme often helps locate the fulcrum. The two kinds of sonnets with their rhyme schemes are again indicated here. Notice where the fulcrum usually occurs in each sonnet type.

Shakespearean Sonnet

A
B   argument one
A
B

C
D   argument two
C
D

E
F   argument three
E
F

      Fulcrum

G   resolution
G

Petrarchan Sonnet

A
B
B
A   argument
A
B
B
A

      Fulcrum

C
D
C   resolution
C
D
C

As you can see, the Shakespearean sonnet is asymmetrical (twelve lines must be balanced in performance by two) and the Petrarchan sonnet is symmetrical (eight lines in the octave, stanza one and six lines in the sestet, stanza two). If you were performing a Shakespearean sonnet, you would have to deliver the closing couplet slowly and with much intensity to balance all that has gone before. With the Petrarchan sonnet, however, you can give equal emphasis to both sections of the poem, but the second stanza may have a different feel because the fulcrum has prescribed some kind of change.

A change in the meter also helps determine where the fulcrum might occur. Often this change is felt as a change in the pace of the poem. The pace, in turn, is determined by a variety of elements: line ends, punctuation, sound patterns, and types of metrical feet. Look once again at MacLeish's poem "The End of the World."

1 Quite unexpectedly as Vasserot
2 The armless ambidextrian was lighting
3 A match between his great and second toe
4 And Ralph the lion was engaged in biting
5 The neck of Madame Sossman while the drum
6 Pointed, and Teeny was about to cough
7 In waltz-time swinging Jocko by the thumb—
8 Quite unexpectedly the top blew off:

9   And there, there overhead, there, there, hung over
10 Those thousands of white faces, those dazed eyes,
11 There in the starless dark the poise, the hover,
12 There with vast wings across the canceled skies,
13 There in the sudden blackness, the black pall
14 Of nothing, nothing, nothing—nothing at all.

The fulcrum in this poem seems to fall between lines 8 and 9. (This poem combines qualities of both Shakespearean and Petrarchan sonnets. Though it is a Shakespearean sonnet in terms of rhyme scheme, the fulcrum divides the sonnet almost in half, as is true of the Petrarchan sonnet.) The first eight lines are composed primarily of enjambed lines. Lines 1, 2, 3, 4, 5, and 6 are enjambed and help to accelerate the pace. The persona gives us the sense that everything is happening simultaneously (using words like "as," "and," and "while" help create this effect, and using the past progressive tense, as in "was lighting" and "was engaged," gives a sense of action in progress), as in a three-ring circus. After the fulcrum, four end-stopped lines (lines 10, 11, 12, and 14) slow down the pace.

Notice also the punctuation in this poem. Before the fulcrum, only one line contains a caesura—line 6. This lack of punctuation also accelerates the pace. After the fulcrum, there are many caesurae—ten, to be exact, marked by ten punctuation marks. Thus, you will read the second half of this poem more slowly. If the first stanza suggests fast-paced activity, the second stanza suggests the sense of death and destruction. The use of the caesura slows the pace to help communicate this difference.

In the first half of this poem, the poet uses sound combinations which speed the progress of the lines. In the second half, however, the sounds impede the progress. Look, for example, at this line (line 6) from the first half of the poem:

Pointed, and Teeny was about to cough

The /p/, /t/, and /k/ sounds speed up the tempo of the line. Compare this effect with the following line (line 12) from the second half of the poem:

> There with vast wings across the canceled skies,

Here, the /th/, /v/, and /s/ sounds slow down the line.

Though "The End of the World" is written in iambic pentameter, there are variations in meter, beginning with the line before the fulcrum. Lines 1–7 scan fairly regularly. The pace changes at the end of line 8:

> Quite un | expect | edly | the top | blew off :

The final spondee slows down the line because it calls for extra emphasis. When you read this line, the three stressed syllables in a row slow you down to emphasize the explosion and to prepare you for the silence after the explosion. In the second half of the poem, the rhythm is quite varied. Look, for example, at line 9:

> And there, | there o | verhead, | there, there, | hung over

There are two iambic feet in this line, and the line is stressed much more heavily than any of the lines before the fulcrum.

The fulcrum, then, marks a major change in this poem in image, sound, and meter. The fulcrum indicates a change in a poem (just as the crisis moment does in a play), and the change must be shown in performance. During the silence that precedes the change, you will want to show what exactly motivates that change to occur. In "The End of the World," for example, after line 8 you would want to remember that explosion— see and hear and feel the devastation—and then begin line 9.[6]

Climaxes

One last consideration of the how of a poem is the development of climaxes. Poems contain two kinds of climaxes: emotional and logical. *Emotional climaxes* occur whenever there is an increase or surge of emotion on the part of the speaker. A poem may have many emotional climaxes or none at all. There is usually one *logical climax* in every poem. The logical climax is the point in the poem when the action reaches its logical conclusion; consequently, it is usually at or near the end of the poem. Look again at the Osborne poem "Lost Key. Again." You might decide that the anxiety in line 13, "But I've got junk to do" signals an emotional climax as well as the fulcrum. The logical climax is lines 16–18 where the speaker reflects on what he or she has been doing rather than getting "junk done."

WHY DOES THE SPEAKER SPEAK?

The purpose behind the speaker's words really depends on the kind of poem under study. In a lyric poem, for example, the persona is usually thinking or describing, trying to resolve a personal dilemma or share an emotional experience. Your performance should try to capture this dilemma or emotional experience, and you must be aware of the degree of tensiveness in the speaker.

Dramatic poems involve the creation of dramatized characters. In dramatic poetry, the speaker may be sharing thoughts, telling a story, or participating in a dialogue with another character. Dramatic poetry calls for you to create the character and to depict his or her beliefs, values, attitudes, and intentions.

Narrative poetry tells a story. The speaker's purpose could be to entertain, to inform, or to persuade. Ask yourself what the narrator would like us to think after the story is over. The narrator's purpose could be to make something appear funny, to make something clear, or to gain our sympathy.

As you analyze the why of the poem, consider the speaker's purpose, the speaker's motivation in doing and saying what he or she does and says, and the speaker's audience—whom the speaker is addressing.

PUTTING IT ALL TOGETHER

Apply the questions that follow to the poem you have selected to perform. (We suggest that you rehearse the poem several times before attempting to answer these questions.)

1. What will you say in your introduction (if you use an introduction) to prepare the audience for your interpretation of this poem?
2. What is the significance of the title of the poem?
3. What kind of poem is this generically: lyric? dramatic? narrative?
4. If lyric, what kind of lyric poem is it? elegy? ode? sonnet? confessional? reflective? descriptive?
5. If dramatic, what kind of dramatic poem is it? dramatic lyric? dramatic narrative? dramatic monologue? dramatic soliloquy? dramatic dialogue?
6. If narrative, what kind of narrative poem is it? ballad? metrical tale? epic?
7. Who seems to be speaking? To whom does he or she seem to be speaking?
8. What is the speaker modal classification of this poem? lyric? dramatic? epic?
9. Is this poem modally mixed? Consider the audience mode: when is the lyric voice heard? When is the dramatic voice heard? When is the epic voice

heard? How does this knowledge affect performance decisions in terms of focus, placement, and so forth?

10. What is the poem about? Does the speaker speak literally or figuratively?
11. Where is the speaker as he or she speaks?
12. Does the speaker speak in the present, past, or future? Is there progression of time?
13. What are the primary sensory appeals in this poem? How can these images be communicated in performance? What do the types of images tell you about the nature of the speaker?
14. What are the primary literary images in this poem? How do these images help determine the nature of the speaker? of his or her message? of his or her audience?
15. How is tone color used? What are the primary alliterative sounds? What are the primary assonantal and consonantal sounds? How do these sounds underline sense?
16. Is there a rhyme scheme? What is it?
17. Scan the poem. What is the prevailing meter? What is the prevailing line length? Are there substitutions? Where are the caesurae? Where are the overrides?
18. Which lines are enjambed and which are end-stopped? How does knowing this information affect your performance?
19. Where does the fulcrum occur? Is the poem symmetrical or asymmetrical?
20. Are there any emotional climaxes? Where is the logical climax?
21. Through what other "texts" did you interpret the poem? How did your past experiences, interests, and preoccupations influence your understanding of the poem?

SELECTED POEMS APPROPRIATE FOR PERFORMANCE

The following poems would be good choices for performance. As we stated earlier, many others exist. Use this list to begin your search for a poem to perform.

Maya Angelou	"Phenomenal Woman," "To a Husband"
Matthew Arnold	"Dover Beach"
W. H. Auden	"In Memory of W. B. Yeats," "The Unknown Citizen"
Gwendolyn Brooks	"The Ballad of Rudolph Reed," "The

	Ballad of Pearl May Lee," "To Be In Love"
Robert Browning	"My Last Duchess," "Soliloquy of the Spanish Cloister," "Porphyria's Lover"
Charles Bukowski	"The City in the Sea"
Joseph Ceravolo	"The Wind is Blowing West"
Alex Comfort	"The Atoll in the Mind"
Robert Creeley	"The Hill," "Dancing"
E. E. Cummings	"in Just-," "anyone lived in a pretty how town," "somewhere i have never traveled"
Emily Dickinson	"Because I Could Not Stop For Death," "I Felt a Funeral," "After Great Pain"
Diane Di Prima	"The Jungle," "Goodbye Nkrumah"
T. S. Eliot	"The Hollow Men"
D. J. Enright	"Of Growing Old," "Changing the Subject," "Sightseeing," "They Who Take the Word"
Ian Evadson	"Workless Waif or Poverty in Passing"
Mari Evans	"Status Symbol"
Robert Frost	"Wild Grapes," "Home Burial," "Death of the Hired Man," "Mending Wall," "Stopping by Woods on a Snowy Evening," "The Road Not Taken"
Nikki Giovanni	"Nikki-Rosa," "12 Gates to the City," "Beautiful Black Men"
Joy Harjo	"The Woman Hanging from the Thirteenth Floor," "I Give You Back," "She Had Some Horses"
Anthony Hecht	"Samuel Sewall"
John Keats	"To Autumn," "Ode on a Grecian Urn"
Robert Kelly	"The Sound"
Joanne Kyger	"My Father Died This Spring," "The Pigs for Circe in May," "Of All Things for You To Go Away Mad' "
Philip Larkin	"Next, Please"
Denise Levertov	"Bedtime," "The Mutes," "Matins," "To the Snake"

Don L. Lee	"But he was cool or he even stopped for green lights"
Vachel Lindsay	"The Congo"
Michael McClure	"Canticle," "Peyote Poem"
James Merrill	"The Mad Scene"
W. S. Merwin	"December: Of Aphrodite"
Robin Morgan	"The Invisible Woman"
Lisel Mueller	"Alive Together"
Howard Nemerov	"The Goose Fish"
Pablo Neruda	"The Word," "Poetry," "We are Many"
Wilfred Owen	"Dulce et Decorum Est"
Octavio Paz	"Two Bodies," "In Uxmalm," "San Ildefonso Nocturne"
Marge Piercy	"A Work of Artifice," "Barbie Doll"
Sylvia Plath	"Lady Lazarus," "Daddy," "The Applicant," "Tulips"
Adrienne Rich	"Storm Warnings," "Diving into the Wreck," "A Woman Mourned by Daughters," "Living in Sin"
Theodore Roethke	"Old Lady's Winter Words," "My Papa's Waltz"
Sonia Sanchez	"A Poem for My Father"
Carl Sandburg	"Chicago," "Freedom is a Habit"
Anne Sexton	"Ringing the Bells," "Pain for a Daughter," "For My Lover, Returning to His Wife"
William Shakespeare	any two sonnets
Percy Bysshe Shelley	"Ode to the West Wind"
Gary Snyder	"Meeting the Mountains"
Alfred, Lord Tennyson	"Ulysses"
Dylan Thomas	"Do Not Go Gentle into that Good Night," "Fern Hill," "Poem in October"
Cesar Vallejo	"Down to the Dregs," "Have You Anything to Say in Your Defense"
Richard Wilbur	"The Juggler," "Beasts," "Grace"
William Butler Yeats	"The Second Coming," "Among School Children"

The remaining two chapters of this book concentrate on additional literary forms available for performance and on experimental and group forms of interpretation.

SUMMARY

Poetry is an artistic creation in verse—a delicately crafted art form to which you give voice and body in performance. When beginning your study of poetry, ask yourself what the significance of the poem's title is. What valuable information does the title reveal?

Then ask, Who is speaking? and Who is being addressed? The answers to these questions can often be discovered by deciding the genre or what kind of poem you are studying: lyric (sonnet, descriptive lyric, reflective lyric, elegy, ode, confessional), dramatic (dramatic lyric, dramatic narrative, dramatic monologue, dramatic soliloquy, dramatic dialogue), or narrative (ballad, metrical tale, epic).

Once you have determined a poem's generic and modal classifications, examine the kind of action in which the speaker is engaged. Is the speaker emoting? thinking aloud? struggling as a result of a conflict? telling a story? Is the action literal or figurative? How much tensiveness is created in the poem? What is the time element? Where is the speaker as he or she speaks? How does the speaker use language? How are sensory imagery, literary imagery, tone color, and meter used to underline sense?

The rhythmic basis of a poem is detected by scanning—marking the lines for their stressed and unstressed syllables—and then dividing the lines into metrical feet. This is called foot prosody.

Variety in a metrical pattern may be provided by using caesurae, substitutions, variation at line ends, and overrides.

The fulcrum is an important element to analyze when preparing a poem for performance. The fulcrum marks a change in the poem, a change that may be marked by thought, speaker, imagery, sound, or meter, among others.

Notes

1. In reality, no syllable that is sounded is unstressed. It is more accurate to say that some syllables receive lighter stress and some receive heavier stress.
2. Charlotte I. Lee and Frank Galati, *Oral Interpretation*, 5th ed. (Boston: Houghton Mifflin, 1987), pp. 501–2, 505, 517.
3. Gwendolyn Brooks, *Report from Part One* (Detroit: Broadside Press, 1972), p. 185.
4. A stanza is a unit which forms a division of a poem and is equivalent to a paragraph in prose. It usually represents a unit of sound and sense. Stanzas are measured according to the number of lines they contain. A two-line stanza, for example, is called a couplet, a three-line stanza is called a tercet, and a four-line stanza is called a quatrain. In some Shakespearean sonnets, for example, the rhyme scheme (ABAB CDCD EFEF GG) often makes obvious the stanzaic divisions. The first three stanzas are quatrains, and the last stanza is a rhymed couplet. In many Petrarchan sonnets, the rhyme scheme (ABBAABBA CDCCDC) makes obvious a different kind of stanzaic division. The first stanza of eight lines is an octave, and the second stanza of six lines is a sestet.

5. John Ciardi, *How Does a Poem Mean?* (Boston: Houghton Mifflin, 1975), p. 360.
6. In addition to changes in image, sound, and meter, the fulcrum can be indicated in a number of other ways. The fulcrum may be indicated by a change in time (Frost's "The Road Not Taken" and Roethke's "Old Lady's Winter Words"); by a change in mood and pace (MacLeish's "The End of the World"); by the inclusion of key words such as *but, yet,* and *now;* and by the speaker's coming to a resolution in thinking (Donne's "Death Be Not Proud"), among others.

performance (although it is often true that writers have publication at a later date in the back of their minds and are aware of possible public consumption as they write), and occasionally a selection is too dry or uninteresting for the audience. In general, you will probably be safe if you choose literature that you like, understand, and feel has some audience appeal. This will greatly enhance its performance potential.

One important consideration when studying any selection is the nature of the speaker. The identification of the speaker is often a very complex matter when performing the literature discussed in this chapter. Many of these literary forms are written in the lyric mode—someone very much like the writer seems to be speaking, often in a less disguised way than in any literature discussed so far. Does this mean, then, that your responsibility as a performer is to create the writer? The answer is complicated but is often a matter of emphasis.

If the emphasis is on the specific nature of the speaker—if the writer's personality is distinctly emphasized and is inseparable from the text—then suggesting the specific nature of this speaker (not impersonating the writer—there is a difference between impersonation and interpretation; only the latter can illuminate) would be necessary. These lyric speakers are the writer's images of themselves at the time they were writing—their personae or masks. Although the writer and speaker are similar and may have much in common, you still are suggesting a persona, not the writer. If the text and not the performance is to be featured, you must focus on the nature of the speaker created in the work and not on how well you can imitate the real man or woman. In many cases, writers have not accurately described a situation or presented unbiased images of themselves. As was true with confessional poets, essayists, too, often exaggerate, alter, or underplay personal experiences in an attempt to universalize them or to be humorous or satiric. No matter how similar authors and the speakers they create may seem to be, there is always a difference between the writer *of* the work and the speaker *in* the work. We do not, for instance, confuse the real James Thurber for the student we meet in Thurber's autobiographical "University Days"; we know that Thurber has heightened events to produce a comic effect. A close textual study will tell you what you need to know to create these lyric personae. When performing any personal literary material, though, some research into the life of the writer can provide valuable insights that add to the performance.

Usually, however, what is said in the texts considered in this chapter is more important than who says it. As Bacon writes, "the work of literature . . . has a life of its own; it is not tied to its creator."[1] Bacon explains that the interpreter's responsibility is to become the text—to embody the experience in it. If the experience is emphasized, you need not worry about suggesting a specific, defined speaker. Unless the text makes specific reference to a particular speaker, focus on communicating the experience.

One additional point should be mentioned. Some beginners desire, when performing diaries, letters, and some postmodern literature, to simulate the writer engaged in the writing process. This usually does not work well (although the presence of a script to suggest the speaker's diary, letter, or story may be useful). It is the result of this process, not the writing itself, that grabs our attention and interest. Trying to show the writer writing is never very believable and usually results in a painfully slow (if believability is desired) delivery.

Let us now briefly discuss each of these literary forms and investigate some additional considerations you should make when preparing them for performance. At the end of each discussion, you will find selections which are particularly good for performance.

Letters

A letter is an account of personal experience with a specific audience in mind. Although most letters are personal, some may be less personal (writers may write letters with eventual publication at the back of their minds) depending on the nature of the writer-audience relationship. Sylvia Plath writes personal letters to her mother in *Letters Home,* and Robert and Elizabeth Barrett Browning reveal an emotional and professional attraction in their first exchange of letters, but Flannery O'Connor writes a less intimate (though just as deeply felt) letter "To a Professor of English" and his class who, in her opinion, completely misunderstood her story, "A Good Man Is Hard to Find." Although some letters may be intended for a public audience (letters to the editor, for example), most letters involve the writer's address to one specific other. The nature of this specific audience (as well as the letter's content) affects performance, as you speak differently to people you know intimately than to strangers. The emotional involvement of the speaker, then, is affected by the identification of the audience as well as by the degree of directness or indirectness, how much is self-disclosed, and so forth. Usually the addressee is not physically present, and the speaker imagines the audience and the potential response. Experiment with focus. Try using open focus if a public, group audience is suggested. You may use inner-closed or semi-closed focus to suggest a private utterance to a specific, absent auditor.

Since most letters were not meant to be performed, you should devise some rationale to substantiate or justify your performance. Could you, for example, be reading the letter aloud as a kind of mental proofreading? Could you be reading the letter aloud to assure yourself that you have expressed yourself accurately or as intended? Could you be orally composing the letter in preparation for a later written version? All of these performance analogues are possibilities. Another possibility for the performance of the letter is to allow the addressee to read it so that you get the words, style, and attitude of the writer in addition to the responses and attitude of the recipient. This can provide a rich performance experience, but it may not be appropriate for all letters. Try reading your letter several ways to see what works best.

Letter selections for performance

From LETTERS HOME

Sylvia Plath writes to her mother Aurelia.

Wellesley, Mass.
August 30, 1954

Dearest Mother,

Thought I'd sit down on this cold, clouded day to write you a note about affairs here since last I talked to you. Practically speaking, all has run off well. I've cooked meals for Gordon all weekend and learned a good deal.

 We had a very lazy weekend, doing absolutely nothing except eating, talking, reading, sunning, and listening to records, and I again realized that it takes a few weeks of utter relaxation to put one in shape in between big pushes of work.

 . . . I was in a mood to pamper myself this weekend and so went to bed early and read J. D. Salinger and Carson McCullers' short story collections in the sun. I just didn't feel like disciplining myself to more difficult intellectual reading. This coming week, however, I hope to start Dostoevsky in Cambridge and pick up German again, which I dropped for this week after the B exam, as if I'd been burned.

 . . . I do want you to know how I appreciate time for a retreat of sorts here. Of course, the house is lonely without you, but I have been such a social being so continually since last winter (the month of June being an intensification, not a cessation, of my social obligations and contacts) that I really feel the need to be in a social vacuum by myself for a few days when I [can] move solely at my own lazy momentum with no people around. Naturally, it is only too easy to want company to alleviate the necessity for self-examination and planning, but I am at the point now where I have to fight for solitude, and it thus becomes a precious, if challenging, responsibility.

 . . . Meanwhile, I want you to know that I love you really very much and have wished occasionally that I could just whisk on a magic carpet to the Cape to give you an impulsive bearhug, because you are, and always will be, so dear to my innermost heart.

 Much love to all.

Sivvy

Letter to Elizabeth Barrett from Robert Browning

To Elizabeth Barrett

New Cross, Hatcham, Surrey

[January 10, 1845]

I love your verses with all my heart, dear Miss Barrett,—and this is no off-hand com-plimentary letter that I shall write,—whatever else, no prompt matter-of-course recog-nition of your genius, and there a graceful and natural end of the thing. Since the day last week when I first read your poems, I quite laugh to remember how I have been turning and turning again in my mind what I should be able to tell you of their effect upon me, for in the first flush of delight I thought I would this once get out of my habit of purely passive enjoyment, when I do really enjoy, and thoroughly justify my admiration—perhaps even, as a loyal fellow-craftsman should, try and find fault and do you some little good to be proud of hereafter!—but nothing comes of it all—so into me has it gone, and part of me has it become, this great living poetry of yours, not a flower of which but took root and grew. . . . I do, as I say, love these books with all my heart—and I love you too. Do you know I was once not very far from seeing—really seeing you? Mr. Kenyon said to me one morning 'Would you like to see Miss Barrett?' then he went to announce me,—then he returned. . . . you were too unwell, and now it is years ago, and I feel as at some untoward passage in my travels, as if I had been close, so close, to some world's-wonder in chapel or crypt, only a screen to push and I might have entered, but there was some slight, so it now seems, slight and just suffi-cient bar to admission, and the half-opened door shut, and I went home my thou-sands of miles, and the sight was never to be?

    Well, these Poems were to be, and this true thankful joy and pride with which I feel myself,

Yours ever faithfully,
Robert Browning

Letter from Elizabeth Barrett to Robert Browning

To Robert Browning

50 Wimpole Street

January 11, 1845

I thank you, dear Mr. Browning, from the bottom of my heart. You meant to give me pleasure by your letter—and even if the object had not been answered, I ought still to thank you. But it is thoroughly answered. Such a letter from such a hand! Sympathy is dear—very dear to me: but the sympathy of a poet, and of such a poet, is the quintessence of sympathy to me! Will you take back my gratitude for it?

. . . Is it indeed true that I was so near to the pleasure and honour of making your acquaintance? and can it be true that you look back upon the lost opportunity with any regret? *But*—you know—if you had entered the 'crypt,' you might have caught cold, or been tired to death, and *wished* yourself "a thousand miles off"; which would have been worse than travelling them. It is not my interest, however, to put such thoughts in your head about its being 'all for the best'; and I would rather hope (as I do) that what I lost by one chance I may recover by some future one.

. . . I am writing too much,—and notwithstanding that I am writing too much, I will write of one thing more. I will say that I am your debtor, not only for this cordial letter and for all the pleasure which came with it, but in other ways, and those the highest: and I will say that while I live to follow this divine art of poetry in proportion to my love for it and my devotion to it, I must be a devout admirer and student of your works. This is in my heart to say to you—and I say it.

And, for the rest, I am proud to remain

Your obliged and faithful
Elizabeth B. Barrett

The following letter by Flannery O'Connor was written in response to a letter she received from a professor of English. The professor, his colleagues, and ninety university students had attempted to interpret O'Connor's story "A Good Man Is Hard to Find" with little success. They finally decided that the appearance of the Misfit— the escaped convict who kills the entire Bailey family as they trek to Florida for a vacation—is not "real" whereas the incidents of the first half of the story are real. The professor decided that Bailey dreams or imagines the accident where the family meets the Misfit and that Bailey plays the role of the Misfit in the second half of the story. He wanted to know when reality becomes unreality in the story.

Flannery O'Connor replied:

To a Professor of English

28 March 61

The interpretation of your ninety students and three teachers is fantastic and about as far from my intentions as it could get to be. If it were a legitimate interpretation, the story would be little more than a trick and its interest would be simply for abnormal psychology. I am not interested in abnormal psychology.

There is a change of tension from the first part of the story to the second where the Misfit enters, but this is no lessening of reality. This story is, of course, not meant to be realistic in the sense that it portrays the everyday doings of people in Georgia. It is stylized and its conventions are comic even though its meaning is serious.

Bailey's only importance is as the Grandmother's boy and the driver of the car. It is the Grandmother who first recognizes the Misfit and who is most concerned with him throughout. The story is a duel of sorts between the Grandmother and her superficial beliefs and the Misfit's more profoundly felt involvement with Christ's action which set the world off balance for him.

The meaning of a story should go on expanding for the reader the more he thinks about it, but meaning cannot be captured in an interpretation. If teachers are in the habit of approaching a story as if it were a research problem for which any answer is believable so long as it is not obvious, then I think students will never learn to enjoy fiction. Too much interpretation is certainly worse than too little, and where feeling for a story is absent, theory will not supply it.

My tone is not meant to be obnoxious. I am in a state of shock.

Flannery O'Connor

Diaries

Diaries are personal accounts of the writer's day-to-day observations of real life events. Diaries tend to be private explorations of behavior, recordings of personal experiences of historical events, rationales, purgations, and so on. Unlike letters, diaries tend to be more honest, for the diarist often chronicles events for his or her own benefit, and diaries tend to be more true to events than memoirs, for example, which are often composed after some time has passed. Diaries often seem less selective than letters. Whereas the letter writer chooses among events to communicate—usually events in the physical rather than an imaginative world—omitting some details, enlarging upon others, the diarist records all that he or she observes from the seemingly mundane to the catastrophic, from the personal to the public. Diaries also move, not in large sweeps of time, like a history or an autobiography, but at the pace of natural life set by the rhythm of waking and sleeping. In both the letter and the diary, the speaker mode is lyric—someone very much like the composer is speaking. Consequently, historical and biographical research would help produce a richer interpretation.

When fiction writers create diaries, an imaginative world is created. The speaker is not the writer, but a character who keeps a diary within the context of the work, such as in Alice Walker's *The Color Purple.* With this diary, the characterization of the speaker, Celie, is essential. (Celie is not Alice Walker—though they may have qualities in common. Perhaps an even better example of a work in which you must distinguish between writer and speaker is Twain's "The Diary of Adam and Eve.") With diaries like these, research into the life and times of the writer may not be as important as in the case of nonfictional diaries (though this kind of research is always useful). The world of *The Color Purple* is created within the novel—that is the *only* place it has ever existed (other than in the mind of the writer or in the mind of the reader). The worlds of Samuel Pepys, Anne Frank, Davy Crockett, Thomas Merton, or Countess Tolstoy really *did* exist in the physical world. For these latter works, the performer must know something about the writer's time and place.

One main difference between the letter and the diary is the intended audience. Whereas a letter usually has a specific addressee who is not the writer, the "audience" for a diary is often the writer himself or herself. Samuel Pepys's famous *Diary,* for example, was, according to Richard Garnett, never intended for public viewing. Garnett writes, "A man of sense, and Pepys was a man of great good sense, would never . . . have knowingly exhibited himself in a series of ludicrous positions."[2] The diary writer is one potential audience for a diary, but God (as in *The Color Purple*) or the diary itself ("Dear Diary") may be possible addressees as well.

When performing diaries, then, it is essential to discover the nature of the audience. If the writer seems to be addressing himself or herself, inner-closed focus may be used. Semi-closed focus may be used if the addressee seems to be God or the diary itself, and the speaker seems to be addressing these audiences as if they were physically present. In the case of Bob Greene's diary entries from *Be True to Your School,* for example, there may be two audiences to consider. When he originally wrote the diary—back in 1964—Greene was writing primarily for himself. As he edited these entries for publication in his 1987 book, he had a mass audience in mind—an audience who, for example, would need to be told that Greene was one of the editors of the *Torch.* When a diary, entries in a diary, or individual lines in a diary seem to be written for the benefit of someone other than the writer, use open focus—but always consider who this general audience might be, how you would like them to respond, and how they might respond to this shared information.

Again, since diaries are usually not intended for performance, try to find a justification for performing them. For what reason could you justify performing a diary entry?

Diary selections for performance

These are excerpts from Samuel Pepys's *Diary,* all relating to Pepys's reactions to viewing Shakespearean plays.

DIARY   Samuel Pepys

September 29th, 1662 (Michaelmas Day)

This day my oaths for drinking of wine and going to plays are out, and so I do resolve to take a liberty today, and then to fall to them again. To the King's Theatre, where we saw "Midsummer's Night's Dream" which I had never seen before, nor shall ever again, for it is the most insipid ridiculous play that ever I saw in my life. I saw, I confess, some good dancing and some handsome women, and which was all my pleasure.

January 6th, 1663 (Twelfth Day)

. . .

So to my brother's, where Creed and I and my wife dined with Tom; and after dinner to the Duke's house, and there saw "Twelfth Night" acted well, though it be but a silly play, and not related at all to the name or day.

August 13, 1664

. . .

Mr. Creed dining with me I got him to give my wife and me a play this afternoon, lending him money to do it, which is a fallacy that I have found now once, to avoyde my vowe with, but never to be more practised I swear; and to the new play at the Duke's house of "Henry the Fifth;" a most noble play, writ by my Lord Orrery; wherein Betterton, Harris, and Ianthe's parts are most incomparably wrote and one, and the whole play the most full of height and raptures of wit and sense, that ever I heard; having but one incongruity, or what did not please me in it, that is, that King Harry promises to plead for Tudor to their Mistresse, Princesse Katherine of France, more than when it comes to it he seems to do; and Tudor refused by her with some kind of indignity, not with a difficulty and honour that it ought to have been done in to him.

November 2nd, 1667

Up, and to the office, where busy all the morning; at noon home, and after dinner my wife and Willett and I to the King's playhouse, and there saw "Henry the Fourth": and contrary to expectation, was pleased in nothing more than Cartwright's speaking of Falstaffe's speech about "What is Honour?" The house full of Parliament-men, it being holyday with them: and it was observable how a gentleman of good habit, sitting just before us, eating of some fruit in the midst of the play, did drop down as dead, being choked; but with much ado Orange Moll did thrust her finger down his throat and brought him to life again. After the play we home, and I busy at the office late, and then home to supper and to bed.

From BE TRUE TO YOUR SCHOOL: A DIARY OF 1964   Bob Greene

May 4

I got out of school this morning to go to this Mental Health Conference downtown at the YWCA; the school sent me because I'm an editor of the *Torch*.

It wasn't much; just a lot of students from all the schools around Columbus sitting around a room listening to experts talking about the importance of mental health.

There was this really cool girl, though; she kept staring at me, and I couldn't help but notice. Finally there was a five-minute break, and she came over to where I was sitting.

She said, "Didn't you get your picture in the *Dispatch* for looking like Ringo Starr?"

I thought she was making fun of my nose, so I just mumbled something and turned the other way.

At tennis practice I played Gary Herwald in singles. I won the first set 6–4 and we were tied 10–10 in the second set when time ran out. We're supposed to continue it.

After practice Dan and I talked about Chuck and Jack's trip to Cleveland. We're both going crazy with envy. We decided that we're going to go up to Cleveland this weekend and try to get together with the same girls Chuck and Jack were with.

Our parents would never let us go if we told them why we're going, of course. Plus, if they found out that we have nowhere to stay, they'd never let us out of the house. So Dan's going to tell his parents that we're staying with relatives of mine; I'm going to tell my parents that we're staying with relatives of Dan's. Then one of us will borrow one of our parents' cars, and we'll just sleep in the car like Chuck and Jack did.

I can't wait.

Reprinted with the permission of Atheneum Publishers, an imprint of Macmillan Publishing Company, from *Be True to Your School: A Diary of 1964* by Bob Greene. Copyright © 1987 John Deadline Enterprises, Inc.

The following is an excerpt from Alice Walker's *The Color Purple*—the character, Celie, is writing to God.

Dear God,

Shug Avery is coming to town! She coming with her orkestra. She going to sing in the Lucky Star out on Coalman road. Mr. _____ going to hear her. He dress all up in front the glass, look at himself, then undress and dress all over again. He slick back his hair with pomade, then wash it out again. He been spitting on his shoes and hitting it with a quick rag.

He tell me, Wash this. Iron that. Look for this. Look for that. Find this. Find that. He groan over holes in his sock.

I move round darning and ironing, finding hanskers. Anything happening? I ast.

What you mean? he say, like he mad. Just trying to git some of the hick farmer off myself. Any other woman be glad.

I'm is glad, I say.

What you mean? he ast.

You looks nice, I say. Any woman be proud.

You think so? he say.

First time he ast me. I'm so surprise, by time I say Yeah, he out on the porch, trying to shave where the light better.

I walk round all day with the announcement burning a hole in my pocket. It pink. The trees tween the turn off to our road and the store is lit up with them. He got bout five dozen in his trunk.

Shug Avery standing upside a piano, elbow crook, hand on her hip. She wearing a hat like Indian Chiefs. Her mouth open showing all her teef and don't nothing seem to be troubling her mind. Come one, come all, it say. The Queen Honeybee is back in town.

Lord, I wants to go so bad. Not to dance. Not to drink. Not to play card. Not even to hear Shug Avery sing. I just be thankful to lay eyes on her.

Essays

The essay is a relatively short literary composition of a personal nature that deals with a single subject, often with a clearly organized beginning, middle, and end. There are many different kinds of essays, and each kind suggests an appropriate performance style. The humorous essay makes its point through wit, satire, and comicality (Swift's "A Modest Proposal"). The expository essay sets out to develop an idea to instruct or inform (Iyer's "The Masks of Minority Terrorism"). The personal or familiar essay is highly lyrical and relates firsthand experiences often by relating them to appropriate external objects (Didion's "On Going Home"). Again, though the writer may seem to be speaking in the essay, the idea expressed is usually more important to communicate than the identity of the speaker. Defining the writer's style will help you decide on appropriate performance analogues.

The speaker mode of most essays is, as previously suggested, lyric. The audience mode is based on shifts in speaker awareness or lack of awareness of audience. The audience mode of an essay (as well as of letters and diaries) may shift from self-realization (lyric) to character imitation or address (dramatic) to event narration or description (epic).

Unlike most diaries and letters, essays are often written with a mass audience in mind and open focus is usually appropriate as a performance analogue. As Wallace Bacon writes in relation to the essay, "Rather than creating a world of its own, as the literary work does, it [the essay] tends to join the reader in the actual world to talk about something in which narrator and reader have a common interest—to create one side of a dialogue in which the reader supplies the other half."[3] The Didion essay, "On Going Home," though, seems to be very private as the writer muses on what home means to her. Inner-closed focus might be appropriate for much of this essay, although there are many moments when Didion seems to be aware of an audience outside of herself (for example, the opening passages describe her whereabouts and her family primarily for the benefit of the reader or audience). Swift's "A Modest Proposal" has a specific audience in a specific locale in mind. With this essay, try to turn the present audience into the audience Swift intended. Swift employs satire and his intention is to laugh people out of their follies and crimes. His audience must be intelligent. If not, they will miss the irony and assume that his essay is serious. What could you say in the introduction that would make Swift's intention clear? The Iyer article is a reaction to the controversy surrounding the casting of a European actor to play the role of a Eurasian in the Broadway production of *Miss Saigon*. Although Iyer has a mass audience in mind, the impetus for his article is a specific incident with which some might not be familiar. He uses this incident, however, as a jumping-off point to discuss the implications of racial discrimination in any context.

Some essays, then, are for such a particular audience that they preclude universal identification. An essay dealing with lack of water in the desert southwest, for example, might have limited appeal to an audience of northeasterners. Essays, too, are not intended for performance, and not all essays are appropriate for performance. Be sure to choose an essay with potential audience appeal.

Essay selections for performance

From ON GOING HOME   Joan Didion

I am home for my daughter's first birthday. By "home" I do not mean the house in Los Angeles where my husband and I and the baby live, but the place where my family is, in the Central Valley of California. It is a vital although troublesome distinction. My husband likes my family but is uneasy in their house, because once there I fall into their ways, which are difficult, oblique, deliberately inarticulate, not my husband's ways. We live in dusty houses ("D-U-S-T," he once wrote with his finger on surfaces all over the house, but no one noticed it) filled with mementos quite without value to him (what could the Canton dessert plates mean to him? how could he have known about the assay scales, why should he care if he did know?), and we appear to talk exclusively about people we know who have been committed to mental hospitals, about people we know who have been booked on drunk-driving charges, and about property, particularly about property, land, price per acre and C–2 zoning and assessments and freeway access. My brother does not understand my husband's inability to perceive the advantage in the rather common real-estate transaction known as "sale-leasebacks," and my husband in turn does not understand why so many of the people he hears about in my father's house have recently been committed to mental hospitals or booked on drunk-driving charges. Nor does he understand that when we talk about sale-leasebacks and right-of-way condemnations we are talking in code about the things we like best, the yellow fields and the cottonwoods and the rivers rising and falling and the mountain roads closing when the heavy snow comes in. We miss each other's points, have another drink and regard the fire. My brother refers to my husband, in his presence, as "Joan's husband." Marriage is the classic betrayal.

Or perhaps it is not any more. Sometimes I think that those of us who are now in our thirties were born into the last generation to carry the burden of "home," to find in family life the source of all tension and drama. I had by all objective accounts a "normal" and a "happy" family situation, and yet I was almost thirty years old before I could talk to my family on the telephone without crying after I had hung up. We did not fight. Nothing was wrong.

And yet some nameless anxiety colored the emotional charges between me and the place that I came from. The question of whether or not you could go home again was a very real part of the sentimental and largely literary baggage with which we left home in the fifties; I suspect that it is irrelevant to the children born of the fragmentation after World War II. A few weeks ago in a San Francisco bar I saw a pretty young girl on crystal take off her clothes and dance for the cash prize in an "amateur-topless" contest. There was no particular sense of the moment about this, none of the effect of romantic degradation, of "dark journey," for which my generation strived so assiduously. What sense could that girl possibly make of, say, *Long Day's Journey Into Night?* Who is beside the point?

That I am trapped in this particular irrelevancy is never more apparent to me than when I am home. Paralyzed by the neurotic lassitude engendered by meeting one's past at every turn, around very corner, inside every cupboard, I go aimlessly from room to room. I decide to meet it head-on and clean out a drawer, and I spread the contents on the bed. A bathing suit I wore the summer I was seventeen. A letter of rejection from *The Nation,* an aerial photograph of the site for a shopping center my father did not build in 1954. Three teacups hand-painted with cabbage roses and signed "E. M.," my grandmother's initials. There is no final solution for letters of rejection from *The Nation* and teacups hand-painted in 1900. Nor is there any answer to snapshots of one's grandfather as a young man on skis, surveying around Donner Pass in the year 1910. I smooth out the snapshot and look into his face, and do and do not see my own. I close the drawer, and have another cup of coffee with my mother. We get along very well, veterans of a guerrilla war we never understood.

From A MODEST PROPOSAL   Jonathan Swift

It is a melancholy object to those who walk through this great town or travel in the country, when they see the streets, the roads, and cabin doors crowded with beggars of the female sex, followed by three, four, or six children, all in rags, and importuning every passenger for an alms. These mothers, instead of being able to work for their honest livelihood, are forced to employ all their time in strolling, to beg sustenance for their helpless infants, who, as they grow up, either turn thieves for want of work or leave their dear native country to fight for the Pretender in Spain, or sell themselves to the Barbados.

I think it is agreed by all parties that this prodigious number of children in the arms or on the backs or at the heels of their mothers, and frequently of their fathers, is in the present deplorable state of the kingdom a very great additional grievance; and therefore whoever could find out a fair, cheap, and easy method of making these children sound, useful members of the commonwealth would deserve so well of the public as to have his statue set up for a preserver of the nation.

But my intention is very far from being confined to provide only for the children of professed beggars; it is of a much greater extent, and shall take in the whole number of infants at a certain age who are born of parents in effect as little able to support them as those who demand our charity in the streets.

As to my own part, having turned my thoughts for many years upon this important subject and maturely weighed the several schemes of other projectors, I have always found them grossly mistaken in their computation. It is true a child just dropped from its dam may be supported by her milk for a solar year with little other nourishment, at most not above the value of two shillings, which the mother may certainly get, or the value in scraps, by her lawful occupation of begging; and it is exactly at one year old that I propose to provide for them in such a manner as, instead of being a charge upon their parents or the parish, or wanting food and raiment for the rest of their lives, they shall, on the contrary, contribute to the feeding and partly to the clothing of many thousands.

There is likewise another great advantage in my scheme, that it will prevent those voluntary abortions and that horrid practice of women murdering their bastard children, alas, too frequent among us, sacrificing the poor innocent babes, I doubt, more to avoid the expense than the shame, which would move tears and pity in the most savage and inhuman breast.

The number of souls in this kingdom being usually reckoned one million and a half, of these I calculate there may be about two hundred thousand couples whose wives are breeders; from which number I subtract thirty thousand couples who are able to maintain their own children, although I apprehend there cannot be so many under the present distresses of the kingdom; but this being granted, there will remain a hundred and seventy thousand breeders. I again subtract fifty thousand for those women who miscarry, or whose children die by accident or disease within the year. There only remain a hundred and twenty thousand children of poor parents annually born: the question therefore is how this number shall be reared and provided for, which, as I have already said, under the present situation of affairs, is utterly impossible by all the methods hitherto proposed; for we can neither employ them in handicraft or agriculture: we neither build houses (I mean in the country) nor cultivate land; they can very seldom pick up a livelihood by stealing till they arrive at six years old, except where they are of towardly parts; although I confess they earn the rudiments much earlier, during which time they can however be properly looked upon only as probationers, as I have been informed by a principal gentleman in the country of Cavan, who protested to me that he even knew about one or two instances under the age of six, even in a part of the kingdom so renowned for the quickest proficiency in that art.

I am assured by our merchants that a boy or a girl before twelve years old is no salable commodity, and even when they come to this age, they will not yield above three pounds, or three pounds and half a crown at most, on the Exchange, which cannot turn to account either to the parents or kingdom, the charge of nutriment and rags having been at least four times that value.

I shall now therefore humbly propose my own thoughts, which I hope will not be liable to the least objection.

I have been assured by a very knowing American of my acquaintance in London, that a young healthy child well nursed is at a year old a most delicious, nourishing, and wholesome food, whether stewed, roasted, baked, or boiled; and I make no doubt that it will equally serve in a fricassee or a ragout.

I do therefore humbly offer it to public consideration that, of the hundred and twenty thousand children already computed, twenty thousand may be reserved for breed, whereof only one fourth part to be males, which is more than we allow to sheep, black cattle, or swine; and my reason is that these children are seldom the fruits of marriage, a circumstance not much regarded by our savages; therefore one male will be sufficient to serve four females. That the remaining hundred thousand may at a year old be offered in sale to the persons of quality and fortune through the kingdom, always advising the mother to let them suck plentifully in the last month, so as to render them plump and fat for a good table. A child will make two dishes at an entertainment for friends; and when the family dines alone, the fore or hind quarter will make a reasonable dish, and seasoned with a little pepper or salt will be very good boiled on the fourth day, especially in winter.

. . .

I profess in the sincerity of my heart that I have not the least personal interest in endeavoring to promote this necessary work, having no other motive than the *public good of my country, by advancing our trade, providing for infants, relieving the poor, and giving some pleasure to the rich.* I have no children by which I can propose to get a single penny; the youngest being nine years old, and my wife past child-bearing. (1729)

THE MASKS OF MINORITY TERRORISM   Pico Iyer

When Actors' Equity briefly decided three weeks ago that the part of a Eurasian in the play *Miss Saigon* could not be taken by a European, its board members provided some of the best entertainment seen on Broadway recently. It was not just that they were asserting an Orwellian principle: All races are equal, but some are more equal than others. Nor even that they were threatening to deprive thousands of playgoers of a drama that promised to shed some light on precisely such cross-cultural nuances; nor even that they were more or less ensuring—if the principle were to be applied fairly—that most Asian-American actors would have to sit around in limbo and wait for the next production of *The Mikado*. They were also raising some highly intriguing questions. How can John Gielgud play Prospero when Doug Henning is at hand? Should future Shakespeares—even future August Wilsons—stock their plays with middle-class whites so as to have the largest pool of actors from which to choose? And next time we stage *Moby Dick*, will there be cries that the title part be taken by a card-carrying leviathan?

The quickly reversed decision, which effectively proclaimed that actors should do everything but act, was a short-running farce. But when the same kind of minority terrorism is launched offstage, as is more and more the case, the consequences are less comical. Jimmy Breslin, long famous as a champion of the dispossessed, speaks thoughtlessly and finds himself vilified as a "racist." Spike Lee, an uncommonly intelligent filmmaker whenever he remains behind the camera, maintains that films about blacks should be directed by blacks (what does this mean for *The Bear*, one wonders, or for *Snow White and the Seven Dwarfs?*).

The whole issue, in fact, seems to betray a particularly American conundrum: the enjoyment of one freedom means encroachment on another; you can't school all of the people all of the time. Older, and less earnest, countries like Britain or Japan live relatively easily with racial inequalities. But America, with its evergreen eagerness to do the right thing, tries to remedy the world with an innocence that can become more dangerous than cruelty. All of us, when we make decisions—which is to say, discriminations—judge in part on appearances. All of us treat Savile Row-suited lawyers differently from kids in T shirts, give preference to the people that we like—or to the people that are most like us—and make differing assumptions about a Texan and a Yankee. To wish this were not so is natural; to claim it is not so is hypocrisy.

But state-sponsored favoritism is something different. As an Asian minority myself, I know of nothing more demeaning than being chosen for a job, or even a role, on the basis of my race. Nor is the accompanying assumption—that I need a helping hand because my ancestors were born outside Europe—very comforting. Are those of us lucky enough to be born minorities to be forgiven our transgressions, protected from insults and encouraged to act as if we cannot take responsibility for our actions (it wasn't my fault I failed the exam; society made me do it)? Are we, in fact, to cling to a state of childlike dependency? As an alien from India, I choose to live in America precisely because it is a place where aliens from India are, in principle, treated no better (and no worse) than anyone else. Selecting an Asian actor, say, over a better-qualified white one (or, for that matter, a white over a better-qualified Asian, as is alleged to happen with certain university admissions) does nobody a service: not the Asian, whose lack of qualifications will be rapidly shown up; not the white, whose sense of racial brotherhood is hardly likely to be quickened by being the victim of discrimination himself; not the company, or audience, which may understandably resent losing quality to quotas.

Affirmative action, in fact—so noble in intention—is mostly a denial: a denial of the fact that we are all born different; a denial of a person's right to get the position he deserves; a denial of everyone's ability to transcend, or live apart from, the conditions of his birth. Most of all, it is a denial of the very virtues of opportunity and self-determination that are the morning stars of this democracy. People around the world still long to migrate to America because it is a place, traditionally and ideally, where people can say what they think, become what they dream and succeed—or fail—on the basis of their merits. Now, though, with more and more people telling us not to say what we think and to support everyone except the majority of Americans, the country is in danger of becoming something else: the land of the free, with an asterisk.

Biographies, Autobiographies, Histories

A biography is a text in which someone writes X's life story, and an autobiography is X's own version of his or her own life story, while a history is someone's account of what has happened either to a people or a country. In terms of the speaker modal classification of these forms, biographies are usually epic (the author writes about another); autobiographies are usually lyric (the author writes about self); and histories are usually epic (the author writes about other people or a country). In the biography, a speaker very much like the writer usually addresses the reader directly, and other characters seemingly speak for themselves. We assume that the point of view of a biography is objective since the writer is speaking about someone else. An autobiography has a lyric feel as the writer speaks about himself or herself. Although characters often speak in an autobiography, they are depicted from the writer's subjective point of view. The history chronicles past events and usually employs a third-person narrator as well as characters. Occasionally histories are told from a first-person perspective where the narrator is a defined character, such as in Gore Vidal's fictional biographical history *Burr*.

It is always important to keep in mind the "fiction" in these "nonfiction" works, as the perspective of the writer greatly colors what and how much we learn. Editor Lee Gutkind admits this in "Permission to Lie?", her introductory essay in the aptly titled *Creative Nonfiction.* She writes:

> For a memoir about her family, a novelist and former journalist whom I know manipulated the transition from fiction to nonfiction. When she began her book, she felt blocked by the perceived conflict between the two genres, unable to comfortably employ the novelistic techniques of scene, dialog and description. And so, in order to get started, she granted herself permission to lie.
>
> The author did not intend to make up facts or tell stories that weren't true, a violation of the promise inherent in all nonfiction. But the narrow range of

creative options traditionally granted to a journalist inhibited her. Giving herself "permission to lie" allowed three-dimensional thought and scenic expression in a novelistic context. She did not permit her writing momentum to be interrupted by the literal truth.[4]

Some writers admit the "fiction" in their nonfiction works, others do not. Dominick Dunne's book on the O. J. Simpson trial, entitled *Another City, Not My Own* which is subtitled *A Novel in the Form of a Memoir,* details Dunne's factual account of the trial infused with his own impressions and feelings. He admits that only 90 percent of what he writes is really true. Truman Capote describes his *In Cold Blood* as a "nonfiction novel," wherein he combines the techniques of fiction and journalism to re-create the murder by Richard Hickock and Perry Smith of the Clutter family in Holcomb, Kansas, in November 1959. Meyer Levin calls his *Compulsion* a "contemporary historical novel or a documentary novel." In his text, he recounts the case of Leopold and Loeb—two teenage boys who murdered a 14-year-old boy in Chicago in 1924. In the book, Levin changes the names of all involved and adds information about what Leopold and Loeb may have been thinking which could only be speculation. Shakespeare's history plays, like *Richard III* and *Julius Caesar,* deal loosely with real historical figures. Although a biography (often told from the first-person minor character point of view or the third-person observer point of view) and a history (often told from the third-person observer point of view) may seem to be more objective than the autobiography (usually told from the first-person major character point of view), all three forms are subject to a literal or implied "I/Eye" determining what we know and how we know it. The hand of the maker is always selecting and arranging. Writers have certain feelings about their subjects which affect the way the "facts" are presented. This can be seen throughout *Anyone's Daughter,* Shana Alexander's account of Patty Hearst's abduction in 1974. Alexander prefaces her work by confessing her personal interest in and identification with Patty Hearst:

> I understood her [Patty Hearst] because in some way she was the girl I had been, and in some way I was also her mother. I understood that a mother-daughter struggle was at the core of her story, something similar to what had happened to me and my mother, and to myself and my own daughter, whom I was losing now. One of these daughters was taken entirely by accident. But all three were in rebellion and revolt.[5]

In this passage, Ms. Alexander openly admits that she writes from a subjective perspective and that her dual identification with Patty Hearst affected everything she wrote. Consequently, understanding the point of view—the attitude—of the author/speaker/narrator is a necessary first step in the analysis of both biography and autobiography. Ask yourself, in the case of biography: How does the writer feel about his or her subject? How does the writer's attitude affect and color the way he or she writes? How does the writer want me to feel about his or her subject? In Dotson Radar's biography of Tennessee Williams, *Tennessee: Cry of the Heart,* the title alone signals Radar's feelings about this genius writer whom he befriended. Radar reveals the intimate details of Williams's life from Radar's personal, firsthand perspective.

In the case of autobiography, analyze the difference between the man or woman as writer and as subject of his or her own autobiography. Is this strictly nonfiction? What do these writers want us to feel about them? What is their vested interest, if any? What causes these writers to put their lives on the page for public consumption? How reliable an account are we getting? How does author reliability affect performance?

For histories, it might be useful to try to read more than one version of the historical event(s) depicted. Then, if there are inconsistencies, consider how and why the writer may have deviated from the "real facts" and what his or her particular bias is. How does the writer's bias shape our understanding of the events? How does this affect performance? Capote admits that his *In Cold Blood* is a journalistic novel. How does this blending of fact and fiction alter our view of the "history"?

When considering the audience for biographies, autobiographies, and histories, try to decide who the intended audience might be. Who would be willing, as Bacon writes, to create the other side of the dialogue suggested between speaker and reader? Some people might be very interested in the life of a particular person or the events that took place in a particular country. Some people might be excited about the possibility of a temporary identification with a famous person, experiencing that person's triumphs, suffering along with that person without having to feel the actual pain. Who, for example, might be the intended audience for Lee Iacocca's book entitled *Iacocca: An Autobiography?* If your audience does not seem to want to hold up their end of the dialogue, what can you do in your introduction or performance to change their minds?

Biography, autobiography, and history selections for performance

From TENNESSEE: CRY OF THE HEART   Dotson Rader

I first met Tennessee Williams shortly after he got out of what he called Barnacle Hospital (actually Barnes Hospital) in St. Louis, where he had been confined by his brother, Dakin, in 1969. Tennessee had flipped out on copious amounts of Doriden, Mellaril, Seconal, Ritalin, Demerol, amphetamines, and too much sorrow in Key West.

He thought his house was surrounded by assassins, rifles pointing at him through the thick foliage, terrorists lurking inside the walls. He feared that he was going the way of his friend, playwright William Inge, who had his own horrific difficulties with booze and pills, and who also drifted in and out of the same paranoid fog now enveloping Tennessee.

"I felt like a sleepwalker in a nightmare, unable to wake up," he said later.

In a drug-induced stupor, he fell against a hot stove in his patio, knocking over a pot of boiling water, and badly burning himself. He felt nothing. Dakin was called in St. Louis, and flew to Key West, where he had Tennessee baptized a Roman Catholic at St. Mary, Star of the Sea Church—an event lost forever in one of the boozy black holes of his mind. Then Dakin hauled him to the nuthouse.

He was first settled in the hospital's posh Queenly Tower, a place aptly named, he remembered, given the sexual proclivities of some of the staff. When he tried to flee the asylum, he was forcefully transferred to the violent ward. Later he was locked in an isolation cell for fighting with other inmates over what they would watch on the communal television set. Tennessee liked soap operas, and the other loonies wanted to see game shows; a row ensued, and the orderlies dragged him off and shut him away in a padded cell. There he had a series of convulsions, suffered two coronaries, and nearly died. For all that and more he never forgave his brother, Dakin, and it inculcated in him a fear of going mad that never left him.

Years later, near the end of his life, when Tennessee did something particularly odd—dress in pajamas for a formal dinner or agree to marry another man or wander around town in a fright wig pretending to be his sister, Miss Rose—I would laugh and try as gently as possible to dissuade him, all the while knowing that when the peculiarity of his action finally sank in, he would take it as evidence that his pilot light was about to burn out and Barnacle Hospital lay ahead as the last stop on his trolley line.

Excerpt from *TENNESSEE: Cry of the Heart: An Intimate Memoir of Tennessee Williams,* by Dotson Radar. Copyright © 1985 by Dotson Radar. Reprinted by permission of Doubleday, a division of Bantam, Doubleday, Dell Publishing Group.

From IACOCCA: AN AUTOBIOGRAPHY   Lee Iacocca (with William Novak)

In 1975, Henry Ford started his month-by-month premeditated plan to destroy me. Until then, he had pretty well left me alone. But in that year he started having chest pains, and he really didn't look well. It was then that King Henry began to realize his mortality.

He turned animal. I imagine his first impulse was: "I don't want that Italian interloper taking over. What's going to happen to the family business if I get a heart attack and die? Before I know it, he'll sneak in here one night, take my name off the building, and turn this place into the Iacocca Motor Company. Where does that leave my son, Edsel?"

When Henry thought I'd steal the family jewels, he had to get rid of me. But he didn't have the guts to just go ahead and do his own dirty work. Besides, he knew he'd never get away with it. Instead, he played Machiavelli, determined to humiliate me into quitting.

Henry dropped his first bomb while I was away. Early in 1975, I was out of the country for a couple of weeks on a whirlwind tour of the Middle East, part of a delegation of business leaders brought over by *Time* magazine to get a better understanding of Israel and the Arab world.

When I returned to the United States on February 3, I was surprised to find Chalmers Goyert, my executive assistant, waiting for me at J.F.K. Airport in New York.

"What's up?" I asked.

"We've got big problems," he told me.

We sure did. I listened as Goyert outlined the incredible events that had taken place during my absence. Just a few days earlier, while a group of us had been meeting with King Faisal in Saudi Arabia, King Henry had suddenly called a special meeting of top management.

The effects of that meeting are still being felt today. Henry was worried about the OPEC situation. The man who had taken the credit for turning the Ford Motor Company around after World War II was beside himself with fear. The Arabs had come charging up the hill, and he just couldn't take it.

Convinced that a major depression was imminent, he ordered $2 billion scratched from future production programs. With this decision, he summarily eliminated many of the products that would have made us competitive—such necessities as small cars and front-wheel-drive technology.

During the meeting, Henry had announced: "I am the Sewell Avery of the Ford Motor Company." It was an ominous reference.

Sewell Avery had been the head of Montgomery Ward, an ultra-conservative manager who had decided not to allocate any money for future development after World War II. He was sure the world was coming to an end and America was doomed. His decision proved to be a disaster for Montgomery Ward, because Sears started knocking the hell out of them.

Henry's announcement had similar implications for us.

As for me, it wasn't hard to read the writing on the wall. Henry had waited until I was thousands of miles away in order to call a meeting where he usurped my power and responsibility—and where he also went against everything I believed in.

Henry did enormous damage to the company that day. Ford's Topaz and Tempo, the small, front-wheel-drive cars that finally went on sale in May of 1983, should have been ready four or five years earlier when the public was clamoring for small cars. But Ford's response to the 1973 oil crisis wasn't even *planned* until 1979.

I was furious. OPEC had already made clear that without small cars we were dead. GM and Chrysler were working fast and furious to bring out their own subcompacts. And while this was going on, the head of the Ford Motor Company had stuck his head in the sand.

From IN COLD BLOOD   Truman Capote

The travelers stopped for dinner at a restaurant in Great Bend. Perry, down to his last fifteen dollars, was ready to settle for root beer and a sandwich, but Dick said no, they needed a solid "tuck-in," and never mind the cost, the tab was his. They ordered two steaks medium rare, baked potatoes, French fries, fried onions, succotash, side dishes of macaroni and hominy, salad with Thousand Island dressing, cinnamon rolls, apple pie and ice cream, and coffee. To top it off, they visited a drugstore and selected cigars; in the same drugstore, they bought two thick rolls of adhesive tape.

As the black Chevrolet regained the highway and hurried on across a countryside imperceptibly ascending toward the colder, cracker-dry climate of the high wheat plains, Perry closed his eyes and dozed off into a food-dazed semi-slumber, from which he woke to hear a voice reading the eleven-o'clock news. He rolled down a window and bathed his face in the flood of frosty air. Dick told him they were in Finney County. "We crossed the line ten miles back," he said. The car was going very fast. Signs, their messages ignited by the car's headlights, flared up, flew by: "See the Polar Bears," "Burtis Motors," "World's Largest FREE Swimpool," "Wheat Lands Motel," and, finally, a bit before street lamps began, "Howdy, Stranger! Welcome to Garden City. A Friendly Place."

They skirted the northern rim of the town. No one was abroad at this nearly midnight hour, and nothing was open except a string of desolately brilliant service stations. Dick turned into one—Hurd's Phillips 66. A youngster appeared, and asked, "Fill her up?" Dick nodded, and Perry, getting out of the car, went inside the station, where he locked himself in the men's room. His legs pained him, as they often did; they hurt as though his old accident had happened five minutes before. He shook three aspirins out of a bottle, chewed them slowly (for he liked the taste), and then drank water from the basin tap. He sat down on the toilet, stretched out his legs and rubbed them, massaging the almost unbendable knees. Dick had said they were almost there—"only seven miles more." He unzipped a pocket of his windbreaker and brought out a paper sack; inside it were the recently purchased rubber gloves. They were glue-covered, sticky and thin, and as he inched them on, one tore—not a dangerous tear, just a split between the fingers, but it seemed to him an omen.

The doorknob turned, rattled. Dick said, "Want some candy? They got a candy machine out here."

"No."

"You O.K.?"

"I'm fine."

"Don't be all night."

Dick dropped a dime in a vending machine, pulled the lever, and picked up a bag of jelly beans; munching, he wandered back to the car and lounged there watching the young attendant's efforts to rid the windshield of Kansas dust and the slime of battered insects. The attendant, whose name was James Spor, felt uneasy. Dick's eyes and sullen expression and Perry's strange, prolonged sojourn in the lavatory disturbed him. (The next day he reported to his employer, "We had some tough customers in here last night," but he did not think, then or for the longest while, to connect the visitors with the tragedy in Holcomb.)

From *In Cold Blood* by Truman Capote. Copyright © 1965 by Truman Capote. Reprinted by permission of Random House, Inc.

Children's Literature

There is very little difference between the analysis and performance of the literature included throughout this text and children's literature. Children's literature includes prose, poetry, and drama and is analyzed and performed in much the same way as already described for "adult" prose, poetry, and drama. We will consider selecting "good" children's literature to perform, and the variety of audiences for whom one might perform.

In general, the best children's literature has many of the following characteristics: a strong rhythm, clever use of rhyme, a monster, a young hero, suspense, repetition, humor, appeal to the senses, alliteration, a satisfactory conclusion with poetic justice, and a strong appeal to the imagination which encourages creative participation on the part of the audience. Some experts believe that a text slightly above the children's level of understanding is preferable to one on their level or below, as texts above their level of understanding expand their experiences, challenge them, and enhance their reading skills and language comprehension. Feel free to deviate from this advice, however, based on your knowledge of your particular audience. Newberry Award books—winners of the best children's books each year—are, of course, always a good choice. Consult the list of texts at the end of Chapter 2, which includes anthologies of materials good for performance. Be sure that you do not make generalizations about the interest and attention spans of children. They will often surprise you with the sophistication of their tastes and choices.

When selecting stories to perform for children, Robert M. Post suggests that they "should have unified and complete plots that have definite beginnings and endings, that are full of action, and that can be easily grasped; characters and settings that are vivid and believable, even in fantasies; and dialogue that is realistic even when the plots, characters, and settings are not."[6] In children's stories, the major character usually has a problem which he or she sets out to solve. The climax occurs when the problem is solved, and the story usually ends "happily ever after." Children's stories often present morals as well—*subtly or unsubtly*—depending on the text. Folk tales, fairy tales, and fantasies are especially good for performance as many of them were orally composed and presented and so translate well in performance. Fantasies, especially, appeal strongly to the imagination. Recently, excellent realistic literature has joined other types of children's literature on the bookshelves. Writers like Robert Cormier and Judy Blume, for example, create wonderful realistic fiction for "young adults."

Children's plays should include strong characterizations, lots of action, and clever dialogue. Many plays that you might not consider appropriate might actually be if you do not underestimate what the audience can understand or appreciate. As Dan Sullivan, a critic for the *Los Angeles Times,* once wrote in relation to children's plays, "Children's theatre is theatre, just as children's food is food—served in smaller quantities, less spicy, simpler (perhaps), but basically the stuff that keeps grownups going."

Nursery rhymes and verse are excellent choices for performance. The strong rhythms and rhymes in nursery rhymes appeal to children and teach them valuable information simultaneously. There are hundreds of wonderful children's poems. Post suggests:

> General criteria for selecting verse for children revolve around *what* is said and *how* it is said. The poetry should deal with significant, relevant subjects developed in some depth or complexity. We must be alert to such dangers as racism and sexism which seem to abound in children's literature, especially in older works, and which may be more harmful than in adult literature since the young child cannot be aware of it. The poet's choice of words, both for meaning and for sound, is an important consideration in choosing literature. Vocabulary is an especially important concern although we must not underestimate our young listeners.[7]

In general, look for the same qualities that make poetry for adults good: poems where sound, meter, and image underline sense. As stated above, children are especially fond of poems with strong rhythm and rhyme.

The introduction for a children's literature performance is most effective if the children are included. If, for example, you are performing Maurice Sendak's story *Where the Wild Things Are,* you could begin the introduction by asking, "How many of you have ever been sent to bed without your supper?" This should not be a rhetorical question; let the children share some experiences with you so that they believe you really care about their responses. Most children's literature entertains but also teaches moral lessons. During the introduction, help the children know what you think is important in the story, what they should listen for. In Sendak's story, you could say something like, "Maybe this story will help us see that we should not take our home or family for granted." (If you are performing children's literature for an adult audience, you must decide ahead of time who your intended audience is to be and prepare your introduction and performance with this audience in mind. Should you want an adult audience to respond to a children's literature selection as if they were children, you must prepare them to make this transformation in the introduction. You could say something like, "I take you back to the days when you were eight years old," or "Remember childhood," or "It's story time again, boys and girls, gather around me so we can continue to find out more about 'The Emperor's New Clothes.'")

When you perform children's literature for children, try to minimize barriers as much as possible. If you use a script, know the text well enough that you can maintain as much eye contact with your audience as possible. Post suggests that even dialogue lines could effectively be delivered directly to the children. Keep the children close to you—perhaps on the floor in front of you as you sit in a chair. In addition, you can enhance a child's engagement with the imaginative world of the text by your degree of enthusiasm for it, your directness of delivery (by either dispensing with the script or by minimizing its use), and by your ability to physically and vocally characterize each character. Children especially appreciate distinctive voices and bodies, expansive gestures, and a wide spectrum of vocal inflection. Try to imagine that the children will perform sections of the work once you have finished. Their degree of characterization is often dependent on how well you presented the characters.

As you perform, be aware of the children's feedback. If they want to laugh, let them. If they want to ask questions, let them. Sometimes it is appropriate for a dialogue to take place between the performer and the audience if a word or section of a text is not clear. Occasionally it is a good idea to let the child audience join in the telling if, for example, a word or phrase is repeated throughout, as in Judith Viorst's *Alexander and the Terrible, Horrible, No Good, Very Bad Day* or Sendak's *Where the Wild Things Are.*

If an illustrated book is performed, especially a Caldecott winner (an award given each year to the best-illustrated children's book), show the pictures—by holding the book so the children can see them, by enlarging them and putting them on poster board, by projecting them with an opaque projector, or by putting copies of the pictures on a flannel board. The children will want to see the pictures, and if you don't show them the illustrations, they may creep closer and closer until they are looking over your shoulder.

When children's literature is performed for children, the goal is to encourage the child's active imagination—his or her joining into the world the writer has created.

This is a serious responsibility. Often the first hearing of a story, poem, play, fable, and so on, stays with a child and immediately becomes THE way the work is remembered and ultimately the RIGHT way to perform it. Children who are read to, often and well, become better readers themselves. If adults read well and often to children, they bridge the gap between the children's appreciation of literature and the children's ability to read themselves.

While children often appreciate exaggeration of sound and structure and a performance with vocal variety and large, broad physical reinforcement, adults usually enjoy a more subtle, less literal translation. And, indeed, adults do enjoy the performance of children's literature. Remember, most children's literature was written by adults, and there is often a second level of meaning which can be emphasized in a performance for an adult audience. Think about *Alice in Wonderland,* for example. How would a performance of this work for children differ from one performed for adults?

If you decide to perform a children's literature selection in your interpretation class, be sure to establish in the introduction who you imagine the class to be. Do you want them to listen and respond as adults or as children? If children, establish their age and how much of the story they are supposed to know already. Often adults delight in transforming into children for you, but you may have to encourage them to do so by asking them questions during the introduction (or during the performance) as if they were children. Once you begin your selection, work on maintaining the child-audience relationship.

When you perform children's literature for a mixed audience of adults and children, it would probably be best to perform with the child audience in mind as they may be the more challenging audience to keep interested.

The worlds projected in children's literature (both the fantastic and the realistic) open the door to a child's as well as an adult's imagination and provide wonderful material for performance. Many children's stories, for example, are really metaphors for life experiences. They make life hold still. They may also be easier to understand and thus to perform. The expressiveness necessitated by many children's selections provides excellent practice for the performer who may be shy, inhibited, or nervous.

Children's literature selections for performance

JABBERWOCKY   Lewis Carroll

'Twas brillig, and the slithy toves
Did gyre and gimble in the wabe:
All mimsy were the borogoves,
And the mome raths outgrabe.

"Beware the Jabberwock, my son!
The jaws that bite, the claws that catch!
Beware the Jubjub bird, and shun
The frumious Bandersnatch!"

He took his vorpal sword in hand:
Long time the manxome foe he sought—
So rested he by the Tumtum tree,
And stood awhile in thought.

And, as in uffish thought he stood,
The Jabberwock, with eyes of flame,
Came whiffling through the tulgey wood.
And burbled as it came!

One, two! One, two! And through and through
The vorpal blade went snicker-snack!
He left it dead, and with its head
He went galumphing back.

"And hast thou slain the Jabberwock?
Come to my arms, my beamish boy!
O frabjous day! Callooh! Callay!"
He chortled in his joy.

'Twas brillig, and the slithy toves
Did gyre and gimble in the wabe:
All mimsy were the borogoves,
And the mome raths outgrabe.

Humpty Dumpty's Interpretation of "Jabberwocky"

From THROUGH THE LOOKING GLASS   Lewis Carroll

"You seem very clever at explaining words, Sir," said Alice. "Would you kindly tell me the meaning of the poem called 'Jabberwocky'?"

"Let's hear it," said Humpty Dumpty. "I can explain all the poems that ever were invented—and a good many that haven't been invented just yet."

This sounded very hopeful, so Alice repeated the first verse:—
" 'Twas brillig, and the slithy toves
Did gyre and gimble in the wabe:
All mimsy were the borogoves,
And the mome raths outgrabe."

"That's enough to begin with," Humpty Dumpty interrupted: "there are plenty of hard words there. '*Brillig*' means four o'clock in the afternoon—the time when you begin *broiling* things for dinner."

"That'll do very well," said Alice: "and '*slithy*'?"

"Well, '*slithy*' means 'lithe and slimy.' 'Lithe' is the same as 'active.' You see it's like a portmanteau—there are two meanings packed up into one word."

"I see it now," Alice remarked thoughtfully: "and what are '*toves*'?"

"Well, '*toves*' are something like badgers—they're something like lizards—and they're something like corkscrews."

"They must be very curious-looking creatures."

"They are that," said Humpty Dumpty; "also they make their nests under sun-dials—also they live on cheese."

"And what's to '*gyre*' and to '*gimble*'?"

"To '*gyre*' is to go round and round like a gyroscope. To '*gimble*' is to make holes like a gimlet."

'And '*the wabe*' is the grass-plot round a sun-dial, I suppose?" said Alice, surprised at her own ingenuity.

"Of course it is. It's called '*wabe*' you know, because it goes a long way before it, and a long way behind it—"

"And a long way beyond it on each side," Alice added.

"Exactly so. Well then, '*mimsy*' is 'flimsy and miserable' (there's another portmanteau for you). And a '*borogove*' is a thin shabby-looking bird with its feathers sticking out all round—something like a live mop."

"And then '*mome raths*'?" said Alice. "I'm afraid I'm giving you a great deal of trouble."

"Well, a '*rath*' is a sort of green pig: but '*mome*' I'm not certain about. I think it's short for 'from home'—meaning that they'd lost their way, you know."

"And what does '*outgrabe*' mean?"

"Well, '*outgribing*' is something between bellowing and whistling, with a kind of sneeze in the middle: however, you'll hear it done, maybe—down in the wood yonder—and, when you've heard it, you'll be *quite* content."

GODFREY GORDON GUSTAVUS GORE   William Brighty Rands

Godfrey Gordon Gustavus Gore—
No doubt you have heard the name before—
Was a boy who never would shut a door!

The wind might whistle, the wind might roar,
And teeth be aching and throats be sore,
But still he never would shut the door.

His father would beg, his mother implore,
"Godfrey Gordon Gustavus Gore,
We really *do* wish you would shut the door!"

Their hands they wrung, their hair they tore;
But Godfrey Gordon Gustavus Gore
Was deaf as the buoy out at the Nore.

When he walked forth the folks would roar,
"Godfrey Gordon Gustavus Gore,
Why don't you think to shut the door?"

They rigged out a Shutter with sail and oar,
And threatened to pack off Gustavus Gore
On a voyage of penance to Singapore.

But he begged for mercy, and said, "No more!
Pray do not send me to Singapore
On a Shutter, and then I will shut the door!"

"You will?" said his parents; "then keep on shore!
But mind you do! For the plague is sore
Of a fellow that never will shut the door,
Godfrey Gordon Gustavus Gore!"

THE ELVES AND THE SHOEMAKER   The Brothers Grimm, translated
by Edgar Taylor

There was once a shoemaker who worked very hard and was very honest, but still he could not earn enough to live upon, and at last all he had in the world was gone, except just leather enough to make one pair of shoes.

Then he cut them all ready to make up the next day, meaning to get up early in the morning to work. His conscience was clear and his heart light amidst all his troubles; so he went peaceably to bed, left all his cares to heaven, and fell asleep.

In the morning, after he had said his prayers, he set himself down to his work, when to his great wonder, there stood the shoes, all ready made, upon the table. The good man knew not what to say or think of this strange event. He looked at the workmanship; there was not one false stitch in the whole job, and all was so neat and true that it was a complete masterpiece.

That same day a customer came in, and the shoes pleased him so well that he willingly paid a price higher than usual for them; and the poor shoemaker with the money bought leather enough to make two pairs more. In the evening he cut out the work, and went to bed early that he might get up and begin betimes next day. But he was saved all the trouble, for when he got up in the morning the work was finished ready to his hand.

Presently in came buyers, who paid him handsomely for his goods, so that he bought leather enough for four pairs more. He cut out the work again over night, and found it finished in the morning as before; and so it went on for some time; what was got ready in the evening was always done by daybreak, and the good man soon became thriving and prosperous again.

One evening about Christmas time, as he and his wife were sitting over the fire chatting together, he said to her, "I should like to sit up and watch to-night, that we may see who it is that comes and does my work for me." The wife liked the thought; so they left a light burning, and hid themselves in the corner of the room behind a curtain and watched to see what would happen.

As soon as it was midnight, there came two little naked dwarfs; and they sat themselves upon the shoemaker's bench, took up all the work that was cut out, and began to ply with their little fingers, stitching and rapping and tapping away at such a rate that the shoemaker was all amazement, and could not take his eyes off for a moment. And on they went till the job was quite finished, and the shoes stood ready to use upon the table. This was long before daybreak; and then they bustled away as quick as lightning.

The next day the wife said to the shoemaker, "These little wights have made us rich, and we ought to be thankful to them, and do them a good office in return. I am quite vexed to see them run about as they do; they have nothing upon their backs to keep off the cold. I'll tell you what, I will make each of them a shirt, and a coat and waistcoat, and a pair of pantaloons into the bargain; you make each of them a little pair of shoes."

The thought pleased the good shoemaker very much; and one evening, when all the things were ready, they laid them on the table instead of the work that they used to cut out, and then went and hid themselves to watch what the little elves would do.

About midnight the elves came in and were going to sit down to their work as usual; but when they saw the clothes lying for them, they laughed and were greatly delighted. Then they dressed themselves in the twinkling of an eye, and danced and capered and sprang about as merry as could be, till at last they danced out at the door and over the green; and the shoemaker saw them no more; but everything went well with him from that time forward, as long as he lived.

Postmodern Literature

Postmodern literature is a construct begun after World War II which has three primary characteristics: (1) there is a reflexive or metafictional sense to this literature—often these texts concentrate on language and the writer's playing with language, and many times their subject matter is the writing process itself; (2) this literature often has no causal plot line with a clear beginning, middle, and end; and (3) this literature rarely has closure—the work just stops rather than supplying a satisfying ending. Postmodern texts, according to Ihab Hassan, are disjunctive and open in form, and emphasize language play and contingency or chance. They create the sense that the language is a performance in itself, and that audience participation is essential to completing the task of discovering what the text "means" because of unfilled gaps and indeterminacies.[8] Of course, we fill in gaps in "traditional" literature all the time. We decide, for example, whether a character's grin is friendly, mischievous, or ominous; we sense that a character feels energetic and happy when he tucks a fresh red carnation into his buttonhole. But in postmodern literature we are asked to make much greater contributions. Look, for example, at the following excerpt from the end of postmodern writer Italo Calvino's short story "The Form of Space,' which manifests many of Hassan's characteristics of postmodern literature.

From THE FORM OF SPACE   Italo Calvino

What you might consider straight, one-dimensional lines were similar, in effect, to lines of handwriting made on a white page by a pen that shifts words and fragments of sentences from one line to another, with insertions and cross-references, in the haste to finish an exposition which has gone through successive, approximate drafts, always unsatisfactory; and so we pursued each other, Lieutenant Fenimore and I, hiding behind the loops of the *l*'s, especially the *l*'s of the word "parallel," in order to shoot and take cover from the bullets and pretend to be dead and wait, say, till Fenimore went past in order to trip him up and drag him by his feet, slamming his chin against the bottoms of the *v*'s and the *u*'s and the *m*'s and the *n*'s which, written all evenly in an italic and, became a bumpy succession of holes in the pavement (for example in the expression "unmeasurable universe"), leaving him stretched out in a place all trampled with erasings and x-ings, then standing up there again, stained with clotted ink, to run toward Ursula H'x, who was trying to act sly, slipping behind the tails of the *f* which trail off until they become wisps, but I could seize her by the hair and bend her against a *d* or a *t* just as I write them now, in haste, bent, so you can recline against them, then we might dig a niche for ourselves down in a *g*, in the *g* of "big," a subterranean den which can be adapted as we choose to our dimensions, being made more cozy and almost invisible or else arranged more horizontally so you can stretch out in it. Whereas naturally the same lines, rather than remain series of letters and words, can easily be drawn out in their black thread and unwound in continuous, parallel, straight lines which mean nothing beyond themselves in their constant flow, never meeting, just as we never meet in our constant fall: I, Ursula H'x, Lieutenant Fenimore, and all the others.

As found in *Cosmic Comics*, translated from the Italian by William Weaver. A Harvest/HBJ Book, A Helen and Kurt Wolff Book, Harcourt Brace Jovanovich, Publishers, San Diego, New York, London. English translation 1968 by Harcourt Brace Jovanovich, Inc., and Jonathan Cape Limited.

As Hassan suggests, postmodern literature is a literature of indeterminacies. Lack of closure, writing in the "margins," a sense of play—these are the postmodern characteristics which function to create the "gap" where texts interact with other texts.

Postmodern literature glorifies in disrupting our normal expectations and revels in shocking or surprising us. Postmodern texts take advantage of what has gone before, but they are also revolutionary—not satisfied with the status quo. Postmodern writers seek new alternatives, new solutions to contemporary theories of language.

One of the most exciting aspects of postmodern texts is that they challenge the performer to develop new performance analogues and styles. Postmodern literature and contemporary literary theories motivate the interpreter to explore and experience the play of language in radically new ways, shifting the focus to the absences and the hidden agendas generated, which language, as an indeterminate field of signification, inevitably provides. Performance art—discussed later in this chapter—is one vehicle for the performance of postmodern texts. As you read the following selections, let your imagination play in order to create new performance possibilities and analogues.

Postmodern selections for performance

From BURIED CHILD   Sam Shepard

This play takes place in the midwestern living room of Dodge and Halie's rural home. The family is made up of Dodge, the dying father; Halie, the adulterous mother; two sons—Tilden, a functional illiterate, and Bradley, an amputee; and the grandson, Vincent (Tilden's son), who returns to his childhood home, in search of his roots and his personal identity, with his girlfriend, Shelly. The following scene is from Act 1 of this three-act drama. The scene begins as Tilden enters carrying several ears of corn.

Dodge:	*(to Tilden)* Where'd you get that?
Tilden:	Picked it.
Dodge:	You picked all that? *(Tilden nods.)*
Dodge:	You expecting company?
Tilden:	No.
Dodge:	Where'd you pick it from?
Tilden:	Right out back.
Dodge:	Out back where!
Tilden:	Right out in back.
Dodge:	There's nothing out there!
Tilden:	There's corn.
Dodge:	There hasn't been corn out there since about nineteen thirty five! That's the last time I planted corn out there!
Tilden:	It's out there now.
Dodge:	*(yelling at stairs)* Halie!
Halie's Voice:	Yes dear!
Dodge:	Tilden's brought a whole bunch of corn in here! There's no corn out in back is there?
Tilden:	*(to himself)* There's tons of corn.

Halie's Voice:	Not that I know of!
Dodge:	That's what I thought.
Halie's Voice:	Not since about nineteen thirty five!
Dodge:	*(to Tilden)* That's right. Nineteen thirty five.
Tilden:	It's out there now.
Dodge:	You go and take that corn back to wherever you got it from!
Tilden:	*(After pause, staring at Dodge)* It's picked. I picked it all in the rain. Once it's picked you can't put it back.
Dodge:	I haven't had trouble with neighbors here for fifty-seven years. I don't even know who the neighbors are! And I don't wanna know! Now go put that corn back where it came from!
	Tilden stares at Dodge then walks slowly over to him and dumps all the corn on Dodge's lap and steps back. Dodge stares at the corn then back to Tilden. Long pause.
Dodge:	Are you having trouble here, Tilden? Are you in some kind of trouble?
Tilden:	I'm not in any trouble.
Dodge:	You can tell me if you are. I'm still your father.
Tilden:	I know you're still my father.
Dodge:	I know you had a little trouble back in New Mexico. That's why you came out here.
Tilden:	I never had any trouble.
Dodge:	Tilden, your mother told me all about it.
Tilden:	What'd she tell you?
	Tilden pulls some chewing tobacco out of his jacket and bites off a plug.
Dodge:	I don't have to repeat what she told me! She told me all about it!
Tilden:	Can I bring my chair in from the kitchen?
Dodge:	What?
Tilden:	Can I bring in my chair from the kitchen?
Dodge:	Sure. Bring your chair in.

HOW EVERYTHING HAPPENS (BASED ON A STUDY OF THE WAVE)
May Swenson

                                                                happen.
                                                        to
                                                up
                                        stacking
                                is
                        something
When nothing is happening

When it happens
                    something
                        pulls
                            back
                                not
                                  to
                                    happen.
When   has happened.
     pulling back   stacking up
           happens
      has happened   stacks up.
When it   something   nothing
                    pulls back while
Then nothing is happening.
                                  happens.
                         and
                  forward
             pushes
        up
     stacks
  something
Then

ACROSTIC   Anonymous

These may be read two or three wayes [sic].

Your face	Your tongue	your wit
so faire	so smooth	so sharp
first drew	then mov'd	then knit
mine eye	Mine eare	My heart
thus drawn	thus mov'd	thus knit
affects	hangs on	yeelds to
Your face	Your tongue	your wit

(The third way, incidentally, goes from right to left and from left to right in alternate lines, in imitation of the ancient Greek manner of writing called boustrophedon, "as the ox turns in plowing.")

As found in *Speaking Pictures: A Gallery of Pictorial Poetry from the Sixteenth Century to the Present* edited by Milton Klonsky, New York: Harmony Books (a division of Crown Publishers, Inc.), 1975, p. 56.

PERFORMANCE STYLES

Now that you have tried your hand at what might be considered "traditional" interpretation performances, you may want to try experimenting. There are unlimited possibilities that you might explore to further your understanding of text in performance. You are limited only by the extent of your imagination and creativity. We will now focus on four specialized forms of performance you might experiment with: program performances, media performances, personal narratives, and performance art.

The Program Performance

In the performances you have done so far, you have most likely shared one piece of literature with an audience. When you wish to investigate a particular theme (love, hate, war, marriage), writer (Shaw, Seuss, Simon), literary style (sonnet, ode, fable, parody), or literary period (Romantic, Victorian, Postmodern) in more depth, you may do so by combining various pieces of literature into a longer program. As you select materials, you become aware of the similarities and differences within a thematic program, in one writer's style, or in literary types and periods. As you program, you act as an "author," deciding which selections to include and how best to arrange them.

Programming is a very creative and exciting way to study literature. You communicate your personal feelings about a certain theme, writer, or literary style or period by the selections you choose and by the way you order them, in addition to the manner in which you perform them. When you combine several literary selections, you create new ideas and reveal new connotations through the juxtaposition of one selection with another. If, for example, you perform a selection about divorce before performing a selection depicting idealistic love, the effect created by the second selection is altered by its juxtaposition with the first selection. An ambiguous, difficult selection may be made more comprehensible by its juxtaposition with another selection on the same theme. The versatility of writers like Eudora Welty, William Carlos Williams, or Gwendolyn Brooks, for example, may be investigated by performing more than one selection by that particular author.

Successful programmed performances have been done by combining two selections on a theme or by the same writer. Here are some programmed performance combinations:

"The Christmas Horses" by Laura Ingalls Wilder with "The Boy Who Laughed at Santa Claus" by Ogden Nash.
"Do Not Go Gentle into That Good Night" by Dylan Thomas with *No Exit* by Jean-Paul Sartre.
"The Road Not Taken" by Robert Frost with "The Wise Men" also by Frost.
"The House of Shadows" by Mary Elizabeth Counselman with *The Ghost Story* by John Pielmeier.
"Shooting an Elephant" by George Orwell with "The Hollow Men" by T. S. Eliot.
"The Ballad of the Landlord" by Langston Hughes with "What Berry Found" from *The Sport of the Gods* by Paul Lawrence Dunbar.
"Infant Sorrow" by William Blake with "In the Gloaming" by Alice Elliott Dark.
Duet for One by Tom Kempenski with "With Rue My Heart is Laden" by A. E. Housman.
Othello by Shakespeare with "Love" by Ray Croft.

The creation of a program performance involves the following nine steps, usually, though not always, in this order:

1. Select a theme, writer, literary style, or literary period to investigate.
2. Narrow the scope of the program or devise an assertion which helps to narrow your selection choices (for example, if your theme is love, your assertion might be "love for animals is the only real love"; if your program is on "sonnets," you might decide to limit your choices to sonnets depicting nature).
3. Decide on the purpose of your program (to inform, persuade, activate, entertain, shock, horrify, or achieve some other end).
4. Choose the material you wish to include (usually by finding more than you will need and then eliminating selections based on what you want the program to say and on time limitations).
5. Analyze the material you have chosen using the dramatistic and modal types of analysis.
6. Organize the material.
7. Compose an introduction and transitions.
8. Rehearse your material.
9. Perform.

The following is a sample program performance which illustrates one possible structure. The program begins with an introduction that explains the theme, tells how many selections will be performed, and then relates the first selection to the theme.

The first selection is then performed, followed by a transition which relates the second selection to the theme and to the first selection. The second selection is then performed, followed by the second transition and the performance of the third selection.

Sample program performance: Introduction

The depiction and characterization of witches has changed throughout time. The following three selections examine the evolution of the concept of "witch." Witches are commonly depicted as frightening manifestations of evil, or, as Macbeth describes them, "secret, black, and midnight hags," with a tremendous power to foresee our destiny. They are demons who live in a dark world and represent the evil in nature meant to corrupt human will. In this scene, Macbeth asks the witches to conjure up his future, which they do with a series of three apparitions.

From MACBETH   William Shakespeare

Macbeth: How now, you secret, black, and midnight hags!
What is't you do?
   All: A deed without a name.
Macbeth: I conjure you, by that which you profess,
Howe'er you come to know it, answer me.
Though you untie the winds and let them fight
Against the churches; though the yesty waves
Confound and swallow navigation up;
Though bladed corn be lodged and trees blown down;
Though castles topple on their warders' heads;
Though palaces and pyramids do slope
Their heads to their foundations; though the treasure
Of nature's germens tumble all together,
Even till destruction sicken—answer me
To what I ask you.
   1. Witch: Speak.
   2. Witch: Demand.
   3. Witch: We'll answer.
   1. Witch: Say, if thou'dst rather hear it from our mouths,
Or from our masters?
Macbeth: Call 'em, let me see 'em.
      (Thunder. First Apparition: an armed Head.)
   1. Witch: He knows thy thought.
Hear his speech, but say thou naught.
  1. Apparition: Macbeth! Macbeth! Macbeth! Beware Macduff,
Beware the Thane of Fife. Dismiss me. Enough. *(Descends)*

Macbeth: Whate'er thou art, for thy good caution thanks
Thou hast harped my fear aright. But one word more—
1. Witch: He will not be commanded. Here's another,
More potent than the first.
(Thunder. Second Apparition: a Bloody Child.)
2. Apparition: Macbeth! Macbeth! Macbeth!
Macbeth: Had I three ears, I'd hear thee.
2. Apparition: Be bloody, bold, and resolute, laugh to scorn
The power of man, for none of woman born
Shall harm Macbeth.   *(Descends)*
Macbeth: Then live, Macduff. What need I fear of thee?
But yet I'll make assurance double sure,
And take a bond of fate. Thou shalt not live,
That I may tell pale-hearted fear it lies,
And sleep in spite of thunder.
(Thunder. Third Apparition: a Child Crowned, with a tree in his hand.)
What is this
That rises like the issue of a king,
And wears upon his baby brow the round
And top of sovereignty?
All: Listen, but speak not to 't.
3. Apparition: Be lion-mettled, proud, and take no care
Who chafes, who frets, or where conspirers are.
Macbeth shall never vanquished be until
Great Birnam Wood to high Dunsinane Hill
Shall come against him.   *(Descends)*
Macbeth: That will never be.
Who can impress the forest, bid the tree
Unfix his earthbound root? Sweet bodements! Good!
Rebellion's head, rise never till the wood
Of Birnam rise, and our high-placed Macbeth
Shall live the lease of nature, pay his breath
To time and mortal custom. Yet my heart
Throbs to know one thing. Tell me, if your art
Can tell so much. Shall Banquo's issue ever
Reign in this kingdom?
All: Seek to know no more.

Transition

In *Macbeth,* the witches are certainly not members of the community; they appear
and disappear at will and exist in a netherworld. In Nathaniel Hawthorne's *The*

Scarlet Letter, Mistress Hibbins is a reputed witch who also happens to be the sister of the Governor of Boston, and because of this she possesses a grudging respectability. She lives in town but visits the forest to serve her master. She is able, then, to function both in the light and dark worlds. She, like the witches in *Macbeth*, is both feared and taken seriously, but whereas the witches in Shakespeare's play smile while Macbeth essentially causes his own downfall, Mistress Hibbins actively seeks to steal the soul of Hester Prynne's mysterious daughter, Pearl.

From THE SCARLET LETTER   Nathaniel Hawthorne

Little Pearl's unwonted mood of sentiment lasted no longer; she laughed, and went capering down the hall, so airily, that old Mr. Wilson raised a question whether even her tiptoes touched the floor.

"The little baggage hath witchcraft in her, I profess," said he to Mr. Dimmesdale. "She needs no old woman's broomstick to fly withal!"

"A strange child!" remarked old Roger Chillingworth. "It is easy to see the mother's part in her. Would it be beyond a philosopher's research, think ye, gentlemen, to analyze that child's nature, and, from its make and mould, to give a shrewd guess at the father?"

"Nay; it would be sinful, in such a question, to follow the clew of profane philosophy," said Mr. Wilson. "Better to fast and pray upon it; and still better, it may be, to leave the mystery as we find it, unless Providence reveal it of its own accord. Thereby, every good Christian man hath a title to show a father's kindness towards the poor, deserted babe."

The affair being so satisfactorily concluded, Hester Prynne, with Pearl, departed from the house. As they descended the steps, it is averred that the lattice of a chamber-window was thrown open, and forth into the sunny day was thrust the face of Mistress Hibbins, Governor Bellingham's bitter-tempered sister, and the same who, a few years later, was executed as a witch.

"Hist, hist!" said she, while her ill-omened physiognomy seemed to cast a shadow over the cheerful newness of the house. "Wilt thou go with us to-night? There will be a merry company in the forest; and I wellnigh promised the Black Man that comely Hester Prynne should make one."

"Make my excuse to him, so please you!" answered Hester, with a triumphant smile, "I must tarry at home, and keep watch over my little Pearl. Had they taken her from me, I would willingly have gone with thee into the forest, and signed my name in the Black Man's book too, and that with mine own blood!"

"We shall have thee there anon!" said the witch-lady, frowning, as she drew back her head.

Levin, Harry (Editor), *The Scarlet Letter* by Nathaniel Hawthorne, Riverside Edition. Copyright © 1960 by Houghton Mifflin Company. Used with permission.

Transition

The last selection, "For Witches" by Susan Sutheim, takes us into the present, where "witches" are simply women who try to function in the real world despite the handicaps and powerlessness of their everyday lives. But beware—when their functioning is made too difficult, their tempers flare and a veiled curse is heard.

FOR WITCHES   Susan Sutheim

today
i lost my temper.

temper, when one talks of metal
means strong,
perfect.

temper, for humans,
means angry
irrational
bad.

today i found my temper.
i said,
you step on my head
for 27 years you step on my head
and though i have been trained
to excuse you for your inevitable
clumsiness
today i think
i prefer my head to your clumsiness.

today i began
to find myself.
tomorrow
perhaps
i will begin
to find
you.

First published in *Women: A Journal of Liberation,* Fall 1969, and is reprinted by permission of the Journal.

When organizing selections for a program performance, remember the following guidelines:

1. It is usually a good idea to place your shortest selection first so your program will have a sense of build. If you use many different selections, alternate shorter and longer selections for the sake of pacing and variety.
2. If you have a number of selections, try to vary them in terms of tone and mood, if possible, to keep audience interest and attention.
3. Place the selection that makes the deepest impression and which has the most important or persuasive statement at the end.

In addition to the program performances just discussed, there are other program performance possibilities. For example, you can select one poem and perform it two or three different ways. You can combine thematic programs with author, period, or style programs. If you are skilled in a foreign language, you can perform a selection in its original language and then translate it, or vice versa.

The Media Performance

Any performance can be enhanced by incorporating other media forms in your presentation. Adding elements such as taped or live music, paintings, computer graphics, film, video, photographs, or PowerPoint™ slides, to name just a few, turns the presentation into a mixed-media performance. These additions can greatly enrich the text if the media are well chosen and employed. We have already defined literature as a potential cause of experiences. Marshall McLuhan tells us that "all media are active metaphors in their power to translate experience into new forms."[9] By using other media forms, you can facilitate the audience's understanding and appreciation of a text and increase their involvement in your performance. The more stimuli that bombard our senses, the more likely we are to become involved, depending, of course, on the quality of the stimuli.

If you decide to prepare a media performance, ask yourself what kinds of media will best enhance your chosen text. Will electronic aids—music, video, film, slides—be useful? Will the showing of a particular painting, photograph, or illustration help the audience to gain understanding or appreciation of the text? What about using mime or dance? "Artists in various fields," says McLuhan, "are always the first to discover how to enable one medium to use or to release the power of another."[10] Interpreters are artists and they can discover and release the power in a literary text by experimenting with various kinds of media.

Read the following poems aloud and see whether you can determine how other media forms can be incorporated to highlight them and release their power.

I HAVE COME TO CLAIM   Judy Grahn

I have come to claim
Marilyn Monroe's body
for the sake of my own
dig it up, hand it over,
cram it in this paper sack.
hubba. hubba. hubba
look at those luscious
long brown bones, that wide and crusty
pelvis. ha ha, oh she wanted so much to be serious
but she never stops smiling now.
Has she lost her mind?

Marilyn, be serious—they're taking
your picture, and they're taking the pictures
of eight young women in New York City
who murdered themselves for being pretty
by the same method as you, the very
next day, after you!
I have claimed their bodies too,
they smile up out of my paper sack
like brainless cinderellas.

The reporters are furious, they're asking
me questions
what right does a woman have
to Marilyn Monroe's body? and what
am I doing for lunch? They think I
mean to eat you. Their teeth are lurid
and they want to pose me, leaning
on the shovel, nude. Don't squint.
But when one of the reporters comes too close
I beat him, bust his camera
with your long, smooth thigh
and with your lovely knucklebone
I break his eye.

Long ago you wanted to write poems.
Be serious, Marilyn
I am going to take you in this paper sack
around the world, and
write on it:—the poems of Marilyn Monroe—
Dedicated to all princes,

the male poets who were so sorry to see you go.
before they had a crack at you.
They wept for you, and also
they wanted to stuff you
while you had a little meat left
in useful places;
but they were too slow.

Now I shall take them my paper sack
and we shall act out a poem together.
"How would you like to see Marilyn Monroe
in action, smiling, and without her clothes?"
We shall wait long enough to see them make familiar faces
and then I shall beat them with your skull.
hubba. hubba. hubba. hubba. hubba.
Marilyn, be serious
Today I have come to claim your body for my own.

I WANDERED LONELY AS A CLOUD   William Wordsworth

I wandered lonely as a cloud
That floats on high o'er vales and hills,
When all at once I saw a crowd,
A host of golden daffodils,
Beside the lake, beneath the trees
Fluttering and dancing in the breeze.

Continuous as the stars that shine
And twinkle on the Milky Way,
They stretched in never-ending line
Along the margin of the bay:
Ten thousand saw I at a glance
Tossing their heads in sprightly dance.

The waves beside them danced, but they
Outdid the sparkling waves in glee:
A poet could not but be gay
In such a jocund company!
I gazed—and gazed—but little thought
What wealth the show to me had brought:

> For oft, when on my couch I lie
> In vacant or in pensive mood,
> They flash upon that inward eye
> Which is the bliss of solitude;
> And then my heart with pleasure fills,
> And dances with the daffodils.

Some cautions should be kept in mind when you perform literature incorporating other media forms. The most practical advice is to be sure your equipment (recorder, projector, monitor, and so on) is in good working order *before* you come to class. Make sure you have an extension cord should you need one, charged batteries, and so forth. Be sure that the media you choose do indeed enhance the text. You should not use media for the sake of using media. You should use media because the use adds to the audience's and your own awareness, understanding, and appreciation of the text. In addition to these cautions there are specific concerns that relate to the type of medium you may use.

When you are using music, be sure that the literature is the primary focus and that the music is kept in the background as a mood setter, tension underliner, or environmental enhancer. Be sure the volume is adjusted beforehand—not too loud, not too soft. If the music is very familiar to the audience, they might begin humming along and stop listening to you or they may start free associating, remembering when they first heard the song—make allowances for this. If you use music with lyrics, the audience might find it difficult to listen both to the text and to the song's lyrics. For this reason, it is probably best to use only instrumental music. Be sure the rhythm of the text determines your pace and not the tempo of the music.

When you are using slides, be sure the audience does not have to struggle between attending to your slides and to your performance simultaneously. Decide how you can show the slides so that the audience's attention is not split between you and the slides. You may want to show some slides to establish the theme or the mood, do part of the performance, show more slides, and then finish your performance. You may start your performance, show slides, end the performance, and then show more slides. If you decide to show the slides and perform at the same time, be sure to pause while a slide is changed to give the audience time to see it before continuing your performance—or use blank slides when you want the audience's attention on you. Remember, sight is our keenest sense and visual stimuli tend to dominate our attention. If given the choice between concentrating on a primarily visual stimulus or on a primarily auditory stimulus, we usually choose the visual stimulus.

When you are using paintings, photographs, or illustrations, ask yourself these questions: If I use a painting, photograph, or illustration, do I want to keep it on view throughout my performance or will its permanent presence be too distracting? Are my visual aids large enough to be seen? Do I show my paintings, photographs, or illustrations before, during, or after the line or lines they relate to?

If you use video or film, again, you must find a way to keep the literature the primary focus. You could make a video of yourself performing, incorporating other media in the tape. You could show part of a film, freeze a frame, and, using the light from the film projector as your "spotlight," perform your selection, and then finish the movie. Incorporating video and film in this way makes you a part of the mixed media.

If you use dance or mime, you might want to perform your text first and then dance or mime your interpretation of the selection, or vice versa. It is difficult but certainly not impossible to perform the literature and the mime or dance simultaneously, but much rehearsal would be necessary.

Recent advances in Information Technology have created new opportunities for exploring various types of media in performance. Today, a wealth of technologies allows artists to combine text image, sound, and even smell into performances. Music conquered the image, image illuminated text, and the personal computer allowed artists to combine media in new and exciting ways. The Internet is a valuable source for media materials. In addition to valuable information about writers and their works, you can find web pages which include photos and appropriate illustrations. Go, for example, to http://www3pitt.edu/~novosel/owen.html. Here you will find a picture of poet Wilfred Owen and copies of the poems "Dulce et Decorum Est," "Anthem for Doomed Youth," "The Parable of the Old Man and the Young," and "Strange Meeting" complete with appropriate illustrations. *Be wary, though. Information you find on the Internet is not necessarily gospel. Anyone can enter information on the Net; finding it there doesn't make it accurate or factual. Check out the information you use for its validity and reliability.*

In addition to web-based multimedia outlets, individual artists can use specific applications to incorporate text, sound, and image into a performance with relative ease. Microsoft's PowerPoint™ is among the most accessible and powerful presentational software. Performers can also preprogram the timing and pace of the presentation so that dancing or mime is included as part of the performance. Such tools, however, require some technical skill and a time commitment.

If you are interested in using PowerPoint™ in your performance, you will first need a computer and a licensed copy of the program. You can cut and paste texts from your regular word processing program or simply type the text yourself in the slides. PowerPoint™ allows users to define many different styles of slide types, arrangements, and backgrounds. You can even include special effects with the text. There is, for example, a typewriter effect that slowly types out the text you have entered, even seeming to correct a mistake made when the wrong key was hit. After you have chosen an appropriate style of slide for the type of text you are performing, you can embed prepared files of movies, songs, and other visual and auditory effects. Each of these elements can be set to play when you click on the icon in the slide or preprogrammed to play at certain times after the slide becomes active. Many programs are available to capture, create, and edit sound and video files for use in PowerPoint™ presentations. You should choose one that saves files for cross-platform applications, however, as you may be faced with an IBM computer in the performance venue after you created all your effects on a MAC computer. (PowerPoint™ is cross-platform; a good program for sound and video is Apple's Quicktime™ player and editor.)

One final thought on the use of PowerPoint™ or other computer-based presentational applications. Most programs offer extensive tutorials and on-line help that can be very useful to a neophyte, but nothing replaces learning the material for yourself. The computers, projectors, and Internet hookups can be expensive and troublesome, though they are getting both cheaper and more reliable every day. Nevertheless, great care and planning should precede any use of hi-tech in a performance.

No matter what kinds of media you use, keep the literature the primary focus. In addition to the points just mentioned, the media should serve one or more of the following purposes:

1. To help establish the mood or theme.
2. To illustrate main points or ideas.
3. To provide subtextual reinforcement.
4. To build intensity.
5. To underline the crisis and climax moments.
6. To help the audience visualize ambiguous moments in the text.

Personal Narratives

Personal narratives are the autobiographical stories you tell every day. Stories are heightened forms of discourse and through them you are able to preserve your familial ties and your cultural heritage. Your personal narratives are ethnographic studies of who you are and where you came from. Rather than being responsible for interpreting the text of another, you have personal authorship and ownership of the stories you tell. When you present a personal narrative, you indicate a willingness to share parts of yourself with others.

Learning to structure a personal narrative so that it has broader implications makes it possible for others to appreciate, relate to, and perhaps learn from your experience. You learn from the experience as well. Organizing your life events into oral stories helps you make sense out of them—helps you objectify them.

But what exactly is a narrative? According to Robert Scholes:

> A narration involves a selection of events for the telling. They must offer sufficient continuity of subject matter to make their chronological sequence significant, and they must be presented as having happened already. When the telling provides this sequence with a certain kind of shape and a certain level of human interest, we are in the presence not merely of narrative but of story. A

story is a narrative with a certain very specific syntactic shape (beginning-middle-end or situation-transformation-situation) and with a subject matter which allows for or encourages the projection of human values upon this material. Virtually all stories are about human beings or humanoid creatures. Those that are not invariably humanize their material through metaphor and metonymy.[11]

As Kristin M. Langellier states, "personal narratives emerge from oral culture and traditions rather than written and literary traditions."[12] The oral tradition is long and established. Homer stood on a hillside long ago, composing and performing oral epic songs; he was, in a sense, the first oral interpreter. But Homer was both composer and performer. With the performance of personal narratives, you emulate this fine tradition by both creating and performing your own story—you activate your memory and keep your own personal history alive. The tradition of storytelling provided an opportunity for elders, for example, to instill moral values and openmindedness in their audiences. It provides contemporary storytellers, like Garrison Keillor, an opportunity to entertain large audiences as well as to make Lake Wobegone an icon of American popular culture. Spalding Gray, actor, writer, and monologist, stresses the importance of keeping the personal story alive in an interview in *Dramatics* magazine:

> Personal storytelling is very important to me because we've become so mediaized that we begin to think that the stories the stars tell on Johnny Carson are more important than ours. And whenever I interview people, interview the audience on stage, and I draw their stories out, the audience begins to realize that it's a radical move. That everyone has interesting stories if they can learn how to shape them. If I am a preacher or a proselytizer at all, it's to say, "Get together with friends, tell stories, listen. Turn off the TV, put down the book, listen to a story." Because the more we are fragmented and the more people are moved around and are in motion and the bigger this country gets and the more media-ized it gets, tied together only through television, the more healing it is to tell personal stories about your day. It gives you a personal history, and it gives you a sense of existence and place.[13]

To prepare a personal narrative, decide on a story from your past that you would like to share with an audience. If you do not feel comfortable presenting the story extemporaneously, perhaps from a prepared outline, you may write the story down. Although it is easier to structure, analyze, and revise your story if it is in print, you will lose something by transforming this memory out of the oral dynamic and into a more fixed print medium. Be careful that writing down and reordering the story does not harm its original orality. How can you maintain the sense of the spontaneity of story "telling" rather than "reading" a personal story?

Decide on the point of view from which you want to tell your story. Do you want to tell it from the first-person major character point of view, where you are the major character? Do you want to tell it from the point of view of someone in your family or from the point of view of a friend or associate? Do you want to tell it from an omniscient or observer point of view? You might try rehearsing the story several different ways to see how point of view affects both the story itself and the telling of the story.

You might also consider the temporal structure of your story. Is the story to be primarily scenic? How will you use summary and description?

Here is an example of a personal narrative prepared by a Japanese foreign exchange student.

A PERSONAL NARRATIVE—"My High School Days in America"

(This personal narrative was composed by a Japanese student attending a university in Tokyo who prefers to maintain her anonymity. She wrote this story for an interpretation festival in Japan, and, although it was written for a Japanese audience, the experience she relates is universal. The personal narrative is reproduced here with her permission.)

The state of South Dakota, which I don't think many of you know, is where I lived for two years. When you imagine America, what comes to your mind? Many of you might think of California, New York, or Florida. South Dakota is just the middle of nowhere compared to those famous states. But for me, it became one of the most memorable places in my life.

I was only seventeen back then, so happy to be selected as an exchange student, and so excited to go to a foreign country for the first time. I dreamed what it would be like living in America. Everything seemed so wonderful, great, and perfect in my mind: nice host family, a big house, being popular at school, having lots of friends, going to parties on Friday nights. Well, maybe I'll have a boyfriend named Michael. (That was the only typical American name I knew.) My imagination went on and on and on. I could hardly wait. At that moment, I never doubted that the excitement would disappear so easily. But it did.

My days in America started. Unlike what I imagined, the reality was nothing but a pain. I knew I had to talk to people to make friends at school, but I was so scared. I continually said to myself, "Will they understand me? If I say something wrong, they might laugh at me. I don't want to be embarrassed." So I always carried a dictionary with me, everywhere. Did it help me to make friends? No. A dictionary won't speak up for you, will it? It's not a dictionary we can count on, but our own courage. I learned not to expect someone to come up to me and say, "Oh, you seem so lonely," or "This must be too difficult for you, let me help you out." It doesn't work that way.

Anyway, no one was close enough to call "my friend." I hated going to school because I had no friends. I had nowhere to belong. I hated school. I hated mornings, and at night I worried about the next day. The only thing that made me happy was the airmail letters from Japan. I read them over and over. I never recognized before how comfortable and safe I was living in my own country, surrounded by my own culture and my loving family. I missed Japan. Strangely, though I missed Japan, I couldn't be proud of being Japanese. People called me "chink" several times. I think they meant Chinese, but not in a nice way. And once I was called, "a foreign, imported girl." My black hair, slanted eyes, flat nose, and the Japanese accent when I spoke English, all became the targets of people's curiosity. Some people made fun of me, maybe because I was different. But that is definitely not an excuse to hurt someone's feelings. I was hurt and very upset.

If this were the end of my story, you would think my high school days were horrible, but believe it or not, they turned out to be the best times of my life. Going through those difficulties, I became mentally stronger and much more outgoing. I joined the high school volleyball team, sang in the chorus, and took part in the school play. I taught Japanese language, Japanese culture, and origami (paper folding) to younger students. By trying to get involved, I started to fit in. I made friends with almost everyone, and I didn't care about being different any more. I truly enjoyed American life from the bottom of my heart.

As a result of this experience, I learned a lesson: "Be positive, be confident, and be proud of yourself." I believe that is the secret to success.

Class Exercise

Select an incident from your past that you would like to share with the class. Share this personal narrative with them, and then ask the class to tell you how they responded to the story. What did you learn about yourself as a result of the selection, preparation, and delivery of the story? What did the class learn about you? What did the class learn about themselves? Through what "texts" did they interpret your story? How was the performance of this story different from the performance of prose fiction? Did you feel more or less comfortable? Why do you think so?

Performance Art

Gregory Battcox has said:

> Before man was aware of art he was aware of himself. Awareness of the person is, then, the first art. In performance art the figure of the artist is the tool for the art. It *is* the art.[14]

The category of "performance art" is the most contemporary—identified as starting in the 1970s—and the most difficult to define of all the styles discussed in this chapter. Although performance art may be unfamiliar to you, the phenomenon exists all over the world. One of the primary intentions of the performance artist is to eliminate the distinction between the artist and what he or she produces—there is a congruence of text and self. As Battcock suggests, the artist is the art. In traditional interpretation, there is usually a clear distinction between performer and text. Performance artists try to minimize this distinction (just as postmodern writers minimize the distinction between writer and writing) by encouraging performers to create their own "texts" or to try for an even stronger merger of text and performer—breaking down the dichotomy between life and art. Some label performance artists narcissists because they seem to revel in their need to express themselves, but artists have been expressing themselves for centuries and the result can be a kind of healing of the performer's psyche as well as entertainment for the audience. As performance artists reveal and lay bare personal images and stories, they provoke the audience into re-examining their lives. Performance artists often attempt to shock, stun, or assault audiences to force them to reassess their notions of what constitutes "art."

Performance artists defy traditional conventions and create new ones. They tap into the creative impulses of their right brains to unleash personal images through performance. The images they create need not obey any norms we usually attribute to art. There need not be causality, linearity, or sequence; fantasy and releasing another level of consciousness reign. British performance artist David Cale recently presented in New York his one-person performance of *Lillian*—the life of an ordinary woman who works in a bookstore but never reads books. *Wake Up and Smell the Coffee* written and performed by Eric Bogosian was presented at the Jane Street Theater in New York. According to Bruce Weber's *The New York Times* review, Bogosian enters "as a shrieking pro wrestler . . . , he quickly dons a New Age persona and becomes a touchy-feely version of himself, then switches to Regis Philbin's evil twin for a surreal rendition of "Who Wants to be a Millionaire." Peter Marks's *The New York Times* review of *City Water Tunnel No. 3* written and performed by Marty Pottenger (a carpenter who spent 20 years in the building trade) suggests that no subject is immune from dramatization. He writes, ". . . against all odds, Marty Pottenger establishes a city water-delivery system as the backdrop for an often lyrical show that speaks with intimate knowledge, and yes, even love, about holes in the ground and the people who drill them." Lisa Kron, a performance artist as well as a storyteller, creates personal and risky works like *101 Humiliating Stories* and her most recent *2.5 Minute Ride.* In his *The New York Times* review of the latter work, Ben Brantley writes:

> "2.5 Minute Ride" boldly assumes the task of looking for the connections between two very different family outings: a recent trip to an Ohio amusement park and Ms. Kron's visit six years ago with her septuagenarian father to the Auschwitz concentration camp, where her grandparents were killed. There's no way you can draw a straight line between these excursions, and Ms. Kron doesn't try.

Later, Brantley describes the "slide show" that Ms. Kron uses to create a picture of her father: ". . . the 'slide show' Ms. Kron uses in her performance, in which she alludes to visual images, even tracing photographic details with a pointer, [is only] the light of the projector." Thus, the audience is encouraged to use their imaginations; to listen to Kron's words and create their own vivid images.

One of our most prolific and talented performance artists is Anna Deavere Smith (now a regular on "The West Wing" and "The Practice"). She is a skilled solo performer as well as a social documentarian. She has created three shows that are the result of hours of interviews and precise characterizations. Amy Gamerman in the *Wall Street Journal* says that Deavere Smith's "great gift is her ability to capture the voices—spoken voices in all their gloriously revealing disorder—not tidy, written ones—of living people." Deavere Smith assays all the roles in what she calls her "search for the American character." The first chapters were "Fires in the Mirror" (about the tension between Jews and blacks in Brooklyn's Crown Heights neighborhood) and "Twilight: Los Angeles, 1992" (about the Rodney King riots). Her latest endeavor is "House Arrest" which is about the presidency and centers on her interviews with people in and around the Clinton administration, including Mr. Clinton himself.

Although Robert Nickas is talking primarily about visual artists in the following paragraph, see if you can relate his ideas to the solo (or group) performance:

> Performance, like Conceptual art, would enable the artist to shun mere pictorial values in favor of true visual communication: art as a vehicle for ideas and action. All of this meant that art no longer had to perform to established formats, and it would never be quite the same again.[15]

Nickas suggests the social and political nature of much performance art. Performance artists often create works around the AIDS issue, workers' rights, feminism, sexism, or racial intolerance to raise consciousness, expand awareness, and give voice to the powerless. Performance becomes a means of social change. More and more areas of daily life are considered grist for the performance artist's mill. As Richard Schechner writes, ". . . there is theater in the theater; theater in ordinary life; events in ordinary life that can be interpreted as theater; events from ordinary life that can be brought into the theater where they exist both as theater and as continuation of ordinary life. . . ."[16]

There is no simple way to describe what performance art is or should be. Every performance artist defines the form, and often himself or herself, in the process—the performer creates the event. The performance artist's spaces may not be those traditionally employed. "Found" spaces are transformed into theatrical venues. Performance art could involve prose, drama, poetry, programming, media, dance, mime, children's literature, personal narratives, or simply life or fantasy images that you would like to release—in short, all of the texts and performance styles already discussed throughout this text.

The performance of much postmodern literature would almost by necessity demand a kind of performance art transformation. In fact, you cannot have post-modern performances without performance art, but you can have postmodern per-formances without postmodern literature. But, as stated above, we need not be limited to postmodern texts. The following describes a performance art piece depicting the essence of Shakespeare's *Julius Caesar*. This piece was created for "A Performance of Shakespeare" class.

A performance art piece of *Julius Caesar* reported by Shawn Stoner

In approaching this presentation, our group's first objective was to do something different—exciting. Our first decision was to perform the presentation in the round—as though the class were in a coliseum. We also wanted to use a strobe light. We decided on a strobe because it tends to create a kind of alternate reality, as you receive flashes of information.

Our intention was to parallel current politics with the events depicted in *Julius Caesar*—in order to point out the similarities.

We visualized the performance as a kind of dance—there would be music, sound effects, costumes, and movement. We wanted to re-create the assassination of Caesar because we felt that was the central image of the play. We visualized Caesar coming into the center of the performance space, turning slowly to look at everyone. The senators, who would be standing in the corner, would then begin to circle him with imaginary daggers behind their backs as rhythmic, drumlike music swelled. Finally, all of them would thrust forward and begin to stab him, with Brutus being last. There would be a long look of recognition between them; then Caesar would fall. This is where we began. Then, when we began looking for sound effects, we found a CD of famous speeches. This was the impetus for our underscoring of the political ramifications of the play. We chose speeches by presi-dents who had assassination attempts made on their lives.

On the day our group was to perform the essence of the play *Julius Caesar*, the desks were arranged around the perimeter of the classroom. A strobe light was taped to the ceiling over the center of the space. The lights were turned out, the strobe was turned on, and Caesar (in toga) walked to the center. As he stood center, we heard the voice of John F. Kennedy giving his "In Your Hands My Fellow Citizens" speech. All of the conspirators were in the corner with their backs turned. Then we heard Kennedy's "Ask Not What Your Country Can Do for You" speech and then "Let us Never Negotiate Out of Fear." At this point, a music selection from Manheim Steamroller's Album "7"—Chakra #1—began. Next we heard "Beware the Ides of March." Then, Brutus's speech about carving up Caesar was heard. At this point, the conspirators turned and faced Caesar. Franklin Roosevelt's voice said, "The only thing we have to fear. . . ." The conspirators started to circle Caesar slowly, with imaginary daggers behind their backs. In the background was the sound of a heart beating. The heartbeat became conga drums as the conspirators stepped forward to stab Caesar. There was a loud gong crash as Brutus stepped forward and stabbed Caesar—the other conspirators dropped to the floor. We heard, "Et tu, Brute," and Caesar fell. There was a howling wind as the conspirators walked away, leaving Caesar's body and Brutus. Brutus looked at his hands as Kennedy's voice gave his "Let the Word Go Forth" speech, followed by Roosevelt's "The Hand That Held the Dagger" speech, and last, Nixon's "I'm Not a Crook."

Though much performance art is done by solo artists, there are also group performances. Both solo and group performance artists intend to assault, move, arrest, or stun us. Shawn Stoner's performance art piece employed a group of performers whose intention was not to [re]produce a scene from *Julius Caesar,* but to draw parallels between the Roman world of the play and American political figures. It was a metonymic production.

In Chapter 1, we spoke of the differences between metaphoric and metonymic performances. Whereas metaphoric performances affirm, respect, or conserve the perceived integrity of a text; metonymic performances subvert, challenge, or transgress beyond this perceived integrity. Metonymic performances are readings against the grain—interpretations which are unorthodox, unexpected, or sometimes even weird. The same discussion applies to metaphoric and metonymic productions. Rather than a duplication of a text, metonymic directors alter the original text, often in an attempt to make it convey some personal, social, or political message. They tap into their right brain consciousness and free their imaginations to create new works or to make old works say new things.

Metonymic productions have become quite popular of late—especially with adaptations of the plays of William Shakespeare. Arguably the most metonymic of productions was Peter Brook's 1970 version of Shakespeare's *A Midsummer Night's Dream* which incorporated circus routines within a set that was a huge white box. The Lookingglass Theatre in Chicago presented a 90-minute adaptation of *Hamlet* using three actors and two hand puppets. *Hamlet! The Musical* was Second City's take on the play including pop culture and show tunes. Consider four films by Kenneth Branagh. His directorial debut was *Henry V* (1989) followed by *Much Ado About Nothing* (1993). Accounting for the changes that must be made when moving from one medium to another, both of these were metaphoric films in that they upheld the perceived integrity of the original texts. Branagh's next two films were both metonymic. His 242-minute (a shorter version was also released) film version of *Hamlet* (1996) was a newly unexpurgated script—a melding of the Folio and quarto texts—the first time that had been done. The film included glimpses of characters not dramatized in the play, such as Priam and Hecuba, and updated the story to the second half of the nineteenth century. Branagh's *Love's Labour's Lost* (2000) went in the opposite direction by including only approximately 25 percent of the original text, and turning it into a musical by having the cast sing such classics as "I Get a Kick Out of You" and "There's No Business Like Show Business." In his review of *Love's Labour's Lost*, *Chicago Sun Times* film critic Roger Ebert wrote that "Branagh here cuts and slashes through Shakespeare's text with an editorial machete." Ebert continues, ". . . by starting the action in 1939 and providing World War II as a backdrop, Branagh has not enriched either the play or the war, but fit them together with an awkward join."

These kind of performances and productions can be very exciting and thought provoking, but, as Ebert suggests, they must be handled with care. When engaged in creating a metonymic production, you should ask the same questions posed in Chapter 1 for metonymic solo performances: What critical stance am I assuming? What am I trying to say about this text and why? What new element of the text have I discovered? How can I turn that discovery into performance?

Class Exercise

Select a play that you have read and that you feel others in class might have read. Decide what you believe the theme of the play is—the essence or central idea of the play, not a plot summary. (For example, if the play you select is *The Glass Menagerie*, you could decide that the essence is "the frailty of the human spirit.") Then, find a way to present this essence to the class. You may employ any medium you desire, including mime, visual art, song, dance, slides, or any combination of these. When you are done, see if the class can determine what play you had in mind.

SUMMARY

This first half of this chapter explains the techniques involved in analyzing and performing various literary forms, including letters, diaries, essays, autobiographies, biographies, histories, children's literature, and postmodern literature.

Although letters, diaries, essays, autobiographies, biographies, and histories are considered nonfiction forms, they all contain a certain bias or perspective that dictates what we are told. Consider this special perspective as you prepare these forms for performance.

Children's literature—prose, poems, and plays—provides excellent material for performance. Be sure to select the best literature to perform, for example, Newberry or Caldecott winners. When you perform children's literature, you will find that vocal flexibility and a wide expenditure of gesture are often necessary. Be sure to consider your audience. Are you performing children's literature for children? adults? a mixed group? How will this affect your performance?

Postmodern literature disrupts, shocks, and surprises us. It breaks conventions and establishes its own rules. This literature challenges the interpreter and offers exciting opportunities for performance.

The second half of this chapter focuses on various performance styles, including the program performance, the media performance, personal narratives, and performance art.

The program performance combines literature on the same theme, by the same author, of the same literary style, or from the same literary period. The program performance is an exciting way to study a theme, author, literary style, or literary period in more depth.

The media performance combines literature and some other media element, for example, music, slides, video, film, photographs, illustrations, mime, and dance. Be sure when you use media elements that the media supplement the text and do not distract or take focus away from the literature.

The personal narrative is a story structured like a short story but composed by the performer based on his or her own experience. The personal narrative is a wonderful way to share family tales and keep our heritage alive.

Performance art is a way of presenting a variety of "texts" by eliminating the distinction between artist and creation. Many performance artists are interested in social change and, thus, have political agendas. Performance art is a way to unleash personal fantasies or stories and is an excellent vehicle for manifesting postmodern texts, among others.

Metaphoric performances or productions tend to uphold and respect the perceived integrity of the text, whereas metonymic productions tend to challenge or transgress beyond the "like" to the "similar to."

Notes

1. Wallace A. Bacon, *The Art of Interpretation*, 3rd ed. (New York: Holt, Rinehart & Winston, 1979), p. 418.
2. Ernest Rhys, ed., *The Diary of Samuel Pepys* with a note by Richard Garnett. (London; J. M. Dent & Sons, 1927), p. vii.
3. Bacon, *The Art of Interpretation*, p. 412.
4. Lee Gutkind, ed., *Creative Nonfiction* (Nutley, NJ: Creative Nonfiction Foundation, 1996), p. 1.
5. Shana Alexander, *Anyone's Daughter: The Times and Trials of Patty Hearst* (New York: Viking, 1979), p. 3.
6. Robert M. Post, "Interpreting Literature for Young Children," *Communication Education* 32 (July 1983): 285–91.
7. Ibid., p. 287.
8. Ihab Hassan, *The Dismemberment of Orpheus: Toward a Post Modern Literature*, 2nd ed. (Madison: The University of Wisconsin Press, 1982), pp. 267–68.
9. Marshall McLuhan, *Understanding Media: The Extensions of Man*, 2nd ed. (New York: New American Library, 1964), p. 64.
10. Ibid., p. 62.
11. Robert Scholes, "Afterthoughts on Narrative: Language, Narrative, and Anti-Narrative," in *On Narrative*, edited by W. J. T. Mitchell (Chicago: University of Chicago Press, 1981), p. 206.

12. Kristin M. Langellier, "Personal Narratives and Performance," in *Renewal & Revision: The Future of Interpretation,* ed. Ted Colson (Denton, TX: NB Omega Publication, 1986), p. 140.

13. Jeffrey Goldman, "Dancing with the Audience: A Conversation with Spalding Gray, Actor, Writer, Monologist, and Connoisseur of Neuroses," *Dramatics* 63 (November 1991): 24–29.

14. Gregory Battcock and Robert Nickas, eds., *The Art of Performance: A Critical Anthology* (New York: E. P. Dutton, 1984), p. ix.

15. Ibid., pp. x–xi.

16. Richard Schechner, *Between Theater and Anthropology* (Philadelphia: University of Pennsylvania Press, 1985), p. 311.

10

Your Role as Group Performer: Readers Theatre and Chamber Theatre

Pet. Marry, so I mean, sweet Katherine, in thy bed.   260
And therefore, setting all this chat aside,
Thus in plain terms: your father hath consented
That you shall be my wife; your dowry 'greed on;
And will you, nill you, I will marry you.
Now, Kate, I am a husband for your turn,   265
For by this light, whereby I see thy beauty,
Thy beauty that doth make me like thee well,
Thou must be married to no man but me.
For I am he am born to tame you, Kate,
And bring you from a wild Kate to a Kate   270
Conformable as other household Kates.

        Enter BAPTISTA, GREMIO, TRANIO.

Here comes your father. Never make denial;
I must and will have Katherine to my wife.
Bap. Now, Signor Petruchio, how speed you with my
    daughter?
Pet. How but well, sir? How but well?   275
It were impossible I should speed amiss.
Bap. Why, how now, daughter Katherine? In your dumps?
Kath. Call you me daughter? Now I promise you
You have show'd a tender fatherly regard
To wish me wed to one half lunatic,   280
A madcap ruffian and a swearing Jack,
That thinks with oaths to face the matter out.

270. wild Kate] F; wild Kat Fe-4.   271. S.D.] F (after l. 268).   Tranio] Q;
Tranio F.

Cf. Ado. i. i. 57-3, and Jonson,   274. how speed you . . . ?] How are
Cynthia's Revels H. & S. iv. i. 5.   you getting on?
247. Katherina implies that Petruchio   277. In your dumps?] Are you feeling
has no more than minimum wisdom.   depressed? A 'dump' was originally
264. will you, nill you] one way or   a mournful melody or song, though
another, willy-nilly OED. Will . . . .   little is known about them (there is a

Although this text focuses on the solo performer, one of the real pleasures of interpretation is working on a performance in a group. Readers theatre and chamber theatre are exciting forms of group performance that allow you to hone your solo performance skills. (For a more extensive study, consult the bibliography of selected texts at the end of this chapter.)

Group forms of interpretation usually involve two or more performers. (Exceptions to this are full-length, one-man or one-woman shows, which have enjoyed an increased popularity of late. On and Off Broadway, Lily Tomlin's *The Search for Signs of Intelligent Life in the Universe,* Whoopi Goldberg's one-woman show, which included satirical political routines as well as some straight drama, the recent exploration of Truman Capote called *Tru,* starring Robert Morse, Lonette McKee in *Lady Day at Emerson's Bar & Grill,* Phyllis Newman in *The Madwoman of Central Park West,* Zoe Caldwell in *Lillian,* Claudia Shear in *Blown Sideways Through Life,* and works by Anna Deavere Smith such as *Fires in the Mirror* are all experimental scripts which resemble readers theatre compiled scripts in their composition and presentation.) Whereas in solo interpretation a performer may be his or her own director, in readers theatre and chamber theatre there is usually an outside director—usually the person who arranged, compiled, or adapted the script. In addition, both these group forms are highly presentational. What do we mean by "presentational"?

Presentational productions are nonrealistic performances which depend on the audience's ability to participate by imagining elements that are only suggested. Presentational productions rarely attempt to depict reality or a realistic impression of life. In many of these types of productions, props are imagined, not literalized, and sets are synecdochic—employing a part to suggest the whole (for example, a twig represents a whole tree). Performers usually use offstage focus, which extends the dimensions of the stage to include the audience's active participation. *Presentational* is not a designation exclusive to readers theatre and chamber theatre, however, as the plays of the Greeks and Romans, medieval productions, and the plays of Shakespeare, Wilder, and Brecht, among others, as well as musicals all have presentational aspects.

In presentational productions, then, many elements break the conventions of representational (realistic) theatre:

1. Nondramatic literature (literature not originally intended for the stage) is often performed.
2. Performers primarily use offstage focus, addressing the audience and projecting scenes out front.
3. Performers may carry scripts, though this is not because they do not know their lines—scripts, if used, are used symbolically to suggest elements in the text.
4. Performers may play more than one role.

GHETTO—a presentational staging of the play by Joshua Sobol presented at Ball State University, directed by Judy E. Yordon. (Ball State University photo.)

5. Two performers (or more) may play the same role.
6. Spectacle elements are often suggested rather than literalized. The set is usually kept fairly bare: stools, music stands, boxes, platforms, and lecterns are often used, but often they are used symbolically to represent other things.
7. Actors are not necessarily type cast, which permits cross-gender performances and color-blind casting.

EXPERIMENTAL GROUP PERFORMANCE POSSIBILITIES

As we stated in Chapter 1, the field of interpretation is growing tremendously, in terms of what we perform and how we perform it as well as how we create scripts and the kinds of "texts" that may be included in scripts. Traditional readers theatre and chamber theatre deal primarily with literary texts. But authors may develop experimental scripts from a variety of sources other than literary texts. Many of these experimental scripts are primarily based on oral expression, and many do not begin with a prepared script but with what may be called everyday life performances. If you wanted to record the experiences of artists, coal miners, railroad engineers, ministers, or farmers, for example, you could do field research and make tape and/or video recordings to document the personal histories of these people. Then you could transcribe, edit, and structure the material into script form. You could also study a particular culture or minority group and turn the results of that ethnographic study into a performance. These scripts feature the "other"—the subject of the script—and help us to appreciate and become more aware of various cultures and lifestyles. Oral narratives may be taped, transcribed, and presented as a way of understanding the stories of the "other." Scripting of these stories can benefit from the study of narrative fiction—of how stories are structured—and by the chamber theatre techniques outlined in this chapter.

Other experimental scripts feature everyday conversations. These scripts transcribe real-life conversations to study the subtleties of spontaneous discourse and the reality of how we communicate with one another. Many of these scripts are developed in rehearsal as cast members improvise from a core idea or refine gathered materials. Useful information on how to develop these types of experimental scripts may be found in the following: Ron Pelias's *Performance Studies: The Interpretation of Aesthetic Texts*, Elizabeth C. Fine's *The Folklore Text: From Performance to Print*, John Heritage and J. Maxwell Atkinson's *Structures of Social Action: Studies in Conversation Analysis*, Bryan K. Crow's "Conversational Performance and the Performance of Conversation" in *The Drama Review* 3 (1988), and Judy E. Yordon's *Experimental Theatre: Creating and Staging Texts*. In short, you are limited only by your imagination in creating and presenting group productions.

As we already stated, the focus of this chapter is on traditional readers theatre and chamber theatre (although elements of experimental production forms could be included within traditional scripts). Traditional readers theatre stages literature of all kinds; oral as well as literary texts may be included. Chamber theatre stages primarily prose fiction texts. Figure 10.1 shows the relationships among readers theatre, chamber theatre, and traditional theatre in terms of the types of "texts" staged.

Readers Theatre

Readers theatre is a flexible, creative medium for presenting all kinds of literary texts. (There are variant spellings of this group form of performance—most commonly *reader's theatre*—but *readers theatre* is the most accurate, as it is not a theatre for one reader but a theatre for all readers and it is not a possessive term.)

Readers theatre productions are presentational, and, therefore, are staged in such a way as to incorporate the audience's ability to imagine. In recent years, the popularity of readers theatre has grown tremendously; some pieces, like *Cats*, a compilation of poems by T. S. Eliot, appear on Broadway. In professional theatre, the

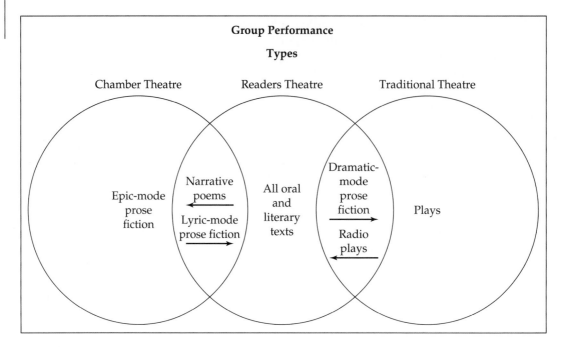

Figure 10.1

staged reading—a kind of readers theatre—of a new play is often done to give potential directors, producers, backers, and the playwright an opportunity to hear how the play sounds and flows.

Students enjoy acting in readers theatre productions because they have an opportunity to present rarely performed texts and because readers theatre offers interesting challenges to the performer. Script creators usually double as directors. They enjoy the creative challenge of writing and staging "original" scripts which empower the creator to assume the role of "author." Let us briefly look at the conventions of traditional readers theatre.

The earliest readers theatre productions made almost no use of spectacle or movement and were very formally staged. Readers—formally attired—often sat on stools behind music stands or lecterns and read from manuscripts. We have experimented much since those early productions. Readers theatre practitioners now believe that there must be some visual appeal for present-day theatre audiences, and they successfully employ spectacle and special effects. Staging underscores the particular text being performed, and manuscripts are often discarded. Today's readers theatre productions pose a dual responsibility on readers theatre directors. They must make sure that the *readers* keep the text as the featured[1] element of the production. However, they must also keep the *theatre* in readers theatre in mind.

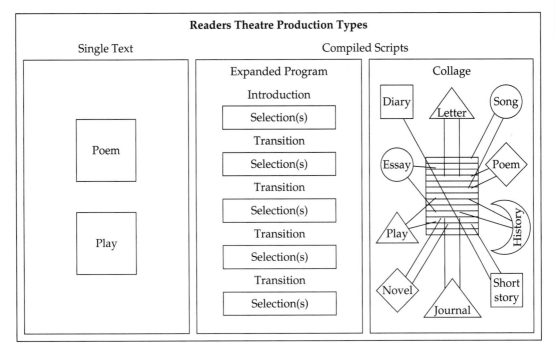

Figure 10.2

Figure 10.2 illustrates three traditional readers theatre production types: single text, expanded program compiled script, and collage compiled script.

There are essentially two kinds of readers theatre compiled scripts. The first is the expanded program where materials are gathered together by some common bond, but each selection maintains its original context and remains an identifiable unit. The "seams" show where one selection ends and the next begins. In collage[2] compiled scripts, each selection or part of a selection becomes part of a new context and usually seams do not show. Let us first discuss the single text production.

Single text production

One way to begin experimenting with the readers theatre form is to work on a group performance of a single text. Poems—even poems that seem to have only one speaker—may be creatively orchestrated for group performance based on any number of considerations. Depending on the type of poem you are working with, there are many creative ways to divide the lines among performers. On the most basic level, if you are working with a modally epic poem, the narrator may take the narrative lines and the characters may take the dialogue lines. If you are working with a dramatic text with more than one speaker, give each speaker his or her own lines to say. If you are working with a dramatic text with only one speaker, such as "My Last Duchess" by Robert Browning, see if you can hear different voices within or suggested by the Duke's language. Could you, for example, divide lines based on different attitudes the Duke projects? Could you divide lines based on the manifestation of the Duke's anima versus animus? Could you divide lines based on what the Duke plans to say, and what just slips out? Could you divide the lines among the various characters mentioned by the Duke (Fra Pandolf, the last Duchess, the Count, the Count's emissary, the Count's daughter)? Line divisions will, of course, be based on your interpretation of the poem, but possibilities are limitless. If you are working on a lyric text, you have a variety of ways to divide the lines. You could divide lines based on varying image structures, sound patterns, or attitudes, for example. Look at the way the following poem has been divided between two voices (male and female) to indicate the ending of a relationship.

A BOOK OF MUSIC   Jack Spicer

Both: Coming at an end, the lovers
           Are exhausted like two swimmers. **Her:** Where
           Did it end? **Him:** There is no telling. No love is
           Like an ocean with the dizzy procession of the waves' boundaries
           From which two can emerge exhausted, **Her:** nor long goodbye
Both: Like death
           Coming at an end. **Her:** Rather, I would say, like a length of coiled rope
Him: Which does not disguise in the final twists of its lengths
           Its endings.
 Her: But, you will say, we loved
Him: And some parts of us loved
 Her: And the rest of us will remain
Both: Two persons. **Both** (him echoing her): Yes
           Poetry ends **Both** (together, sharply): like a rope.

"A Book of Music" by Jack Spicer from *The Collected Books of Jack Spicer* © 1975 by the Estate of Jack Spicer, by permission of Black Sparrow Press.

Often plays are staged in the readers theatre format. Many of the earliest readers theatre productions were plays staged using the conventions of economy and suggestion. When you stage a play, you must be careful in selecting the play; your choice must benefit from being staged in a readers theatre format. Usually a play which makes its primary appeal to the ear is a good one for readers theatre. Radio plays are good, as are plays which cannot successfully be staged in conventional theatre because they require either too many sets or too many performers. Since

84 CHARING CROSS ROAD—a presentational production of the novel by Helene Hanff presented at Ball State University, directed by Gilbert Bloom. (Ball State University photo.)

readers theatre emphasizes the audience's participation in the creation of the scenes, plays too demanding in the area of special effects and spectacle elements can be successfully done in readers theatre. We often underestimate the audience's ability to imagine. Some plays easily done in readers theatre style are *Equus, Our Town, The Elephant Man, Amadeus,* most of the plays of Bertolt Brecht and William Shakespeare, and Dylan Thomas's *Under Milk Wood.* In the program note for a production of the Thomas "play for voices," the director wrote:

> This production of *Under Milk Wood* is being staged in a presentational style called readers theatre. Readers theatre is a group form of interpretation which stresses economy and suggestion of character and action. In keeping with these conventions, the sixty-three inhabitants of the town of Milk Wood will be presented by eight actors and actresses. Through vocal and physical suggestion, these eight performers present characters whose interactions exist essentially in your imagination. Readers theatre has been called "the theatre of the mind" because of the active participation asked of each audience member. The audience members are asked to create each separate character and locale

in their minds, and to visualize, for example, a bench as a bed, tombstone, or bucket. No illusion of a real town is attempted; the audience members are free to imagine their own Milk Wood.

The expanded program

A second type of readers theatre script is the expanded program compiled script. *Compile* means "to put together" or "to juxtapose" texts. In this type of production, performers can investigate a theme, the works of an author, or a literary style or period in more depth than a solo performer can. Once again, the purpose might be to entertain, inform, shock, activate, or persuade, and the audience who attend the production should be considered when the script is prepared. As with the solo program performance, selections are usually presented with an introduction and narrative transitions which are generally drawn from research into the author's life, works, and writing style. The expanded program often employs simple staging, and as always, the emphasis is on the literature being performed.

Here are examples of expanded programs and formats to give you an idea of the variety of possibilities.

Thematic Program   "Save the Whales." This was a production intent on changing the audience's mind regarding the senseless slaughter of whales. The creator used numerous media forms, and the production was staged with the audience onstage and the actors surrounding them.

"How Do I Love Thee." Portraits of Elizabeth Barrett and Robert Browning using poetry, drama, and letters. The famous title sonnet became the pair's marriage vows.

"The Gladdest Things in the Toyroom." This production analyzed the theme of marriage: why people get married and what happens when a marriage goes sour. The material was from R. D. Laing's book *Knots,* May Swenson's book *Iconographs,* and concrete poetry.

Single Author Program   *Twain by the Tale.* This is a professional script, compiled by Dennis Smee and available through a publisher (Bakers Plays), which features the works of Mark Twain.

"The Mystery and Manners of Flannery O'Connor." This is a collection of the works of this Southern writer showing primarily her preoccupation with religion and her Southern life-style.

Literary Style or Literary Period Program   "Love Sonnets." This is a survey of the sonnet form from Shakespeare to E. E. Cummings.

Story Theatre. This is a professional script written by Paul Sills which includes the improvised telling of favorite fables and is available through a publisher (Bakers).

"Genius, Grace, Correctness: Topics in Restoration and Eighteenth-Century Literature." This is a study of the literature of the period mentioned in the title and focuses on John Locke, John Dryden, Joseph Addison, and John Bunyan.

The collage script

The collage compiled script is the newest and perhaps the most challenging type of traditional readers theatre form—both for the performers and for the compiler-director. As earlier stated, in an expanded program, each literary selection is a recognizably separate part of the whole. Each selection is usually read in its entirety, when possible, with introductory and transitional material provided to show how selections relate to each other and to the program's theme. In a collage compiled script, however, often only fragments of literary selections are used: a stanza from a poem, a few paragraphs from a short story or novel, a newspaper headline, a diary entry, a few lines of dialogue from a play, and so forth. The compiler-director, then, may choose any type of literature as source material: prose fiction, essays, drama, poetry, letters, diaries, newspapers, song lyrics, journals, interview transcripts, and each is recognized only as a part of the greater whole. The audience should not be concerned with individual selections by individual authors; they should be concerned with understanding the script's overall theme or message, to which each selection contributes. The selections or fragments of selections work together as though there were only one source, and the script flows seamlessly revealing the compiler's intention.

When you create a collage compiled script, the first thing is to choose the theme or idea you wish to convey. As with the thematic extended program, many themes are available: love, death, hate, war, loneliness, insanity, holidays, relationships, and so on. Once you have selected a theme, narrow it down and decide on the particular assertion or hypothesis you want to investigate, just as for the solo program performance. Then, after you have selected your theme and narrowed its scope, determine your specific purpose (to entertain, inform, or persuade) and begin to gather materials. Gather more than you will need. It is easier to eliminate selections or parts of selections than to search for and add more later.

Once you have collected enough literature, analyze, edit, arrange, and rearrange the materials so that your attitude toward your theme is clear. Although you must strive to maintain your perceived intent of the source material as much as possible, you can put the source material into a larger context that may change or widen its dimensions. Occasionally, a selection may be understood more clearly when it appears in a new context within a collage script. Emily Dickinson's poem "It Sifts from Leaden Sieves," for example, is ambiguous and depends almost entirely on the reader's decision as to what the "It" of the title refers. In one compiled script on madness, this poem was included within a cutting from Conrad Aiken's short story "Silent Snow, Secret Snow." This story employs snow as a metaphor for a young boy's increasing madness. When the Dickinson poem was included in this new context, the "It" lost its ambiguity as the character in the story spoke this poem to describe his new world of snow.

As you gather materials, consider the eventual modal classification of your script. A modally lyric script focuses on the investigation of one man or one woman. A lyric-mode collage script could also be a biographical investigation of a famous person. The cast could represent a part of this man or woman's mind, past, present, or future. A dramatic-mode script centers on individualized characters who are involved in some sort of conflict situation. A script which is epic in mode contains both a narrator and characters. Modally epic scripts feature a narrator who tells a story and usually include defined characters.

Probably the most difficult aspect of the collage script is deciding on a structural format for linking all the pieces of literature together. Structure is what gives the content of your script form and definition. When you are considering structure, you can look toward three broad areas for assistance: composition structure (the way in which literature is put together), speech structure (the way in which a speech is put together), and music structure (the way music is composed).

Composition Structure Among the plots of short stories, novels, plays, and narrative poems, two types of structures are most common: causal structure and contingent structure. (Review the information on plot structures in Chapters 6 and 7 of this text.)

In causal structure, B happens because A happened, and C happens because B happened. In other words, all events in the story, play, or poem can be traced back to an incident that has already occurred. Most causal plots follow the order we cited earlier: exposition, development of conflict, crisis, resolution of conflict, climax, and denouement. With this type of structure, the audience is able to follow the cause-effect relationship and the logical flow of your argument. Use this type of structure for compiled scripts which are basically narrative in nature.

The contingent structure can be used when you do not want to emphasize logical or causal connections between phenomena. This type of structuring often involves associative moments common to stream-of-consciousness literature, such as the works of Virginia Woolf and James Joyce. In the fiction of these writers, incidents happen and thoughts are triggered from no apparent cause or motivation. An idea in a character's mind triggers another seemingly unrelated idea which then triggers another, and so on. When you daydream, you often engage in free association, that is, you let your mind flow from one idea to another seemingly without any outside stimulus. James Thurber's short story "The Secret Life of Walter Mitty" is full of free association as Mitty allows noises or happenings in the real world he feels trapped in to transport him to the fantasy world he prefers.

With the contingent structure, you may start with A, then go to C, then to F, then to B, then back to A again. There is structure, but the structure is not the causal structure we are primarily accustomed to. Ideas relate to each other, but not in a logical, narrative connection. Many lyric-mode scripts of an abstract nature have contingent structures. Use this type of structure when you want to investigate the seeming randomness of everyday life, an abstract idea, or show the complexity of the human mind.

Speech Structure   Speech composition formats provide additional structures for compilation scripts. For a basically informative script, you may want to try this pattern: (1) introduction, (2) preview of main points, (3) body, (4) review of main points, and (5) conclusion.

Use expository literature in the introduction, and then write the preview of the script's main points, or take sections from the material in the body of the script to use in the preview. Most of the literary selections go into the body of your script, and the main points are repeated again in the review. You could save a selection that capsulizes the theme for the conclusion.

For a script with a rhetorical or persuasive intent, try this structural pattern, called Monroe's Motivated Sequence: (1) attention, (2) need, (3) satisfaction, (4) visualization, and (5) action.[3]

The attention step introduces your theme and attempts to capture the audience's interest. The need step attempts to show the audience that there is a difficult problem to be solved. The satisfaction step proposes a solution that will satisfy the need and alleviate the problem. The visualization step tries to show the audience how much better off they will be if your solution is put into effect or how much worse off they will be if it is not put into effect. The action step gives specific information as to what this particular audience can do to effect change. (The song "Trouble" in the musical *Music Man* follows the Motivated Sequence structure.)

Music Structure   The last kind of organizational structure is borrowed from musical formats. Music provides four kinds of structures: sonata, rondo, theme and variation, and antiphonal.

The sonata form is the basic life pattern: (A) we are born, (B) we live, and (A) we die. You could also describe the sonata form as beginning with Exposition, then Development, and ending with Recapitulation. With this format, you begin with the major idea (A) and then develop a related but different or contrasting idea (B). At the end of the script, you come back to the main idea (A), but it is usually different or at least changed (A´) because of what happened in the developmental stage (B). For example, in A, a newly married couple starts married life, full of idealistic dreams for the future. In B, the script examines some of the realities and decisions this married couple must face. In A´, you could show that the married couple has developed a new understanding and sees the future more realistically or has decided not to stay together, depending on your assertion.

The rondo form follows the ABACADA (and so forth) pattern. With this form, you begin with A, the main idea, then offer new or contrasting ideas on the A theme, and alternate these ideas throughout the script. If, for example, you compile a script on the Great Depression, your A or main statement could be: The Depression helped some people, but hurt others—*crash.* Your B, C, D, and so forth, could be examples from literature showing characters who were hurt and others who were strengthened through or even benefited from their experiences in the Depression. Your A will be a repetition or restatement of the initial A, ending each time with the word *crash*—signifying the stock market crash of 1929. A variation of the rondo is the augmented script. With augmented scripts, you begin with one recognizable text (e.g., the Bible, the Gettysburg Address, the preface to the Constitution, a well-known song, a soliloquy from *Hamlet,* and so on) that specifically relates to your theme, and you "augment" it or make it larger by interweaving lines from other texts within the original text. The original text is the A, and the lines from other texts are your B, C, D, etc.

The theme-and-variation format presents the theme at the beginning of the script and then offers variants on the theme throughout the production. Your initial theme might involve the conventional marriage. You might then show variations on this theme by using literary selections, song lyrics, diaries, and newspaper articles that depict alternatives to conventional marriage: communal living, persons living together outside of marriage, gay couples, extended family living, and so forth.

Antiphonal patterns follow the ABABAB format. This format usually involves an argument involving two conflicting points of view. For example, your A literary selections could involve characters who have opted to go to college; your B selections could involve characters who have opted to go to work rather than to college. The A and B sections alternate, with each side presenting its point of view. Within each A and B section, you may use one or many different literary selections, so compilation may be needed within each A and B unit as well as the script as a whole. When dealing with the antiphonal pattern, deciding whether to finish with the A or B argument can be very significant.

Once the collage compiled script is structured, the compiler-director must then orchestrate the script. Orchestration involves deciding who will take each line. One way to do this is to divide the script into attitudinal voices. How many performers you cast will depend upon the number of attitudes or individual characters represented in your finished script. If, for example, your theme is the draft, one character (or attitude) could be in favor of the draft, one could be against it, one could be apathetic, and one could be a flag-waving patriot. As you go through your script to orchestrate it, you label each line depending on its attitude toward the draft. In addition to attitudinal voices, there are other ways to orchestrate your script. You could decide to create atmospheric voices (wind, rain, ghosts, creaking noises, and so on), qualities (death, love, romance, religion), or nonhuman speakers (train, computer, robot, animals), among others.

Once the script is orchestrated, the compiler-director must stage the production in the best way possible to make the unique statement clear. In staging, remember

JANE EYRE—a chamber theatre adaptation of the novel by Charlotte Brontë presented at Ball State University, adapted and directed by Judy E. Yordon. (Ball State University photo.)

that the primary appeal is usually auditory, focus is normally depicted offstage, no literal entrances or exits need be used, and economy and suggestion are usually necessary. This does not mean, however, that performers must remain static. The production should be staged so that the physical element of the production underscores the vocal. Deviate from these conventions to best meet the demands of your script.

Chamber Theatre

The second type of group production form is called chamber theatre. Chamber theatre was defined and developed in the early 1940s by Robert S. Breen of Northwestern University. Breen developed this form of narrative theatre as a vehicle for the staging of narrative fiction—short stories and novels. Since Breen defined the form, it has become very popular and chamber theatre productions (though not often designated as chamber theatre productions) have appeared all over the United States and Europe. A chamber theatre production of *Grapes of Wrath*, adapted and directed by Frank Galati, a student of Breen's, made a successful appearance on Broadway. Both the production and the director won Tony awards. Galati's new adaptation of E. L. Doctorow's novel *Ragtime* made it to Broadway. *Nicholas Nickleby* was also a successful chamber theatre adaptation of the novel by Charles Dickens. Steppenwolf Theatre Company in Chicago has distinguished itself in the production of original adaptations of novels. Galati's adaptation of *Grapes of Wrath* was originally produced at Steppenwolf, as well as excellent productions of Burgess's *A Clockwork Orange,* Faulkner's *As I Lay Dying,* and Vonnegut's *Slaughterhouse-Five.* An inspired production of *Dr. Jekyll and Mr. Hyde* played in London, and toured throughout the United States. The musical *Seussical* is an adaptation of stories by Dr. Seuss.

In a chamber theatre production, the nature and behavior of the narrator, his or her reasons for and manner of telling the story, are the central and major concerns. The narrator's point of view is the controlling element to consider in the adaptation process and in the staging of the story. Narrators who refer to themselves as "I" behave and interact in a different manner from narrators who show and tell their stories from the third-person perspective.

As we stated in Chapter 6, most prose fiction works are written in the past tense and in the epic mode. The director of a chamber theatre production should consider the temporal mode of the story and decide if there is a difference between the virtual-present *telling* of the story and the virtual-past *showing* of the remembered events. Whereas most plays are written in the present tense and project the illusion of a witnessed event, most prose fiction is written in the past tense and projects the illusion of vicarious experience. The remembered scenes must be presented through the narrator's point of view: we are not seeing events as they happen.

Prose fiction written in the epic mode is best suited to chamber theatre, as the strong relationship between narrator and characters representative of epic-mode literature is what chamber theatre attempts to feature. The director of a chamber theatre production is guided by the narrator's attitude toward and relationship with each character when staging. The narrator shows his or her personal bias by moving close to or staying far from the characters in the story and, in the case of omniscient or observer narrators, by assuming any one of a variety of roles: director, moralizer, puppeteer, camera-eye, reporter, double, alter ego, sympathizer, or judge, among others. To clarify the epic mode in performance, the narrator can use offstage focus when telling the story and have the characters use onstage focus when reliving the virtual-past scenes. This combination of offstage and onstage focuses emphasizes the tensiveness in epic-mode literature and often heightens the conflict within the story.

When turning a story into a chamber theatre script, you do not rewrite the story or change the tense or the point of view. You adapt what is there for dramatic presentation by deciding who will say each line or part of each line. Epic-mode lines—lines that further the plot line—are usually taken by the narrator and delivered using offstage, open focus. Dramatic-mode lines—dialogue—are taken by the characters using onstage focus. Lines written in the lyric mode pose the most problems for adaptors. A lyric-mode line written from the narrator's perspective and in the narrator's vocabulary and syntax is usually said by the narrator using offstage, open focus. Lyric-mode lines written from the character's perspective and in the character's vocabulary and syntax are usually said by the character and delivered with inner-closed focus (to self), open focus (to audience), or closed focus (to another character), depending on the line. Characters say these lines as written, *even though they may be speaking about themselves in the third person and in the past tense.*

Though these modal distinctions will help you begin the adaptation process, you are likely to come across lines that cause problems. As you go through a prose fiction work, you should ask yourself on any given line, From whose perspective is this line? Whose vocabulary and syntax are represented? Let this information help you in making line divisions.

A sample chamber theatre adaptation of "The Open Window"

A sample script may make this discussion of line divisions in chamber theatre clear to you. The following script is an adaptation of the story we analyzed in Chapter 6, "The Open Window." Look at this adaptation and compare it with the original story to see how the story was transformed into a chamber theatre script.

THE OPEN WINDOW   Saki (H. H. Munro)

Adapted for Chamber Theatre
by Judy E. Yordon

Stage empty except for Narrator. Framton knocks on door at left. Narrator answers door, removes Framton's hat and coat and hangs them up, asks his name, receives Framton's letters of introduction, and seats him in chair stage left. Framton seems nervous and uneasy. Narrator stands above Framton as Vera enters left. Narrator hands her letters of introduction which she hastily scans and returns to narrator.

Vera:	My aunt will be down presently, Mr. Nuttel; in the meantime you must try and put up with me.
Narrator:	*(to audience)* Framton Nuttel endeavoured to say the correct something
Framton:	*(to Narrator)* which should duly flatter the niece of the moment
Narrator:	*(to Framton)* without unduly discounting the aunt that was to come. *(He steps down to talk to the audience.)* Privately he doubted more than ever whether these formal visits on a succession of total strangers would do much towards helping the nerve cure which he was supposed to be undergoing.

(Framton's sister, who has been hiding behind Framton's chair, appears and stands above Framton.)

Sister: I know how it will be

Narrator: his sister had said when he was preparing to migrate to this rural retreat;

Sister: you will bury yourself down there and not speak to a living soul, and your nerves will be worse than ever from moping. I shall give you letters *(She drops letters on Framton, which the narrator picks up and puts in his pocket.)* of introduction to all the people I know there. Some of them, as far as I can remember, were quite nice. (Sister exits off right.)

Framton: *(to no one in particular)* Framton wondered whether Mrs. Sappleton

Narrator: *(To audience)* the lady to whom he was presenting one of the letters of introduction

Framton: came into the nice division.

Vera: Do you know many of the people round here? *(to the audience)* asked the niece, when she judged that they had had sufficient silent communion.

Framton: Hardly a soul. My sister was staying here, at the rectory, you know some four years ago, and she gave me letters of introduction to some of the people here. *(Narrator hands Framton one of the letters of introduction which Framton hands to Vera.)*

Vera: Then you know practically nothing about my aunt? *(Vera does not look at the letter, takes it, and hands it to Narrator.)*

Framton: Only her name and address.

Narrator: *(to audience)* He was wondering whether Mrs. Sappleton was in the married or widowed state.

Framton: *(to Narrator)* An undefinable something about the room seemed to suggest masculine habitation.

Vera: Her great tragedy happened just three years ago, that would be since your sister's time.

Framton: Her tragedy?

Narrator: *(to audience)* Somehow in this restful country spot tragedies seemed out of place.

Vera: You may wonder why we keep that window wide open on an October afternoon. *(She points downstage center at an imaginary open window.)*

Framton: It is quite warm for the time of the year, but has that window got something to do with the tragedy?

Vera: Out through that window, three years ago to a day, her husband and her two young brothers went off for the day's shooting. They never came back. In crossing the moor to their favourite snipe-shooting ground they were all three engulfed in a treacherous piece of bog. It had been that dreadful wet summer, you know, and places that were safe in other years gave way suddenly without warning. Their bodies were never recovered. That was the dreadful part of it. *(She now loses her self-possessed note and becomes falteringly human.)* Poor aunt always thinks that they will come back someday, they and the little brown spaniel that was lost with them, and walk in at that window just as they used to do. That is why the window is kept open every evening till it is quite dusk. Poor dear aunt, she has often told me how they went out, her husband with his white waterproof coat over his arm, and Ronnie, her youngest brother, singing, "Bertie, why do you bound?" as he always did to tease her, because she said it got on her nerves. Do you know, sometimes on still quiet evenings like this, I almost get a creepy feeling that they will all walk in through that window— *(She breaks off with a shudder. Framton is aghast.)*

Narrator:	It was relief to Framton when the aunt bustled into the room *(Mrs. Sappleton rushes in talking a mile a minute and making apologies to Framton as the Narrator talks to the audience.)* with a whirl of apologies for being late in making her appearance.
Mrs. Sappleton:	I hope Vera has been amusing you?
Framton:	She has been very interesting.
Mrs. Sappleton:	I hope you don't mind the open window, my husband and brothers will be home directly from shooting, and they always come in this way. They've been out for snipe in the marshes today, so they'll make a fine mess over my poor carpets. So like you menfolk, isn't it? *(Framton attempts to answer, but cannot. Mrs. Sappleton continues talking about the "scarcity of birds" and the "prospects for duck in the winter" as the Narrator speaks to the audience.)*
Narrator:	She rattled on cheerfully about the shooting and the scarcity of birds, and the prospects for duck in the winter.
Framton:	*(to Narrator, horrified):* To Framton it was all purely horrible.
Narrator:	*(To audience)* He made a desperate but only partially successful effort to turn the talk on to a less ghastly topic; *(Framton does try several other topics, the weather, his health, etc., while the Narrator speaks.)* he was conscious that his hostess was giving him only a fragment of her attention, and her eyes were constantly straying past him to the open window and the lawn beyond.
Framton:	*(To Narrator)* It was certainly an unfortunate coincidence that he should have paid his visit on this tragic anniversary. *(Framton turns to Mrs. Sappleton and raises his voice to gain her attention in an attempt to once more change the subject.)* The doctors agree in ordering me

	complete rest, and absence of mental excitement, and avoidance of anything in the nature of violent physical exercise.
Narrator:	*(To audience, with patient indulgence)* Framton laboured under the tolerably wide-spread delusion that total strangers and chance acquaintances are hungry for the least detail of one's ailments and infirmities, their cause and cure.
Framton:	On the matter of diet they are not so much in agreement.
Mrs. Sappleton:	No? *(She says this in a voice which only replaced a yawn at the last moment. We hear Ronnie say "Bertie, why do you bound," and we see three figures slowly coming out of the audience toward the open window.)*
Narrator:	Then Mrs. Sappleton suddenly brightened into alert attention— but not to what Framton was saying.
Mrs. Sappleton:	Here they are at last! Just in time for tea, and don't they look as if they were muddy up to the eyes!
Narrator:	Framton shivered slightly and turned towards the niece with a look intended to convey sympathetic comprehension.
Framton:	*(Looking at Vera)* The child was staring out through the open window with dazed horror in her eyes.
Narrator:	*(To audience)* In a chill shock of nameless fear Framton swung around in his seat and looked in the same direction. *(Framton crosses downstage to look out the open window.)* In the deepening twilight three figures were walking across the lawn towards the window;
Framton:	they all carried guns under their arms,
Narrator:	and one of them was additionally burdened with a white coat hung over his shoulders.
Framton:	A tired brown spaniel kept close at their heels.
Narrator:	Noiselessly they neared the house, and then a hoarse young voice chanted out of the dusk:
Voice One:	I said, "Bertie, why do you bound?" *(Framton runs to where Narrator has hung up his hat and coat, gathers them up, and the Narrator helps Framton make a quick exit out front door off right.)*
Framton:	Framton grabbed wildly at his hat and coat;
Narrator:	*(Coming downstage to look out the open window at Framton)* the hall-door, the gravel-drive, and the front gate were dimly noted stages in his headlong retreat. A cyclist coming along the road had to run into the hedge to avoid imminent collision.
Voice Two:	Here we are, my dear, fairly muddy, but most of it's dry. *(Mr. Sappleton addresses Narrator, who, we can surmise, assumes the role of the butler in the house.)* Who was that who bolted out as we came up? *(and before the Narrator can answer, while the Narrator is removing the men's soiled jackets)*

Mrs. Sappleton:	A most extraordinary man, a Mr. Nuttel, could only talk about his illnesses, and dashed off without a word of good-bye or apology when you arrived. One would think he had seen a ghost. *(Vera and Narrator exchange quick, knowing glances.)*
Vera:	I expect it was the spaniel. *(She speaks very calmly.)* He told me he had a horror of dogs. He was once hunted into a cemetery some where on the banks of the Ganges by a pack of pariah dogs, and had to spend the night in a newly dug grave with the creatures snarling and grinning and foaming just above him. Enough to make anyone lose their nerve.
Narrator:	*(to audience, with a smile)* Romance at short notice was her speciality.

The point of view of "The Open Window" is third-person limited omniscient. The narrator in this story is primarily omniscient with Framton and only slightly with the niece, Vera. In this adaptation, the narrator functions as a kind of butler in the house and exhibits a polite alliance with the guest, Framton. Consequently, the narrator and Framton share lyric lines and deliver lines to each other. The line "asked the niece, when she judged that they had had sufficient silent communion" is given to the niece to suggest that she and the narrator have a relationship and to keep the ending a surprise.

Staging in chamber theatre

When staging a chamber theatre production, you have two factors to keep in mind: the movements of the narrator in the virtual present and the movements of the narrator and the characters in the virtual-past scenes. As stated earlier, the narrator mediates between the audience and the scenes onstage and uses both onstage and offstage focus. The scenes in the virtual past are staged with onstage focus and resemble conventional theatre moreso than does the staging in readers theatre. Characters in the virtual-past scenes relate to each other in a manner similar to the way characters react in conventional theatre except that the narrator is in the scene, is often addressed by the characters, often addresses them, and may participate in the action. The narrator rarely stands off to one side; he or she becomes the major component of staging. Breen, creator of the chamber theatre technique, explains that the narrator should begin center stage and then move in accordance with his or her perspective. The narrator's point of view determines where he or she stands, whom he or she identifies with, how involved or uninvolved he or she is with the events related, and so on. Move the narrator close to or distant from characters to correspond with his or her sympathies. In addition, the narrator has a responsibility to the audience. Who does the narrator think this audience is? What does this narrator want or need from this audience? Why does the narrator tell this story to this audience? What response does the narrator hope to receive? Analyze the relationships the narrator has with each character as well as with the audience to determine staging.

Performers may make realistic entrances and exits, and may use costuming, lighting, set, set pieces, and props, if the narration does not make these elements clear. Often the description in a story or novel is so vivid that few spectacle elements are necessary to help the audience imagine the scene. Remember in your staging to consider both the locale of the narrator in the virtual present—if that locale is significant—and the locale of the virtual-past scenes. In "Why I Live at the P.O." by Eudora Welty, for example, although Sister, the narrator, is in the post office during the virtual-present telling of the story, the majority of the story occurs in her home. The post office might take very little stage space, whereas the home environment would dominate. Analyze setting, as often present and past locales are not the same, and both may need to be conveyed.

One of chamber theatre's major staging principles is *alienation.* Alienation is an element of presentational theatre and was used by Bertolt Brecht as an aspect of his epic theatre. Alienation devices are the devices used in a production to eliminate the illusion of reality. Brecht felt that the audience needed to be constantly reminded that they were watching a play. He wanted to prevent the audience from identifying too closely with any character because he often had a political or rhetorical point to make, and he wanted his audience to think and not get too emotionally involved. In chamber theatre productions, the actors are "presenting" the characters the narrator creates, and alienation helps achieve this effect. An alienation device is anything used in a production to draw attention to the artifice of the stage and away from verisimilitude. Chamber theatre often employs the following alienation devices, depending on the text and the director's concept:

1. Narrators and characters may carry scripts (however, the presence of the script is rare in most productions).
2. Narrators and characters may use offstage focus.
3. Narrators and characters may be bifurcated. (*Bifurcation* is the casting of two performers to play one role. This technique is often used to show the attitudinal, emotional, or psychological divisions within one person.)
4. Characters in a chamber theatre production often speak of themselves in the third person and in the past tense. This device shows the closeness between the characters and the narrator, alienates or separates the character from the experience, and underscores the sense that the performer is presenting, not being, the character.
5. Spectacle elements are often mimed or suggested.
6. Actors are usually not type cast, permitting cross-gender performances and color-blind casting.

THE SCARLETT LETTER—a chamber theatre adaptation of the novel by Nathaniel Hawthorne presented at Ball State University, adapted and directed by Judy E. Yordon. (Ball State University photo.)

Chamber theatre gives us a way to understand narrative point of view. The solo performer of prose fiction generally does not have much trouble projecting the dialogue in a story but often has problems performing the narrative passages. The solo performer is not always able to make summary and description as exciting or compelling as the dialogue—the scenic moments. The group performance of chamber theatre often solves this problem, because the narrator is played by an actor or actress whose role must be clarified. The director should usually cast the strongest performer in the important role of the narrator, and the director must give this person assistance in developing the narrator's unique personality and relationships with the other characters in the scene. In addition, the narrator, in conjunction with the director, must decide who the audience might be. The narrator must be able to find the best way to facilitate the general audience's transformation into the audience appropriate for this text. Descriptive and narrative passages that may have once seemed only long and tedious suddenly become clues in determining the narrator's personality and the audience's identity.

SUMMARY

There are two forms of group interpretation: readers theatre and chamber theatre. Both readers theatre and chamber theatre are presentational, nonrealistic forms of production which include the audience's imaginative participation as a scripting and staging principle. Readers theatre is the staging of all kinds of literature. Readers theatre productions emphasize the experience in the text and appeal to the audience's ability to imagine. There are three kinds of potential readers theatre scripts: single text, expanded program compiled scripts, and collage compiled scripts.

Chamber theatre, like readers theatre, is a presentational theatre form. Chamber theatre is the adaptation of prose fiction (short stories and novels) for the stage. Chamber theatre maintains the narrator as the central character, the past tense, and the epic mode in which most prose fiction is written.

SELECTED TEXTS ON (OR INCLUDING INFORMATION ON) GROUP INTERPRETATION

Bacon, Wallace A. *The Art of Interpretation*. 3rd ed. New York: Holt, Rinehart & Winston, 1979, pp. 457–72.

Breen, Robert S. *Chamber Theatre*. Evanston, IL: Wm. Caxton, 1978.

Coger, Leslie Irene, and White, Melvin R. *Readers Theatre Handbook: A Dramatic Approach to Literature*. 3rd ed. Glenview, IL: Scott, Foresman, 1982.

Fine, Elizabeth C. *The Folklore Text: From Performance to Print*. Bloomington: Indiana University Press, 1984.

Haas, Richard, et al. *Theatres for Interpretation*. Ann Arbor, MI: Roberts Burton, 1976.

Kaye, Marvin, ed. *From Page to Stage: Selecting and Adapting Literature for Readers Theatre*. Garden City, NY: The Fireside Theatre, 1996.

Kaye, Marvin, compiler. *Readers Theatre: What It Is, How to Stage It and Four Award-winning Scripts*. Newark, NJ: Wildside Press, 1995.

Kleinau, Marion L., and McHughes, Janet Larsen. *Theatres for Literature*. Sherman Oaks, CA: Alfred Publishing, 1980.

Lee, Charlotte I., and Gura, Timothy J. *Oral Interpretation*. 9th ed. Boston: Houghton Mifflin, 1997, pp. 436–52.

Long, Beverly Whitaker; Hudson, Lee; and Jeffrey, Phillis Rienstra. *Group Performance of Literature*. Englewood Cliffs, NJ: Prentice Hall, 1977.

Maclay, Joanna H. *Readers Theatre: Toward a Grammar of Practice.* New York: Random House, 1971.

Yordon, Judy E. *Experimental Theatre: Creating and Staging Texts.* Prospect Heights, IL: Waveland Press, 1997.

Notes

1. Joanna Maclay speaks of "featuring the text" in *Readers Theatre: Toward a Grammar of Practice* (New York: Random House, 1971).
2. See Marion L. Kleinau and Janet Larsen McHughes, *Theatres for Literature* (Sherman Oaks, CA: Alfred Publishing, 1980), especially chapter 6.
3. Alan H. Monroe, *Principles and Types of Speech,* rev. ed. (New York: Scott, Foresman, 1939), pp. 208–23.

Appendix

CAREER OPPORTUNITIES IN PERFORMANCE STUDIES

It is our hope that your interest in interpretation/performance studies will continue once you have completed your college studies. What you learn in interpretation/performance studies classes and through involvement in extracurricular activities can help to prepare you for a variety of careers in many different fields. This is especially true now that the field of interpretation/performance studies has widened its definitions of (and consequently its interests in) "text" and "performance" to include considerations that touch many other fields of endeavor. This chapter focuses on some career possibilities for a student trained in interpretation/performance studies. As Louis E. Catron, professor of theatre at the College of William and Mary, put it, "Few people choose to set out on a difficult, demanding four-year course of [performance] study because it will make them good candidates for employment in other fields. But it will."[1] Although many of the careers we discuss require an advanced degree in interpretation/performance studies or training in a related area, they remain future possibilities for motivated students willing to spend time preparing themselves.

Students often ask, "What can I do with course work or a degree in performance studies?" In addition to the exposure to good literature and to the benefits of the performance experience which contribute to your total education, performance studies training prepares students not only for a professional career in performance but also for careers in related areas.

PROFESSIONAL CAREERS IN PERFORMANCE STUDIES

Although professional careers in performance studies continue to materialize rapidly, at present these careers are limited to two areas: teaching and professional performance.

Teaching Careers

Training in performance studies is beneficial in elementary, high school, and college classrooms. In the elementary classroom, the performance studies-trained teacher is able to use both solo- and group-performance techniques to become a more effective language arts teacher. The oral reading skills of elementary students are often neglected. Your knowledge of oral reading and your ability to help students understand what they read are invaluable skills. You will be able to help students bring expression to what they read as well. Oral performance improves silent reading skills and can also stimulate creative writing about literature. Kenneth Koch conducts poetry-writing workshops with elementary children and his success is partially attributable to his use of oral performance. In his two books *Wishes, Lies and Dreams* and *Rose, Where Did You Get That Red?* Koch suggests the use of children's oral reading to inspire creative writing. During a reading class, the performance studies-trained teacher may use dramatic performance to interest both the performer and the audience in the story, play, or poem under study. Students tend to remember the literature for a longer period of time, and they tend to learn more from the work as a result of their personal involvement.

Elementary teachers are often called upon to direct assembly programs. The teacher trained in performance studies can present a student performance hour, a program of performances on a theme, or a readers theatre or chamber theatre production, for example, as an assembly program. Few spectacle accoutrements are required for these types of productions, and the students gain experience in the performance techniques for different kinds of literature. The performance situation provides the student with a chance to develop poise, to improve diction and vocal and physical control, as well as to learn vicariously about the experiences of others. Performance allows students to engage in perspective taking—the opportunity to learn about others, including a variety of cultures and minority groups. In addition, participation in performance studies activities encourages a child's communication skills—both as a solo performer sharing literature with an audience and as a group performer working with classmates.

Testimonials to the effectiveness of performance studies in the elementary classroom abound. One innovative teacher began a readers theatre company at his elementary school. Lyndee Alton's company includes third-grade through eighth-grade students who love literature and performance. Alton believes that his students' participation in readers theatre has measurably improved their reading skills. Doris Haenny, an elementary school librarian, has been an enthusiastic supporter of readers theatre for elementary school students since she completed a readers theatre workshop. Haenny believes that readers theatre helps "elementary school children with reading skills, literature appreciation and their self-images."[2]

As you work with performance studies activities, you may want to try a bubble factory in your classroom.[3] A huge bubble is constructed and inflated to fit any space and is decorated to suggest the setting for a particular literary selection, for example. Students sit inside the bubble and become part of the scene. This experience helps students develop their imaginations in both oral and written expression.

There are many opportunities to use your performance studies skills in the high school classroom. High schools that do not offer a separate class in interpretation usually offer a unit on interpretation/performance studies in an English, theatre, or speech communication class (often handled by the same teacher in the same class).

Performance studies is easily integrated into the English classroom. Instead of only writing about literature, students perform the literary selections under study and share them with the entire class. This activity helps students to see their written analysis as a means to an end rather than as an end in itself. The dramatic presentation of their selections closely involves the students in literature and makes the classroom a stimulating and creative environment. When students are empowered to devise and support their own interpretation of a literary text, they begin to develop self-confidence in dealing with literature and are motivated to tackle more difficult selections. The fear of being "wrong" is eliminated, and students are encouraged to be more creative and experimental. In addition, students learn to work independently and to discover for themselves why a writer used this sound here and that image there. Literature becomes a more personal, human endeavor as students are trained to study the intertextuality of a selection. Through what personal texts do I read this text? How have my past experiences, interests, hobbies, and preoccupations influenced the way I view any text?

In the theatre arts classroom, where the student receives training in the art of acting, inclusion of a unit in performance studies is essential. In the acting class, the student develops sensitivity to the feelings, attitudes, and thought patterns of characters in plays. Performance studies not only helps acting students discover those feelings, attitudes, and thought patterns, but also helps them learn how to project these qualities. The solo performance of a scene from a play can be a valuable experience for the actor before taking on a role in that play. Solo performance helps the student-actor see the play as a whole, develop a concept for every character in the scene, and learn to create each character vocally, physically, and psychologically; it also gives the performer a chance to be his or her own director. This knowledge is invaluable when the student then tackles just one role in the play. The student comes to the role with a greater sense of the play as a whole and with a more informed sense of what the other characters in a scene think and feel.

In addition, the performance studies experience introduces the acting student to other kinds of literary texts as well as plays. The study of prose fiction and narrative point of view can assist the student when performing in many plays in which a character assumes a narrative role (for example, *Our Town, Into the Woods, Evita, Grapes of Wrath, Equus, Agnes of God, Nicholas Nickleby*). The study of poetry can help students prepare roles in verse plays like those of Maxwell Anderson or William Shakespeare.

In the speech communication classroom, performance studies activities provide variety in assignments, increase the speaker's self-confidence, improve poise, and give the student a chance to speak before a group without having to share personal feelings or ideas. This last advantage is one reason many public speaking teachers begin by assigning an interpretation performance rather than a public speech. Many beginning students suffer from reticence and are uncomfortable when they have to begin by composing and delivering their own speech. The performance techniques of the interpreter are similar to those of the public speaker, and participation in interpretation gives the public speaker a related performance experience.

Classroom teaching of performance studies offers related activities. Many states have forensic leagues which sponsor individual events tournaments. These tournaments often offer interpretation events. High school teachers trained in interpretation coach students in preparation for competition. Students may compete in events like dramatic interpretation (serious prose or drama), humorous interpretation (comedic prose or drama), poetry interpretation, interpretation analysis (performance plus explication), and dramatic duo interpretation (two interpreters perform a scene from a play). While the students compete, their coaches judge the interpretations of students from other high schools. As a coach, your responsibility is to help your students select, cut, analyze, and rehearse their selections and to give constructive criticism. As a judge, you are usually asked to write your reactions to each performance on a ballot, and the ballots are given to the students after the competition ends. Integration of performance studies with the speech communication, theatre, and English curricula is a definite benefit to the students. Interpretation makes drama students better performers and audience members, speech students better speakers and listeners, and English students more discerning readers.

Before you can teach performance studies on the college or university level, you will have to acquire an advanced degree. Many fine schools offer master's and doctor's degrees in performance studies. The additional coursework intensifies your study and prepares you to teach a variety of courses. In many colleges and universities, more than one course in performance studies is offered, and both solo performance and group performance are emphasized. College and university performance studies teachers must know the intricacies of performing prose fiction, poetry, drama, letters, diaries, histories, and nonliterary (oral) texts, among others, as well as have the directing skills to create and produce group productions, including readers theatre, chamber theatre, and ethnographic scripts.

If you are interested in teaching speech communication, English, or theatre on the college or university level, consider how performance studies can be integrated with these areas. Often interpretation units are included in speech communication classes as a way to help students use literature in public speeches, to help them develop an extemporaneous delivery style, and to help them understand the nature of speaker-audience relationships. In the English classroom, interpretation assignments can help bring literature to life and increase the student's understanding of speakers and their particular points of view. Actors and actresses must be able to interpret their roles, and they need the kind of close textual study that the interpretation experience provides.

Acting Careers

If you do not want to teach performance studies, you might decide that your interest is more in the area of professional performance. The opportunities in this area grow every day, and your chances depend on training, talent, luck, and determination. Your interest may lead you in the direction of either solo or group performance. The one-man or one-woman show is enjoying a resurgence both on and off Broadway. Actors who perform one-man or one-woman shows are solo interpreters. Performers like Hal Holbrook in *Mark Twain Tonight*, Vincent Price as Oscar Wilde in *Diversions and Delights*, James Whitmore as Harry Truman in *Give 'Em Hell, Harry*, Robert Morse as Truman Capote in *Tru*, Julie Harris as Emily Dickinson in *The Belle of Amherst*, Lily Tomlin in *The Search for Signs of Intelligent Life in the Universe*, Whoopi Goldberg in her one-woman show, which included satirical political routines as well as some straight drama, Eric Bogosian in *Pounding Nails in the Floor with My Forehead*, Lonette McKee in *Lady Day at Emerson's Bar & Grill*, Phyllis Newman in *The Madwoman of Central Park West*, Zoe Caldwell in *Lillian*, Claudia Shear in *Blown Sideways Through Life*, and Anna Deavere Smith in "Fires in the Mirror," "Twilight: Los Angeles, 1992," and "House Arrest" are skilled interpreters, able to embody literary and/or historical figures and encourage the audience's participation in the creation of the necessary spectacle elements. Interpretation also prepares you to compile or construct your own scripts.

Solo performers are popular on college campuses and offer shows on a variety of themes. If you enjoy solo performance, you can get your own show together on a theme or writer that interests you. (See John S. Gentile's *Cast of One: One-Person Shows from the Chautauqua Platform to the Broadway Stage*.) To survive as a solo performer, your first responsibility is to get the best training possible in interpretation. As you prepare your show, consider potential audience interest, as well as your own interests. Compose a flyer or a brochure to publicize your show and send the brochure to clubs, organizations, churches, sororities, and fraternities and to college, university, and high school speech and drama teachers.

The trained performer might also find a professional career in radio or television. Radio broadcasters can benefit from performance studies training, which helps them interpret a script written by someone else quickly and accurately. Radio and television students with a background in performance studies often seem more self-confident on the air or on camera, are more expressive and articulate, and do a better job reading copy. Careers in in-service workshops and in-service teaching are also possible, as well as making television commercials, radio dramas, and voiceovers.

If your interest is in professional group performance, many opportunities are available. Small theatres all over the United States experiment with diverse theatre forms, including readers theatre and chamber theatre–type productions. Small professional companies like the Peanut Butter Readers travel all over the United States performing shows for elementary and high school audiences. The Peanut Butter Readers offer workshops and training in interpretation in an attempt to foster an interest in experiencing literature through performance. A group called Theatre Voices has been in the commercial readers theatre business for over twenty years. Another group, "Script in Hand Company," is a readers theatre company, operating out of Brooklyn, New York. Chamber Repertory Theatre, out of Boston, Massachusetts, is a professional touring company that engages in national tours annually. They perform for students of literature, drama, and language arts, presenting such works as "The Tell Tale Heart," "The Necklace," and *The Legend of Sleepy Hollow.*

There are also companies that stage full-length chamber theatre and readers theatre productions and that hold open auditions. In Chicago, for example, there is a company called Novel Ventures which produces adaptations of novels only. In New York City a group of professional and amateur interpreters have united to form The Open Book—a company which performs readers theatre and chamber theatre productions for many different types of audiences. Their group has received recognition from professional actors and is now being sponsored by Jose Ferrer and Beverly Pemberthy.

The number of Broadway and off-Broadway productions which incorporate readers theatre and chamber theatre techniques in script and staging has increased enormously. Productions like *For Colored Girls Who Have Considered Suicide When the Rainbow Is Enuf, The Robber Bridegroom, The Elephant Man, The Belle of Amherst, Amadeus, Evita, Les Miserables, Chess, Into the Woods, The Grapes of Wrath, Miss Saigon, Dr. Jekyll and Mr. Hyde, The Secret Garden, Six Degrees of Separation, Ragtime,* and *Getting Out,* among others, include presentational staging, narrators, offstage focus, address to the audience, bifurcation, multiple casting, and suggested or mimed props and set pieces. Students trained in interpretation are able both to perform in productions of this nature and to compose and direct scripts for performance by others.

Performance Studies and Related Fields

In addition to professional careers, performance studies students can use their training in therapy-related careers, business-related careers, church-related careers, in the world of publishing, and in other related areas.

Therapy-related careers

Students trained to understand literature and the potential of the performance experience can often use this training to help others express and deal with their problems. Performance studies-related activities can be used with physically and mentally challenged persons, with aged persons, and with prisoners.

Work with Challenged Persons   There are many outlets for the interpreter's work with challenged persons. You can work as a teacher or as an activities therapist in schools, hospitals, or community centers. Working with literature can help challenged persons foster a positive self-concept, work productively with other members in group projects, and express their frustrations and joys through a character who may manifest similar characteristics. The physical limitations of physically challenged people do not inhibit their involvement in interpretation activities. Physically challenged persons can successfully participate in solo performance and in readers theatre productions, in chamber theatre productions, in radio plays, and in choral reading presentations. At Wright State University in Dayton, Ohio, for example, William Rickert, a professor of interpretation, works with challenged performers in readers theatre productions. He calls his group the Rolling Stock Company. Rickert believes that because readers theatre is such a flexible medium, it does not demand of challenged performers anything that they cannot give. Rickert is discovering that "handicapped performers can be powerfully expressive, and that the aesthetic stimulation and personal gratification from casting handicapped performers far outweigh any necessary practical accommodations."[4]

A major part of the diverse and complicated process of counseling, for example, is helping clients develop and maintain positive mental health. One technique to accomplish this is to "prescribe" certain poems to help individuals cope with specific feelings. In the case of a depressed client, for example, the trained therapist might recommend "On His Blindness" by John Milton. For a client dealing with the loss of a parent, Dylan Thomas's "Do Not Go Gentle into that Good Night" is a good choice. To treat a client experiencing anxiety, the therapist might recommend that the client read "The Road Not Taken" by Robert Frost which deals with coping with anxiety. By reading these poems, clients may gain insights into their own feelings. In addition, the reading—or performing—of various poems can convey to the clients that they are not alone—that others have had similar experiences, suffered from similar problems. Clients often find this knowledge comforting and healing.

Mentally challenged persons have as much appreciation of and love for literature as anyone else. They enjoy participating in a production as well as being part of an audience. Solo performance or participation in group production gives the mentally challenged person a sense of personal achievement. In addition, participation can improve reading skills and boost self-confidence. Group work can provide valuable communicative experiences. Donald Heady, a former professor at Ball State University, ran a Sheltered Workshop in Muncie, Indiana, where he worked with challenged performers in various dramatic activities. Heady believed that his doctor's degree in interpretation was tremendously beneficial in his work with developmentally disabled individuals. Heady said that "those who had previously found reading extremely difficult and remembered many negative experiences surrounding the study of reading, suddenly were able to achieve through 'performing' literature a whole new attitude toward the subject. Especially obvious has been their growth in speech skills as they prepare for performance."[5] The results of Heady's work are recorded in a film entitled *The Human Tree Players*, which is available from Ball State University and is distributed free by the National Committee: Arts for the Handicapped.

Work with Aged Persons   Students trained in performance studies have also worked successfully with aged persons. Mary Ann Hartman at the University of Maine–Orono pioneered this idea; Beth Hartman, her daughter, and Burton Alho of the University of Maine Equal Employment Office in Orono are continuing her work. Hartman and Alho work with nontraditional performers in oral history and interpretation. They use scripts orally composed by aged and challenged persons which are aimed at changing public policy. The elderly are a valuable source of stories, songs, and folklore that often remains untapped. Students who have majored or minored in performance studies are trained to tap this source of oral literature by recording these stories and songs and turning them into scripts. Don Heady, mentioned earlier, began a theatre group for the "fiftysomething" generation called the Third Age Theatre Company, now directed by Frank Gray of Ball State University. The scripts for this group include oral histories, letters, and oral narratives composed by group members. In addition to using these oral texts, Gray is especially interested in working with literature in which the elderly are the heroes or heroines. His group has successfully staged such books as Dr. Seuss's *You Are Only Old Once* and *In the Ever After: Fairy Tales and the Second Half of Life* by Allan B. Chinen. Every two years, Gray takes his Third Age Theatre cast members to the Senior Theatre Festival. Groups from all over the United States bring productions; many are compilation scripts composed of original stories and songs.

In addition to his work with children in the motivation of creative writing, Kenneth Koch has also worked with senior citizens. In a book entitled *I Never Told Anybody: Teaching Poetry in a Nursing Home,* Koch details how to work with the aged in the composition of poetry. Koch taught poetry writing at the American Nursing Home in New York City. He worked with twenty-five students ranging in age from seventy to ninety-five years and discovered that after barriers were overcome (some students were in continual pain, some were blind, some suffered from memory loss) the participants were very happy to write poetry. Koch's poetry-writing technique incorporates oral performance. He writes about his use of oral composition and oral performance in the preface to his book: "The students told us their poems aloud, and we wrote them down. . . . The students' hesitancy and fear were much alleviated by our encouragement and admiration. My reading the poems aloud at the end of each class was an important part of this. It helped them to see that what they wrote was poetry and could be talked about seriously and admired."[6] Interpretation-trained students can accomplish these same results by working with writers in nursing homes, Young Men's Christian Associations, Hadassah, community centers, and retirement communities, among others. Positions are available in many of these settings for performance studies-trained people, who record the oral literature of the aged members and turn the literature into scripts they can share with each other. Visits to such places as Greenfield Village in Dearborn, Michigan, and Conner's Prairie Settlement outside of Indianapolis, Indiana, also show how successfully older people can interpret literature. These places give "Living History" presentations in which members of the community dress as famous people—Thomas Edison, George Washington, a pioneer settler—and present dramatic interpretations of the history of the area for visitors. You can participate in such living history exhibitions, or you can help prepare other performers on a volunteer basis.

There are many opportunities for theatre-trained individuals to work with Elderhostel groups throughout the world. In 1975 Marty Khowlton, a social activist and educator, linked the European hosteling concept with the residential emphasis of Scandinavian Folk Schools and created a new kind of learning program for older adults. He called it Elderhostel, and although it began in America (there are programs in every American state), there are programs in every Canadian province as well as in over 70 foreign countries, and more than 2,300 educational institutions are involved. Elderhostel provides educational adventures for individuals 55 years of age or older in a variety of activities. Elderhostel groups need trained individuals to work with theatre classes, to accompany groups on theatre trips, and to present workshops, among other art-related activities. For more information about Elderhostel, write to Elderhostel Inc., 75 Federal Street, Boston, MA 02110-1941.

Work with Prisoners   As a student of performance studies, you can use your skills as an activities director in a prison. Activities therapy and poetry therapy, in particular, have been successfully integrated into prison programs. Trained individuals have brought in readers theatre and chamber theatre productions for the prisoners to witness and comment on, and students have worked with prisoners on their own performances and productions.

At Menard Psychiatric Center correction facility in Chester, Illinois, performance activities were successfully integrated into the prison program in the early 1970s. Leigh Steiner-Crane was the first person to be employed full time as an interpretation-trained therapist. Steiner-Crane used communication arts and interpretation performance to help the prisoners become more self-actualized. Prisoners at Menard wrote their own poetry and performed it, engaged in sociodramas, and participated in bimonthly performance hours. The prisoners were receptive to the therapy and increased their creative potential.[7]

In Arizona, performance studies professor David Williams successfully uses poetry with the prisoners in Arizona penal institutions. His students annually tour the Arizona State Prison and the Minimum Security Prison. In addition, the Arizona Center for Women has a company called Women's Entertainment Theatre which is funded by the Arizona Department of Corrections, the Arizona Commission on the Arts, and Project CULTURE (a project of the American

Correctional Association). Their production, "No Loser, No Weeper," which toured prisons throughout Arizona, was a compilation of poetry, original work, and music. Similar programs have started in North Carolina and in Kentucky, among other states.

These kinds of programs provide prisoners with an acceptable outlet for frustrations, anxieties, and other feelings. The programs are a part of a total rehabilitation program and give prisoners a chance to use their imaginations. If this type of activity interests you, look into starting an activities program at the prison closest to your general area, if a program does not already exist.

Business-related careers

If your area of interest is business, performance studies can also be of benefit to you. More and more the business world is appreciating the creative contributions of fine-arts majors. Richard Gurin, president and CEO of Binney & Smith, Inc., and a member of the National Alliance of Business, expresses a growing consensus among business leaders:

> After a long business career, I have become increasingly concerned that the basic problem gripping the American workplace is not interest rates or inflation; those come and go with the business cycle. More deeply rooted is . . . the crisis of creativity. Ideas . . . are what built American business. And it is the arts that build ideas and nurture a place in the mind for them to grow . . . Arts . . . programs can help repair weaknesses in American education and better prepare workers for the twenty-first century.[8]

John Brademas, in his "Remarks" before the American Council on the Arts Conference on "Arts Education for the 21st Century American Economy" in Louisville, Kentucky, on September 16, 1994, commented on the need for a connection between business and the arts because both are focused on "products" or "performance" or "both."[9] Qualities in fine-arts students that business people appreciate include a sense of self-discipline, ability to work under pressure, curiosity, wonder, satisfaction, an ability to create contexts for deeper messages, critical thinking skills, toleration for ambiguity, goal orientation, and an ability to take the initiative and to make nuanced judgments and interpretations.

In addition, to bringing your artistic skills into the traditional business world, you can, for example, be a cultural specialist within a business structure, helping a firm which has dealings with literary texts. In a book store, you can be responsible for ordering literature. In the newspaper business, your experience in performance studies qualifies you to write theatre or book reviews. In advertising and public relations, your skills at scripting materials can help you prepare advertising campaigns and adapt to specific audiences.

Students trained in performance studies can often work at improving employee communication skills in companies. Janet Elsea, president of Communication Skills, Inc., a Washington, D.C., consulting firm, has a doctor's degree in interpretation. She uses interpreters theatre techniques as a regular part of her work. Elsea runs an Effective Speaking Seminar, conducts workshops for employees of public broadcasting stations, and directs skill development programs. In each situation, Elsea uses her interpretation experience by asking participants to read aloud and role play. She also uses vocal exercises and scripting techniques adapted from traditional interpreters theatre practice. Because performers know about role playing, they are often able to help business people clarify interpersonal relations and perceptions. Interpreters, who are used to seeing the world through another's eyes, can help business people deal with others. Performance studies-trained individuals work for or run their own consulting companies, helping businesses improve their communication skills and strategies. Some of these individuals are John Korinek, Dale Ludwig, Eric Dishman, and Janet Larsen Palmer, who is the president of Communication Excellence Institute in San Dimas, California.

Religious careers

If your interest is religion, you will find performance skills invaluable in both composing and delivering sermons and in using group interpretation to dramatize Biblical parables, spiritual dramas, and related literature. One branch of interpretation called *hermeneutics* is the science of the interpretation of a Biblical text. If you have religious aspirations, a course in performance studies can help you write sermons and deliver them with enthusiasm, verve, and sense of performance. Some places of worship even look for trained persons to conduct presentations as part of a total liturgical program. Seminaries now offer degrees in religion and the arts and in worship and dance.

Productions are sometimes brought into services to make a Biblical text more dramatic and more personal. Instead of just hearing a sermon, the worshipers see one as well. Recently, a church brought in a readers theatre production which combined literature by Shakespeare, Kierkegaard, and Charles Schulz! As an interpreter in a church setting, imagine how you can bring the mysteries of salvation, the beauty and meaning of a parable, or a moment in the history of God's people to life through solo performance and group presentation. A temple recently requested that scenes from the Holocaust play *Ghetto* be staged as part of their Friday night service.

Publishing or sales careers

The world of publishing can use performance studies-trained students in at least two capacities: as editors of textbooks in the humanities and as salespersons.

Your knowledge of the structures of literature and of performance will be useful in editing and evaluating textbooks. One interpretation-trained student whom we know works for a publishing company in New York City as a freelance editor of theatre, English, and speech communication textbooks.

A background in performance studies will help you in sales. You might be a salesperson selling textbooks to college and university professors in the English, performance studies, theatre, and speech communication fields, for example. Your performance experience teaches you how to read a text for its basic ideas and structure. This information will help you present any textbook to potential buyers. Your performance experience should also help you give a more persuasive and enthusiastic sales presentation, in any area of sales.

ADDITIONAL CAREER POSSIBILITIES

Because performance studies is such a diverse area of study, your training provides useful experiences that apply to many different professions and careers. Some of these include creative writing, anthropology, recreation, and consulting.

Creative Writing

The close textual study of literature which the art of interpretation demands is excellent preparation for creative writers. Interpretation students study how language moves, how works are structured, how images and sounds enhance or underscore meaning, how rhyme and rhythm work to underscore sense, and so forth. These considerations are essential to a creative writer. Interpretation makes you look at literature in terms of the implied audience. Writers, too, write for a specific audience and can therefore benefit from the audience analysis that interpreters engage in. Writers skilled in the creation of original readers theatre or chamber theatre scripts now have an outlet for publication. Fireside Theatre sponsors an annual readers theatre scriptwriting contest. Winning scripts are published in Fireside Theatre's *Readers Theatre,* edited by Marvin Kaye, artistic director of The Open Book theatre company in New York.

Anthropology

Anthropologists engage in "observing, describing, and interpreting the diverse features of man."[10] Social anthropologists, in particular, study customs and behaviors of people exemplified in oral literature, folklore and myth, children's games, and religious ritual.

Performers are deeply interested in the oral tradition—our social and literary heritage. Before the advent of printing, literature existed exclusively in acoustic space, and "interpreters" were entertainers who composed and sang oral epic songs. We carry on that tradition today. Our interest in the oral tradition extends to the study of our own heritage (much of which is found in folklore and myths) as well as to ethnographic studies of other, less familiar groups. Today's performance studies students receive personal training in the preservation of this heritage. Since performance is now defined much more broadly than before, students are trained to perceive "performance" in everyday conversation, festivals, parades, political rallies, and so on, somewhat as anthropologists do. As Richard Schechner attests in *Between Theatre & Anthropology*, "If 'everyday life' is theatre, then people doing ordinary things are performers."[11] The study of the connections between performance and anthropology expands our knowledge of the other, and makes us more aware of how people interact in the everyday world. Schechner writes, "Whether practitioners and scholars of either discipline like it or not, there are points of contact between anthropology and theatre; and there are likely to be more coming."[12] Schechner posits possible research areas for those interested in both theatre and anthropology:

> To what degree are performers of rituals—the deer dancers of the Arizona Yaqui or the Korean shamans . . . aware of the performing-arts aspects of their sacred work? Also, what about large-scale performative events that cannot really be easily classified as belonging to either ritual or theatre or politics? I mean performances like the Ramlilas of northern India . . . and the Ta'Ziyeh passion plays of Iran. Is contact a one-way or even a two-way operation? Some anthropologists, Turner foremost among them, began "performing anthropology" . . . and some theater people, Peter Brook, Jerzy Grotowski, and Eugenio Barba, especially, explored . . . "theatre anthropology" . . . [13]

Performance studies students are trained to gather ethnographic information and preserve it. They are also trained observers of the performances of others. This information can be used to compile scripts based on oral literature. Jean Haskell Speer and Elizabeth Fine, performance studies professors, make folk literature and the translation from everyday "performances" to printed scripts their primary field of study. Their work in this area helps other interpreters know how to conduct interviews to gather oral literature, as well as how to transcribe from the oral mode to the print mode. Our training in the observation of human behavior and our interest in oral history makes us excellent potential social anthropologists.

Recreation

The integration of performance studies in recreational settings is relatively new, but it is growing in popularity. At some universities where recreational programs are strong, recreation majors often minor in performance studies to help them feel comfortable "performing" and to help them make presentations more lively. Recreational guides are often called upon to give tours of parks and facilities and to take campers on nature hikes. When they can use performance techniques or include literature in their presentations, the guides often achieve better results.

Consulting

Often performance studies-trained individuals are called upon to serve as consultants to help those who speak before large groups of people hone their skills. Business people, executives, salespeople, for example, are often called upon to make presentations. They can benefit from learning the skills of the performer. Recently, the Indiana Prosecuting Attorney's office called for performance studies students to work with new lawyers to improve their communication skills before juries. Performers who understand the nature of proxemics—how space communicates; know how to analyze goals, obstacles, and strategies; and know how to best use their voices and bodies to communicate effectively can serve as consultants in a variety of arenas.

Although many of the careers described in this appendix require advanced work (and often an advanced degree), this study has immediate rewards. For one, it helps you see literature more closely and more personally, which is invaluable. In addition, you learn to work with a variety of different kinds of texts, as well as how to create your own personal texts and original scripts. You develop an understanding of performance on stage as well as in life. There are few professions which do not call for some kind of performance or communication activity.

You now have the wisdom to know how to prepare a selection for performance and the skill to perform it. You have considered possibilities for future applications of your skills. The virtue is in the doing. Enjoy!

Notes

1. Louis E. Catron, "What Theatre Majors Learn," *Dramatics* (December 1991): 11.
2. Doris Haenny, "It Happens in the Library," *Readers Theatre (News)* 7 (Spring–Summer 1980): 44.
3. Janet Larsen McHughes, "The Bubble as a Creative Environment for Drama," *Communication Education* 26 (September 1977): 214–20.
4. William Rickert, "Readers Theatre on Wheels," *Readers Theatre (News)* 7 (Spring–Summer 1980): 8.
5. Donald Heady, private interview, Ball State University, February 10, 1981.
6. Kenneth Koch, *I Never Told Anybody: Teaching Poetry Writing in a Nursing Home* (New York: Random House, 1977), pp. 6–7.
7. Leigh Steiner-Crane, "Poetic Self-Actualization: Creative Stimulation for Rehabilitation and Reintegration," *Journal of the Illinois Speech and Theatre Association* 28 (Fall 1974): 21–27.

8. "Educating for the Workplace through the Arts," *BusinessWeek*, October 28, 1996, p. 2

9. Ibid., p. 5.

10. *Encyclopaedia Britannica*, 15th ed., "Anthropology." s.v.

11. Richard Schechner, *Between Theatre & Anthropology* (Philadelphia: University of Pennsylvania Press, 1985), p. 248.

12. Ibid., p. 3.

13. Ibid., p. 4.

Glossary

Aesthetic Distance   The emotional/psychological or physical distance between performer and text and between performer and audience.

Alienation   An effect created by Bertolt Brecht in his epic theatre to destroy the illusion of reality. An alienation device, often employed in chamber theatre, is anything that draws attention to the artifice of the stage and away from verisimilitude, such as a narrator addressing the audience.

Alliteration   The repetition of identical consonant sounds in stressed syllables, usually at the beginning of words in close proximity, throughout a poem.

Allusion   A reference to a person, place, or thing outside the literary work. Writers usually allude to characters or events in mythology, the Bible, another literary work, or to a contemporary or historical event.

Analogue   (See Performance Analogue)

Anapest   A type of metrical foot which contains two unstressed syllables followed by a stressed syllable.

Apostrophe   An address to an inanimate object, a muse, God, or an absent or deceased person or character.

Archetypal Analysis   A literary theory which examines the literature in relation to mythological motifs and patterns.

Aside   Short lines addressed by a character directly to the audience. The conventional aside allows one character to speak to the audience and not be heard by the other performers on stage.

Assonance   The repetition of identical vowel sounds in words in close proximity throughout a work.

Audience Mode   The analysis of literature based on the relationship between the speaker and his or her audience. Individual lines or moments are *dramatic* if a character speaks to another character, *epic* if the speaker addresses the general audience, and *lyric* if the speaker addresses private thoughts aloud to himself or herself, or if the speaker addresses a muse, God, an absent or deceased person, or an inanimate object.

Ballad   A tightly metered narrative poem which tells a story with stark images, often with a refrain.

Barrier   Anything which inhibits communication from taking place between performer and audience. There are three kinds of barriers: *external*, which are situational barriers such as a disturbance outside the room; *internal*, which are related to disturbances within a performer or an audience member such as inability to concentrate because one is too tired; and *semantic*, which are text- or performance-centered, such as when the selection is too simplistic or too complex.

Bifurcation   The casting of two performers to play one role.

Biographical Analysis   A literary theory that examines the relationship between

413

the writer's life and the literature the writer creates.

Body Act   The transformation the performer makes to project the physical, social, psychological, and moral dimensions of each character in a scene.

Body Fact   A performer's physical, social, psychological, and moral makeup.

Caesura   A pause within a poetic line, usually marked by punctuation.

Causal   A type of plot structure where events are motivated by preceding events.

Chamber Theatre   A form of presentational theatre defined and developed by Robert S. Breen for the staging of prose fiction.

Character   Dramatized speakers, categorized as flat, static, round, or dynamic, and analyzed physically, socially, psychologically, and morally.

Character Placement   The assigning of specific locations in and directly above the audience for each character who speaks dialogue lines.

Climax   The highest point of action.

Collage Compiled Script   A type of readers theatre script which juxtaposes various literary selections together so that they become part of a larger whole and so that the script reveals only one seamless message—that of the compiler.

Confessional Poem   A highly lyric poem that seems like autobiography in verse.

Conflict   The tension in plays caused by a character struggling with himself or herself, with another character or characters, or with his or her environment.

Contingent   A type of plot structure where events happen seemingly at random.

Convention   A convention is, in essence, an agreed upon lie—an understanding between artists and audience that something will be accepted as real or natural even if it seems unreal or unnatural. When a character in a play speaks an aside, for example, the convention permits the audience members to believe that only they can hear what is said.

Conventional Verse   Poetry with a discernible metrical pattern, a consistent line length or line length pattern, and approximately the same number of lines in each stanza.

Crisis   The turning point.

Dactyl   A type of metrical foot which contains one stressed syllable followed by two unstressed syllables.

Deconstruction Analysis   A literary theory which analyzes a text by examining the necessary gaps which occur whenever language is used.

Denouement   The section of the plot which ties up loose ends and often projects the action into the future.

Description   When narrators elaborate on the narrative line, making events take longer and seem more detailed than they actually were: discourse time is greater than story time.

Descriptive Lyric   A general type of lyric poem written in the present tense.

Diction   The language of a play, according to Aristotle. Martin Joos defines five styles of language: frozen, formal, consultative, casual, and intimate. *Frozen* language is characteristic of language in print. *Formal* language is used by characters who do not know each other well or who have a superior/inferior relationship. *Consultative* language is the norm of spoken English, spoken by acquaintances. *Casual* language is spoken by friends or by people who share common interests and, thus, use jargon understood only by the participants. *Intimate* is the language of lovers, of those who spend much close, private time together.

Direct Discourse   Dialogue, the recorded speech of characters.

Discourse Time   The time it takes for the narrator to verbalize the events of a story.

Dissolve Technique   A technique for keeping characters differentiated without using character placement. With dissolve, one character simply begins speaking when the previous character finishes with no transition or artificial shift of placement.

Drama   Plays written with characters, implied action, and dialogue, and usually intended for actors to perform on a stage.

Dramatic Dialogue   A type of dramatic poem in which two defined characters address each other.

Dramatic Lyric   A type of dramatic poem in which a clearly defined character(s) speaks the sympathies, values, or attitudes of the poet.

Dramatic Monologue   A type of dramatic poem in which one character speaks to a silent character.

Dramatic Narrative   A type of dramatic poem in which a defined character tells a story.

Dramatic Poetry   One of the three genres of poetry, along with lyric and narrative. Dramatic poetry centers on a dramatized speaker who is in some sort of conflict situation. There are five kinds of dramatic-genre poems: dramatic dialogues, dramatic lyrics, dramatic monologues, dramatic narratives, and dramatic soliloquies.

Dramatistic Analysis   Approaching the study of a text by asking who is speaking, to whom, about what, where, when, how, and why.

Dynamic Character   A character who undergoes change from the beginning of the story to the end.

Elegy   A type of serious lyric poem written in memory of someone—often someone famous—who has died.

Emotional Climax   A moment in a poem when there is an increase or surge of emotion. There may be many or no emotional climaxes, depending on the performer's interpretation of the situation in the poem.

Empathy   Literally, to feel with another. Empathy is to feel a oneness, physically, vocally, mentally, and so on with the speaker in a text.

End-stopped Line   A line of verse which ends with some kind of punctuation mark.

Enjambed Line   A line of verse which is run on—there is no punctuation at the end and the thought carries over to the next line.

Epic Poem   A very long narrative poem which centers on the accomplishments of a traditional or historical hero who faces and meets trials to aid a race or a nation.

Evaluative Response   A possible response during an after-performance critique that indicates that the audience has made a judgment about the relative goodness, appropriateness, effectiveness, or rightness of the performer's presentation.

Expanded Program Compiled Script   A type of readers theatre script where materials are gathered together by some common bond, but unlike the collage compiled script, each selection maintains its original context and remains an identifiable unit.

Exposition   That element of plot which establishes the time frame, introduces the characters, and sets the scene.

Feminist Analysis   A literary theory which approaches a text in terms of the portrayal of women and the power relations in which they are involved.

Flat Character   A character who has one prevailing trait or characteristic.

Focus   Where the performer looks during performance, determined by the nature of the speaker-audience relationship. Focus may be classified as offstage and onstage and as closed, inner-closed, open, and semi-closed. *Offstage* focus occurs when the performer projects the scene out front—breaking the imaginary fourth wall of the realistic portrayal. *Onstage* focus is the focus of representational theatre, where performers see only each other on stage and not the audience, creating the imaginary fourth wall. *Closed* focus is a type of offstage focus used by a performer when a defined character speaks to another defined character. *Inner-closed* focus is used when the speaker is addressing himself or herself, thinking aloud. The performer looks around the room without catching anyone's eye. *Open* focus is used when the speaker addresses the audience. *Semi-closed* focus is used when the speaker addresses a muse, or God, an absent or deceased person, or an inanimate object—in short, anyone or anything that is not present and responding.

Foot Prosody   When the meter of a poem is based on the type and number of metrical feet in a line. Foot prosody is the most common type of metrical prosody and the type most often representative of conventional verse.

Free Verse   Poetry whose patterns are not as easy to recognize as those in conventional verse. Free-verse poetry does not scan easily, as it usually includes a variety of metrical feet and line lengths.

Fulcrum   A moment of silence that marks a major change in image, sound, meter, thought, point of view, tone, or mood within a poem.

Genre   A French word meaning "kind" or "type." There are three primary literary genres—prose, poetry, and drama.

Goal   The motivation, intention, or objective of a character in a play. Goals involve the character's needs or wants and should be stated as action verbs, e.g., "I want to buy a Cadillac."

GOS   (See "goal," "obstacle," "strategy.")

Hyperbole   An exaggerated statement employing inflated language.

Iamb   The most often employed type of metrical foot which contains one unstressed syllable followed by a stressed syllable.

Imagery   The writer's use of language symbols to reconstruct objects or experiences which stimulate sense impressions in the mind of the reader.

Indirect Discourse   The narrator reports what a character once said, felt, hoped, or thought.

Individuality   A characteristic of good literature. A text has individuality if it has a distinctive style and language, in short, if it has a unique way of expressing a universal theme.

Interpretation   In general, the process of studying and performing texts. More specifically, in this textbook, interpretation is defined as an artistic process of studying literature through performance and sharing that study with an audience.

Interpretive Response   A possible response during an after-performance critique that indicates that the audience's response is to teach, to tell the performer what his or her interpretation means.

Intertextuality   The idea that we read and understand texts by relating them to other texts we have read, to other experiences we have had, and to our interests and preoccupations, based on our personal ownership of language.

Jargon   The specialized vocabulary used and understood only by the members of a particular group of people.

Kinesthetic   A type of sensory image which relates to muscular involvement, awareness of body position, and tension.

Kinetic   A type of sensory image which relates to the expenditure of energy, physical movement.

Literary Imagery   Figurative language; images a writer uses to make a work clearer, fresher, or more vital, usually through some means of comparison or by relating to something outside the poem.

Literature   According to Wellek and Warren, literature is "a potential cause of experiences."

Litotes   An understatement in which the affirmative is implied by denying its opposite.

Logical Climax   What the poem logically comes to, or the point that the poem logically reaches, often at the end of the poem.

Lyric Poetry   One of the three genres of poetry, along with dramatic and narrative. In lyric poetry, a persona speaks, and this speaker is often highly personal, emotional, and contemplative. There are two general categories of lyric poems: descriptive and reflective. In addition, there are confessionals, elegies, odes, and sonnets.

Marxist Analysis   A literary theory which examines a text in terms of its production, including the means and the authority by which it is produced—based on principles devised by Karl Marx.

Media Performance   Enhancing a performance by the addition of other media forms, such as taped or live music, slides, film, or video.

Metaphor   A type of literary image in which a comparison is made—something is said to be the same as something else.

Metaphoric Performance   A performance of a text that affirms, respects, or conserves the perceived integrity of that text.

Metonymic Performance   A performance of a text that subverts, challenges, or transgresses beyond the perceived integrity of that text. Metonymic performances are often extremely personal, daring, and idiosyncratic.

Metonymy   Using one word or image to represent another the first is closely associated with.

Metrical Tale   A relatively long narrative poem which tells a completely developed story in verse.

Modal Approach   A way of studying literature by investigating who is speaking and who is addressed.

Mood   The atmosphere the narrator creates when telling the story.

Motif   Any image repeated often enough to become significant.

Motivation   That which prompts a character to behave in a certain way. Motivation is related to what the character wants or needs.

Music   According to Aristotle, music is an element of drama which encompasses two concerns: actual music (either live or recorded) as well as the beauty of the language used—the rhythm, sound qualities, and so forth.

Narratee   The implied audience in a short story or novel.

Narrative Poetry   One of the three genres of poetry, along with dramatic and lyric. Narrative poetry centers on a narrator telling a story. There are basically three kinds of narrative poems: ballads, metrical tales, and epics.

Narrator   A storyteller; the speaker in narrative literature.

New Historical Criticism   A type of literary analysis that examines the social and political contexts that situate a text in a particular ideological framework.

Obstacle   An obstacle is anything that prevents a character from achieving his or her goal. If a character's goal is to buy a Cadillac, an obstacle might be lack of funds.

Ode   A relatively long lyric poem, often celebrating a specific occasion or praising an object or idea.

Onomatopoeia   An element of tone color which involves words that sound like their meanings—that imitate actual sounds, like "buzz."

Overrides   An element that produces metrical variety. An override results, if,

when scanning a poem, a bar line divides a word.

Oxymoron   A contradiction that seemingly cannot be resolved, like "parting is such sweet sorrow."

Paradox   A seemingly contradictory statement that turns out to be partly true, like "loving hate."

Performance   Performance is a human activity involving fixed texts such as literary texts and those used in stage, film, and television and more spontaneous texts, including everyday conversation, cultural rituals, and storytelling.

Performance Analogue   A translation of an analytic decision into a performance choice.

Performance Art   A contemporary performance mode (beginning in the 1970s) which attempts to eliminate the distinction between artist and art. Performance artists defy traditional conventions and often have social or political agendas.

Performance Studies   Performance studies is an interdisciplinary field of knowledge that focuses on elements of texts, performers, and audiences, individually or in groups, to advance understanding of the aesthetic, historical, psychological, political, and sociocultural dimensions of performance and performative events.

Persona   An undefined speaker in a text who seems to be the writer's disguised self.

Personal Narratives   Personal, autobiographical stories, including the stories we tell every day.

Personification   Occurs when human characteristics are bestowed on inanimate objects, abstract qualities, and animals.

Phoneme   The smallest unit of sound in the English language. When analyzing the tone color in a poem, look for the repetition of like phonemes.

Plot   The sequence of events in a story or play. There are primarily two types of plots, causal and contingent. The plot of a play was, to Aristotle, the most important element.

Poetry   Poetry is highly imagistic, written in condensed language, stylized syntax, and figures of speech not found in ordinary communication; it is crystallized experience.

Point of View   The perspective from which a story is seen and told. Involves how, when, and where the narrator tells the story, and the narrator's degree of personal involvement. There are primarily four types of point of view: *First-person major character* is when the narrator is telling a personal story in which he or she was the central character and uses the pronoun "I." *First-person minor character* is when the narrator is telling a personal story in which he or she was not the central character and uses "I." *Third-person observer* is when the narrator remains outside the story and objectively relates the events; *Third-person omniscient* is when the narrator tells the story and reveals what all the characters are feeling or thinking (total omniscience) or what some of the characters are feeling or thinking (limited omniscience). One additional point of view is *second person*—common in postmodern fiction—which deals with the slippery "you."

Postmodern Literature   Literature since World War II which is disjunctive and open in form, emphasizes language play, contingency or chance, and is filled with indeterminacies. Postmodern texts disrupt our normal expectations and revel in shock or surprise.

Presentational Theatre   A type of theatre which depends on the audience's ability to imagine suggested elements. Presentational productions make no attempt to re-create reality or a realistic impression of life. They openly acknowledge that we are watching a performance. Includes both readers theatre and chamber theatre.

Primary Cadence   A complete sentence in a poem, marked by (.), (?), or (!).

Probing Response   A possible response during an after-performance critique that indicates that the audience's intent is to seek further information by asking questions.

Program Performance   A combination of literature which focuses on a particular theme, writer, literary style, or literary period.

Prose   There are two subgenres within this genre: prose fiction and prose nonfiction. *Fiction* is narrative literature that creates an imaginary reality, as in short stories and novels; *nonfiction* relates fact or theory, such as letters, diaries, essays, and so on.

Prosody   The art of patterning in poetry.

Psychoanalytic Analysis   A literary theory which analyzes literature as well as the state of mind of the writer in terms of Freudian psychology and principles.

Pyrrhic   A type of metrical foot containing two unstressed syllables.

Raisonneur   The character in a play who is the most reasonable and who often represents the playwright's attitudes, beliefs, and opinions.

Reader-Response Analysis A literary theory which analyzes a text according to a reader's expectations.

Readers Theatre Readers theatre, a type of presentational theatre, is a flexible, creative medium for presenting all kinds of literary texts with emphasis on the experience in the literature.

Reflective Lyric A general type of lyric poem written in the past tense.

Representational Theatre Unlike presentational theatre, representational theatre attempts a slice-of-life realism, providing the audience with the specific spectacle details that conform to the playwright's stated expectations.

Rhetorical Analysis A literary theory which concerns itself with the persuasive-communicative strategies within the literary text and with the effect the work has on its audience/readers.

Rhyme An element of poetry which provides unity by keeping thought groups together. There are many kinds of rhyme: *end rhyme* is when the rhyming words occur at the ends of lines; *eye rhyme* is when two words that at one time rhymed, and look as if they still do, no longer rhyme because over time the pronunciation of one of the words has changed; *full rhyme* exists when words have the same vowel and succeeding sounds with different preceding sounds. *Half rhyme* is a type of approximate rhyme where one of the three conditions for full rhyme is not met, and *internal rhyme* occurs within lines.

Round Character A character who has many traits and characteristics, who is multidimensional.

Scansion The analysis of poetic meter ascertained by marking lines for their stressed and unstressed syllables.

Scene Occurs when discourse time (the time the narrator takes to tell the story) is equal to story time (the time it took for the events actually to occur).

Sensory Imagery Images in a text which appeal to our sense of sight (vision), hearing (audition), taste (gustation), smell (olfaction), touch (taction), movement (kinetic), muscular involvement, awareness of body position and tension (kinesthetic), and hot and cold (thermal).

Sensory Showing Sharing images in a text with an audience so that they will be able to reconstruct them in their imaginations.

Simile A comparison using "like," "as," or "as if." A simile usually implies a less exact comparison than a metaphor does.

Soliloquy A character, usually alone onstage, speaks his or her thoughts aloud. A soliloquy is usually longer than an aside.

Sonnet A lyric poem of fourteen lines written in iambic pentameter with a prescribed rhyme scheme.

Speaker Mode Classifying an entire literary selection in terms of who is speaking. *Dramatic* is when the speaker is a defined character, distinctly not the writer. *Epic* is when both a narrator and a character(s) speak. *Lyric* is when an undefined persona speaks who seems to be like the writer.

Spectacle Spectacle includes all the visual and auditory elements of a play—set, props, costumes, makeup, music, sound, lighting, and so forth.

Spectacle Act   What the solo performer can do to persuade an audience to imagine a play's spectacle.

Spectacle Fact   All the visual and auditory accoutrements the playwright intended to accompany the play in production.

Spondee   A type of metrical foot containing two stressed syllables.

Stanza   A unit which forms a division of a poem, equivalent to a paragraph in prose.

Static Character   A character who does not undergo any change.

Stichomythia   Alternating one-line speeches and replies which call for fast-paced delivery.

Story Time   The time it took in the past for the events to occur in a story or novel.

Strategy   A plan created by a character to overcome an obstacle and achieve a goal. If a character's goal is to buy a Cadillac but he or she lacks funds, a strategy is to get a second job and save more money.

Stream of Consciousness   A type of literary work in which events are triggered by the mental associations of the narrator or of a character, such as in works by James Joyce and Virginia Woolf.

Stress Prosody   When the meter of a poem is based on the number of stresses per line.

Structural Analysis   A literary theory which examines the fundamental structures underlying the patterns of a text.

Style   The narrator's manner of telling the story, such as gothic, convoluted, or bathetic.

Subtext   Konstantin Stanislavski's term for the implied message communicated underneath or between the lines of dialogue, realized by careful study of the text.

Suggestion   A quality of good literature involving ambiguities and indeterminacies. Suggestion is apparent when everything in a text is not spelled out and the reader has to fill in the gaps. Another definition of "suggestion" involves the interpreter's attempts to employ economy when performing.

Summary   When the narrator shortens events or capsulizes long sequences of time: discourse time is shorter than story time.

Supportive Response   A possible response during an after-performance critique that indicates the audience's intent is to reassure or pacify the performer.

Syllabic Prosody   When the meter of a poem is based on the number of syllables per line.

Sympathy   Literally, to feel for another. You understand what the other is feeling, but you maintain a bit more distance than you do when you empathize.

Synecdoche   A type of literary image in which a part is used to suggest the whole.

Tag Lines   The "he saids" and "she saids" normally associated with lines of direct discourse. The author uses tag lines to help the reader know who is speaking.

Tensiveness   The elements within a literary text which give it life. The contrasting rhythms, the movements in and out of characters' minds, the combination of different sounds and images, and the conflict situations within and between characters are all tensive elements.

Theme The basic idea or moral the writer tries to convey.

Thought According to Aristotle, thought is the theme of the play—the message the playwright would like to communicate.

Tone The author's attitude toward the work, such as ironic, sympathetic, or humorous.

Tone Color The repetition of like sounds throughout a poem. There are five elements of tone color: alliteration, assonance, consonance, onomatopoeia, and rhyme.

Triggering The stimulation of thoughts during moments of free association.

Understanding Response A possible response during an after-performance critique that indicates the audience's intent is only to ask the performer whether they correctly understood what the performer intended.

Universality A quality of good literature. A text is universal if it deals with common themes most people can relate to, such as love, hate, war, childhood, and death.

Virtual Past The time in which the events of a story occurred.

Virtual Present The time in which the narrator tells the story.

Visual Prosody When the rhythm of a poem relies on the picture the words and spaces make on the page.

Bibliography

Chapter 1

Bacon, Wallace A. *The Art of Interpretation.* 3rd ed. New York: Holt, Rinehart & Winston, 1979.
Baldick, Chris. *The Concise Oxford Dictionary of Literary Terms.* Oxford: Oxford University Press, 1990.
Gray, Paul H., and Van Oosting, James. *Performance in Life and Literature.* Boston: Allyn and Bacon, 1997.
Hjort, Mette, and Laver, Sue. *Emotion and the Arts.* New York: Oxford University Press, 1997.
Lee, Charlotte I., and Gura, Timothy J. *Oral Interpretation.* 9th ed. Boston: Houghton Mifflin, 1997.
Matravers, Derek: *Art and Emotion.* New York: Oxford University Press, 1998.
Pelias, Ron. *Performance Studies: The Interpretation of Aesthetic Texts.* New York: St. Martin's Press, 1992.
Rosenblatt, Louise M. *The Reader, The Text, The Poem: The Transactional Theory of the Literary Work.* Carbondale, IL: Southern Illinois University Press, 1978.
Scholes, Robert. *Textual Power.* New Haven: Yale University Press, 1985.

Chapter 2

Bacon, Wallace A., and Breen, Robert S. *Literature as Experience.* New York: McGraw-Hill, 1959.
Cunningham, Cornelius Corman. *Literature as a Fine Art: Analysis and Interpretation.* New York: Ronald Press, 1941.
Geiger, Don. *The Sound, Sense, and Performance of Literature.* Chicago: Scott, Foresman, 1963.
Greetham, D. C. *Theories of the Text.* New York: Oxford University Press, 1998.
Strelka, Joseph P., ed. *Theories of Literary Genre.* University Park: The Pennsylvania State University Press, 1978.
Valentine, Kristin B., and Valentine, D. E. *Interlocking Pieces: Twenty Questions for Understanding Literature.* 3rd ed. Dubuque, IA: Kendall-Hunt, 1991.
Wellek, René, and Warren, Austin. *Theory of Literature.* 3rd ed. New York: Harcourt, Brace & World, 1956.

Chapter 3

Abrams, M. H. *The Mirror and the Lamp.* New York: Oxford University Press, 1953.
Atkins, G. Douglas, and Morrow, Laura. *Contemporary Literary Theory.* Amherst: University of Massachusetts Press, 1989.
Bakhtin, Mikhail. *The Dialogic Imagination: Four Essays by M. M. Bakhtin.* Edited by Michael Holquist, translated by Emerson and Holquist. Austin: University of Texas Press, 1981.
Barthes, Roland. *The Pleasure of the Text.* Translated by Richard Miller. New York: Farrar, 1973.
Bloom, Harold. *Deconstruction and Criticism.* Herndon, VA: The Continuum International Publishing Group Inc., 2000.
Cooke, Brett, and Turner, Frederick, eds. *Biopetics: Evolutionary Explorations in the Arts.* Herndon, VA: The Continuum International Publishing Group Inc., 2000.
Corbett, Edward P. J., ed. *Rhetorical Analyses of Literary Works.* New York: Oxford University Press, 1969.
Culler, Jonathan. *Literary Theory: A Very Short Introduction.* New York: Oxford University Press, 1998.

424

Eagleton, Terry. *Literary Theory: An Introduction.* Minneapolis: University of Minnesota Press, 1983.

Foster, Hal. *The Anti-Aesthetic: Essays on Postmodern Culture.* Seattle: Bay Press, 1983.

Foucault, Michel. *This Is Not a Pipe.* Berkeley: University of California Press, 1982.

Frye, Northrop. *The Well-Tempered Critic.* Bloomington, IN: Indiana University Press, 1963.

Gilbert, Allan H., ed. *Literary Criticism: Plato to Dryden.* Detroit: Wayne State University Press, 1962.

Gilbert, Allan H., ed. *Literary Criticism: Pope to Croce.* Detroit: Wayne State University Press, 1962.

Gray, Paul H. "The Uses of Theory." *Text and Performance Quarterly* 11 (1991): 267–77. (This edition of *Text and Performance Quarterly* focuses specifically on literary theory and interpretation.)

Hall, Vernon, Jr. *A Short History of Criticism.* New York: New York University Press, Gotham Library, 1963.

Hawthorne, Jeremy. *A Glossary of Contemporary Literary Theory.* New York: Oxford University Press, 1998.

Lodge, David, ed. *Modern Criticism and Theory: A Reader.* London: Longman, 1988.

Long, Beverly Whitaker. "Performance Criticism and Questions of Value." *Text and Performance Quarterly* 2 (1991): 105–15.

Park-Fuller, Linda. "Voices: Bakhtin's Heteroglossia and Polyphony, and the Performance of Narrative Literature." *Literature in Performance* 7 (1986): 1–12.

Post, Robert M. "Dramatistic Analysis of Literature." *Illinois Schools Journal* 58 (Fall 1978): 28–36.

Richter, David H. *Falling into Theory: Conflicting Views on Reading Literature.* Boston: Bedford Books, 1994.

Selden, Raman. *A Reader's Guide to Contemporary Literary Theory.* Lexington, Kentucky: The University Press of Kentucky, 1985.

Showalter, Elaine. *The New Feminist Criticism: Essays on Women, Literature, & Theory.* New York: Pantheon, 1985.

Strelka, Joseph P., ed. *Literary Criticism and Philosophy.* University Park: The Pennsylvania State University Press, 1983.

Thompkins, Jane P., ed. *Reader-Response Criticism: From Formalism to Post-Structuralism.* Baltimore, MD: Johns Hopkins University Press, 1980.

Valentine, Kristin B., and Valentine, D. E. *Interlocking Pieces: Twenty Questions for Understanding Literature.* 3rd ed. Dubuque, IA: Kendall-Hunt, 1991.

Chapter 4

Bacon, Wallace A. *The Art of Interpretation.* 3rd ed. New York: Holt, Rinehart & Winston, 1979.

Doll, Howard D. "Non-Verbal Communication and Oral Interpretation." In *Studies in Interpretation,* vol. 2, edited by Esther M. Doyle and Virginia Hastings Floyd. Amsterdam: Rodopi N. V., 1977.

Heinberg, Paul. *Voice Training for Speaking and Reading Aloud.* New York: Ronald Press, 1964.

Kahan, Stanley. *Introduction to Acting.* Boston: Allyn and Bacon, Inc., 1985.

Katz, Robert L. *Empathy: Its Nature and Uses.* New York: Macmillan, 1963.

Klein, Maxine. *Time, Space and Design for Actors.* Boston: Houghton Mifflin, 1975.

Knapp, Mark L. *Nonverbal Communication in Human Interaction.* New York: Holt, Rinehart & Winston, 1972.

Lee, Charlotte A., and Gura, Timothy J. *Oral Interpretation.* 9th ed. Boston: Houghton Mifflin, 1997.

Lessach, Arthur. *The Use and Training of the Human Voice.* 2nd ed. New York: D. B. S., 1967.

Lomas, C. W. "The Psychology of Stage Fright." *Quarterly Journal of Speech* 23 (February 1937): 35–44.

Machlin, Evangeline. *Speech for the Stage.* Rev. ed. New York: Theatre Arts Books, 1966.

Richmond, Virginia P., and McCroskey, James C. *Communication: Apprehension, Avoidance, and Effectiveness,* 2nd ed. Scottsdale, AZ: Gorsuch Scarisbrick, 1989.

Roland, David. *The Confident Performer.* Portsmouth: Heinemann, 1997.

Chapter 5

Abercrombie, Nicholas. *Audiences: A Sociological Theory of Performance and Imagination.* Thousand Oaks, CA: Sage Publications, Inc., 1998.

Bennett, Susan. *Theatre Audiences.* 2nd ed. New York: Routledge, 1997.

Blau, Herbert. *The Audience.* Baltimore, MD: Johns Hopkins University Press, 1990.

Campbell, Paul N. "The Well-Tempered Audience." *Central States Speech Journal* 32 (Spring 1981): 35–44.

Gillespie, Patti Peete. "The Performing Audience." *Southern Speech Communication Journal* 46 (Winter 1981): 124–38.

Johnson, David W. *Reaching Out: Interpersonal Effectiveness and Self-Actualization.* Englewood Cliffs, NJ: Prentice Hall, 1972.

Langellier, Kristin M. "A Phenomenological Approach to Audience." *Literature in Performance* 3 (April 1983): 34–39.

Long, Beverly Whitaker. "Evaluating Performed Literature." In *Studies in Interpretation,* vol. 2, edited by Esther M. Doyle and Virginia Hastings Floyd. Amsterdam: Rodopi N. V., 1977.

Loxley, Robert. "Roles of the Audience: The Aesthetic and Social Dimensions of the Performance Event." *Literature in Performance* 3 (April 1983): 40–44.

Mattingly, Alethea. "The Listener and the Interpreter's Style." *Western Speech Journal* 28 (Summer 1964): 154–59.

McQuail, Denis. *Audience Analysis.* Thousand Oaks, CA: Sage Publications, Inc., 1997.

Reynolds, Jerry. "Audience." *Western Speech Journal* 33 (Fall 1969): 241–48.

Warland, Steven Guy; Travernicht, Maxine M.; and Gruner, Charles R. "Audience Response to Visual Stimuli in Oral Interpretation." *Southern Speech Communication Journal* 32 (Summer 1967): 289–95.

Williams, David A. "Audience Response and the Interpreter." In *Studies in Interpretation,* vol. 2, edited by Esther M. Doyle and Virginia Hastings Floyd. Amsterdam: Rodopi N. V., 1977.

Wolvin, Andrew D., and Coakley, Carolyn Gwynn. *Listening.* 2nd ed. Dubuque, IA: Wm. C. Brown, 1985.

Chapter 6

Allison, John M., Jr. "Narrative Time: A Phenomenological Reconsideration." *Text and Performance Quarterly* 14 (April 1994): 108–125.

Bakhtin, Mikhail. *The Dialogic Imagination: Four Essays by M. M. Bakhtin.* Edited by Michael Holquist, translated by Emerson and Holquist. Austin: University of Texas Press, 1981.

Bauman, Richard. Story, *Performance, and Event: Contextual Studies of Oral Narrative.* New York: Cambridge University Press, 1986.

Bentley, Phyllis. *Some Observations on the Art of the Narrative.* New York: Macmillan, 1947.

Booth, Wayne C. *The Company We Keep: An Ethics of Fiction.* Berkeley: University of California Press, 1988.

Booth, Wayne C. *The Rhetoric of Fiction.* 2nd ed. Chicago: University of Chicago Press, 1983.

Capecci, John. "Performing the Second-Person." *Text and Performance Quarterly* 9, no. 1 (1989): 42–52.

Chesebro, James W. "Text, Narration, Media." *Text and Performance Quarterly* 9 (1989): 1–22.

Currie, Mark, ed. *Metafiction.* New York: Longman, 1995.

Emmott, Catherine. *Narrative Comprehension.* New York: Oxford University Press, 1997.

Espinola, Judith C. "The Nature, Function, and Performance of Indirect Discourse in Prose Fiction." *Speech Monographs* 41 (August 1974): 193–204.

Forster, E. M. *Aspects of the Novel.* New York: Harcourt, Brace & World, 1927.

426

Gelley, Alexander. *Narrative Crossings: Theory and Pragmatics of Prose Fiction.* Baltimore, MD: The Johns Hopkins University Press, 1987.

Gibson, Walker. *Tough, Sweet & Stuffy: An Essay on Modern American Prose Styles.* Bloomington, IN: Indiana University Press, 1966.

Gura, Timothy J. "Beginning Interpreters as Third-Person Narrators." *Communication Education* 32 (July 1983): 312–14.

Hanne, Michael. *The Power of the Story: Fiction and Political Change.* Herndon, VA: The Continuum International Publishing Group Inc., 2000.

Hawthorn, Jeremy. *Studying the Novel: An Introduction,* 3rd ed. New York: Oxford University Press, 1997.

Heston, Lilla. "A Note on Prose Fiction: The Performance of Dialogue Tags." *Speech Teacher* 22 (January 1973): 69–72.

Heston, Lilla. "The Solo Performance of Prose Fiction." *Speech Teacher* 24 (September 1975): 269–77.

Isaacs, Neil D., and Leiter, Louis, eds. *Approaches to the Short Story.* San Francisco: Chandler, 1963.

Lanser, Susan Snaider. *The Narrative Act: Point of View in Prose Fiction.* Princeton, NJ: Princeton University Press, 1981.

Lodge, David. *After Bakhtin: Essays on Fiction and Criticism.* London: Routledge, 1990.

Lodge, David. *The Art of Fiction.* New York: Viking, 1993.

Maclay, Joanna H. "The Aesthetics of Time in Narrative Fiction." *Speech Teacher* 18 (September 1969): 194–96.

Maclay, Joanna H. "The Interpreter and Modern Fiction: Problems in Point of View and Structural Tensiveness." In *Studies in Interpretation,* vol. 1, edited by Esther M. Doyle and Virginia Hastings Floyd. Amsterdam: Rodopi N. V., 1972.

Mitchell, W. J. T., ed. *On Narrative.* Chicago: The University of Chicago Press, 1981.

Oliver, Douglas L. *Poetry and Narrative in Performance.* New York: St. Martin's Press, 1989.

Parks, Tim. *Translating Style.* Herndon, VA: The Continuum International Publishing Group Inc., 2000.

Raban, Jonathan. *The Technique of Modern Fiction: Essays in Practical Criticism.* South Bend, IN: University of Notre Dame Press, 1969.

Scholes, Robert. *Approaches to the Novel.* San Francisco: Chandler, 1966.

Scholes, Robert, and Kellogg, Robert. *The Nature of Narrative.* London: Oxford University Press, 1966.

Urgo, Joseph R. *Novel Frames: Literature as Guide to Race, Sex, and History in American Culture.* Jackson: University Press of Mississippi, 1991.

Van Oosting, James. "Some Observations upon the Common Aesthetics of Story Writing and the Solo Performance of Prose Fiction." *Literature in Performance* 2 (November 1981): 66–75.

Yordon, Judy E. "Defining Potential Roles of Minimally-Defined Narrators in Prose Fiction Texts." *Indiana Theatre Bulletin* 8 (1987): 3–10.

Chapter 7

Adler, Stella. *The Technique of Acting.* New York: Bantam, 1990.

Auslander, Philip. *From Acting to Performance: Essays in Modernism and Postmodernism.* New York: Routledge, 1997.

Battcock, Gregory, and Nickas, Robert, eds. *The Art of Performance: A Critical Anthology.* New York: E. P. Dutton, 1984.

Bentley, Eric. *The Playwright as Thinker: A Study of Drama in Modern Times.* New York: Reynal & Hitchock, 1946.

Bentley, Eric. *The Life of Drama.* New York: Atheneum, 1965.

Berry, Cicely. *The Actor and His Text.* London: Harrap Ltd., 1987.

Berry, Cicely. *Voice and the Actor.* New York: Macmillan, 1974.

Brandt, George W., ed. *Modern Theories of Drama: A Selection of Writings on Drama and Theatre.* New York: Oxford University Press, 1998.

Brooks, Cleanth, and Heilman, Robert B., eds. *Understanding Drama.* New York: Holt, Rinehart & Winston, 1945.

Carnovsky, Morris, with Peter Sander. *The Actor's Eye.* New York: Performing Arts Journal Publications, 1984.

Culpeper, Jonathan; Short, Mick; and Verdonk, Peter, eds. *Exploring the Language of Drama: From Text to Context.* New York: Routledge, 1998.

Floyd, Virginia Hastings. "Point of View in Modern Drama." In *Studies in Interpretation,* vol. 2, edited by Esther M. Doyle and Virginia Hastings Floyd. Amsterdam: Rodopi N. V., 1977.

Gassner, John. *Form and Idea in Modern Theatre.* New York: Holt, Rinehart & Winston, 1956.

Gentile, John S. "Early Examples of the Biographical One-Person Show Genre: *Emlyn Williams as Charles Dickens* and Hal Holbrook's *Mark Twain Tonight!" Literature in Performance* 6 (November 1985): 42–53.

Gura, Timothy J. "The Solo Performance and Drama." *Speech Teacher* 24 (September 1975): 278–81.

Hagen Uta, with Haskel Frankel. *Respect for Acting.* New York: Macmillan, 1973.

Heffner, Hubert; Selden, Samuel; and Sellman, H. S. *Modern Theatre Practice.* 5th ed. New York: Appleton-Century-Crofts, 1973.

Linklater, Kristin. *Freeing the Natural Voice.* New York: Drama Book Specialists Publications, 1976.

Lynch, James J. *The Language of the Heart: the Body's Response to Human Dialogue.* New York: Basic Books, 1985.

McGraw, Charles. *Acting Is Believing: A Basic Method for Beginners.* 2nd ed. New York: Holt, Rinehart & Winston, 1966.

Roloff, Lee. "The Roles of the Interpreter and the Actor." *Speech Teacher* 22 (March 1973): 144–47.

Rubin, Lucile S., ed. *Movement for the Actor.* New York: Drama Book Specialists Publications, 1980.

Schechner, Richard. *Environmental Theatre.* New York: Hawthorn Books, 1973.

Schechner, Richard. *Public Domain.* Indianapolis: Bobbs-Merrill, 1969.

Stanislavski, Konstantin. *An Actor Prepares.* Translated by Elizabeth Reynolds Hapgood. New York: Theatre Arts Books, 1948.

Stanislavski, Konstantin. *Building a Character.* Translated by Elizabeth Reynolds Hapgood. New York: Theatre Arts Books, 1977.

Styan, J. L. *The Elements of the Drama.* New York: Cambridge University Press, 1960.

Wallis, Mick, and Shepherd, Simon. *Studying Plays.* New York: Oxford University Press, 1998.

Chapter 8

Bloom, Edward A.; Philbrick, Charles H.; and Blistein, Elmer M. *The Order of Poetry: An Introduction.* New York: Odyssey Press, 1961.

Brooks, Cleanth. *The Well-Wrought Urn.* New York: Harcourt, Brace & World, 1947.

Brown, Susan H., and Lashbrook, William B. "An Experimental Study in the Preservation of Poetry Shape." *Western Journal of Speech Communication* 44 (Spring 1980): 146–52.

Ciardi, John, and Williams, Miller. *How Does a Poem Mean?* Boston: Houghton Mifflin, 1975.

Geiger, Don. "Emotion in Poetry: The Oral Interpreter's Special Responsibility." *Southern Speech Journal* 21 (Fall 1955): 31–38.

Gross, Harvey. *Sound and Form in Modern Poetry.* Ann Arbor: University of Michigan Press, 1973.

Higgins, Dick. "Early Sound Poetry." *Literature in Performance* 5 (April 1985): 42–48.

Lakoff, George, and Johnson, Mark. *Metaphors We Live By.* Chicago: The University of Chicago Press, 1980.

Lee, Charlotte I., and Gura, Timothy J. *Oral Interpretation.* 9th ed. Boston: Houghton Mifflin, 1997.

Overstreet, Robert. "Preservation of Line Shape in the Performance of a Poem." *Southern Speech Communication Journal* 45 (Spring 1980): 73–84.

Nagy, Gregory. *Poetry as Performance: Homer and Beyond.* New York: Cambridge University Press, 1996.

Perry, John Oliver. *Approaches to the Poem.* San Francisco: Chandler, 1965.

Post, Robert M. "Performing Syllabic Verse." *Literature in Performance* 4 (April 1984): 10–19.

Rickert, William E. "Semantic Consequences of Rhyme." *Literature in Performance* 4 (April 1984): 1–9.

Ricks, Christopher. *Essays in Appreciation.* New York: Oxford University Press, 1996.

Salper, Donald R. "The Sound of a Poem." *Quarterly Journal of Speech* 57 (Spring 1977): 129–33.

Salper, Donald R. "Onomatopoeia, Gesture and Synaesthesia in the Perception of Poetic Meaning." In *Studies in Interpretation,* vol. 2, edited by Esther M. Doyle and Virginia Hastings Floyd. Amsterdam: Rodopi N. V., 1977.

Sanders, Gerald. *A Poetry Primer.* New York: Farrar, Straus, 1935.

Skinner, John F. "Semantic Play in the Poetry of Howard Nemerov." *Literature in Performance* 6 (April 1986): 44–59.

Spender, Stephen. *The Making of a Poem.* New York: W. W. Norton, 1962.

Chapter 9

Appignanesi, Richard, and Garratt, Chris. *Introducing Postmodernism.* New York: Totem Books, 1996.

Atwood, Ann. *My Own Rhythm: An Approach to Haiku.* New York: Scribner, 1973.

Bacon, Wallace A. *The Art of Interpretation.* 3rd ed. New York: Holt, Rinehart & Winston, 1979.

Battcock, Gregory, and Nickas, Robert, eds. *The Art of Performance.* New York: E. P. Dutton, 1984.

Bauer, Caroline Feller. *Handbook for Storytellers.* Chicago: American Library Association, 1977.

Bauman, Richard, ed. *Folklore, Cultural Performances, and Popular Entertainments.* New York: Oxford University Press, 1992.

Bauman, Richard. *Story, Performance, and Event.* New York: Cambridge University Press, 1986.

Bauman, Richard. *Verbal Art as Performance.* Prospect Heights, IL: Waveland Press, 1977.

Berger, Arthur Asa. *Narratives in Popular Culture, Media, and Everyday Life.* Thousand Oaks, CA: Sage Publications, Inc., 1996.

Best, Steve, and Kellner, Douglas. *Postmodern Theory: Critical Interrogations.* New York: The Guilford Press, 1991.

Brewton, John E., and Comps, Sarah W. *Index to Children's Poetry.* New York: H. W. Wilson, 1965.

Cameron, Eleanor. *The Green and Burning Tree: On the Writing and Enjoyment of Children's Books.* Boston: Little, Brown, 1969.

Carlson, Marvin. *Performance: A Critical Introduction.* New York: Routledge, 1996.

Comeaux, Patricia. "Experiential Possibilities for Bringing Children and Poetry Together." *Communication Education* 30 (Spring 1981): 174–79.

Conrad, Edna, and Van Dyke, Mary. *History on the Stage: Children Make Plays from Historical Novels.* New York: Van Nostrand Reinhold, 1971.

Cook, Elizabeth. *The Ordinary and the Fabulous: An Introduction to Myths, Legends, and Fairy Tales for Teachers and Storytellers.* New York: Cambridge University Press, 1969.

Cullinan, Bernice E., and Person, Diane G., eds. *Encyclopedia of Children's Literature.* Herndon, VA: The Continuum International Publishing Group Inc., 2000.

Diamond, Elin, ed. *Performance and Cultural Politics.* New York: Routledge, 1996.

Fensch, Thomas, ed. *Nonfiction for the 1990s.* Hinsdale, NJ: Lawrence Erlbaum Associates, 1991.

Fine, Elizabeth C., *The Folklore Text: From Performance to Print.* Bloomington: Indiana University Press, 1984.

Fine, Elizabeth C., and Speer, Jean Haskell, eds. *Performance, Culture, and Identity.* Westport, CT: Praeger, 1992.

Folklore: An Annotated Bibliography and Index to Single Editions. Compiled by Elsie B. Ziegler. New York: Faxon, 1973.

Gamble, Teri, and Gamble, Michael. *Oral Interpretation: The Meeting of Self and Literature.* Skokie, IL: National Textbook, 1976.

Garner, Thurmon. "Playing the Dozens: Folklore as Strategies for Living." *Quarterly Journal of Speech* 69 (February 1983): 47–57.

Goldberg, Roselee. *Performance Art: From Futurism to the Present.* New York: Harry N. Abrams, 1988.

Hutch, Richard A. *The Meaning of Lives: Biography, Autobiography and the Spiritual Quest.* Herndon, VA: The Continuum International Publishing Group Inc., 2000.

Jones, Amelia, and Stephenson, Andrew, eds. *Performing the Body/Performing the Text.* New York: Routledge, 2000.

Kaye, Nick. *Site Specific Art: Performance, Place and Documentation.* New York: Routledge, 2000.

Kershaw, Baz. *The Radical in Performance: Between Brecht and Baudrillard.* New York: Routledge, 2000.

Langellier, Kristin. "Personal Narratives: Perspectives on Theory and Research." *Text and Performance Quarterly* 9 (October 1989): 243–76.

Livo, Norma J., and Rietz, Sandra A. *Storytelling: Process and Practice.* Littleton, CO: Libraries Unlimited, 1986.

McLuhan, Marshall. *Understanding Media: The Extensions of Man.* New York: New American Library, 1964.

Pecora, Norma Odom. *The Business of Children's Entertainment.* New York: Guilford Publications Inc., 1997.

Pollock, Della. "Telling the Told: Performing Like a Family." *The Oral History Review* 18 (Fall 1990): 1–36.

Post, Robert M. "Interpreting Literature for Young Children." *Communication Education* 32 (July 1983): 285–92.

Read, Alan. *Theatre and Everyday Life.* New York: Routledge, 1995.

Reeves, Marjorie. *Pursuing the Muses: Education and Culture Studied in Two Collections of Family Papers, 1700–1900.* Herndon, VA: The Continuum International Publishing Group Inc., 2000.

Rosenberg, Helane S., and Predergast, Christine. *Theatre for Young People: A Sense of Occasion.* New York: Holt, Rinehart & Winston, 1983.

Sawyer, Ruth. *The Way of the Storyteller.* Rev. ed. New York: The Viking Press, 1962.

Sayre, Henry. *The Object of Performance.* Chicago: University of Chicago Press, 1989.

Schechner, Richard. *Between Theater and Anthropology.* Philadelphia: University of Pennsylvania Press, 1985.

Schechner, Richard, and Appel, Willa, eds. *By Means of Performance: Intercultural Studies of Theatre and Ritual.* New York: Cambridge University Press, 1990.

Shedlock, Marie L. *The Art of the Storyteller.* Dover, 1951.

Stahl, Sandra Dolby. *Literary Folkloristics and the Personal Narrative.* Bloomington: Indiana University Press, 1989.

Stern, Carol Simpson, and Henderson, Bruce. *Performance: Texts and Contexts.* New York: Longman, 1993.

Taft-Kaufman, Jill. "Other Ways: Postmodernism and Performance Praxis," *Southern Communication Journal* 60 (1995): 222–32.

Tyas, Billi. *Child Drama in Action: A Practical Manual for Teachers.* New York: Drama Book Specialists, 1971.

Williams, David, ed. *Collaborative Theatre: The 'Theatre du Soleil' Sourcebook.* Translated by Eric Prenowitz and David Williams. New York: Routledge, 1999.

Chapter 10

(This list includes articles on group interpretation as well as some texts on related areas. For texts on or including information on group interpretation, see the end of Chapter 10.)

Abel, Leslie Gillian, and Post, Robert M. "Towards a Poor Readers Theatre." *Quarterly Journal of Speech* 559 (December 1973): 436–42.

Bacon, Wallace A. "Readers Theatre as a Humanizing Process." *Readers Theatre (News)* (Fall 1975): 3, 11.

Bowen, Elbert R. "Adapting the Novel for the Production in Readers Chamber Theatre." In *Studies in Interpretation*, vol. 2, edited by Esther M. Doyle and Virginia Hastings Floyd. Amsterdam: Rodopi N. V., 1977.

Bowman, Michael S. "Novelizing the Stage: Chamber Theatre After Breen and Bakhtin." *Text and Performance Quarterly* 15 (January 1995): 1–23.

Brecht, Bertolt. "A Short Organum for the Theatre." In *Brecht on Theatre*, edited and translated by John Willet. New York: Hill and Wang, 1964.

Brecht, Bertolt. "The Modern Theatre is the Epic Theatre." In *Brecht on Theatre*, edited and translated by John Willet. New York: Hill and Wang, 1964.

Brown, Joseph Epolito, and Stump, Nancy Palmer. "Genre Theory and the Practice of Readers Theatre." *Speech Teacher* 23 (January 1974): 1–8.

Coger, Leslie Irene. "Theatre for Oral Interpreters." *Speech Teacher* 12 (November 1963): 304–7.

Crook, Tim. *Radio Drama*. New York: Routledge, 1999.

Donovan, Jane. "Audience Roles in a Compiled Readers Theatre Script: 'Who Are *You* This Time.'" Paper presented at SCA Convention, Boston, November 1987.

Ellis, Donald G., and Donahue, William A., eds. *Contemporary Issues in Language and Discourse Processes*. Hillsdale, NJ: Lawrence Erlbaum Associates, 1986.

Fine, Elizabeth C. *The Folklore Text: From Performance to Print*. Bloomington: Indiana University Press, 1984.

Heritage, John, and Atkinson, J. Maxwell. *Structures of Social Action: Studies in Conversation Analysis*. Port Chester, New York: Cambridge University Press, 1985.

Heston, Lilla A. "A Note on Prose Fiction: The Performance of Dialogue Tags." *Speech Teacher* 22 (January 1973): 69–72.

Hirschfeld-Medalia, Adeline. "Stylized Movement in Interpreters Theatre." *Communication Education* 25 (March 1976): 111–20.

HopKins, Mary Frances, and Bouldin, Brent. "Professional Group Performance of Non-Dramatic Literature in New York." In *Performance of Literature in Historical Perspectives*, edited by David W. Thompson. Lanham, MD: University Press of America, Inc., 1983.

King, Judy Yordon. "Chamber Theatre by Any Other Name . . . ?" *Speech Teacher* 21 (September 1972): 193–96.

Kleinau, Marion L., and Kleinau, Marvin D. "Scene Location in Readers' Theatre: Static or Dynamic?" *Speech Teacher* 14 (September 1965): 193–99.

Logan, Christie A. "Form and Rhythm in Compilation Productions: Progressing the Audience's Field of Experience." Paper presented at SCA Convention, Boston, November, 1987.

Ludwig, Dale. "Performing the Authorial Novel: A Chamber Theatre Production of *Joseph Andrews*." *Literature in Performance* 6 (April 1986): 71–82.

Macarthur, David E. "Readers' Theatre: Variations on a Theme." *Speech Teacher* 13 (January 1964): 47–51.

Meyer, Janice Jones. "'Bartleby the Scrivener': Performing the Narrator's Inner Conflict in Chamber Theatre." *Communication Education* 26 (November 1977): 348–51.

Miller, Cynthia A. "Concepts for Adapting and Directing a Readers Theatre Production: Symbolism, Synecdoche and Metonymy." *Communication Education* 33 (October 1984): 343–50.

Miller, Lynn Christine. "The Subjective Camera and Staging Psychological Fiction." *Literature in Performance* 2 (April 1982): 35–45.

Narula, Uma, and Pearce, W. Barnett, eds. *Cultures, Politics, and Research Programs: An International Assessment of Practical Problems in Field Research*. Hinsdale, NJ: Lawrence Erlbaum Associates, 1990.

Parella, Gilda. "Through the 'I' of the Beholder: A Rationale for Physicalization in the Performance of Narratives." *Central States Speech Journal* 25 (Winter 1974): 296–302.

Pearse, James Allen. "Montage: A Paradigm for Readers Theatre." In *Studies in Interpretation*, vol. 2, edited by Esther M. Doyle and Virginia Hastings Floyd. Amsterdam: Rodopi, N.V., 1977.

Pelias, Ronald J. "The Use and Misuse of Multiple Casting." *Western Journal of Speech Communication* 43 (Summer 1979): 224–30.

Schneider, Raymond. "The Visible Metaphor." *Communication Education* 25 (March 1976): 121–26.

Sturges, Christine A. "The Effect of a Narrator's Presence on Audience Response to Character in the Staging of Narrative Literature." *Speech Teacher* 24 (January 1975): 46–52.

Taft-Kaufman, Jill. "Creative Collaboration: The Rehearsal Process in Chamber Theatre." *Communication Education* 32 (October 1983): 428–34.

Wade, Alan. "From Text to Television: A Chamber Theatre Approach." *Literature in Performance* 2 (April 1982): 23–34.

Young, Jerry D. "Evaluating a Readers Theatre Production." *Speech Teacher* 19 (January 1970): 37–42.

Zachary, Samuel J. "A Language Rationale for Conventional Readers Theatre of the Deaf." *Literature in Performance* 5 (November 1984): 20–28.

INDEXES

Author-Title Index

Subject Index